Ludus Literarius, or the Grammar Schoole

Presented to the
LIBRARY *of the*
UNIVERSITY OF TORONTO
by

O.I.S.E.

LUDUS LITERARIUS

OR

THE GRAMMAR SCHOOLE

By JOHN BRINSLEY

Edited with Introduction
and Bibliographical notes

By E. T. CAMPAGNAC

LIVERPOOL
THE UNIVERSITY PRESS
LONDON
CONSTABLE & CO. LTD.
1917

LB
1025
B74
1917

1449

INTRODUCTION

WHEN a craftsman makes a plain, full and fearless statement about his work, if he has been engaged in it long enough to have gained practical mastery, and wisely enough to have made routine itself the instrument of ever-renewed inquiry, then, even though he be a man of moderate ability, he offers to his fellows, themselves occupied in the same business, a storehouse from which the best of them and the ablest, contemporary or of later times, may draw something that will entertain or warn or help them. And if he has any notable vigour of mind or force of character, he provides, not a little, but very much for their profit and guidance. Indeed, if fortune is kind to him and to the world he may then appeal to a far wider audience; for such a man, writing with the frankness and the reserve of disciplined emotion of what he thoroughly knows, passes at once beyond what is special to his own avocation,—not, of course, by wandering away from what is proper to it into vague and idle generalities, beyond its just boundaries, but rather by exhibiting in his large and detailed treatment both the peculiar qualities of his own profession and not less its relation to the common business of other men, the business, in fact, of living in an orderly world.

This is the best and in truth the only justification for any work; that being in itself worth doing and of a sort to engross the whole of a man's powers, demanding from him a concentrated devotion, it shall be a part of the general activity of men, and contribute to their welfare. If it is thus related, a condition of its serving the public weal is that from the world, to which it yields its harvest, it draws its own varied nourishment. It must needs be that men, who ply their several businesses in the world, take some colour from their occupation, their hands subdued to what they work in; but if their whole minds and hearts are subdued also (as would appear to be the melancholy lot of some, to judge by their looks), then we may be sure that they are not getting from the generous and inexhaustible sources of life what they need, and consequently are themselves failing to reinvigorate and replenish the wells of human gladness and power. Teachers, of all men, are those who need most to maintain this exchange, not as a form of barter, but as a condition of usefulness and of enjoyment, for they more certainly than others hold an office which should make them at once the pensioners and the benefactors of Society. From the Society in which they live they must receive what they are to impart to their pupils; and to that Society it is their business to restore what it gave enhanced in value and reality.

Society, or the world, expects teachers to equip their pupils with some knowledge and some skill and with some ideas too which will set them upon using that knowledge and that skill for its, and their own benefit. Without this equipment we know that men cannot take their place in the world, as partners in its work and companions in its pleasures. Without this they will be at least burdensome and perhaps, or probably, actively mischievous. And what this equipment is we imagine ourselves to have learnt from long experience, our own and our ancestors', from general experience of affairs and from the special experience which we have gained, each one of us and each group of us, in the particular path along which we have traced our lives. But there must, we know, for economy and efficiency be a division of labour, and if we, who are so rich in experience, were to pause to impart our experience at first hand to our children, we should be cutting at the roots of our own growth and strength; let us, we say, merchants, lawyers, doctors; let us, members of philanthropic or other committees, guardians, social workers, busy hostesses; let us pursue without let or hindrance these duties to which aptitude and inclination guide us, and to which we are bound by our strong public spirit, and let others, whose scope is not the same as ours, devote themselves to teaching the young the elements, the simple and common elements of knowledge and of skill from which our own distinctive gifts have sprung as from a common root in a common soil.

To this teachers may make reply that conscious that they do not possess the qualities and have not enjoyed the special experience which are ours, and willing to do the simple and elementary work which we are pleased to assign them, they must beg our help. They must beg us to let them see our qualities in operation, to tell us something of our experience; in a word, if they are to prepare our children for our place, they must have some glimpse, at any rate, of the place which we now occupy, and which our children will in turn occupy in days to come.

The author of the book which is now republished announces upon his title-page that he wrote it "for the perpetual benefit of Church and Commonwealth." It is a great claim to make. For what is the book? It is the detailed account written by a schoolmaster of his work—"Interesting at best," we might be disposed to say, "to a few of his contemporary fellow practitioners; useful perhaps to novices in the same profession; a valuable exercise in self-criticism for himself." The writer professes to have enquired into the practice of other men "most profitable schoolmasters and other learned" and to have put to trial what he gathered from them: and "very praiseworthy and painstaking" we may call him; "a most conscientious and laborious man." No doubt he would have treasured our mild encomium; but it is clear that his aim is directed to a larger end than we have considered appropriate to his powers. He writes "for the perpetual benefit of Church and Commonwealth."

We are accustomed to set, or to discover, a barrier between the scholar and the man of the world; we seldom find or look to find in the teacher a man of affairs; but according to Brinsley the scholar is, in fact, a man of the world not less than another, provided he is doing his proper work well; and the teacher a man of affairs, provided he teaches. What, then, is the proper work of a scholar? It is to interpret the world to itself, to preserve its best meaning, and to carry on the high traditions of the past into the future by maintaining through differences of succeeding forms, as generation follows passing generation, the elements of sanity, chivalry and endurance which have combined to make the life of a people great. And what is the proper work of a teacher? It is the same as that of a scholar. It is because we have come to dissociate the conception of a scholar from that of a teacher that we have separated both from "the world" and from "affairs."

Brinsley insists, it is the basis of his whole theory of education, that society is one, and that every part of it enjoys the dignity, since it shares with the rest the obligation, of upholding and enriching the common life of the whole.

I do not propose to analyse or summarise his treatise. That has been done by others before me, and admirably by Professor Foster Watson, whose books are well known. The treatise itself has long been inaccessible, except to those students who have the good fortune to be near a great library. They, if they have used their opportunities, will be aware that Brinsley has himself provided his book with a table of Contents which is a full analysis and conspectus of his subject and his argument. Now, thanks to the generous aid of some of my friends, the whole work is again at the disposal of those who may wish to read it. Brinsley began his book, as we may see from his first page, "at the desire of some worthy favorers of learning." It is pleasant to record that this edition could not have been brought out, especially in these difficult days, but for the encouragement and help of other, not less worthy, "favorers of learning" in our own time. My own thanks, already expressed to them, I now repeat, and I am sure that thanks will be paid not less readily by students of education, and scholars who wish to explore a passage, still too little studied, in the history of classical learning and teaching in this country.

These are difficult days; but we have in these days been, as a people, more ready than in serener seasons to probe our system of education. It has been under or immediately after the stress of a great war that the main advances have in the past been made in English (and not only in English) education. For a great war knits people together, breaking down conventional divisions, and impelling every one to give a true account of himself and of his ability to meet a national need at the peril of suffering a national disaster. It makes men intolerant of artifice and subterfuge; we must openly confess what we are and where we are. We take stock of our resources and we make them known to our fellow-countrymen. At a real crisis, though it will not be pretended that all idle and inconsiderate speech is silenced, yet the volume of sincere and truthful speech is marvellously increased. Learning, because we must learn, what our possessions and our powers are, we learn also what are our defects and our disabilities. We learn to make use, for the common good, of possessions imperfectly employed, because selfishly employed, or employed not at all, but merely and disastrously hoarded; we learn to exert and to develop powers hitherto dormant, and to spend them productively and to the best advantage. We speak of reconstruction. Among our possessions not the least precious is the funded experience of men like Brinsley, specialists of wide outlook and far-sighted patriotism, who minding their own business have minded it all the more heedfully because they saw in it their best mode of public service. Such men refuse to run in blinkers, but they run straight, and the straighter because their view is large.

I have said that I shall not offer an epitome of a book which I trust will now be read by many who have not known of its existence, and even by those who have often referred to it and repeated commonly quoted extracts. But

I must return again to the title-page for a word, which is worth a special commemoration. We are prone to distinguish between work and play, between business and enjoyment. Brinsley entitles his book "Ludus Literarius," and assures us that it will shew us "how to proceede from the first entrance into learning to the highest perfection required in the Grammar Schooles, with ease, certainty and delight both to Masters and Schollers."

It is not unnatural to pupils or their teachers to seek "ease" and ensue it; but "certainty," which I take to mean accuracy, precision, scholarship, does not always consort with ease, either for those who are making their gradual, dusty way towards learning, or for those who have already attained and are already perfect. Some accurate scholars are painful men, and yet, not "painful" in the sense in which Brinsley would have taken that word; for he speaks (p. 307) of painfulness and delight in the same breath, and puts love, faithfulness and painfulness together (p. 311). I suppose that the best thing that a man can do for his fellows is to increase their vitality; it will not, I trust, be deemed improper to say of any teacher that he comes (if he has any business to come at all) that those to whom he comes may "have life and have it more abundantly." Not much, perhaps, he may be able to add, but something, and that life. And it will be granted that a man who gives "delight" gives life.

Brinsley tells us very little of "child-nature"; a good stable-man tells us little or nothing about "horse-nature," a good gardener is commonly reticent about "plant-nature." It was his business to teach boys Latin and Greek; other matters, too; but these above others; and to keep his pupils in order, and to make them behave decently; and, so it would appear, his experience proved that if he could delight them he would win his goal more surely than if he did not. The aphorisms of a practical man are worth shelves full of pretty guess-work; his words count, they stand for realities. Brinsley indicates that a school master should be, and implies that he should look, cheerful.

The book is cast in the form of a dialogue; the speakers are Spoudeus and Philoponus, contemporaries at College twenty years ago, and both since those days engaged in teaching. There is little indeed of dramatic vigour or verve in the conversation which they hold; but the names of the two men are worth noting, suggesting as they must to us of a later age the aptitude and force of the titles which Bunyan was presently to give to his characters. Spoudeus is full of zeal and devotion, but—there is no other word—a fussy man; he has aged so much that it is only his voice and not his "favour" that Philoponus recognises when they first meet after that long interval: "Cares and troubles have made me aged long before my time," admits Spoudeus (p. 2). Philoponus for his part has not been unacquainted with the griefs and vexations which many a schoolmaster suffers; but his early disappointments set him upon speculation and enquiry: "I set myself," he says (p. 3), "to seek out the best way of teaching, by inquiring, conferring and practising continually all the most likely courses which I could hear or devise"; and as a happy result he claims "that I take ordinarily more true delight and pleasure in following my children . . . than any one can take in following hawkes and hounds, or in any other the pleasantest recreation, as I verily persuade myself." And he gives an excellent proof that he is not mistaken about himself: "because, after my labour ended, my chiefest delight is in the remembrance thereof." Philoponus clearly has not grown old; he loves his work. But he has not fallen in love, blindly and brutally, with any one rigid method. He is still ready to inquire and to adopt what inquiry and trial suggest of improvement. Spoudeus is fussy, and we can believe, has been tiresome; and among the people whom he has tired is himself; but he is remarkable not so much in this, as in recognising the fact; and he comes with an excellent and amiable frankness to his old friend to learn from him how to be a school master without being (and looking) a martyr.

This is a dialogue; it is the report of a conference *à deux*, of a committee meeting of two persons, both of whom have first hand personal knowledge, gained from many years of continuous work, and who are met to help each other and to increase, if they can, by counsels shared and experiences compared, the value and usefulness of their profession in the service of Church and State. They note,—Spoudeus ruefully, Philoponus with sane amusement,—the slenderness of their emoluments and the obscurity of their position as teachers. But they dispatch all this in a few sentences, and spend their time and their energy upon what is essential, the improvement of teaching, the widening of its scope, the deepening of its influence.

Conferences are much affected in our own day; and the name of committees is legion; but a conference like this, a committee meeting like this, is, probably, rare. At any rate, the proceedings are not given to the world. Books, of course, are written about Education; never so many; but though I know I offer an easy target to the idle marksman, I make bold to say that not every one who writes or speaks about Education, really contributes to it. Not every one who writes about English literature, it may be said, makes literature. This must be conceded; but then it is not beside the mark to enquire, "Why write?" And there is no excuse for writing about a subject unless by writing a man can increase knowledge of it, and efficiency in the use of it, and, what is of cardinal importance, quicken his own and other men's delight in it.

Now Brinsley does more than write about Education; he takes the reader into the class-room, and shows him what is being done there. This is, of course, the best evidence of Brinsley's power as a writer; he provides us with something better than a record; he makes us witnesses of his work. He is not content even with giving an exhibition, a demonstration, as if to visitors who have come upon a special show-day; the reader becomes, for the time, a colleague or a pupil; so vivid, so real, so genuine and unaffected is the author.

He is generous, too, and open-handed; what he has learned by trial he is not loth to bestow upon any who can receive and use the fruit of his labour. On the contrary, he invites us to take (and, it needs to be said quite explicitly), he invited his contemporaries and rivals to take from his store what they would. His methods spring from his principles; he has, therefore, no tricks or "tips," such as those who pursue and achieve a meaner success protect by a vigilant secrecy, or cover by rights of patent. Writing, as he professes to write, for the benefit of the commonwealth, he breaks down, or rather refuses for his own part to build the barriers of professional pride or jealousy, which make a close corporation of what might be a liberal society, sealing it against the genial influences of the larger world, and robbing the world of whatever is best within the little community. When such boundary walls are set up, it is commonly found that the men who have established them to protect themselves and their colleagues from the invasion of aliens, at once establish party walls which separate them from their fellow-craftsmen. The shrewd folly, which treats as aliens those who might be allies from over the border, treats those who are, in name at least, allies as though they were aliens and adversaries. Brinsley has set an example which should be followed. One of the best services which could be rendered to Education would be the unadorned but unabridged statement made by teachers of their own practice. It is true that not every man could make such a record readable by his fellow-practitioners, still less by the public. Unadorned statements are the product of a practised and deliberate art, or else of a childlike simplicity even rarer; and unabridged statements demand patience, of course from their readers, but from their writers not less. Yet the attempt might be a wholesome discipline for those who should find that they had essayed what was beyond their powers. And those who made it and triumphed over the difficulties of their task would deserve (and perhaps some day win) the thanks of readers, few but fit, critical and kindly. A very courageous man among such writers might read his own book; and it can hardly be supposed that he would be unmoved. "Did I," we can imagine him crying to himself in solitude, "really say this and that? Did I teach these matters, and omit those? Was this the order in which I arranged what I offered to my pupils, and this the emphasis which I laid here and again here?" It may be that he would be powerfully

encouraged by reading his own record: he might
"Put in his thumb
And pull out a plum"
and revel in the evidence of his own virtue and ability.

It may be that the record would disturb him. If he were an honest and (as we have assumed) a really courageous man, he would, we make no doubt, find cause both for congratulation and for regret. He would learn much from this revision of his career. Other readers (if others there were) could not read with the same intimacy and knowledge of interest; but being, as they must be, a little remote, they might be able to survey the whole document both more dispassionately and more justly. Quite dispassionately, to be sure, they could not read, if they were to be just; for there before their eyes would be spread a most *human* document; here would be a heart laid bare; but bare only to eyes lit with sympathy; other eyes would not see, for they could not, what was offered. Naked and unashamed would that writer be, and in no need of a covering to screen him from the staring but sightless gaze of persons blinded by suspicion and bigotry, or by stupid curiosity.

Brinsley regarded himself (being a teacher) as a servant of the community; and it will be taken for granted at once that he meant the community of men, of English men, among whom he lived. His conception of Society is, like Plato's, that of an ordered system, in which the several parts fulfil each one a special and appropriate function. He lived in the world, and admits that he liked life's way; but his appetite and taste were the keener and truer, his touch upon affairs more certain and more strong because he lived in another world too; or, to be more exact, because he drew into the world of practical affairs in which he played his part, the air of another region in which he was not less at home. We are prepared to believe that teachers and other persons plying their several businesses are the servants of those who pay them their wages; they are servants of the community as a whole, and fail in their duty and fall from their honour if they allow themselves to become the slaves of their paymasters. But the whole community to which their allegiance is due is vaster than we commonly think. The teacher, so Brinsley proclaims, borrowing noble lines from Theognis, is the " minister and herald of the Muses."

"It behoves the minister and herald of the muses, if he has more than an equal share of knowledge and wisdom, not to grudge it; some things he must search out, and some he must reveal, and others again he must create; since he alone knows what use to make of them."

The passage is not easy to render in English as terse as the Greek; but its sense need not quite escape us. The teacher, like other men, is an inheritor of the wisdom of mankind; yet more properly upon him than on others falls the burden of examining his inheritance: it is a great store; but he must turn it over with his own hands, he must find out what is there, he must devote himself to patient research (μῶσθαι). That is his first duty. It is not his only duty: for part, at least, of what he discovers, he must bring to the knowledge of other men; pointing it out to them; he must expound and illustrate it, (δεικνύναι). And if he is to rise to the height of his calling he must do more than this; his researches have provided him with material, but his treatment must be, sometimes, creative: what he has won by laborious investigation he must make to live afresh; he must be no mere showman but an artist (ποιεῖν).

It would be hard to find a more comprehensive account of the functions of a teacher. You cannot add to it; but you can take nothing away. We may acknowledge (as indeed we must) that these three functions, of research, of exposition, of creative activity are fulfilled in varying degrees by various men. Some have special aptitude (and opportunity) for research, and little of either for exposition, and perhaps less still for invention; others, a more numerous class and one far more dangerous to themselves and their listeners, possess and cultivate a special gift of exposition; they may overcultivate a thin and shallow soil; they may try to produce heavy and abundant crops from roots that have no depth; but if they are sincere and humorous they will do no harm, but only good; and some exposition is necessary for a man's own health, unless he will choke himself in a plethoric silence; others, the rarest these, can breathe upon dead bones and make them live.

The name of "teacher" is most commonly given to and assumed by those who belong to the second group; it is even conceded to persons who have the gift of words but are as impatient of research as they are incapable of creation. These whose place is in the third group are called poets, prophets, fanatics, artists, revolutionaries or madmen, while those who fill the meagre ranks of the first are called (what they sometimes are) dull fellows. Brinsley freely weaves Theognis' verses on his banner; he is no teacher who cannot, in some measure, do all these things; he alone who combines these attributes of the investigator, the revealer, the creator, fully deserves the title of teacher.

Sir Joshua Reynolds has excellent good counsel for those who would use a book like Brinsley's—and first of all counsel *to* use it.

"A student" he says in the second of his Discourses delivered to the Royal Academy, "unacquainted with the attempts of former adventurers is always apt to over-rate his own abilities, to mistake the most trifling excursions for discoveries of moment, and every coast new to him for a new-found country. If by chance he passes beyond his usual limits, he congratulates his own arrival at those regions which they who have steered a better course have long left behind them."

"Adventurers" has the right flavour: they

are men, however, plodding, punctual and punctilious who have yet had the heart to run a risk: it is of artists that Reynolds is speaking, and no man (however laborious) is an artist who is afraid of making a fool of himself or of having his pains for his reward. Not less certainly may it be said that no artist makes a fool of himself for nothing. But the "safe" man is no artist, and arrives nowhere, for he never starts. It is upon the records of adventurous journeys that we must look, if we are to keep our humility or avoid a just ridicule. How many "new movements" in education would have been unheralded and unsung (may we not say, unadvertised?) if those who have recently made them had been at the trouble to make themselves familiar with what in earlier centuries had been attained? To be sure, every generation, like every individual man, must begin for himself; but not quite at the beginning for the accumulated results of his fore-runners have a little raised the level on which he stands; he may at least learn more rapidly than those who have gone before him; he may travel not only more quickly but more easily over ground that has been broken by pioneers; saving his energy and his time for a real advance. Such an advance is, to be sure, in part a re-interpretation to a new age of what has been said and done in a preceding age; but it may be more than that; on the basis of re-interpretation fresh heights may be reached. But men "unacquainted with the attempts,"—let alone the achievements—of their precursors, may win some notoriety for themselves, but fail to carry forward the causes which they profess (with such sincerity as is to be combined with simple ignorance) to espouse and champion.

Brinsley offers us a book of educational theory—theory, it is true, translated into practice and illustrated by it, but theory, from title to termination. Many teachers make little of theory, not realising that no action is possible without some theory, a poor theory, a mistaken, or a very little or—a true theory. What they mean, perhaps, is that they are so much satisfied with their own practice that they are unwilling to reflect upon other men's theory. Now just as no practice can be had without some theory, so no theory can be had without some practice. The distinction, loudly proclaimed by the vulgar, between theory or vision and practice or conduct is without warrant. A man will not achieve a wide view unless he has climbed to a height; theorists, in fact, are commonly men of all others the most patient of toil.

Brinsley offers to his readers a point of view; but he shews them also the steps by which he has won it. They may be disposed to follow his steps; but even if not, they will direct their course to his position or a position even higher all the more surely if they consider precisely what he has done. And for trial, for practice in its secondary sense, of experiment and discipline, undertaken for the sake of technical facility it is often useful quite exactly to follow the steps of a master. For with facility in performance there may come a certain facility in criticism; the mind, like the muscles, may become alert, relieved of grossness and freed from hebetude. Sir Joshua Reynolds has sound words on this topic, addressed to students of painting but not inapplicable to teachers:

"Some who have never raised their minds to the consideration of the real dignity of Art, and who rate the works of an artist in proportion as they excel or are defective in the mechanical parts, look on theory as something that may enable them to talk but not paint better; and confining themselves entirely to mechanical practice, very assiduously toil on in the drudgery of copying; and think they make a rapid progress while they faithfully exhibit the minutest part of a favourite picture. This appears to me a very tedious, and I think a very erroneous method of proceeding."

It would be hard to find a stronger, or yet a more temperate warning against the unintelligent use of models, against the custom, not yet killed, according to which stupid or shy pupils with infinite trouble learn to do what stupid masters (not shy) have come by habit to do only too well. But there is an intelligent use of models: and this Reynolds (like Brinsley) advocates. "For my own part," says Reynolds in the Sixth Discourse, "I confess, I am not only very much disposed to maintain the absolute necessity of imitation in the first stages of the art, but am of opinion, that the study of other masters, which I here call imitation, may be extended throughout our whole lives, without any danger of the inconveniences with which it is charged, of enfeebling the mind or preventing us from giving that original air which every work undoubtedly ought always to have."

And again, in the same discourse, "Invention is one of the great marks of genius: but if we consult experience, we shall find, that it is by being conversant with the inventions of others that we learn to invent; as by reading the thoughts of others that we learn to think."

But the quarrel of practical, successful and even good teachers with theory and theorists is due to other causes than vanity or laziness. They probably distrust a theory which is based upon inadequate experience, and resent the intrusion of the advocates of such a theory. Here they are right, though they might pleasantly remind themselves that a wise man may learn of a fool. But they can have no decent quarrel with Brinsley on this ground; for theorist as he is, he is so steeped in practice, so full of it, that an inattentive reader might suppose that he was no theorist at all, that he was merely recording things done, setting them down as in a catalogue or index. In fact, Brinsley does much more than this; his review of his own procedure is made in order to help another man; and in order to help he must reveal, as far as he can, the principles which have governed his procedure. We have already seen what his starting point is : it is the belief that education is a process by which a man is brought and brings himself to the full development, possession and use of his powers ; and that all this is possible only in Society, and in the service of Society, for which he has a double name, Church and Commonwealth. This is his starting point ; clearly it is also his goal ; for the end of all effort is the realisation of the hope which prompted it. Towards this end, then, he makes his way ; and pausing, when his friend comes to ask his advice and help, at the point which he has reached after many years of experience he declares two things ; first, simply, that these have been the steps which he has taken, the methods which he has employed, and second, that these steps, these methods, will lead other persons to the same results. Now it is this second declaration, made not in these words, but made both directly and by implication throughout the book that is of special moment. Is it true? That is the question.

A formula in which a chemist or an architect concisely states the results of long and minute investigation, may be applied by other men who have not undertaken, and are incapable of undertaking such an investigation : and if it is correctly applied in precisely the circumstances in which it is intended to be applied, and to certain definitely named and understood materials, the results will fulfil anticipation.

But, it is argued, when we have to deal not with the things with which a chemist or an architect deals in circumstances prescribed and recognised, but with human minds and the products of human minds, human ideas, then the whole problem is at once changed. The circumstances cannot be prescribed, and the forces with which we are concerned are not invariable. And accordingly though a formula might be and in fact is appropriate for one kind of work, it is wholly inadmissible in the other. It is a strong argument, but it may be, and everywhere is, met by another not less strong. Certain modes of life and forms of conduct are desired by men; and they are desired because they illustrate and embody certain kinds of character, which also are firmly and in their main outlines clearly conceived—conceived not by "specialists," but by ordinary men. There are some general and common standards (not the highest, it may be) recognised and enforced by the general and common sense of a Society. A Society gives to itself an account of itself, and it is an account in which it sets out what it is and what it desires to be. On the whole, it desires to be, to continue to be what it is and has been; but even the most complacent of men have before their eyes or their imagination a picture of themselves as, with improvement, they may become; and by improvement they mean the development of their natural gifts. The English may, and at the present moment do, set high value upon the French character;

but they do not desire to become French; they desire to become better Englishmen, by which (both naturally and justly) they mean, more *English* Englishmen than ever they were before. Or if a man, not now regarding himself as English or French, but as human, contemplates his own possible improvement, he is bound to state his ambition in such terms as these: he has the ambition, being human to become still more human. Now when people send their children to school, they expect the schoolmasters to make them, being already English, more English than ever; to acquire, cultivate and develop those qualities which express themselves in an English way of life; or, a rare person may, while wishing all this or instead of wishing this, desire his child, being human to become more completely and perfectly human.

This, not less, is the task which teachers accept. And if they have never satisfied the large and various demands which it makes upon them, and if some have been less happy and less efficient than others, it is to be said that their success has been enough to encourage Society to continue their trust, and beg them to go on with what they have so long had in hand. The studies of the class-room, the organisation of the school, these are matters into which most men are as little apt to enquire as into the ingredients and processes of cooking of their favourite pudding. They leave these to the schoolmaster and to the cook, concerning themselves with the result.

Teachers decide not with complete, but with large freedom upon subjects and the treatment, arrangement, co-ordination of subjects, with a view to the result. It must then be presumed that their decisions are made, after experiment, because they have found out that certain subjects, treated in certain ways, tend towards the result or even actually reach it. May they not, then, express what they have got by trial, repeated and prolonged, in a formula, which will serve others who have the same result in view, but have come less near to attaining it?

A chemist can supply us with a formula for producing an explosive; may not a teacher offer a formula for educating a boy? A teacher is not a chemist, and a boy—one must, on reflection, admit—is not really and merely an explosive. The chemist in any particular enquiry aims at a definite object, and knows whether he has attained it or not: the teacher aims at a mark which is moving, and tries to reach a goal which for ever recedes as he advances. Again a chemist deals with elements the properties of which he either knows or may reasonably hope to know completely, and which remain constant: the teacher is concerned with a nature which he can never thoroughly explore, the depths of which he can never sound and which varies: the chemist, leaving his laboratory, may be sure that the British Public will not invade it during his absence, and add to or take from his test-tubes what seems good to it: the teacher enjoys no such security : on the contrary, he knows that his pupil, lessons over, will leave him and plunge at once into a world of influences, some friendly to the purposes of the school, others hostile; influences hardening, or enervating, ennobling or debasing; influences known and unknown, and even the known of potency incalculable.

We need not try further to illustrate the difficulties which beset a teacher; if he can never win success such as is the reward and pride of other men, he yet pursues his way and overcomes, if not all his difficulties, some of them; and if none of them entirely, some of them partially; and his partial triumph encourages him still to go on, and compels the slow and even grudging admiration and arrests and keeps the confidence of the world, which still entrusts to him its children and its hopes. His slow and broken progress is the measure of the progress of the world; the school is a microcosm, the University a little world, and never so much a world as when those who dwell in it humorously apprehend its littleness, and so transcend its limits and break its bounds. For them, the world is a University, from which no subject of human interest is or can be excluded.

The comparison which has been drawn between the teacher and the chemist has not been quite fair to the latter, and must now be corrected. It has been assumed, I think, justly that the chemist is occupied with things in their own nature fixed or, at any rate, fixed within limits of variation such as cannot be assigned to human qualities, but to him at any moment they may be incalculable, for he may not have discovered precisely what their nature is ; and he may arrive at a conclusion (later to be verified) by a happy divination. Even a layman can quote famous examples of this: and the learned could overwhelm him with pertinent instances. But divination, verified, provides a rule; felicitous guess work establishes though it does not create law. And what has been done once can then be done again, and by other men.

Are we to expect that experiment, good fortune, or genius will ever discover a rule, a law, for human nature comparable in exactness and universality to rule and law as we speak and think of them in "science"? The popular, and even the academic, use of the word "science" suggests that we do not expect this. We make a distinction habitually and constantly between scientific and humane studies. And the reason why we persist in making a distinction is that we still wish not only to note but to maintain a difference.

It is true, philologists, critics or literature, historians, and again sociologists and economists claim to use a scientific method, and often with propriety; but as yet the common sentiment of men is against allowing their method, however truly scientific, a scientific result. Scientific, we admit, these men may be in the collection, the arrangement, the comparison of evidence; but when they offer their conclusions we are apt, we of the common world, to discredit them, or at least to keep our judgment in suspense. For the truth is that we should not like to find a law, let us say of human dignity, as certain in its operation and as comprehensive in its range as the law of gravity. We should feel that our liberty, our liberty of error, had been invaded, our right, our right of going wrong, compromised and damaged. That is at the root of our common dislike of scientific conclusions in human affairs; but we oppose to them a second line of attack. We impugn the evidence; at least we say that it is inadequate.

To reconcile the ideas of law and of freedom in human life is the gift of poets; their language alone suffices to hold in harmony the hopes which transcend other and less ample modes of expression. Poets can achieve this and philosophers when they spring for a moment to the level of poetry.

For human freedom is exhibited, not in the conscious evasion or the ignorant neglect of law; but in its interpretation; and here in fact is the difference which may truly be proclaimed between science as it is concerned with man, and science as it is concerned with things. Scientific law makes things intelligible; it is itself made intelligible by man who uses it for his own ends.

But we are very far yet from reaching rule or law in human affairs, though curiously enough, far short of it as we fall, we hour by hour and day by day in the least as well as in the greatest of our affairs act as if the hastily-drawn generalisations which we possess were already trustworthy : we trust them enough to act on them. In private and in public life, we act as if we knew what human nature is, and what would appeal to it. A wise mother in her household, or a great statesman wielding an almost more than human power at a critical moment in his country's history, each of these, and between them every one who has any dealings with his fellows, acts upon a theory of human nature, as exhibited in the instances with which he is concerned. If a mistake is made, we say that it is due to ignorance of human nature ; a fortunate decision we attribute to knowledge of human nature. And not only a wise mother and a great statesman, but a foolish mother and a statesman not great act upon what theory they have, supported by what knowledge they have, of human nature.

Now the main, the central value of Brinsley's work is that it is a study of human nature ; it is a piece of research thoroughly scientific ; he sets down, in detail, without reservation, what he has done, and what reaction or response has been offered by his pupils. We may not accept his conclusions; we may think that they are not based upon adequate evidence, or that the evidence which he adduces is not fully estimated or weighed with a delicacy fine enough for his purpose. It is, then, for us to supplement him. If teachers would regard their processes of work upon human minds with as much care as some of them give to setting forth their results, we should soon have a wealth of material on which to build larger and more solid conclusions; and we should probably learn that in the record of processes all that was valuable about results had already been revealed.

If anyone should fear that this "wealth of material" might become overwhelming he could reassure himself by several considerations. First, he could fortify his courage by remembering how permanent and how generally operative a force resides in human indolence. And then he could reflect that even if every teacher were willing, not every teacher would be able, to set down exactly what he did. A novice in a laboratory may write in his note-book what he does in analysing a flower or in dissecting a frog's leg, and achieve a decent accuracy in the statement (which will include an account of mistakes, as well as of things properly done), and yet have established no claim to be an artist in his writing. He may not wish to be an artist. His teachers, men of the most profound scientific knowledge, may write accounts of the processes which they have learnt by experience to adopt, and of the experience itself which has taught them; they may write clearly, accurately and comprehensively; but they may not wish to be artists, and with few and splendid exceptions, they are not artists; and the clearness, the accuracy, the comprehensiveness of their writing, suffer no diminution or loss. They may fail in attractiveness, in persuasiveness, in charm; but if so, they fail in what they have not attempted, and may very well say that this is no failure at all. But a teacher, who attempted an account of his operations, of his dealing with the human mind, who should achieve clearness accuracy and comprehensiveness of statement (a very high achievement won by no ordinary patience and no ordinary ability) but cannot with all these things attain yet one thing more, artistic presentation, will have left undone the one thing needful. We need not, then, be in alarm; the material which we want for evidence on which to build our principles of education, will be increased, as we trust; but never so much as to cause an *embarras de richesses*.

In the meantime, it is not for us to decry, but rather to revere a man who has done what we, most of us, have not even tried to do. Brinsley has recorded his own practice; he has said quite clearly what were the aims which directed him; he claims, and not boastfully, that his procedure, tested by experiment has helped him to achieve his aims.

Many men, who are clearly and confessedly less laborious, trust more confidently to genius. And they believe that it is the prerogative of genius to be intolerant of question, and are delighted to imagine that they transcend all examination. They say that they do not know, that they certainly cannot explain, *how* they do what they do consummately well. It is a gift.

Now, I am very far from believing that genius

is nothing but an "infinite capacity for taking pains," though I believe that pains are for most men the price of perfection or even of mediocre proficiency. But genius is certainly an infinite capacity of going on, of advancing; genius may fail and die, and the proof of its failure or death is given by its ceasing to surpass itself. And if it is to continue its advance, and prolong its own period of growth, it must strengthen its bases, must deepen and thicken its roots. This is to be done by self-criticism. It may be true, at a given moment, that a man does not know how he has done a thing; but if he is to do it again, both with certainty and with vivacity, still more if he is to do it better, and to do a better thing, then he must find out how he has done it. And he may try to find out, without accusing himself of any distrust of his genius.

I venture once more to quote Sir Joshua Reynolds: in the Third Discourse he writes, appositely to our theme, "Could we teach taste and genius by rules, they would be no longer taste and genius. But though there neither are, nor can be, any precise invariable rules for the exercise, or the acquisition, of these great qualities, yet we may truly say, that they always operate in proportion to our attention in observing the works of nature, to our skill in selecting, and to our care in digesting, methodising and comparing our observations. There are many beauties in our art that seem, at first, to lie without the reach of precept, and yet may easily be reduced to practical principles. . . . Everything which is wrought with certainty is wrought upon some principle. If it is not, it cannot be repeated. If by felicity is meant anything of chance or hazard, or something born with a man, and not earned, I cannot agree with this *great philosopher."

A study of the *Ludus Literarius* may help us to attain a merited "felicity."

Of the life† of John Brinsley little is known. The year of his birth may be guessed to have been 1564 or 5; he was entered at Christ's College, Cambridge, as a sizar, in the Lent term 1580-81, and signed as "John Brinley." He took his B.A. degree in 1584-5 (entered as Brynsley), and his M.A. in 1588. He became a "Minister of the Word," and master of the public school at Ashby-de-la-Zouch in Leicestershire. He had a great reputation for skill as a teacher, and prepared many of his pupils for the universities. Of these one, William Lilly, the astrologer, who was put in Brinsley's charge in 1613, has left us some notes on his teacher in his autobiography. From him we learn that Brinsley "a strict puritan, not conformable wholly to the ceremonies of the Church of England," "was [about 1619] enforced from keeping school, being persecuted by the Bishop's officers: he came

---

* Bacon.
† *See* Dictionary of National Biography.

to London and then lectured in London, where he afterwards died."

His wife was a sister of the Bishop of Norwich, Joseph Hall, the author of "Christ Mystical": his son, also named John Brinsley, and sometimes confused with his father (born in 1600, and entered Emmanuel College, Cambridge, in 1615), was a Puritan Divine, and a voluminous writer.

This edition of the *Ludus Literarius* has been reproduced from that of 1627. I have compared it throughout with the first edition of 1612; the differences between the two are of no importance; but such as they are they can be traced in the following statement:—

The 1612 edition has the "Commendatory Preface" after "Of Grammatical Translations," and then the "Contents in General."

After *Finis*, p. 339, the 1612 edition has: "Studious Reader, I thought meete to give thee notice, that my translation of Sententiæ Pueriles, and of Cato, are now under the Presse; and the former of them, within a day or two, ready to come forth. Expect the other, shortly after."

In the next (back) page are "Postscript". [corrigenda] and "Faults escaped by the Printer."

POSTSCRIPT.

p. 53, l. 3, read "by that"   [not corrected in 1627 ed.]
p. 78, l. 35, for "declension" read "gender"   [not corrected in 1627 ed.]
p. 87, l. 16, for "ever" read "alwaye"   [corrected in 1627 ed.]

Introduction. XXXV.

p. 115, l. 9, put in "so far as I know" [corrected in 1627 ed.]
p. 116, l. 11, put in "so in others, for most part"
[not corrected in 1627 ed.]
p. 191, l. 37, put out "found" [not corrected in 1627 ed.]
p. 202, l. 25, for "*of* Grammatica," read "*at* Grammatica"
[not corrected in 1627 ed.]
p. 220, l. 32, put out "secondly" [not corrected in 1627 ed.]
p. 251, l. 20, for "most" read "many" [not corrected in 1627 ed.]
p. 274, l. 22, put out "kinde" [not corrected in 1627 ed.]
p. 297, l. 35, for "rest" read "rise" [not corrected in 1627 ed.]

FAULTS ESCAPED BY THE PRINTER.

In p. 20, l. 3, the alphabet should have been distinguished by threes: thus, a. b. c.   d. e. f.   g. h. i.   and so for the rest.

Page	Line	False	True	
20	25	thus	this	[corrected in 1627 ed.]
30	24	long	longest	[*longer* in 1627 ed.]
30	36	a booke	bookes	[not corrected in 1627 ed.]
31	22	m. i. t.	m. c. t.	[not corrected in 1627 ed.]
31	30	without	or without	[not corrected in 1627 ed.]
46	1	Third	a third	[not corrected in 1627 ed.]
56	9	of	or	[corrected in 1627 ed.]
59	29	manui felices	manui felici	[*fælici* in 1627 ed.]
63 [69]	3	parsed	poased	[not corrected in 1627 ed.]
63 [69]	27	parsing	poasing	[not corrected in 1627 ed.]
72	23	more	most	[corrected in 1627 ed.
73	1	goe truely	goe surely	[corrected in 1627 ed.]
79	3	speedily	specially	[corrected in 1627 ed.
102 {	12	que	que	[*Quæ* in 1627 ed.]
	18	virtutem	virtutum	[not corrected in 1627 ed.]
	36	weapon	weapons	[not corrected in 1627 ed.]
114	9	must	will	[not corrected in 1627 ed.]
137	2	àscio	ascio	[not corrected in 1627 ed.]
144	3 & 11	vincit	vincet	[line 3 corrected 1627 ed.]
				[line 11 not corrected]

Introduction.

Page	Line	False	True	
179	31	fittest	fitliest	[corrected in 1627 ed.]
181 [183]	17	curiously	cursorily	[corrected in 1627 ed.]
191 [192]	1	in manner	in good manner	[corrected in 1627 ed.]
221	37	so great	great	
231	16	Nomenclaton	Nomenclator	[corrected in 1627 ed.]
234	35	Theoguis	Theognis	[*Theognia* in 1627 ed.]
235	22	bis	this	
236	19 [18]	be also	also	[*also be* in 1627 ed.]
241	13	who	which	[corrected in 1627 ed.]
278	24	oderint	oderunt	[corrected in 1627 ed.]
200	margin, against line 18, for "yongest," read "highest"]			
				[corrected in 1627 ed.]

I hope that the Bibliography which I have made with some care and labour may be of interest and service to students. It is, I believe, complete, if my conjecture that for "Cosarzus," on p. 92 (*see* Bibliographical notes, p. 346), we should read "Cognatus" is justified.

My thanks are due to Dr. P. Giles, Master of Emmanuel College, Cambridge; Professor Foster Watson, Dr. John Sampson, Professor Postgate, and Mr. K. Forbes, for help and advice of many kinds on many points of doubt or difficulty; and I am—once more—under special obligations to Mr. P. S. Allen, of Merton College, Oxford, as much for his encouragement in a task not easy to fulfil in these times, as for the generosity with which he has allowed me to invade his leisure and borrow his learning. I am indebted to Miss D. Allmand for her vigilant and skilful aid in preparing the bibliography and in revising the proofs ; to Miss H. S. Kermode and Mr. H. P. Flewitt for tracing and verifying some references which had escaped me or were beyond my reach ; and to Miss D. Millett, Assistant Secretary of the Liverpool University Press, for the patience and interest with which she has watched and facilitated the production of this book.

E. T. CAMPAGNAC.

Liverpool, *August*, 1917.

LIST OF BRINSLEY'S WORKS.

[For the convenience of students I shew where the books may be found. B.M. signifies British Museum; Bod., Bodleian Library.]

1. LUDUS LITERARIUS; OR THE GRAMMAR SCHOOLE; shewing how to proceede from the first entrance into learning to the highest perfection required in the Grammar Schooles.
    4°, London, 1612 and 1627.
    B.M. and Bod.

2. SENTENTIAE PUERILES, translated grammatically.
    8°, London, 1612.
    Bod.

3. CATO (concerning the precepts of common life), translated grammatically. 8°, London, 1612.
    Bod.

4. CORDERIUS DIALOGUES, translated grammatically.
    8°, London, 1614.
    Bod.

    ———   [Another edition.]   16°, London, 1653.
    B.M.

5. THE TRUE WATCH AND RULE OF LIFE.
    7th edition. 2 parts. 8°, London, 1615.
    B.M. and Bod.

    ———   8th edition. 8°, London, 1619.
    B.M.

    ———   Third part out of Ezekiel IX. 4°, London, 1622.
    B.M. and Bod.

    ———   Fourth part "to the plain-hearted seduced by Popery." 8°, London, 1624.
    B.M. and Bod.

6. THE POSING OF THE PARTS; or a most plaine and easie way of examining the accidence and grammar by questions and answers.   4°, London, 1615.
    Bod.

    ———   [Another edition.] 4°, London, 1630.
    B.M.

    ———   10th edition. 4°, London, 1647.
    B.M.
    ———   [Another edition.] 4°, London, 1665.

7. THE FIRST BOOK OF TULLIES OFFICES, translated grammatically, chiefly for the good of schools. 8°, London, 1616.
Bod.

THE FIRST BOOK OF TULLIES OFFICES, translated grammatically; and also according to the propriety of our English tongue. 8°, London, 1631.
B.M.

8. PUERILES CONFABULATIUNCULAE; or Children's Dialogues, little conferences, or talkings together, or dialogues fit for children. 8°, London, 1617.
B.M.

9. A CONSOLATION FOR OUR GRAMMAR SCHOOLS; or a faithful encouragement for laying of a sure foundation of all good learnings in our schools. 4°, London, 1622.
B.M.

10. VIRGIL'S ECLOGUES, with his book on the Ordering of Bees, translated grammatically. 4°, London, 1633.
Bod.

11. STANBRIGII EMBRION RELIMATUM, seu Vocabularium metricum olim a Johanne Stanbrigio digestum, nunc vero locupletatum, defaecatum, legitimo nec non rotundo plerumque carmine exultans, & in majorem Pueritiae balbutientis usum undequaque accomodatum. 4°, London, 1647.
B.M. and Bod.

LUDUS LITERARIUS;
OR,
THE GRAMMAR
SCHOOLE;

SHEWING HOW TO PRO-
ceede from the first entrance into learning, to the highest perfection required in the
GRAMMAR SCHOOLES, with ease, certainty and
delight both to Masters and Schollers; onely according to
our common Grammar, and ordinary
Classicall Authours:

BEGUN TO BE SOUGHT OUT AT
the desire of some worthy favorers of learning, by searching the experiments of sundry most profitable Schoolemasters and other learned, and confirmed by tryall:

Intended for the helping of the younger sort of Teachers, and of all Schollers, with all other desirous of learning; for
the perpetuall benefit of Church and Common-wealth.

It offereth it selfe to all to whom it may doe good, or of whom it
may receive good to bring it towards perfection.

Χρὴ Μουσῶν θεράποντα καὶ ἄγγελον, εἴ τι περισσὸν
Εἰδείη, σοφίης μὴ φθονερὸν τελέθειν,
Ἀλλὰ τὰ μὲν μῶσθαι, τὰ δὲ δεικνύναι, ἄλλα δὲ ποιεῖν,
Τί σφιν χρήσηται μοῦνος ἐπιστάμενος. Theognis.

Nullum munus Reipub. afferre maius meliúsue possumus, quàm si doceamus atque erudimus iuuentutem. Cic. 3. de Divin.

Quærendi defatigatio turpis est, cum id quod quæritur sit pulcherrimum. 2. de Finibus.

AT LONDON,
Imprinted by FELIX KYNGSTON
for *John Bellamie.* 1627.

TO THE HIGH
AND MIGHTY PRINCE,
HENRIE, PRINCE OF
Wales; and to the most Noble and excellent Duke, *Charles,* Duke of *Yorke; J. B.* unfainedly wisheth all grace and glory, and humbly commendeth the Patronage *of his Labours.*

Eing that all of us of this Nation (*most Gracious and Excellent*) do above all people, owe unto the Highest, our lives and Religion, with all our blessings; and next under him, to his Anoynted, your most royall Father, our dread Soveraigne; to whom he hath given us, by whose hand he hath so miraculously saved us, & doth still preserve us alive in the midst of our enemies: we are therfore every one alwaies bound (in what thing

The Epistle Dedicatory.

thing soever he shall inable us thereunto) to testifie our acknowledgement. Pardon then the desire of your devoted & most affectionate poore servant, if he shall endeavour in all humility, to witnesse his thankefulnesse unto the Lord of heaven, & to his Anoynted, by seeking to adde somwhat unto the Honor, and deserts of his Royall Progenie: even of you, who are the rich gifts of the heavenly bounty, and the flourishing branches of that happy-spreading Cedar. And what is it, which might still more advance you in the eyes and hearts of all the people of your most noble Father's Dominions, then if now from your first yeeres, you might begin to bee the blessed instruments of the Almighty, of an everlasting benefit to the present and all succeeding generations? whereby you might knit all hearts more surely unto the holy God, and his supreme Deputy here amongst us; as also to your selves in Regall issue, and unto yours for ever. Accept therefore, to this purpose (I beseech you) this weake labour thus begun, of searching out, and inquiring of all the speediest, surest and most easie entrance and way to all good learning in our
Gram-

The Epistle Dedicatory.

Grammar schooles. To the end, that those rare helpes of knowledge, which the Lord hath granted to this last Age (some of the principall wherof have bin scarce knowne, or very little practised, so far as I can find; and most of the rest have bin only knowne amongst some few) might by your Princely favours, be made common unto all, for the publike good of the present Age, and of all times to come. The Lord God hath given unto your Highnesse and Excellency, to be borne, and to live in the time of most glorious light and knowledge; in which, if the experiments of sundry of the learnedest, and most happily experienced Schoolemasters and others, were gathered into one short sum, all good learning (which is the chiefest glory of a Nation) would daily flourish more and more, and be conveyed to all places and times; that not only this age present, but also all posterity should have just cause evermore to magnifie the God of glory for you: for how must this needes oblige all sorts, if this heavenly gift of learning, might through you be attained with much more ease, delight, and certainty; and also in shorter time, with lesse charges

The Epistle Dedicatory.

charges to Parents, without that extreme sharpenesse used ordinarily in schooles amongst the poore children? How shall it increase your lasting comfort & honor, if by your Highnesse favours, the work thus entred into, shal soone come to an happy end? For as some very learned and of much experience, have begun already to helpe herein; so others of the chiefest gifts and imployments in this kind, shall not disdaine to lay-to their hands to bring it in time to some perfection. Why should we the liege subjects of *Jesus Christ*, & of this renowned Kingdome, be overgrowne herein, by the servants of Antichrist; many of whom bend all their wits, and joyne their studies, for the greatest advantage of their learning, even in the Grammar schooles, onely to the advancement of Babylō, with the overthrow of this glorious nation, and of all parts of the Church of Christ, to bring us under that yoake againe, or else to utter confusion? Or why should we omit any time or opportunity, which the Lord offereth hereunto? The hope therefore of your poore servant is, that your Highnesse and Excellency will not impute any presumption to
this

The Epistle Dedicatory.

this indeavour, (though thus undertaken by me the unablest of many thousands) but that you will accept it, according to the desire that hath bin in me, to do good thereby to this Church & Nation: And the rather, for the undoubted assurance of the exceeding benefit, which must needs come in time, by the best courses once found out and made publike: and though such a worke have bin long talked of & wished, yet it is still generally neglected. The experience also which the Lord hath shewed, in the readinesse of sundry very learned, in a work of not much lesse difficulty, to helpe most lovingly, with their best advices, to bring still to better perfection, doth give your servāt certaine hope of the like cheerefull assistance herein. Howsoever yet it shall remaine for a testimony of duty to the heavenly Majesty, of thankfulnesse & loyall affection towards our Liege Soveraigne, and you his Royall Progenie: That as you are the worthy sons of a Father most renowned of all the Kings of the earth, for singular learning, & for holding up, and advancing by all meanes the glorious light thereof, and as you are not inferior to any of the Princes of the world in your education and

In the true Watch and Rule of Life, made farre more perfect and plaine in this 5. Editiō.

The Epistle Dedicatory.

and first yeres: so all sorts may through you receive an increase of the same shining light, and all hearts may bee still more firmely bound by your perpetuall benefits. To you thrice happy Prince, I offer it most humbly, as the poore Widowe's mite, amongst the great gifts presented to your Highnesse. And to you, right noble Duke, the study of your servant, if he might but in any one thing further you in that sweete and pleasant way of learning, wherin you are so graciously proceeding. Finally, I trust that it shal ever stand as a true witnesse of an unfained desire towards the perpetuall flourishing of this Nation, with all the Church of CHRIST. And in this humble desire, I commend your Highnesse and Excellency unto him who advanceth and setteth up Kings in their Throne, and hath said that he will honour those who honour him. The whole successe I commit to that Supreme Grace, who looketh at the heart, and accepts the will: whom you desiring to follow, shall reigne with him in that most blessed light eternally.

*Your Highnesse and Grace's
humbly devoted in all loyall and
faithfull observance,*

JO. BRINSLY.

A COMMENDATO-rie Preface.

ARts are the onely helpes towards humane perfection. Those therefore which are the helpes towards the easinesse, maturitie, perfection of Arts, deserve best of mankinde. Whence it is, that God would not suffer the first devisers, so much as of shepheards' tents, of musicall instruments, of Iron-works, to bee unknowne to the world: the last whereof even heathen Antiquitie hath in common judgement continued, without much difference of name, till this day; although I cannot beleeve that any of the heathen gods were so ancient. Yea, hence it is, that the holy Ghost challengeth the faculty even of manuary skill, to his owne gift; as being too good for Nature, and too meritorious of men. That *Bezaleel* and *Aholiab* can worke curiously in silver and gold, for the materiall Tabernacle, is from God's Spirit, and not theirs: How much more is this true, in those sciences which are so essentiall to the Spiritual house of God? As Arts are to perfection of knowledge; so is Grammar to all Artes. Man differs but in speech and reason (that is, Grammar and Logicke) from beasts

A Commendatory Preface.

beasts: whereof reason is of Nature; speech (in respect of the present variatiō) is of humane institution. Neither is it unsafe to say, that this later is the more necessary of the two: For we both have and can use our reason alone; our speech wee cannot, without a guide. I subscribe therefore to the judgement of them, that thinke God was the first Author of letters (which are the simples of this Art) whether by the hand of *Moses*; as *Clement* of Alexandria reports from *Eupolemus*: or rather of the ancienter Progeny of *Seth* in the first world; as *Josephus*. He that gave man the faculty of speech, gave him this meanes, to teach his speech. And if he were so carefull to give man this helpe, while all the world was of one lip (as the Hebrewes speake) how much more, after that miserable confusion of tongues, wherein every man was a Grammar to himselfe, and needed a new Grammar, to be understood of others? It is not therefore unworthy of observation, that God (knowing languages to be the carriage of knowledge) as in his judgement he devided the tongues of those presumptuous builders; so contrarily he sent his Spirit in cloven tongues upon the heads of those master-builders of his Church. What they were suddenly taught of God, we with much leasure and industry learne of men; knowing the tongues so necessarie for all knowledge, that it is well, if but our younger yeeres be spent in this study. How serviceable therefore is this labour, which is here undertaken, and how beneficiall, to make the way unto all learning, both short, and faire! Our Grandfathers were

A Commendatory Preface.

were so long under the ferule, till their beards were growne as long as their pens: this age hath descried a neerer way.; yet not without much difficulty, both to the schollers, & teacher: Now, time, experience, and painfulnes (which are the meanes to bring all things to their height) have taught this Author yet further, how to spare both time and paines this way unto others; and (that which is most to bee approved) without any change of the received groūds. It is the common envy of men, by how much richer treasure they have found, so much more carefully to conceale it. How commendable is the ingenuity of those spirits, which cannot ingrosse good experiments to their private advantage? which had rather do then have good: who can be content to cast at once into the common Bank of the world, what the studious observatiō, inquisition, reading, practice of many yeeres have inriched them withall: That, which this Author hath so freely done; as one that feares not, lest knowledge should have made too easie, or too vulgar. The Jesuites have won much of their reputation, and stolne many hearts with their diligence in this kind. How happy shall it be for the Church & us, if we excite our selves at least to imitate this their forwardnes? We may out-strip thē, if we want not to our selves. Behold here, not feete, but wings, offered to us. Neither are these directions of meere speculation, whose promises are commonly as large, as the performance defective; but such as (for the most part) to the knowledge of my selfe, and many abler Judges, have beene, & are daily answered in his experience, and practice, with more then usuall successe.

What

A Commendatory Preface.

What remaines therefore, but that the thankefull acceptation of men, & his effectuall labours should mutually reflect upon each-other? that he may be incouraged by the one, and they by the other benefited: that what hath beene undertaken and furthered by the grave counsell of many, and wise; and performed by the studious indeavors of one so well deserving; may be both used and perfected to the common good of all, and to the glory of him which giveth, and blesseth all.

Jos. Hall, Dr. *of Divin.*

THE CONTENTS IN GENERALL OF
the chiefe points aymed at, and hoped to be effected by this
WORKE.

*T*O *teach Schollers how to bee able to reade well, and write true Orthography, in a short space.*

2. To make them ready in all points of Accedence and Grammar, to answere any necessary question therein.

3. To say without booke all the usuall and necessary rules to construe the Grammar rules, to give the meaning, use, and order of the Rules; to shew the examples, and to apply them: which being well performed, will make all other learning easie and pleasant.

4. In the severall fourmes and Authors to construe truely, and in propriety of words and sence, to parse of themselves, and to give a right reason of every word why it must bee so, and not otherwise; and to reade the English of the Lectures perfectly out of the Latine.

5. Out

The Contents in generall.

5. *Out of an English Grammaticall translation of their Authors, to make and to construe any part of the Latine, which they have learned to prove that it must be so: and so to reade the Latine out of the English, first, in the plaine Grammaticall order; after, as the wordes are placed in the Author, or in other good composition. Also to parse in Latine, looking onely upon the Translation.*

6. *To take their lectures for themselves, except in the very lowest formes, and first enterers into construction; or to doe it with very Little helpe, in some more difficult things.*

7. *To enter surely in making Latine, without danger of making false Latine, or using any barbarous phrase.*

8. *To make true Latine, and pure* Tullies *phrase, and to prove it to be true and pure. To doe this in ordinary morall matters, by that time that they have bin but two yeeres in construction.*

9. *To make Epistles imitating* Tully, *short and pithy, in* Tullies *Latine, and familiar.*

10. *To translate into English, according to propriety both of words and sense: and out of the English to reade the Latine againe, to prove it, and give a reason of every thing.*

11. *To take a piece of* Tully, *or of any other familiar easie Author, Grammatically translated, and in propriety of words, and to turne the same out of the translation into goood Latine, and very neere unto the words of the Authour; so as in most you shall hardly discerne, whether it be the Authour's Latine, or the scholler's.*

12. *To*

The Contents in generall.

12. *To correct their faults of themselves, when they are but noted out unto them, or a question is asked of them.*

13. *To be able in each fourme (at any time whensoever they shall be apposed of a sudden, in any part of their Authors, which they have learned) to construe, parse, reade into English, and forth of the translation to construe and to reade into the Latine of their Authors ; first, into the naturall order, then into the order of the Author, or neere unto it.*

14. *In* Virgill *or* Horace *to resolve any piece, for all these points of learning, and to doe it in good Latine ;*

In
{
 Construing to give propriety of words and sense.
 Scanning the verses, and giving a reason thereof.
 Shewing the difficulties of Grammar.
 Observing the elegācies in tropes & figures.
 Noting phrases and Epithetes.
}

15. *So to reade over most of the chiefe Latine Poets, as* Virgill, Horace, Persius, &c. *by that time that by reason of their yeeres, they be in any measure thought fit for their discretion, to goe unto the University : yea to goe thorow the rest of themselves, by ordinary helpes.*

16. *In the Greeke Testament to construe perfectly, and parse as in the Latine, to reade the Greeke backe again out of a translation Latine or English : also to construe, parse, and to prove it out of the same. To do the like in* Isocrates, *or any familiar pure Greeke Author ; as also in* Theognis, Hesiod, *or* Homer, *and to resolve as in* Virgill *or* Horace.

17. *In*

The Contents in generall.

17. *In the Hebrew to construe perfectly, and to resolve as in the Greeke Testament; and to reade the Hebrew also out of the translation. Which practice of dayly reading somewhat out of the translations into the Originals, must needes make them both very cunning in the tongues, and also perfect in the texts of the Originals themselves, if it be observed constantly; like as it is in dayly reading Latine out of the Translation.*

18. *To answer most of the difficulties in all Classicall Schoole-Authors; as in* Terence, Virgil, Horace, Persius, *&c.*

19. *To oppose schollerlike in Latine, of any Grammar question necessary, in a good forme of words; both what may bee objected against Lillies rules, and how to defend them.*

20. *To write Theames full of good matter, in pure Latine, and with judgement.*

21. *To enter to make a verse with delight, without any bodging at all; and to furnish with copie of Poeticall phrase, out of* Ovid, Virgil, *and other the best Poets.*

22. *So to imitate and expresse* Ovid *or* Virgil, *as you shall hardly discerne, unlesse you know the places, whether the verses be the Authour's or the scholler's: and to write verses* ex tempore *of any ordinary Theames.*

23. *To pronounce naturally and sweetely, without vain affectation; and to begin to doe it from the lowest fourmes.*

24. *To make right use of the matter of their Authours, besides the Latine; even from the first beginners: as of* Sententiæ *and* Confabulatiunculæ Pueriles, Cato,

The Contents in generall.

Cato, Esop's fables, Tullies Epistles, Tullies Offices, Ovid's Metamorphosis, and so on to the highest. To helpe to furnish them, with variety of the best morall matter, and with understanding, wisedome and precepts of vertue, as they grow; and withall to imprint the Latine so in their minds thereby, as hardly to be forgotten.

25. *To answer concerning the matter contained in their Lectures, in the Latine of their Authors, from the lowest fourmes, and so upward.*

26. *To construe any ordinary* Author *ex tempore.*

27. *To come to that facility and ripenesse, as not onely to translate leasurely, & with some meditation, both into English and Latine, as before in the* Sect. *or Article* 10. *and* 11. *but more also, to reade any easie Author forth of Latine into English, and out of a translation of the same Grammatically translated, to reade it into Latine againe. As Corderius, Terence, Tullies Offices, Tullie de natura Deorum, Apthonius. To doe this in Authors and places which they are not acquainted with, and almost as fast as they are able to reade the Author alone.*

28. *To write fayre in Secretary, Romane, Greeke, Hebrue; as they grow in knowlege of the tongues.*

29. *To know all the principall and necessarie Radices, Greeke and Hebrue; and to be able to proceede in all the learned tongues of themselves, through ordinary helpes, and much more by the worthy helpes & meanes, to be had in the Universities.*

30. *To be acquainted with the grounds of Religion, and the chiefe Histories of the Bible. To take all the substance of the Sermons, for Doctrines, proofes, uses, if they be plainely and orderly delivered: and to set them downe after-*

The Contents in generall.

afterwards in a good Latine stile, or to reade them ex tempore *in Latine, out of the English: To conceive and answer the severall points of the Sermons, and to make a briefe repetition of the whole Sermon without booke.*

31. *To be set in the high way, and to have the rules and grounds, how to attaine to the puritie and perfection of the Latine tongue, by their further labour and practice in the University.*

32. *To grow in our English tongue, according to their ages and growthes in other learning: To utter their minds in the same both in proprietie and purity; and so to be fitted for Divinitie, Law, or what other calling or faculty soever they shall be after imployed in.*

33. *Finally, thus to proceed together with the tongues in the understanding and knowledge of the learning, or matter contained in the same.   To become alike expert, in all good learning meete for their yeeres and studies; that so proceeding still, after they are gone from the Grammar schooles, they may become most exquisite in all kinds of good learning to which they shall be applied.*

These things may be effected in good sort, through God's blessing, in the severall fourms, as the schollers proceed, by so many in each fourme as are apt and industrious, only by the directions following, if they be constantly observed; If the Masters being of any competent sufficiencie, will take meet paines; and if the schollers being set to schoole so soone as they shall bee meete, may be kept to learning ordinarily, having bookes and other necessary helpe & encouragements. That so all schollers of any towardlinesse and diligence may be made absolute Grammarians, and every way fit for the Universitie, by fifteene yeeres of age; or by that time that they shall bee meete by discretion and government.

The Contents in generall.

vernment. And all this to bee done with delight and certaintie, both to master and schollers, with strift and contention amongst the schollers themselves, without that usuall terrour and cruelty, which hath beene practised in many places, and without so much as severitie amongst good natures.

How greatly all this would tend to the furtherance of the publike good, every one may judge; which yet it will doe so much the more, as the Lord shall vouchsafe a further supply, to the several meanes and courses that are thus begun, by adjoyning daily the helpes and experiments of many mo learned men, of whom we conceive good hope, that they will be ready to lend their helping hands, to the perfiting of so good a Worke.

To the loving Reader.

Ourteous Reader, who tenderest the poore Countrey schooles, for which this labour hath been undertaken, or didst ever feele or know the wants in many of them, accept my willing minde for their good. And take this Impression as not set foorth, but chiefely to the end, to have store of Copies, to goe to many learned wel-willers to the Worke, for their helpe: like as it hath heretofore, to sundry much reverenced for their learning and wisedome. Of all whom, I humbly intreate their kinde assistance, for amending that which is amisse; by adding what is wanting, cutting off whatsoever is superfluous, changing what is unbefitting, and reducing every thing into the right order: That it may speedily come forth more plaine and perfect; and thereby, if not themselves, yet their friends may reape some benefit of their labours. For the liberty and boldnesse used in it, consider that it is but a Dialogue to incite & encourage others; as, I tooke it, farre more profitable and delightsome to reade, then

To the loving Reader.

then a bare narration. All who are friendly and unfained favourers of good learning, will (I hope) thinke so of it. It shall wrong no man willingly: farre be that from mee. I will right them againe, so soone as I know it. Be the faults never so many, through my weakenesse and want of meere leasure (as they must needs bee the moe, by my absence from the Presse) yet time, I trust wil reforme them. In the meane while, let my travell and the good things weigh against the rest. For the length of it, remember for whome I write, even the meanest teachers and learners: with whom though I sometime use repetitions, I cannot be over-plaine; sith they commonly get so little of short Treatises, be they never so learned. Cōsider also, that I would hide nothing, which God hath vouchsafed me in my search: that out of all, the most profitable may be selected, & in the mean time the best only used. And for the matter of the Dialogue, take it as that which is desired to be effected in time; and which I hope all shall finde, when once the helpes belonging hereunto, shall be supplied and perfected.

Account this, but as a meere entrance into the work: which if seven yeeres shall bring to perfection fully to accomplish that which is wished, I shall thinke my paines most happily bestowed, if God so farre forth prolong my daies. I seeke not my selfe: if I may doe some little service to God and my Countrey, I have enough. I oppose my selfe to none. Shew my oversight in love, and I will amend it. I prescribe to none: no, not the meanest; but onely desire to learn of all the learned, to helpe the unlearned.

To the loving Reader.

unlearned. In the worke I take nothing to my selfe, but the wants. What I received of others, I received to this end; after full triall made of them, to publish them for the common good. This I have professed from the beginning of my travell. I would also give every one his due particularly, what I have had of him; and will, if it shall bee thought meete. I have promised nothing but my labour: that I have and doe desire to performe to my abilitie and above. The weaker I am, the fitter shall I bee to apply my selfe to the simplest: and the more honour God shall have, if hee shall give that blessing unto it, which I do humbly beg. If any man shall oppose, and detract from these my labours; forasmuch, as he shall therein (as I take it) shew himselfe an enemie to the common good of the present Age, and of all posteritie (the benefit whereof, as God is my witnesse, I have intended principally in these my endeavours) I can but be sorry, and pray for him.

Thine in Christ,

J. B.

To the loving Reader.

For the manner of proceeding used in this worke, it is prescribed in the preface to the reader, which is set before our common Grammar : where it, having shewed the inconvenience of the diversitie of Grammars and teaching, doth direct thus ;

Wherefore it is not amisse, if one seeing by triall an easier and readier way, then the common sort of Teachers doe, would say that he hath proved it, and for the commodity allowed it ; that others not knowing the same, might by experience prove the like, and then by proofe reasonable judge the like : not heereby excluding the better way when it is found ; but in the meane season forbidding the worse.

OF GRAMMATICALL
Translations.

Here is a way (saith Master *Askame*) touched in the first book of *Cicero de Oratore*, which wisely brought into schooles, truly taught, and constantly used, would not onely take wholly away that butcherly feare in making Latines, but would also with ease and pleasure, and in short time, as I know by good experience, worke a true choise and placing of words, a right ordering of sentences, an easie understanding of the tongues, a readinesse to speake, a facility to write, a true judgement both of his owne, and other men's doings, what tongue soever he doth use.

This way, as he sheweth, is by causing the scholler first to understand the matter which hee learneth: secondly, to construe truly: thirdly, to parse exactly: fourthly, to translate into English plainly: fifthly, to translate out of the English into the Latine of the Author againe: and so after to compare with the Author how neere he came unto it. Finally, by much translating both wayes, chiefely
out

Mr. Askam's 1. Booke page. 1.

Of Grammaticall Translations.

out of the English into Latine, as he setteth downe in the beginning of his second booke; and hereby he saw those strange experiments of the increase of learning, which he reporteth of Master *John Whitney*, and others. Now, whereas these things are very hard to bee performed in the common schooles; especially for lacke of time to trie and compare every scholler's translation, and ever giving them new pieces to translate, and those such as are meete for every fourme; by the meanes of these translations of our first schoole Authors, all these things may be performed in every Author and fourme, most certainly & constantly, and with much ease and delight both to Master and Schollers; as I trust will be found. The manner hereof I have set downe in the 8. Chapter, and others following. Therefore since the time that God made these knowne unto me (which was about some foure yeeres agoe or not much above, upon the occasion of a late worthy experiment related unto mee, confirming the testimonie of Master *Askam*) I have laboured in these translations, above all other things, First, to finde out the Grammar rule of construing truly and perfectly, wherby to guide these translations, & whereupon they chiefely depend: Secondly, to find out the particular uses and benefits of them: Thirdly, to finde out and set downe such directions, as whereby to frame the translations to serve for all the uses most plainly: Fourthly, to translate so many of our first Authors after the same manner, as since that time I have had occasion for my schollers in each fourme to reade:
Fifthly,

Of Grammaticall Translations.

Fifthly, to have certaine triall and experience of every thing, so much as in this time I could; and upon triall to commend them to Schooles, to helpe hereby to bring into Schooles that excellent way of learning, which he so highly commendeth, and whereof I have very great hope; and so by them a perpetuall benefit to all schooles and good learning: which I unfainedly wish and pray for.

Advertisement by the Printer.

COurteous Reader, whereas in the later end of this Book it is signified in what forwardnesse the Author's translation of *Sententiæ Pueriles and Cato*, are; take notice also that his booke entituled, *The Poasing of the Accedence*, is since come to my hands, and likely to come forth at the same time with *Cato*.

Ludus Literarius:
OR,
The Grammar Schoole.

CHAP. I.

A Discourse betweene two Schoolemasters, concerning their function. In the end determining a conference about the best way of teaching, and the manner of their proceeding in the same.

SPOUDEUS.   PHILOPONUS.

Spoud.
GOD save you, good Sir: I am glad to see you in health.
Phil. What, mine old acquaintance, M. *Spoudeus?*
Spoud. The very same, Sir.
Phil. Now, I am as right glad to see you well; you are heartily welcome to this my poore house.
Spoud. Sir, I give you many thankes.
Phil. But how have yo done these many yeeres?
Spoud. I thanke God I have had good health, ever since we lived in the Colledge together: but for my time, I have spent it in a fruitlesse, wearisom, and an unthankfull office; in teaching a poore countrey schoole, as I have heard, that your

The Schoolemaster's place ordinarily wearisome, thankelesse.

THE GRAMMAR SCHOOLE

your selfe have also beene imployed in the same kinde of life, and am therefore perswaded, that you have had some experience of my griefe.

Phil. Experience, say you? yea indeed I have had so much experience of that whereof you now complaine, that if all other things were according thereunto, I might bee able to teach very many. But I pray you Sir, what good occasion hath brought you into these parts? It is a wonder to see you in this countrey. I should hardly have knowne you (it is so long since we lived together, now above twentie yeeres, and also for that you seeme to mee so aged) but that I did better remember your voice, then your favour.

They who have felt the evils of labouring without fruit in their calling, will neither spare labour nor cost to helpe the same.

Spoud. Sir, you see the proverbe verified in me; *Cura facit canos.* Cares and troubles have made me aged long before my time. As for my journey, a very great and necessarie occasion hath driven me into these quarters, to come even unto you, to seek your helpe and direction, in a matter wherein (I hope) you may exceedingly pleasure me, without hurt any way, or so much as the least prejudice unto your selfe.

Phil. You might thinke me very unkinde, and forgetfull of our ancient love, if I should not be ready to shew you any kindnesse; especially sith you have taken so long a journey unto me. But I pray you what is the matter?

If for to gaine a little politick experience, or to see fashions, many will adventure both by sea and land, into enemies' countries, to the hazarding ofttimes both of body and soule; how much more ought we to travell at home, amongst our friends, to gaine lasting comfort in our labours?

Spoud. The matter (if you wil give me leave) is this. I have heard that you have long taken great paines in teaching; and that of late yeeres, you have set your selfe wholly to this happy kinde of travell; to finde out the most plaine, easie, and sure waies of teaching, for the benefit both of your selfe, and others: whereby you have attained much happy knowledge in this behalfe. Now my long journey hath been for this same very purpose, to desire some conference with you, and to intreat your loving favour & helpe. I should thinke my selfe for ever bound unto you, if you would vouchsafe to impart unto me some of those experiments, which I have been certainly informed, that by your travels you have obtained. For, I myselfe have so long laboured in this moiling and drudging life, without any fruit

to

THE GRAMMAR SCHOOLE

to speake of, and with so many discouragements and vexa- *Many honest and* tions in stead of any true comfort, that I waxe utterly wea- *painfull Schoole-* rie of my place, and my life is a continuall burden unto me: *masters weary of their places, live* Insomuch as that it causeth me to feare, that God never *in continuall* called me to this function, because I see his blessing so lit- *discontent tho-* tle upon my labours; neither can I finde any delight there- *row lacke of* in: whereas, notwithstanding, I heare of some others, and *knowledge of a* even of our old acquaintance, whom God blesseth great- *good course of teaching.* ly in this calling; though such be verie rare, some one or *Some few God* two spoken of almost in a whole countrey. *much blesseth in*

Phil. Indeed I have travelled in this too unthankefull a *this calling,* calling (as you doe most justly complaine) and that in all *though they be very rare.* this time, since we lived together. In the greatest part wherof, I have been well acquainted with your griefes and vexations; which are no other then doe ordinarily waite upon this our function: yet this I thankfully acknowledge (according to your former speech, and to give you likewise some reviving) that now of late, since I set my selfe more consciounably and earnestly to seeke out the best waies of teaching by inquiring, conferring and practicing constantly all the most likely courses, which I could heare or devise, God hath granted unto me, to finde so great contentation and joy of this same labour in my schoole, that it hath swallowed up the remembrance of all my former grievances. *More true con-* For I doe plainely see such a change, that now I doe not on- *tentment may* ly labour in my place usually without griefe, or any wea- *be found in this* rinesse at all, but that I can take ordinarily more true *calling rightly followed, then in* delight and pleasure in following my children (by obser- *any recreation* ving the earnest strife and emulation which is amongst *whatsoever.* them, which of them shall doe the best, and in the sensible increase of their learning and towardnesse) then anie one can take in following hawkes and hounds, or in anie other the pleasantest recreation, as I verily perswade my selfe. And the rather, because after my labour ended, my *The fruit of this travell, is ever* chiefest delight is in the remembrance thereof; and in *sweetest in the* the consideration of the certaine good, that I know shall *remembrance of* come thereby, both unto Church and Common-wealth: *it after.*

and

THE GRAMMAR SCHOOLE

and also that my labour and service is acceptable to the Lord, though all men should be unthankfull. So that now I am never so well, as when I am most diligent in my place. Yea, I doe seeme to my selfe to find withall so great a blessing upon my labours, above all former times, that if I had knowne the same courses from the beginning, I doe assure my selfe that I had done ten times more good, and my whole life had been full of much sweet contentment, in regard of that which it hath bin. Although my labours have never beene utterly unprofitable, but that I have still sent forth for every yeere, some unto the Universities, and they approved amongst the better sort of those which have come thither: yet this hath beene nothing to that good which I might undoubtedly have done.

Knowledge and practice of the best courses will much augment the blessing of our labours, and fill our lives with contentment

Spoud. Sir, I am perswaded that you speake as you thinke: and therefore I doe grow into greater hope, that you having had so much experience of the griefe in the one, and joy in the other, will be more compassionate of me, and more readie also to impart your experiments with me, to make me partaker of your comfort.

Feeling of the griefe and want of others, will make us more compassionate.

Phil. For communicating unto you, for your helpe and comfort, what God hath made knowne unto me, I take it to be my dutie. We all of us know the danger of hiding our talent, or keeping backe our debt, when the Lord having given us abilitie, doth call upon us to pay it.

We are but Stewards of Gods gifts, and to be accountable for every talent.

Spoud. I thank God unfainedly (good Sir) for this heartie affection, which I doe finde in you, and for this readinesse to communicate with mee the fruits of your travels. You shall see, I hope, that I shall receive them, with like alacritie and thankfulnesse, and be as readie to imploy them to the best, to doe my uttermost service in my place and calling hereafter. So that although my first beginnings have bin small, through ignorance of better courses, yet I trust my after-fruits shall much increase. Hereby my last dayes shall proove my best, and make some amends for that which is past: and also my new comforts shall sweeten all the remainder of my life, and make me likewise to forget the daies

What our affection and resolution should be in receiving any speciall blessing from the Lord: as namely, direction how to walke more fruitfully in our calling.

THE GRAMMAR SCHOOLE

daies that are past. How true is that Proverbe of wise *Salomon*, that heavinesse in the heart of man doth bring it down, but a good word doth rejoyce it? You have revived my heart, and put new spirits into mee, by that which you have already said.

Phil. The Lord will revive you, I hope, and all of us also who labour in this toiling kind; by causing us to find more sound fruit, and pleasant content in our teaching, then ever yet we felt; if we will but set our selves to seeke of him, and readily impart our several experiments for the good of all: if withall we will receive thankefully, and cheerefully put in practice those gracious helpes of so many learned men, which he in this last age of the world hath afforded aboundantly, above all former times, very many whereof lie utterly hid and unknowne to the greatest sort, unto this day: And that partly through lack of care and conscience, to do that good which we might, and ought in our places; partly through extreme unthankfulnes, neglecting the rich gifts of the Lord, so plentifully powred down from heaven upon us, to leave the world more without excuse. But as for mine owne selfe, all that I can promise is, onely my study and desire, to doe you and all other the greatest good that ever I shall be able; and hereunto we have all bound our selves. If I know any thing wherein I have, or you may receive benefit, I acknowledge it wholly where it is due, even to him who giveth liberally to all who seeke him aright, and casteth no man in the teeth. And resting upō his rich bounty for a further supply, if you shall propound in order the particular points, wherein you would wish my advice, I shal very willingly go on with you, and acquaint you with all things which hitherto I have learned in all my search, and more hereafter as his wisdome shall adde unto me.

Spoud. I rejoice in your confidence, & with that so it may bee. In the meane time I like well of your motion, of going thorow in order the principall matters of difficultie. If therefore you shall thinke meete, I shall reduce all to certaine heads, which a friend of mine shewed unto mee of late,

How the way of all good learning may be more easie then ever in former ages.

Many most worthy helps lye utterly hid from the greatest part, onely through neglect.

THE GRAMMAR SCHOOLE

late, set down in a certain Table, which it may be that your selfe have seene.

Phil. Let me heare what was contained in it, and then I shall soone answer you, whether I have seene it or no.

Spoud. There was contained in it, a briefe summe of sundry particular benefits, which may bee brought to Grammar schooles, to make schollers very perfect in every part of good learning meet for their yeeres; and that all both Masters and Schollers may proceede with ease, certainty and delight, to fit all apt Schollers for the Universitie every way, by fifteene yeeres of age. Concerning which severall heads, although it were a most happy worke if they could be attained unto (all of them being in my minde very excellent, and indeed the whole, such a worke as must needs bring a perpetuall benefit, both to Church, and Common-wealth, and that not onely to the present, but to all succeeding ages) yet that I may speake freely, what I conceive of them, many of them seeme very strange unto me. And, although I will not say that they are utterly impossible: yet indeed I take them to be altogether unlikely; considering the continuall paines and vexation that my selfe have undergone, and yet could never come in many of them, neere unto the least part thereof.

Phil. By that little which you have mentioned, I take it that I have seene the very same: and for them I doe not onely thinke it, but also doe know assuredly, that by the Lord's gracious assistance & blessing, through constant diligence they may be all effected; for that I have knowne so much triall of all of them, as is sufficient to induce any man therunto: besides that they doe all stand upon plaine and sure grounds, as I trust I am able to make evident demonstration in each particular, so as any man of understanding may perceive cleerely, that they may be done. Neither doe I doubt but to satisfie you in every point, and to cause you to yeeld unto the evidence hereof, before we part, if you will but onely aske and still shew me wherein you are not satisfied. Moreover, I am so very confident herein, not onely

All the things mentioned in the contents, may be effected through diligence, constancie and God's blessing. See the particulars in the contents set before the books.

upon

THE GRAMMAR SCHOOLE

upon mine owne reason and experience, but because I have knowne the judgements of sundry very learned and experienced both Schoolemasters and others, who have beene acquainted with these selfe-same heads, which you have mentioned, who, though at the first reading of them, they have beene of your judgement, and have thought as you doe, yet within a quarter of an houre after that they have taken a little triall, in some of the most unlikely, and seen the reason of them, have rested fully satisfied and assured of the whole, that all might be done, as standing on the like grounds. And therefore I have no cause to distrust the like successe with your selfe.

Spoud. Sir, if you shall doe this for me, I shall acknowledge my selfe to have received a very great benefit, and be thankfull unto the Lord & to your selfe as his instrument; and doe my uttermost endevour to put them all constantly in practice, that I may confirme them by mine owne experience, and finde the same happy comfort, that your selfe have done.

I will therefore beginne in order according unto those heads, and so propound the questions, how each thing may be done, and desire your answer unto them severally.

Phil. Nay rather, for the manner of proceeding, I take this to be far more easie and commodious to us both, and whereby God may direct this conference so, as to profit many others besides our selves; To go thorow all the whole course of learning, from the first step, beginning at the very first Elements, even at the A.B.C. and so to ascend to the highest top of learning, which can bee required in Grammar schooles; to make a scholler each way fit for the University. Thus to run thorow all the necessary points appertaining to the same, as neere as we can remember; To make hereby the whole way easie and ready to all good learning, and to ranke every head in the right order & proper place, according to the due manner of proceeding in Schooles. So wee may insert these points which you have spoken of; dividing the whole into several Chapters, for the full distinguishing
and

The most easie and profitable manner of proceeding in this conference.

THE GRAMMAR SCHOOLE

and plain setting down of every matter. To the end therefore that I may bee the better guided and occasioned to impart all things unto you, I shall request you, first to propound all the severall points of learning in order, from point to point as wee proceed. Secondly, in the propounding of them, to shew mee in every one, what course you your selfe have taken, wherein you have found so little fruit or comfort, as you complaine, and which you thinke to be most ordinary in the countrey schooles. Wherein you shall faile in omitting any necessary head or Chapter, or in misplacing any, I shall afford you my best direction.

Spoud. I will accomplish your desire so well as I can. I doubt not of your patience, seeing you take mee thus of a suddaine; and that you who have better thought of these things, wil guide me continually, until we have gone thorow the whole.

Phil. I trust you are so perswaded of mee. Therefore I pray you begin.

CHAP. II.
When the Scholler should first be set to the Schoole.

Spoud.

The first point. How soone the childe is to be set to the schoole.

THat I may begin at the very first entrance of the Schoole: let me inquire this of you, how soon you would have your childe set unto the Schoole; for I thinke that worthy to be first knowne, if so be that you purpose to have your scholler fitted for the Universitie, by fifteene yeeres of age.

Phil. I like your reason well, to enter there. But to the intent that I may more fully make knowne unto you, what I thinke, and have found in this behalfe, let mee heare first of you, as I wished in generall, at what age you use in your countrey, to set your children to begin to learne.

Spoud.

THE GRAMMAR SCHOOLE

Spoud. For the time of their entrance with us, in our countrey schooles, it is commonly about seven or eight yeeres old: sixe is very soone. If any beginne so early, they are rather sent to the schoole to keepe them from troubling the house at home, and from danger, and shrewd turnes, then for any great hope and desire their friends have that they should learne any thing in effect. *{The time of the first entrance in countrey schooles, at seven or eight.}*

Phil. I finde that therein first is a very great want generally; for that the child, if hee be of any ordinary towardnesse and capacitie, should begin at five yeere old at the uttermost, or sooner rather. My reasons are these: *{The child of any ordinary towardlinesse, to begin to learne about five yeere old.}*

1. Because that then children will begin to conceive of instruction, and to understand; and bee able not onely to know their letters, to spell and to reade, but also to take a delight therein, and to strive to goe before their fellowes. Experience heerein will quickely teach every one, who shall make triall of it, if so be that they doe follow a right course. *{Reasons. 1 Because they are then meet to conceive of learning, and to delight in it.}*

2. Very reason must needs perswade every one of this. For, if they bee apt much before five yeeres of age, to learne shrewdnesse, and those things which are hurtfull, and which they must bee taught to unlearne againe; why are they not as well fit to learne those things which are good and profitable for them, if they be entred and drawne on in such a manner, as they may take a delight and finde a kinde of sport and play in the same? This delight may and ought to be in all their progresse, and most of all in their first entrance, to make them the better to love the schoole, and learning, as we shall see after. *{2 For that they are apt much sooner to learne shrewdnesse, and those things which are hurtfull.}*

3. Many of them doe learne so much untowardnesse and naughtinesse amongst other rude children, in that time before they come to schoole, that they are worse for it continually after: and also they feele such sweetnesse in play and idlenesse, as they can hardly bee framed to leave it, and to take a delight in their bookes without very much adoe. *{3 To avoid much rudenesse, and that too much sweetnesse which they feele in play and idlenesse.}*

4. This

THE GRAMMAR SCHOOLE

4 This age is most easily bended and accustomed to good things.

4. This first age is that wherein they are most pliant, and may bee bended and fashioned most easily to any good course. And being thus accustomed to good things from their infancie, and kept so much as may be, from all practice and sight of evill, custome becomes unto them another nature. So great a thing it is (according to the old proverbe) to accustome children, even from their tender yeeres; and so undoubtedly true is that common verse,

Quo semel est imbuta recens seruabit odorem testa diu.

5 Two or three yeeres may be gained by this meanes, to fit the sooner for the Universitie, or other imploiments, which is no small benefit.

5. Above all these this is a principall benefit, that by this meanes two or three yeeres may well be gained, to fit your Scholler so much sooner for the Universitie, or for any honest trade or calling. So that a child thus entred rightly, shall doe much more at eight yeeres old, then another so neglected can doe at ten, or it may bee at eleven or twelve. Also many such shall be meete for trades and like imployments, when they have no learning to fit them thereunto. This must needs be a great griefe to the Parents of such, whose children have so lost their time, as it is a joy to others whose children have beene so well brought up, when they see their children compared together.

6 Parents ought to labour to see their children's good education before their eyes, so soone as may be.

6. Lastly, our time being so short, it much concerneth every parent, to see their children to have the best education and instruction, which is the chiefe patrimonie, and the greatest comfort and hope both of the Parents and Children, and also of their houses and posteritie. And this so soone as ever may bee, to fit them for some profitable imploiment for Church or Common-wealth.

Ob.
It will hinder their growth.

Spoud. But they will say with us, that it will hinder the growth of their children to be set to schoole so young.

Ans.
The schoole being rightly used, will not hinder any more then their play.

Phil. Let the schoole be made unto them a place of play: and the children drawn on by that pleasant delight which ought to be, it can then no more hinder their growth then their play doth, but rather further it, when they sit at their ease; besides that continuall experience doth confute this errour.

Ob. 2.

Spoud. Bee it so as you say: yet this is a received opinion, that

THE GRAMMAR SCHOOLE

that it will cause them to hate the schoole, whē they should be set to it in good earnest.

It will cause them to hate learning.

Phil. Nay rather it is clean contràry: for being acquainted with the schoole so young, and with the sport and pleasure which they finde amongst other children there ; and also being kept from feeling the overmuch sweetnesse in play, it shall cause them to love & to delight in the schoole continually, and to goe on without any repining, or so much as thinking of being away from the schoole: whereas they being nuzled up in play abroad, are very hardly reclaimed and weaned from it, to sticke to their bookes indeede.

A. *They will rather love it better.*

Spoud. But yet it is thought that they can get but little learning then, being so very young, and therefore there is the smaller losse of a yeere or two, at that time.

Ob. 3. *It is a small matter to lose a yeere or two then.*

Phil. The losse will bee found in the end, although it bee indeed in the beginning. For looke how many yeeres they lose in the beginning if they bee apt, so many in the end they will bee shorter, of such of their fellowes, who are but of their owne age, and applied all alike being of like capacitie. Therefore, as wee will not let them lose a day, when they growe towards the Universitie, so neither should we when they are young; but prevent this losse, and take the time in the beginning.

A. *The losse of a yeere or two will be found in the end.*

Spoud. We see notwithstanding some very long ere ever they begin, who then goe forward with it the fastest of all.

Ob. 4. *They will learne the faster.*

Phil. It is true in some pregnant wits, and who are industrious: but you shall have others as blockish and dull. Also, for those, if they go so fast in the rudiments & first grounds, how much more would they doe so at the same time in better studies? Neither can they have halfe that learning in all things, which others of like age and aptnesse have, who have been well applyed from their first yeeres.

A. *So in higher learning at these yeeres.*

Spoud. I yeeld to all which you have said in this behalfe ; and I doe see plainely the exceeding benefits, that must needs come hereby, especially in gaining of time ; if they may bee entred in that playing manner, and goe forward

THE GRAMMAR SCHOOLE

ward with alacritie and contention; and moreover so, that they bee not any way overloaded or discouraged, nor yet indangered, by the overcharging of their wits and memories.

Phil. For that take you no feare; you shall (God willing) see the evidence of that, and a plaine direction in every Chapter, how to proceede in that easie and playing kinde. Therefore, if you be satisfied in this, let us come unto the next point.

Spoud. Very gladly Sir: for I long to heare this, how you would teach your child being so yong, to reade so soon and readily.

Phil. I like the point well : proceed according to your order.

CHAP. III.

How the Scholler may be taught to reade English speedily, to fit him the sooner, and better for the Grammar Schoole.

Spoud.

The inconvenience of having the Grammar schooles troubled with teaching A.B.C.

BEfore wee enter into this question, let me put you in minde of one thing, which doth much trouble mee concerning this very matter. That it seemeth to mee an unreasonable thing, that the Grammar Schooles should bee troubled with teaching A.B.C. seeing it is so great a hinderance to those paines which wee should take with our Grammar Schollers, for whom wee are appointed : Because it doth take up almost one halfe of our time, and thereby doth deprive us of a chiefe part of the fruit of our labours; especially when our mindes are so distracted, and our thoughts carried so many wayes, to doe good to all. The very little ones in a towne, in most countrey townes which are of any bignesse

THE GRAMMAR SCHOOLE

nesse, would require a whole man, of themselves, to bee alwaies hearing, poasing & following them, so as they ought to be applyed: for continuall applying in a right course, is in this and all other parts of learning, above all other meanes. And young ones, by a little slaking our hands, run faster backe, then ever they went forward; as boates going up the streame.

Continuall applying in a right course is above all meanes.

Besides, it is an extreme vexation, that we must be toiled amongst such little petties, and in teaching such matters, whereof wee can get no profit, nor take any delight in our labours.

Phil. I am well inured with this grievance, which you speake of, and doe know by long experience your complaint to bee too just in this behalfe. I myselfe have complained of it many a time. For it were much to be wished, that none might bee admitted to the Grammar schooles, untill they were able to reade English: as namely, that they could reade the New Testament perfectly, and that they were in their Accidences, or meet to enter into them. There might bee some other schoole in the towne, for these little ones to enter them. It would helpe some poore man or woman, who knew not how to live otherwise, and who might doe that well, if they were rightly directed. Also it would be such an ease to all Grammar Schoolemasters, as they might doe much more good in their places. Wherefore, all such Schoolemasters who are incumbred with this inconvenience, are not onely to wish, but also to labour to have it reformed in their severall schooles. Yet notwithstanding, where it cannot be redressed, it must be borne with wisdome and patience as an heavy burden. Patience shall make it much more light. And therefore every one is to doe his best indeavour, to know how to make it most easie, if it doe lie upon him. Moreover, seeing we purpose, God willing, to goe thorow all the whole course of learning, and also sith our labour is to finde out the meanes, whereby to make the way plaine, to traine up every childe from the very first entrance into learning, (as was said) untill

How this might be remedied by some other schoole in each towne for this purpose.

The redresse of it to be sought.

To be borne with patience where it cannot be remedied.

THE GRAMMAR SCHOOLE

untill wee have brought him into the Universitie, we cannot omit any point, which may tend unto the fame, much lesse the first steppe of all. For, a child well entred is halfe made: according to that Proverbe, *Principium, dimidium totius*. The foundation well layd, the building must needs goe forward much more happily. This is specially true in learning; wherein children feeling a sweetnesse in the beginning, are very much incouraged, as daily experience will manifest to every one.

Spoud. I see well the necessitie of undergoing this burden, in those places where remedy cannot be had, without greater inconveniences. And therefore, sith that necessitie hath no law, nor for myselfe I know no meanes how to bee freed from it; I pray you let us returne againe unto the point, and let mee still intreat of you your best direction, to make this burden so light as may bee. This is a thing worth the diligence of all, who must be imployed amongst little ones: to wit, to teach children how to read well, and to pronounce their letters truly; as also to spell right, and to know how to write true Orthography in a short space. For (that I may acknowledge the truth, and which hath bin no small discredit unto mee in this behalfe) I have had some who have beene with me, two or three yeeres, before they could reade well. And that which hath yet been much more grievous to me. I have sometimes beene so abashed and ashamed, that I have not knowne what to say, when some being a little discontented, or taking occasion to quarrell about paying my stipend, have cast this in my teeth, that their children have been under me sixe or seven yeeres, and yet have not learned to reade English well. I myselfe have also knowne, that their complaints have been true in part; though I have taken all the paines with them that ever I could devise. Therefore good Sir, set downe as plainely and shortly as you can, how this may be helped. Both myselfe and many others shal be much beholden for your direction in this first entrance. For my maner of entring them, it is that which I take to bee everywhere: to teach & heare them

so

THE GRAMMAR SCHOOLE

so oft over untill they can say a lesson, and so to a new.

Phil. I likewise have been well acquainted with this your trouble: and therefore I will indevour, to afford you so much as I have yet learned, how to avoid these clamours; and how any poore man who will imploy his paines, may learn to teach children to read well in a short time, though this may seeme unbefitting our profession.

First the childe is to be taught, how to call every letter, pronouncing each of them plainely, fully and distinctly; I meane, in a distinct and differing sound, each from others, and also naturally, from the very first entrance to learning. More specially to bee carefull, for the right pronouncing the five vowels, in the first place, as *a, e, i, o, u*. Because these are first and most naturall, and doe make a perfect sound, so that they may bee pronounced fully of themselves; and they being rightly uttered, all the rest are more plaine. After these vowels, to teach them to pronounce every other letter: which are therefore called Consonants, because they cannot make a perfect sound of themselves, without a Vowell.

1 To teach children how to call and pronounce their letters right.

And first the five Vowels.

The Consonants.

This may be done, and also the teaching of children to spell any syllable, before the child do know any letter on the booke; and that, some wise and experienced doe hold the surest and best course. But they are, at least, to be taught to pronounce their letters thus, as they doe learne them; to prevent the griefe and wearisomnesse of teaching them to forget evil customes in pronouncing, which they tooke up in their first ill learning. And so ever in teaching to read, the teachers are to continue the like care of sweet and naturall pronunciation.

Right calling the letters before the children doe know them.

Secondly, for the knowing of the letters (besides that common manner practised in Schooles, which is by oft reading over all the letters forwards and backwards untill they can say them) they may be much furthered thus; That is, by causing the childe to find out, and to shew you which is *a*, which *b*, which *c*, which *f*, and so any other letter. First to finde them in the Alphabet, then in any other place.

2 How to teach children to know the letters the soonest.

To cause them to finde out any letter.

Or

THE GRAMMAR SCHOOLE

The surer way is to learne but one letter at once.

Or if you will let them learne but one letter at once, untill they can readily know or finde out that letter in any place, and after that another in the same manner: This is holden the surer and more easie way: But this at your owne judgement.

3 How to teach to spell.

3. You may helpe them to spell thus, besides that course which is usuall. Let so many as are beginners, or who cannot reade perfectly, stand together, and then poase them without booke, one by one. First, in syllables of two letters, as they are set downe in their A.B.C. and where one misseth, let his next fellow tell: if he cannot, then, let some other. Then examine them in syllables of three letters, after in moe. And ever what syllable they misse, marke it with a dent with the nayle, or a pricke with a pen, or the like: and when you have marked out those wherein they so misse, poase them oft over, not forgetting due praise to them who doe best. One halfe houre would be spent daily in this kind of examining, untill they be perfect in any syllable, or word. To make children to take a delight in spelling, let them spell many syllables together, which differ but only in one letter, as hand, band, land, sand, &c. These syllables and words following, I have observed, to bee of the hardest for children to spell: I will set you them downe together in this short briefe. They may serve for spelling, reading, or writing, and may soone be gotten by being often poased, read or written over.

M. Coots English Schoole-master might be profitable to this purpose, in which booke are syllables, and words of all sorts.
To make children to take delight in spelling.

Some of the hardest syllables to practice children in the spelling of them. These would be written in some little table to poase them oft.

Ac, ec, ca, ce, ci, co, cu, ag, eg, ah, az, ae, ai, au, ga, ge, gi, go, gu, va, wa, we, wee, bac, bace, bag, bage, gage, badge, bau, baye, dawe, dewe, iawe, rac, race, rosse, rose, yell, you, gua, cha, cla, dwa, gla, pha, tha, sca, sha, swa, wra, chra, phra, spha, thra, twa, thwa, able, abs, ach, adge, afle, apt, ath, own, blowe, browe, chrou, dregg, dredge, dwarfe, frogg, gnash, gnaw, plowe, snow, stew, slugge, they, thom, throne, twaine, twigge, schoole, cockle, puddle: pegle, good, golde, gogle, balme, fallen, stolne, scalpe, salfe, thumbe, couple, pearce, charme, chapt, moth, mouth, nymphes, unkle, tenth, strength, height, depth, breadth, weight, joint, laude, beau-

THE GRAMMAR SCHOOLE

beautie, deede, language, guide, feede, feude, vowe, braue, dou, dove, knife, knives, yeoman, ynough, ayre, heyre, doubting, island, yle, buy, league, hatchet, laugh, yeugh, bough, publique, quishon.

These are some of the hardest syllables, as I said: your selfe may adde moe as you meet with them. Also this is to be observed in spelling; that before (on) you spell or write commonly (ti) not (ci) as salvation, not salvacion, though we pronounce it as (ci.) But this is to be knowne chiefly, by the Latine words from whence they come. *Note in spelling.*

Right pronuntiation of words, and continuall practice in spelling, are the surest way to come to spell truely. *Right pronouncing makes right spelling.*

If you pronounce the word false, which you would have your childe to spell, hee spelleth it false: for he spelleth according as it is pronounced to him, or as he useth to pronounce. As for example; aske the childe how hee spelles a strea, (as in many places the countrey manner is to pronounce it) hee will spell strea or stre: but aske him how hee spels a strawe and to pronounce it, and he will spell strawe.

To direct further how to come to perfection in spelling or writing right, I shall have occasion to speake after. *Further direction for spelling after.*

In joining syllables together, they must be taught to utter every syllable by it selfe, truely, plainely, fully, and distinctly, as we heard of the letters before; and so also as that others who heare may understand; ever sounding out the last syllable: as sal-va-ti-on. *4. Joining syllables together.*

Understanding the matter.

Thus they may goe thorow their Abcie, and Primer. And if they reade them twise over, that they may be very perfect in them, it will be the better for them. For, the second reading of any booke doth much incourage children, because it seemeth to be so easie then; and also it doth imprint it the more. Besides that, they will runne it over so fast at the second time, as it wil be no losse of time at all unto them. *Bookes to be first learned of children: Abcie, Primer. Second reading of a booke.*

After these they may reade over other English bookes. Amongst which, the Psalmes in metre would be one, because children will learne that booke with most readinesse *Psalmes in metre.*

and

B

THE GRAMMAR SCHOOLE

Testament.

and delight through the running of the metre, as it is found by experience. Then the Testament, in which the discreet Master may keepe his scholler lesse or more, untill he think him meet to enter into the Accedence.

Schoole of Vertue.

If any require any other little booke meet to enter children; *the Schoole of Vertue* is one of the principall and easiest for the first enterers, being full of precepts of civilitie, and such as children will soone learne and take a delight in, thorow the roundnesse of the metre, as was said before of the singing Psalmes: And after it *the Schoole of goodmanners*, called, *the new Schoole of vertue*, leading the childe as by the hand in the way of all good manners.

Schoole of good manners.

5 In what time children well applyed, may easily learne to reade English.

By these meanes, children if they be well applyed, and continually kept unto it, may be taught so to reade within a yeere or little more, as they may bee meet to enter into their Accedence, by that time that they be six yeere old at the uttermost; especially if they bee in any measure apt, and much practised in spelling the hardest syllables.

Dividing and distinguishing syllables.

For dividing or distinguishing of syllables, this one observation is to be remembred; That what consonants are usually joined in the beginnings of words, those are not to be disjoined and separate in the middest of words, except in Compound words. But of this wee shall speake more fitly after. And thus much may suffice for the present, for the speedy reading of English; for hereof I have had much certaine experience.

Spoud. I cannot justly dislike of any thing which you have said herein, it standeth all with so great reason: chiefely to make children so perfect in the hardest syllables. For, they being perfect in these, must need attain all the rest in a short space. Except onely one thing which you uttered; which indeede seemes a strange Paradox to mee: Namely, that some wise & experienced, would have childrē taught to call and pronounce all their letters, and to spell any syllable before they know a letter on the booke.

Phil. This is very true which you say; it may seeme a Paradox to them who have not tryed it. I my selfe was of
your

THE GRAMMAR SCHOOLE

your minde when I heard it first. Yet setting my selfe to make some triall of it, for the reverence I bare to him of whom I heard it, and for that he shewed me experience of it in a child not foure yeeres old, I found it the easiest, pleasantest and shortest way of all, where one would begin in a private house with little ones playing. The manner is thus.

6 To teach little ones to pronounce their letters, and to spell before they know a letter, is the pleasantest way.

1. You must teach them, as I said, to call their five Vowels, and to pronounce them right: Which they will presently learne, if you doe but onely cause them to repeat them oft over, after you, distinctly together thus: a, e, i, o, u, after the manner of five bels, or as we say; one, two, three, foure, five.

How little ones will presently pronounce their five vowels.

2. Then teach them to put the consonants in order before every vowell, and to repeate them oft over together; as thus: to begin with *b*, and to say, ba, be, bi, bo, bu. So *d*. da, de, di, do, du. *f*. fa, fe, fi, fo, fu. Thus teach them to say all the rest, as it were singing them together, la, le, li, lo, lu; The hardest to the last, as ca, ce, ci, co, cu: and ga, ge, gi, go, gu. In which the sound is a little changed in the second and third syllables. When they can doe all these, then teach them to spell them in order, thus; What spels b-a? If the childe cannot tell, teach him to say thus; b-a, ba: so putting first *b*. before every vowell, to say b-a ba, b-e be, b-i bi, b-o bo, b-u bu. Then aske him againe what spels b-a, and hee will tell you; so all the rest in order. By oft repeating before him, hee will certainly doe it. After this if you aske him how hee spels b-a, he will answer b-a ba. So in all others.

To put the consonants in order before the vowels pronouncing them.

To teach to spell these thus, putting the consonants first.

Next these, teach them to put the vowels first, as to say, ab, eb, ib, ob, ub. Then thus, a-b ab, e-b eb, i-b ib, o-b ob, u-b ub. After, what spelles a-b, e-b, &c. Thus to goe with them backward and forward, crosse, in and out, untill they can spell any word of two letters. Then you may adjoine those of three letters: Afterwards, all the hard syllables, to tell what any of them spels, till they be perfect in all, or as you shall thinke meet. By this meanes, and by a little repeating of the letters of the Alphabet over before them, by three or foure letters together, as they stand in order, so

Repeating the letters of the Alphabet, by roate.

as

THE GRAMMAR SCHOOLE

as they may best sound in the children's eares, they wil soone learne to say all the letters of the A.B.C. if you will. As to repeat them thus: A.b.c.d.e.f.g.h.i.k.l.m.n.o.p.q.r.s.t.u.w. x.y.z.&. To say them thus by roat, will nothing hinder but further them.

To teach them to know their letters as before.

Then they may presently be taught to know the letters upon the booke, either one by one, finding first which is *a*, in the Alphabet; and after in any other place. Then to finde which is *b*, and so through all the rest as you will.

To cause them to know the matter by questions, or oft repeating to them.

Then when they are cunning in their letters and spelling, if you make them to understand the matter which they learne, by questions, for a little at the first, they will goe on in reading, as fast as you will desire. The easier and more familiar the matter is to them, the faster they learne.

Any one who can reade, may thus enter children for reading English.

Thus may any poore man or woman enter the little ones in a towne together; and make an honest poore living of it, or get somwhat towards helping the same. Also the Parents who have any learning, may enter their little ones, playing with them, at dinners, and suppers, or as they sit by the fire, and finde it very pleasant delight.

So they may helpe to gaine their children a yeere or two in learning, at the beginning, & also the Grammar Schooles of this labour and hindrance.

Spoud. You have perswaded mee very much concerning this doubt also. Surely, Sir, howsoever this may seeme but a toy, yet all tender parents will much rejoice in it, and acknowledge it an exceeding benefit, to have their children so entred; and this time being gotten in the beginning, will bee found in the end as you truely said. Yet there is another matter that comes unto my remembrance, about which I have taken no small griefe and discouragement many a time, concerning this point of reading English. I will mention it here, and desire your judgement how to redresse it, although it might happely come in fitter afterwards.

The trouble is this: That when as my children doe first enter into Latine, many of them will forget to reade English,

THE GRAMMAR SCHOOLE

English, and some of them bee worse two or three yeeres after that they have been in construction, then when they began it.

Now if you could teach me how to helpe this likewise, that they might as well goe forward still in reading English as in Latine, I should account this a very great benefit. For, some of their Parents, who use me the kindliest, will bee at me, that their children may every day reade some Chapters of the Bible, to helpe their reading of English. Now this I cannot possibly doe, but they must needs bee hindred in their Latine, in some lessons or necessarie exercises; and either be behinde their fellowes, or else trouble all their fellowes very much, that they cannot goe so fast forward as they should, but stay for these readers. Others being more ignorant or malicious, upon every light occasion, are readie to rage & raile at me, for that their children, as they say, doe get no good under me, but are worse and worse. For, whereas they could have read English perfectly (it may be) when they came to me, now they have forgotten to doe it. Thus am I grieved on every side, and vexed daily, let mee labour never so much, and spend my heart amongst them for to doe them good.

Phil. Sir, herein I can say, as she in the Poet;
Haud ignara mali miseris succurrere disco.

For I have tasted deepely of the same griefe untill verie lately, within this yeere or two. Yet now I seeme to my selfe, to finde as sensible and continuall a growth amongst all my Schollers, in their English tongue as in the Latine. And not onely for the reading of it, but also for understanding it, and abilitie to utter their mindes of any matter, wherewith they are acquainted, or which they learne in Latine; and also how to expresse the meaning of the Latine in proprietie, and puritie of our owne tongue: so that I am quite delivered from that clamour.

But to tell you what I thinke, wherein there seemes unto mee, to bee a verie maine want in all our Grammar schooles generally, or in the most of them ; whereof
I have

8 *The inconvenience of children forgetting to reade English, when they enter first into Latine, and how to avoid it.*
Complaints of Parents for children forgetting English.

Complaint of want of care in our schooles for growth in our owne tongue, as in the Latine.

THE GRAMMAR SCHOOLE

I have heard some great learned men to complaine; That there is no care had in respect, to traine up schollers so, as they may be able to expresse their minds purely and readily in our owne tongue, and to increase in the practice of it, as well as in the Latine or Greeke; whereas our chiefe indevour should be for it, and that for these reasons. 1. Because that language which all sorts and conditions of men amongst us are to have most use of, both in speech and writing, is our owne native tongue. 2. The puritie and elegancie of our owne language, is to be esteemed a chiefe part of the honour of our Nation: which we all ought to advance as much as in us lieth. As when Greece and Rome and other nations have most flourished, their languages also have been most pure: and from those times of Greece and Rome, we fetch our chiefest patterns, for the learning of their tongues. 3. Because of those which are for a time trained up in schooles, there are very few which proceed in learning, in comparison of them that follow other callings.

Spoud. This complaint is not without just cause: for I doe not know any schoole, wherein there is regard had hereof to any purpose; notwithstanding the generall necessitie and use of it, and also the great commendation which it brings to them who have attained it: but I thinke every minute an houre, untill I heare this of you, how my trouble and shame may be avoided, and how I may obtaine this facultie to direct my children, how they may goe thus forward, not only in reading English perfitly, but also in the proprietie, puritie and copie of our English tongue, so as they may utter their mindes commendably of any matter which may concerne them, according to their age and place.

Phil. I will but name the meanes unto you now: for I shall have occasion to shew them all more particularly hereafter. Besides the daily use of distinct reading over their English parts to get them perfectly, and of right reading all other things which they learne in Latine, as your selfe doe know; these meanes following, by the blessing of God will accomplish your desire.

1. The

THE GRAMMAR SCHOOLE

1. The continuall use of the bookes of construing of *Lillies* Rules, by causing them to learne to construe, and to keepe their Grammar rules, onely by the helpe of those translations. This I finde one very good use of these books, besides some other which I shall mention after. *Daily use of Lillies rules construed.*

2. The daily use, and practice of Grammaticall translation in English, of all the Schoole Authours, which the yonger sort doe learne; causing them each day out of those to construe, and repeate, whatsoever they learne. This I also have prooved by happie experience, to be a rare helpe to make young Schollers to grow very much, both in English and Latine. But of all these, for the manner, benefits, and use of them, I shall have occasion to speake at large. *Continuall practice of English Grammaticall translations.*

3. Besides these, they would have every day some practice of writing English heedily, in true Orthographie; as also of translating into English; or, of writing Epistles, or familiar Letters to their friends, as well in English as in Latine. Amongst some of them, the reporting of a Fable in English, or the like matter, trying who can make the best report, doth much further them in this. And generally, amongst all those that can write, the taking of notes of Sermons, and delivering them againe, or making repetitions, is a speciall meanes. Also striving to expresse whatsoever they construe, not onely in proprietie, but in varietie of the finest phrase, who can give the best. This chiefly in the higher fourmes: So reading forth of Latine into English; first in proprietie, then in puritie. By these, and some use of the Historie of the Bible, and the like, which I shall be occasioned to mention after; you may finde their growth, according to your desire, and much above your expectation. *Translating and writing English, with some other Schoole exercises.*

Spoud. Undoubtedly Sir, these must needs be very availeable; because schollers may have hereby, so much use of the English every day, above that which is practised in any Schoole which I have knowne. But for any such translations of the Schoole-Authors, I have not heard of them. Onely

THE GRAMMAR SCHOOLE

Onely I have seene the bookes of construing *Lillies* rules, and some of my children have them, though I feared that it would rather make them idle, being but a truant's booke. Indeed I never conceived so much of them as you say: I shall better thinke of the use thereof.

Phil. There is not the best thing but it may be abused. But for that booke as the others, I shall shew and prove unto you the commodities of them, above all that you would imagine. Experience makes mee confident: Yet to returne unto your selfe, concerning the complaint of the Parents for their children going backward in reading English, when they first learne Latine; the chiefe fault in truth is in the Parents themselves; although wee poore schoolemasters must be sure to beare all. For if such murmuring Parents would but cause their children, every day after dinner or supper, or both, to reade a Chapter of the Bible, or a piece of a Chapter, as leisure would permit, and to doe it constantly; thereby to shew their love to the Lord, and his Word, and their desire to have the Word dwell plentifully in their houses, to have their children trained up in it, as young *Timothy* was; then, I say, this complaint would soon be at an end: for they should either see then, their children to increase in this, or else they should discerne the fault to bee in their children's dulnesse, and not in our neglect. Notwithstanding, sith that they are so very few of whom wee can hope, that they have any care of this dutie in their houses, in respect of all the rest who omit it, and yet all the blame must surely rest on us, it concerneth us so much as we can to redresse it; and therefore use all good meanes, to cut off all occasions of clamours, and of discrediting our selves, and our schooles, and to contend for the greatest profiting of our children, aswell in this, as in any other part of learning; the use of this being, as we heard, most generall and perpetuall.

Spoud. You have directed me very rightly how to answer such Parents: now I shallbe able to shew them where the fault is, & be calling upon them to redresse this at home.

I shall

The chiefe fault of the children going backwards in reading English, when they first learne Latine, is the Parents theselves.

THE GRAMMAR SCHOOLE

I shall also indevour to put all this in use, and more as you make the particulars more fully knowne unto me; and as I shall finde by triall the fruit thereof. But now, that you have thus satisfied me in al these my doubts; I cannot but demand yet one other point, wherein I finde another great want, though not comparable to the former; because there is not so much use of it: which is about the ordinarie numbers or numbring. For I am much troubled about this, that my readers and others above them, are much to seeke in all matters of numbers, whether in figures or in letters. Insomuch, as when they heare the Chapters named in the Church, many of them cannot turne to them, much lesse to the verse.

Phil. This likewise is a verie ordinarie defect, & yet might easily be helped by common meanes, in an houre or two. I call it ordinarie, because you shal have schollers, almost readie to go to the Universitie, who yet can hardly tell you the number of Pages, Sections, Chapters, or other divisions in their bookes, to finde what they should. And it is, as you say, a great & a foule want; because, without the perfect knowledge of these numbers, schollers cannot helpe themselves by the Indices, or Tables of such books, as they should use, for turning to any thing of a sodaine: although it be a matter whereof they should have use all their life long. And to conclude, it is a great neglect, because it is a thing so easie, as that it may be learned in so short a time, only by most usuall meanes, as by these following. For numbers by letters, use but only to appose them, according to the direction in the Latine Grammar at *Orthographia*, and they wil do them presently. As if you aske what I. stands for, what V. what X. what L. &c. And back againe, what letter stands for one, so what for five, or for ten. But especially if you desire to have them very ready herein, cause them to have these written, & then to practise to read them over often, until that they can answer any of them perfectly. Warn them also to remember alwaies, that any number set after a greater, or after the same nūber, doth adde so many mo, as the value of that later number is. As, I. set after X. thus, XI. doth make eleven, XV. fifteene.

An ordinarie fault, that most Schollers are to seeke in matters of common numbers, which they may be taught in an houre or two.

Numbers by letters known easily, yet oft neglected.

THE GRAMMAR SCHOOLE

teen. XX. twentie. But being set before, they doe take away so many as they are: as I. before X. thus, IX. nine.

If you wish an example more at large, this may serve; let each of them that should learne have a briefe of these, after this manner, to shew them all the chiefe numbers. I. one, II. two, III. three, IIII. or IV. foure, V. five, VI. six, VII. seven, VIII. eight, IX. nine, X. tenne, XI. eleven, XII. twelve, XIII. thirteene, XIIII. fourteene, XV. fifteene, XVI. XVII. XVIII. XIX. xx. xxI. xxV. twentie five, xxx. thirtie, XL fortie, L. fiftie, xC. ninetie, C. a hundreth, D. five hundreth, M. a thousand. And thus much shortly for numbring by letters.

Numbers by figures. For the numbers by Figures, this rule must also bee observed; That the Figures doe signifie in the first place so much onely, as if they were alone, or one time so many. In the second place tennes, or ten times so many. In the third place, hundreths, or a hundreth times so many. In the fourth place thousands, or a thousand times so many. In the fift place ten thousands. In the sixt place hundreth thousands; the places being reckoned from the right hand to the left. As for example, 1.2.3.4.5.6.7.8.9. 10.11.12.13.14.15.16.17.18. 19. 20. twentie. 21.22.23, &c. 30. thirtie. 31. 32. 40. fortie. 41. &c. 50. fiftie. 51. 60. sixtie. 70. seventie. 80. eightie. 90. ninetie 100. a hundreth. 101. a hundreth and one. 102. 110. a hundreth and ten. 120. a hundreth and twenty. 130, &c. 200. two hundreth, &c. 1000. a thousand. 10000. ten thousand. 100000. a hundreth thousand.

These being learned backwards and forwards, so that your scholler be able to know each of them, to call them, or name them right, and to finde them out, as the child should finde any letter which he is to learne: in a word, to tell what any of these numbers stand for, or how to set downe any of them; will performe fully so much as is needfull for your ordinarie Grammar scholler. If you do require more for any, you must seeke *Records* Arithmetique, or other like Authors, and set them to the Cyphering schoole.

Spoud.

THE GRAMMAR SCHOOLE

Spoud. This is a defect that I see is most easily supplied by a very little paine and care in examining. I have troubled you overlong in this, being in it selfe so very a trifle, though the want generally be to be blamed. Now therefore let us hasten unto our profession for the Grammar Schoolemaster. For I desire earnestly to be in our own element, as more befitting and beseeming our place.

Phil. I am very willing to make all the haste that we can: for this I see, that though we neither use digressions, nor needlesse words; yet this our conference will prove very long, before that I can make my mind plain unto you: Unlesse I should be so short, as either to be obscure, or to omit many things which I take to be very necessarie: But yet before we come to make entrance into the Latine, if we do keepe order, we are to goe thorow the way of writing, as being more generall, and which chiefly appertaineth also to our English tongue; in respect of our more frequent use of it; I meane chiefely for the writing of our ordinarie hand called the Secretarie hand, which is almost wholly in use amongst us. *Why this Dialogue is so long.*

CHAP. IIII.

How the Master may direct his Schollers to write very faire, though himselfe be no good Pen-man.

Spoud.

TO come therefore unto writing, and the manner of teaching it; That which you affirme may be done herein, cannot but be a very great benefit, and a notable grace to schooles, and also to all learning, if it can be so effected: That all Schollers in generall may be directed to write commendably, and a great part of them which are more apt to write very faire; and that in the severall *Faire writing a great benefit, and ornament to Schooles.*

THE GRAMMAR SCHOOLE

It hath been a received opinion among many, that a good scholler can not be a good writer.

severall hands of the learned tongues, as they doe proceede in every one of them. For many of the best Schollers have beene wont to write very ill; insomuch, as it hath beene a received opinion, as you know, amongst very many, That a good Scholler can hardly be a good pen-man. Moreover you shall find very few good writers in Grammar schooles; unlesse either they have been taught by Scriveners, or by themselves marvellous apt hereunto, and very rare, or where the Master doth apply himselfe chiefly to teach to write.

The trouble of School-masters, for the want of this facultie to teach Schollers to write.

The want of this, hath bin another part of my griefe: for besides the complaint and grudging of the parents; I have also seen, after they have bin a great while with me, that they have not bin able to write so, as to be fit for any trade; but they must after be set to learne of the Scrivener: much lesse have they bin able to write a letter to their friends, or to performe any such businesse with their pen, in any commendable maner. You shall therfore do me no lesse a pleasure, then in the former, if you can direct me, how to help all these evils, and to attaine to that dexteritie, whereof you speake.

Phil. I hope to satisfie you herein also. But first relate unto mee, what courses your selfe have taken, to teach your Schollers to write; whereof you have found so little profit: and after I shall adde, as in the former, what I have learned, to the better effecting hereof.

The ordinary course in Schooles to teach to write.

Spoud. Surely I have done this: I have daily set them copies, so well as I could, which hath bin no small toile unto me: or else I have caused some of my Schollers, or some others to doe it. Also I have made them now and then to write some copies; and it may be, I have corrected them for writing so badly, or guided some of their hands, or shewed them how to amend their letters. This I take to be the most that is done in Schooles ordinarily; unlesse any do procure Scriveners to teach in their townes: whereof we finde no small inconveniences.

Phil. I take it to be as you say, that this is all which is done in most Schooles: and hence so many of us have experience of the like murmurings against us. Now I will let you see

THE GRAMMAR SCHOOLE

see plainly, and as familiarly as I can, how to help this evill, and to attaine this so great a benefit.

1 The Scholler should be set to write, when he enters into his Accidence; so every day to spend an houre in writing, or very neere. *1 When Schollers should begin to write.*

2 There must be speciall care, that every one who is to write, have all necessaries belonging thereunto; as pen, inke, paper, rular, plummet, ruling-pen, pen-knife, &c. *2 To have all necessaries.*

3 The like care must be, that their inke be thin, blacke, cleere; which will not runne abroad, nor blot: their paper good; that is, such as is white, smooth, and which will beare inke, and also that it be made in a book. Their writing books would be kept faire, strait ruled, and each to have a blotting paper to keepe their bookes from soyling, or marring under their hands. *3 Inke and paper of what sort. Writing bookes kept faire.*

4 Cause every one of them to make his own pen; otherwise the making, and mending of pens, will be a very great hinderance, both to the Masters and to the Schollers. Besides that, when they are away from their Masters (if they have not a good pen made before) they will write naught; because they know not how to make their pens themselves. *4 Every one to learne to make his owne pen.*

The best manner of making the pen, is thus: *The manner of making the pen.*

1 Choose the quill of the best and strongest of the wing, which is somewhat harder, and will cleave.

2 Make it cleane with the backe of the pen-knife.

3 Cleane it strait up the backe; first with a cleft, made with your pen-knife: after with another quill put into it, rive it further by little and little, till you see the cleft to be very cleane: so you may make your pen of the best of the quil, and where you see the cleft to be the cleanest, and without teeth. If it doe not cleave without teeth, cleave it with your pen-knife in another place, still neerer the backe: for if it be not strait up the backe, it will very seldome run right. After, make the nebbe and cleft both about one length, somewhat above a barley corne breadth, and small; so as it may let downe the inke, and write cleane. Cut the nebbe first slant downewards to make it thinne, and after strait *Cleft of the pen. The neb of the pen.*

over-

THE GRAMMAR SCHOOLE

overthwart. Make both sides of equall bignesse, unlesse you be cunning to cut that side, which lieth upon the long finger, thinner and shorter; yet so little, as the difference can hardly be discerned. But both of equall length is accounted the surest.

The surest way for making the pen. The speediest and surest way to learne to make the pen, is this. When your Scholler shall have a good pen fit for his hand, and well fashioned; then to view and marke that well, and to trie to make one in all things like unto it. It were good for the learner to procure such a pen made, and to keepe it for a patterne to make others by, untill he be very perfect in it. A childe may soone learne to make his pen; yet, few of age do know how to make their owne pens well; although they have written long and very much: neither can any attaine to write faire without that skill.

How to hold the pen. Next unto this, cause your scholler to hold his pen right, as neere unto the nebbe as he can, his thumbe and two fore-fingers, almost closed together, round about the neb, like unto a Cat's foote, as some of the Scriveners doe terme it.

To carry the pen so lightly as to glide on the paper. Then let him learne to carry his pen as lightly as he can, to glide or swimme upon the paper. So hee shall write the cleanest, fairest, and fastest, and also his pen shall last the longer.

Copies. In stead of setting copies, to have copie books fastened to the top of their bookes. In stead of setting of copies, and to save that endlesse toile, let every one have a little copie booke fastened to the top of his writing booke, with a strong thread of a span long, or thereabout; that alwaies when he writeth, he may lay his copy booke close before him, and that the side of the copy may almost touch the line where he writeth, that his eye may be upon the copie, and upon his letter both together. And also, to the end that ever when he hath done writing, he may put his copie booke into his writing booke againe; so that the copie may never be out of the way, nor the Scholler write without it.

The fittest volume for their writing booke is, to have them in *quarto*.

More-

THE GRAMMAR SCHOOLE

Moreover, the copie bookes would be made thus: Not above two inches in breadth; foure or six copies in a booke, halfe Secretary, halfe Roman. The copie books might be made thus most fitly, as I take it. *Maner of the copie bookes.*

.1 One line of small letters, of each letter one, except in those which have letters of divers kinds, and therein both kinds to be set downe: as i.j.f.s.u.v.

Under the line of small letters, would be set a line of great letters, after the same manner; and under them both a line or two of joyning hand, containing all the letters in them.

Examples of both sorts for the present, untill better can be found, may be these. I meane copies both of Secretarie and Romane, containing all the letters in them.

For Secretarie thus:

Exercise thyselfe much in God's book, with zealous and fervent prayers and requests. *Examples of copies containing all the letters in one line of joyning.*

For Romane thus:

Æquore cur gelido sephyrus fert xenia kymbis?

Respect not the verse, but the use.

Under all these, may be fitly set in very little roome those characters or letters, out of which all the rest of the letters may be framed: as in the small letters in Secretarie, m.i.t. v.z.f. In the great letters, C D So under the Roman copies after the same maner.

In the end of the copie bookes, in a page or two, might be set downe all the hard syllables mentioned before. That by oft writing them over, they might be helped to spell, and to write true Orthographie. And after those, the numbers mentioned, to be able to write or to tell any of them upon the book without it. Then what scholler soever were not able to tell any of them, after a little poasing, were well worthy to be corrected. If such copie books were finely printed, being graven by some cunning workman, and those of the most perfect and plaine formes of letters, that could possibly be procured, in a strong and very white paper, one Booke or two of them would serve a scholler neere all his time, that he should never need to change his hand. *The hardest syllables and principal numbers to be set in the end of the copy books. The copy books to be printed and how, with the benefit of them.*

The

THE GRAMMAR SCHOOLE

Inconvenience of following divers hands.

The often change and following of divers hands, doth as much hinder writing, as often change of Schoolemasters doth hinder learning. Therefore the best is to be chosen at the first, and ever to be stucke unto without alteration, if it may be.

The best written copies to be procured.

In the meane time, untill such copies can be had, some would be procured of the master, to be written by the best Scrivener who can be gotten, after the manner aforesaid, for each scholler to have one to fasten to his booke, and to use as before.

Inconvenience of the lacke of such bookes.

Otherwise when for lacke hereof, the Master, or Usher, or some other Scholler is compelled every day, to write each scholler a new copie; it is both an endlesse toyle, and also an extreme losse of time: beside the inconvenience mentioned, of change of hands, and that few Masters or Ushers are fit pen-men, to write such copies as were necessarie.

Lastly, because through want of such copies, schollers do write ordinarily without direction or pattern, in all their exercises, whereby they either grow to very bad hands, or doe profit in writing, little or not at all.

Faire writing to be practised by all the Schollers once every day.

This exercise of writing faire, would be practised by all the Schollers thorow the Schoole, at least once every day, for an houre's space or neere; and that about one of the clocke: for then commonly their hands are warmest and nimblest.

Now those that write exercises, may take the opportunitie of that time, to write them so faire as they can.

Generall rule in writing; To make all like unto the copie.

In all writing this generall rule would be observed streightly, to cause them to strive to make every letter, as like to the copie letter in all proportion, as the one hand is to the other. And that they never thinke a letter good, untill no difference can be found between it and the copie letter, that it cannot be discerned whether is the better.

To keepe even compasse.

Great care would be had withall, to make every writer to keepe even compasse in the height, greatnesse, and breadth of his letters; that no one letter stand either

too

THE GRAMMAR SCHOOLE

too high or too low, be overlong, or overshort, nor any way too bigge, or too little, too wide, or too narrow.

To the end, that they may write of even height; cause them to rule their bookes with a ruling pen, and then that they make the body of each letter, to touch their rules on both sides, I meane both at the tops and bottomes of the letters; but not to goe one haire breadth higher or lower. Thus by practice the scholler will in time attaine to write very faire of himselfe without any ruling pen. *How to write of even height.*

That every one may rule their bookes thus, cause them to have each his ruling pen, made of a quill, somewhat like unto a pen; but onely that it is to be made with a nocke in the neb or point of it, like the nocke of an arrow, the nebs of the nocke standing just of the breadth of their copie letters asunder, that they may rule their rules meet of the same compasse with their copies. *Each to have his ruling pen, and what ones.*

The points of the nebs of the ruling pens, must not be made over-sharpe, nor pressed downe over-hard in ruling; because they wil then race the paper, and make it that it will not beare inke. They are moreover to rule but a few lines at once: because the lines being drawne but lightly, will soon goe out, and not be seene before that the learners come to write in them. *The neb of the ruling pen, and how to rule with it.*

Also this care must be had in ruling, to carry the ruling pen so even and straight forward, that both the lines which are drawne by it, may be seene together; or else to draw the lines so oft over with the same, untill that both the lines may be well seene. This would be observed carefully, untill that time that they can begin to write even and streight of themselves: for the even compasse doth especially grace a hand, and the faire shew of it will cause children to take a delight in writing faire. *Even writing to be straitly looked to, by the helpe of a ruling pen.*

Every scholler who writeth Latine, should have two of these ruling pens: one for Secretarie, and another for Romane; or else to have one made of iron or brasse, the one end for the one, the other end for the other.

Moreover, the books of all the new beginners or enterers, whilst

THE GRAMMAR SCHOOLE

whilst they write letters, would be ruled well with crosse lines, with the ruling pens on this manner: It is found to direct them very much.

Ruling the books of the yong beginners with crosse lines thus.

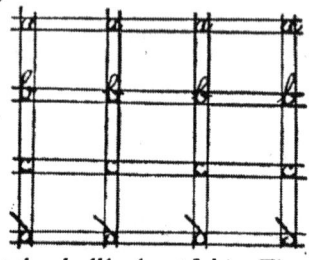

Benefit of this ruling.

Thus their books shall be kept faire. The compasse or the space within the crosse lines, serves to keepe and guide the body of each letter to make it of a just proportion. The straight lines direct and guide the childe to make every stroke straight forward, or up and downe, and also how to frame the head and taile of each letter.

The compasse in greatnesse or neerenesse of the letters.

Thus much for the compasse of the letters; chiefly in the tops and bottomes of the letters.

Now that the letters may not be over bigge or over little, set too neere one another or far off, this may be one good direction;

Cause your scholler to draw his lines, on which he will write his copies, of the very same length with the length of the line of his copy: and then if he writes just so much in his line as is in the copie, it is very like that he makes his letters of a good proportion, not too bigge nor too little, and the compasse even, not one over neere, or far off from another. But if he write more in a shorter space, then is in like space in the copy, he either makes his letters too little, or sets them too neere one another; letters, or words, or both. And so on the other side, if he write lesse in a line, then is in his copy in the same space, and length, then he makes his letters too bigge, or too wide asunder.

The letters would be joyned in every word : yet so, as no one be set over neere another, but just as the copie, observing

THE GRAMMAR SCHOOLE

ving blacks and whites, as the Scrivener tearmeth them. And each word in a sentence, would be set about the breadth of an *a*, or an *o*, from one another.

For writing straight without lines (after that they have practised this a good while, to write with double lines, ruled with the ruling pen, and after with single lines) this may helpe to guide them well; to cause them to hold their elbow so close to their side and so steadily, as they can conveniently; for the elbow so stayd, will guide the hand as a rule, especially in writing fast. Afterwards, looking at the end of the line, as we use to try the straightnesse of an arrow, they shall see easily where it is crooked. Practice will bring facility. *Writing straight without lines.*

These also may be speciall furtherances for the first enterers: When the yong scholler cannot frame his hand to fashion any letter; besides the guiding of his hand, and also the shewing where to begin each letter, & how to draw it, some doe use to draw before them the proportion of their letters, with a piece of chalke upon a boord, or table, or with a piece of black lead upon a paper; and then let the child try how he himselfe can draw the like upon it; and after this to let him to doe it with his pen, following the letter of his booke. *Speciall furtherances for the first enterers in writing. When they cannot frame a letter.*

Or thus; Let him take a dry pen, that cannot blot his book, and therewith cause him to follow that letter in his copie, which he cannot make, drawing upon the copy letter very lightly, & a little turning the side of the pen, where the letter is small; but leaning harder upon it where it is full, & there also turning the broad part of the pen. Onely warne him to be carefull, that he do not hurt the letter in the copy, by his hard leaning upon his pen, or by the overmuch sharpnesse of it. Thus let him follow his copie letter, drawing his pen so oft upon it, untill he thinke his hand will goe like unto it. Then direct him, to try with another pen with inke, whether he can make one like to that of his copie. If he cannot, let him goe to it with his dry pen againe, untill that he can fashion one like unto it. *To follow a letter with a dry pen.*

This also is a speciall observation: That the more leasurely the childe draweth at the beginning, as the Painter doth, *Leasurely drawing at the Painter.*

THE GRAMMAR SCHOOLE

To learn to make one letter well first, then another.

To helpe to write cleane, fast and faire together.

Making flourishes, gliding upon the paper.

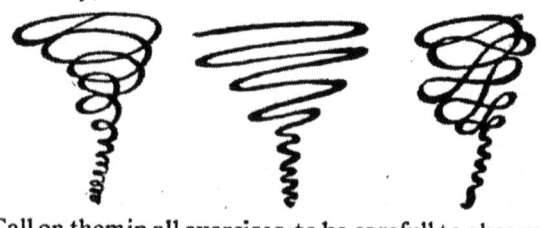

To observe ornaments of writing.

☞ *To make the letters most plaine.*

☞ *Mischiefes of getting a bad hand.*

doth, and the more lightly, the sooner a great deale he shall learne to frame his hand to write faire.

This likewise some good Scriveners observe; to suffer the child to learne to make but one kinde of letter at once, untill they can make that in some good sort, then another: as first *a*, then *b*. But especially to begin with those letters, out of which all the rest may be framed, to make them perfectly, as *m, c, t, v, s*. For so all the rest will be the easier.

To helpe to write cleane, fast and faire together, call oft on your schollers to exercise their hands in making of *f* strokes, that is, dashes of *f*, and *f* thus ff; and the stroake of the great C, and B, thus, $C\mathfrak{D}$

Also some use to cause the learners, to practise their hands to run upon the paper, either with inke or without, untill they be very nimble and cunning to glide upon the paper; and namely, to make certain rude flourishes.

Call on them in all exercises, to be carefull to observe the graces of letters: as the keeping of great letters, accents, points, as comma, colon, period, parenthesis, and whatsoever may serve for the adorning of writing; and evermore to take a delight in writing faire: which delight is in each art the one halfe of the skill; but to fly all long tailes of letters, and to make all their letters so plaine as they can: the plainer the better. Beware that you suffer no one to learne a bad hand, or to make any bad letter, so neere as you are able to prevent it. For it will be found much harder to teach such to forget their bad letters and hands, then to teach other which never learned, to write the good.

So that if you teach such, a better hand, after that they have learned and been long inured to the worse; although they

seeme

THE GRAMMAR SCHOOLE

seeme to have learned to write well, yet unlesse they be holden continually to practise their good hand each day a little, they will fall unto their bad hand againe: so great force hath any evill custome.

This therefore must be our wisedome, to procure from the beginning the most excellent copies, for our schollers, whatsoever they cost; and to keep them constantly to them: they will soone quite the cost both to Master and Scholler. *To procure the most excellent copies from the beginning.*

To the end that any Master may be the better able to teach thus; let him either try to attaine this faculty of writing faire (which much commends a Master) or at least, let him labour to be well acquainted with these directions, or the like: and also let him cause his Schollers to observe them constantly; or so many of them as need shall require. *That the Master may teach his Schollers to write faire, what to be done.*

And to this end, let him use to walke amongst his Schollers as they write all together; & see that they do practise these things duely: but chiefly that every one have his copy book layed close before him; and to marke well wherein any one of them misseth in any letter or stroke, that it is not like to the copie, there to point him to the copie, and to shew him where they differ, or to cause him to compare them himselfe: so to appoint them to be mending their faults, untill their letters be in all things like the copie letters. And what letters they make the worst, to make them so oft over, in some voide place of their booke, or some waste paper, untill those be as good as any of the rest, and like the copy, as was said. Amongst others, to looke specially to these three letters together, *f. g. b.* and to *m.* which being well made, do grace all the rest, and yet are commonly made the worst of all. *To walk amògst the schollers, to see they observe these directions.* *To observe all the bad letters and faults in writing.*

Thus any one of these Schollers, chiefly one of them who write the best, may helpe the Master to direct the rest. *Any Scholler may helpe the Master.*

By these meanes the Schoole-master may bring many of his Schollers to be very good pen-men, and all generally to some competent sufficiencie, to the credit of the Schoole, the good contentment of the parents, and the great benefit of the Schollers, though he cannot write well himselfe, if hee can but onely thus farre forth direct, *The meanest writers may bring many of their schollers to be good pen-men.*

as

THE GRAMMAR SCHOOLE

as to cause his Schollers to follow these observations.

To avoid the evils by wandring Scriveners.

Hereby the Schooles also may be freed from having any need of the Scriveners, which go about the country, at least, which go under the names of Scriveners, & take upon them to teach to write; and doe ofttimes very much hurt in the places where they come. For they draw away the mindes of many of the Schollers from their bookes; even of all such as cannot endure to take paines, nor have any great love of learning, and cause many of good hope to leave the schoole utterly. Besides that, very often, so soone as ever these Scriveners are gone, the schollers whom they have taught, do forget what they seemed to have gotten by them, unlesse they be kept to practise their writing daily.

So that all that cost and time is commonly lost; besides the former inconveniences, that sundry by them lose all the learning which they had gotten. Also most of the yonger sort, who seem to write faire, and so leave the Schoole in a conceit of that which they have gotten by the Scrivener; yet doe write so false Orthography, as is loathsome to see, and ridiculous to reade.

Things necessarily required in commendable writing

For these properties should be joyned together in every pen-man, who would have any approbation; to bee able as well to write a good stile (I meane to indite, and to expresse his mind in some good forme of words, and true Orthography) as to write faire.

The use of Scriveners in the Grammar Schooles, what.

As for the use of Scriveners in the common schooles, it would be this (if any); either to make every scholler his book of copies, to use after the manner prescribed, untill such printed ones can be had: or else to set all the schollers in a good way of writing, for right framing their letters, and the like. To do it only at such times as the Master shall appoint; that it may be without any great hinderance to the schollers for their learning, and warily preventing all the former inconveniences. For schooles and good learning being such a singular benefit, and so great a gift of God to Church and Commonwealth, all hinderances would be wisely foreseene, and heedily prevented.

These

THE GRAMMAR SCHOOLE

These are the special helps which hitherto I have learned, for the direction of schollers in writing: and by these I am assured upon triall, that what is promised in this behalfe, may be effected through God's blessing.

Spoud. Sir, these must needs be very profitable: yet my memory being weake, and they many, I shall hardly thinke of them, to put them in practice. I pray you therefore repeat unto me againe in a word or two, which of them you take to be the principall, and of most continuall use.

Phil. These I take to be the principall, & almost the summe of all; and which would ever be had in memory: that the schollers have good pens, thin ink, faire & good copy books, and those made fast to their bookes, to have them ever laid close before them whē they are to write faire; which would be once every day; and then all of them together. That they have their bookes ruled strait and lightly, and that with ruling pens amongst all the yonger sort: and that therein a care be had, that they ever touch both the lines of the ruling pen with the bodies of their letters. Also that they have their faults shewed them, by pointing them to the copy letters; and where their letters are unlike to the copy, there to cause them to be amending them continually, until they attaine to write as faire as it. To call on them ever to have an eye to the copy, & to have the fashions of the letters in their minds. To take a delight in writing; striving who shall doe the best: to this end, to let their hands glide lightly on the paper; to strive to write very cleane; to make minimes, and such like letters sharpe at tops and bottomes, or just to the proportion of their copies: to hold their pens very low: their elbow something neere their side: to keepe their copies and bookes faire, unblotted and unscrauled: to have void places or waste papers for assaies, &c.

The summe of the principal and most necessary directions for writing, to be e'ver remembred: and therefore here shortly repeated, that we may ha've a briefe notion of them.

Most shortly, these three are almost all in all; good copies, continuall eying them well, a delight in writing: although I thinke it very necessary, that you be acquainted with all the former directions as they are set downe at large, to use them as need shall require. You may soone attain the knowledge

of

THE GRAMMAR SCHOOLE

of them, when you have them written down: the labour of learning them will be nothing to you in regard of the benefit; and much lesse in regard of the long search and observation, which I have used to finde them out.

Spoud. It is true indeed; and I am the more beholden unto you: but give me leave this one word; that which you said even now, may seeme to make very much against the Scriveners.

<small>*This maketh nothing against the honest Scriveners, but to prevent the abuse of shifters, and hurt to schooles.*</small>

Phil. Not at all; it only helpeth to redresse the great abuse by some shifters, who goe under the name of Scriveners; for all good Scriveners have their callings and imployments, wherein to serve to the profit and good of the Commonwealth, and not unto the hurt thereof. This onely may teach us to prevent and avoid those intolerable abuses, and hurts to schooles mentioned; whereof there hath been, and is daily, so much experience.

Spoud. Sir, I cannot but like of your answer; I my selfe have had some experience of the truth of the complaint: it is very necessarie that such evils should be prevented. Now therefore that you have thus shewed me how to make my schollers good pen-men, and that they may grow therein, as in their schoole learning; and thus prepared the way to our Grammar schoole: let us at length come to that which hath been the speciall end of my journey, and wherein our chiefe travel & imployment lyeth. And first let us begin with the rudiments of the Grammar, I meane the Accedence; wherein our first entrance is.

Phil. Very willingly: but first let me acquaint you with certaine generall observations, which concerne our whole course of teaching, and whereof we shall have almost continuall use; lest we be troubled with repeating them often after.

Spoud. It is well advised, that we may doe all things the most shortly, and in the best and easiest order that we can: I pray you therefore shew unto me what those generall observations be.

CHAP.

THE GRAMMAR SCHOOLE

CHAP. V.

Of certaine generall Observations to bee knowne of Schoole-masters, and practised carefully in all Grammar learning chiefely. And first, of causing all things to be done with understanding.

Phil.

FOr the generall Observations, the first may be this: *Schollers are to be taught to do all things with understanding, and to know the matter before in generall.*
1. That Schollers be taught to do all things with understanding; and to be able to give a reason of every matter which they learne. And so in every lecture which they learne in any tongue, first to understand the matter of it, and the lesson will be learned presently.

But before I speake any more of this, I pray you let me heare of you what course you have taken in this point.

Spoud. This first observation seemeth strange unto me, at the very naming of it. I my selfe have used onely this course, and I thinke it to be all that is done in most of our countrey Schooles; To give Lectures to the severall formes, or cause some Scholler to do it. And therein first to reade them over their Lecture, then to construe them, and in the lower formes to parse them. So when they come to say; to heare them whether they can reade, say without booke, construe and parse. More, as I take it, is not much used, for the understanding and making use of them. *The common course to do all things without understanding the reason of them, or how to make use of any thing.*

Phil. I know it to be as you say; and do hold it to be a verie great defect in Schooles generally: yea a farre greater hinderance to learning, then that of letting them to lose so many yeeres, before they begin to learne. For this is a matter which of all other concerneth the credit of Schooles, and furthereth learning wonderfully; to teach Schollers to understand whatsoever they learne, and to be able *The defect hereof exceeding great.*

THE GRAMMAR SCHOOLE

To do all things by reason, brings almost double learning.

able to give a reason of every thing why it is so; and to doe this from the lowest to the highest. My reasons are these:

1. Because if it were rightly knowne, and constantly practised in Schooles, it would bring forth very neere double so much good and sound learning, as is now gotten comonly.

2. It would bring withall, so much ease, pleasure and delight, both to all teachers and learners, and also so much certainety, and cause them to go forward with such cheerefulnesse, boldnesse and contention, as will hardly be beleeved untill it be tried by experience. In a word; It would cause all things to be gotten much more speedily, layed up more safely, and kept more surely in memory. Therefore, that old rule is true;

Legere & non intelligere negligere est.

To reade without understanding and knowledge how to make use, is a neglect of all learning.

To reade and not to understand what we reade, or not to know how to make use of it, is nothing else but a neglect of all good learning, and a meere abuse of the meanes and helps to attaine the same. It is no other thing but a very losse of our precious time, and of all our labour and cost bestowed therein, in regard of that which is read with understanding.

Triall of the difference betweene learning with understanding and without.

We may see triall here of sundry wayes.

1 Schollers examined together, whereof one understandeth, and can give reasons of things, the other not.

1. Let children be examined together; I meane such as of whom one of them alone hath beene taught to do all things by reason and with understanding; so that he is able to give you a plaine reason, and make the right use of every thing, which he hath learned: the other have learned onely to say without booke, to construe and parse; then marke the difference. Although all these learne one and the same Author; yet when they come to the triall, you would thinke that one to have all learning, when you heare him to give a reason of every thing, and that he can make use of all things; all the rest to have almost nothing at all, or at least nothing in regard of that one so taught.

2. In getting a lesson, how to do it soonest, and in the best manner.

2. Prove it thus in getting learning.

Teach your Scholler one lesson which you cause him to understand perfectly before; another of the same matter, whereof he understandeth little or nothing; and then trie whe-

THE GRAMMAR SCHOOLE

whether he will not do that, whereof he understandeth the meaning and reasons, almost in halfe the time, which the other will require. And this also so, as you may evidently discerne it, that he will do it with much more ease, certainety and boldnesse, then he can do the other.

3. We our selves may make triall of it by our owne experience, in construing any difficult piece of Latine, Greeke, or Hebrew, or committing any thing to memorie; whether if so be that we do but understand the matter of it before perfectly, we shall not do it in halfe the time, and with one halfe of the labour, that otherwise it would require.

3. In our owne experience construing or studying out any difficult place in any Author or tongue.

Or if we would write or speake of any thing, let us prove it but thus: If we first understand the matter well, and have it perfectly in our head, whether words to expresse our minds will not follow as of themselves.

To this very purpose, for confirming the truth hereof, and to keepe a continuall remembrance of this point; these three verses of *Horace* were worthy to be written in letters of gold, and to be imprinted in the memorie of every one who is desirous to get the best learning: for so they would indeede prove golden verses, and make undoubtedly golden times;

*Scribendi rectè sapere est & principium & fons :
Rem tibi Socraticæ poterunt ostendere chartæ ;
Verbáque prouisam rem non inuita sequentur.*

The meaning of the verses, I take it to be this: To attaine to this facultie, to be able to write or speake of any matter, and so to come to all excellent learning, the very first and chiefe fountaine, and that which is all in all, is to understand the matter well in the first place. As for store of matter, the writings of learned men (such as *Socrates* was) will furnish you abundantly therewith.

And when you have the matter thoroughly in your head, words will follow, as waters out of a Fountaine, even almost naturally, to expresse your mind in any tongue, which you studie in any right order.

This

THE GRAMMAR SCHOOLE

This will be found to be true in Latine, Greeke, Hebrew, and by a like reason in every other tongue, and in every facultie: whether we would write, speake, learne, resolve, or remember and lay up for ever.

One chiefe cause why Virgil and others writ so eloquently, because they were so ripe in understanding, and had such store of matter.

This was a principall cause that made *Tully, Ovid, Virgil*, and some others so to flow in eloquence; and especially *Virgil*, whom men worthily account the chiefe of all Latine Poets, because they did understand so fully whatsoever they writ of. I might instance this also in Preachers, by our daily experience; of whom some are better able to preach powerfully in two dayes warning, and having words at will, then other in two moneths; and all because the one sort are so full of understanding and matter, the other are so barren thereof.

Trie.

Thus in all these examples, every man may see a plaine demonstration of the truth of these verses of *Horace*, which he no doubt did write upon his owne experience, as every man shall find, who wil set himselfe to make triall. Prove and confirme what tongue soever your Scholler learnes, even from the first reading of English, if he can repeate you the matter, or the summe of it, or have it in his head, trie whether he will not have the words presently. The plentifull experi-

They who find experience, will be desirous to make others partakers.

ence which I have seene, of the sweete delight and fruite of this course, of causing children to do all things with understanding and reason, compared with the fruitlesse toyles and griefes of former times, do make me not onely confident for the thing, but also desirous to make all other partakers of the benefit.

Spoud. I do fully see the evidence of all that which you have said, and therefore I must needs be perswaded of it. I do heartily thanke God for it, and will endevor myselfe to put

It seemeth great difficulty for masters to teach their Schollers to do all things with understanding.

it in practice continually. Only here is the difficulty, how a Schoolemaster may do this, to teach his Scholler so to proceede with understanding, and how to give a reason of every matter which they learne, to make use of all their learning.

Above all, how hee may beginne to fraught young Schollers

THE GRAMMAR SCHOOLE

Schollers with all store of matter, as they goe on: this very much passeth my skill. I should thinke my selfe most happy, to obtaine this knowledge, if it possibly can be done.

Phil. Attend to those things which I shall relate, and I have no doubt, but I shall very much accomplish your desire in this: for our whole conference doth tend chiefely to this end. As all learning is grounded on reason: so in every Chapter I shall endeavour my selfe to manifest the reasons of every thing, and how you may teach others; so farre forth, as hitherto the Lord hath made them knowne unto me. And more hereafter, as I shall learne more. The principall meanes for their understanding, is, by asking short questions of the matter: for so they will understand any thing, which they are to learne. But of that more hereafter in the particular examples; and chiefly, Chap. 23.

Spoud. If you have done then with this, let us goe forward to your next generall observation; and so thorow them all, as briefly as you can.

Phil. My next observation is this: that as I would have them to do all things with understanding; so to learne onely such bookes and matters, as whereof they may have the best use, and that perpetually in all their learning, or in their whole life. For this is well knowne to every one; that things well learned in youth, will be kept most surely all the life long; because in that age they are most easily imprinted, and sticke the longest in fresh memory. And for that cause, children should spend no time unfruitfully in such bookes, as whereof they cannot have both very good and continuall use. This cannot be but a great folly, to mis-spend our precious time in such studies, whereof neither our selves nor others can have benefit after; or else in such, as the knowledge whereof will vanish for want of practice: and much more in those, which will corrupt and hurt in stead of doing good. And therefore all filthy places in the Poets would be wisely passed over, or wearily expounded. It were well if there were an *Index Expurgatorius*, to purge out all the filth out of these by leaving it out, or changing it.

The second generall observation, To learne onely such things, as whereof they may have good and perpetuall use.

Filthy places in Poets omitted.

Third

THE GRAMMAR SCHOOLE

3. To note all hard words, or matters worthy observation.

Third rule, and that generall for all Students, is this: that whatsoever difficult words, or matters of speciall observation, they do reade in any Author, be marked out; I meane all such words or things, as either are hard to them in the learning of them, or which are of some speciall excellency, or use, worthy the noting: or which after that they have beene a certaine time in construction, they have not either learned, or at least they know not where they have learned them. For the marking of them, to do it with little lines under them, or above them, or against such parts of the word wherein the difficulty lieth, or by some prickes, or whatsoever letter or marke may best helpe to call the knowledge of the thing to remembrance; yet so much as may be, without marring of their books. To do this, to the end that they may oft-times reade over these, or examine and meditate of them more seriously, untill that they bee as perfect in them, as in any of the rest of their bookes: for having these, then have they all.

Manner of marking.

This generall in getting all learning.

This would be universall, in getting all kinde of learning; after that children do grow to any discretion to marke such things rightly: you will marvell (if you have not made triall of it) how much they will go thorow, and what sound knowledge they will come unto in any kinde of study; and how soone by this helpe, more then they can do without it. And when they have once gotten it, they may as easily keepe it, and as surely, by oft-times running over those things, which are so noted, above all the rest. This is the reason that you shall have the choysest bookes of most great learned men, and the notablest students, all marked thorow thus, in all matters either obscure, or of principall and most necessary use. And this one chiefe meanes, whereby Schollers may have the difficultest things in their Authours so perfectly, as that whensoever they shall bee examined of a sudden, they shall be very ready, to their great praise, and to the just commendation of the Schoole. For the manner of noting, it is best to note all School bookes with inke; and also all others, which you would have gotten *ad unguem,* as we use to

The bookes of the best students thus noted.

To note bookes of daily use with inke.

THE GRAMMAR SCHOOLE

to say, or whereof we would have daily or long practice; because inke will indure: neither will such bookes be the worse for their noting, but the better, if they be noted with judgement. But for all other bookes which you would have faire againe at your pleasure; note them with a pensil of blacke lead: for that you may rub out againe when you will, with the crums of new wheat bread. *Others with blacke leade thrust into a quill.*

The very little ones, which reade but English, may make some secret markes thus at every hard word; though but with some little dint with their naile: so that they doe not marre their bookes. *How to rub it forth againe.*

Of this I shall speake more particularly in the manner of parsing, Chap. 9.

A fourth observation, is this: That whatsoever bookes or matter Schollers do learne, after they beginne to learne without booke; that they learne them so perfectly, and hold them so surely, by daily repetition and examination, that they may have in their minds such an absolute knowledge of all the words, and matters which they have learned; as wheresoever they shall meete with the same againe, or shall have occasion to use them, they may not neede to be driven to learne then anew; but that they may tell of a sudden where they have learned them, or can repeat the place: and so make their use and benefit of them. *4. To learne all so perfectly, as the former may be instead of a Schoolemaister to the latter.*

To teach the same things twise, or thrise, is a double labour and griefe: but to have all things which they have learned, ever in readinesse, is a singular benefit, and a rare commendation. For besides the preventing of all losse of labour and time, it shall be to the great delight of all who heare them tried, and the exceeding furtherance of their continuall growth in all good learning. *Not to neede to teach the same things twise or thrise over.*

And to effect this yet more fully; acquaint them in all their Lectures and exercises, some one of them or other, who can tell first, to repeate where they have learned every hard word: and that chiefly in their Grammar, if they have learned it there, to have that exceeding perfect; and to marke surely every new word, according to the direction which I have before given. *To tell where they have learned every hard word.*

A

THE GRAMMAR SCHOOLE

5. That the whole Schoole be divided into so few fourmes as may be.

A fift generall observation, and which is not inferiour to any of the former, for the good both of Masters and Schoollers, and the very great benefit of Schooles, is this: that the whole Schoole be divided into so few fourmes as may be, of so many as can any way be fitted to goe together: though they be sixteene, or twenty, yes, fortie in a fourme, it is not the worse.

The reasons of it are most cleere.

Reasons:
1. It is for most part the same labour, to teach twenty in a fourme as to teach two.

1. In most things it is almost the same labour to teach twenty, as to teach two: as in reading all Lectures and rules unto them, in examining all parts and Lectures. Like as it is in Sermons, and Catechisings, where it is the same labour to teach one, that it is to teach a thousand, if all can heare alike. This is very generall, except in exercises of writing; wherin also great advantage may be gotten by this meanes, if right order be observed, as we shall shew after.

2. The fewer fourmes, the more labour may be bestowed in examining every tittle. Examination, a quickner of learning.

2. Secondly, the fewer fourmes there are, the more time may be spent in each fourme; and more labour may be bestowed in examining every tittle necessary. Which worke of continuall examination, is a notable quickner and nourisher of all good learning; helping marvellously understanding, audacity, memory, and provoking emulation of the Schollers: and therefore a principall part of the Master's labour, and of the time in the Schoole, would be imployed in this.

Every one of a fourme shall someway provoke the others by this meanes.

3. By this meanes, every one of a fourme shall someway provoke, or incourage the rest of their fellowes. If they be but dull, the rest will thinke to go before them; but if they be more pregnant and witty, or more painefull and diligent, they shall put spirits into all the rest, and be as a spurre unto them. For there is in our nature an inbred desire to ayme at the best, and to wish to equalize them in each commendable quality; if there be right meanes of direction and incouragement thereunto.

And every one may helpe others.

Also every one of a forme may someway helpe the rest: for none are so dull, but they may happely remember some thing, which none of the rest did.

This

THE GRAMMAR SCHOOLE

This I have seene by experience, to be the very best way; even for those who but reade the Accidence, to put so many of them into a fourm together, as may be: they will both further one another very much, in reading it quickely (each helping and teaching others) and also they may sooner be heard, when every one need but to reade his piece of the same lesson, the rest helping. Thus they will goe through very fast, and be all ready to enter without booke together. Trie, and finding the benefit, you will not alter. *Those who but reade, to be put together so many as can be.*

6. A sixt generall observation, and of no lesse worth then any of the former, may be this: That there be most heedfull care, chiefly amongst all the yongest, that not one of them be any way discouraged, either by bitternesse of speech, or by taunting disgrace; or else by severitie of correction, to cause them to hate the Schoole before they know it, or to distast good learning before they have felt the sweetnesse of it: but in stead hereof, that all things in Schooles be done by emulation, and honest contention, through a wise commending in them everything, which any way deserveth praise, and by giving preeminence in place, or such like rewards. For that Adage is not so ancient as true: *Laus excitat ingenium.* *6. To have a great care that none be discouraged.*

But all to be provoked by emulation, and desire of praise.

There is no such a Whet-stone, to set an edge upon a good wit, or to incourage an ingenuous nature to learning as praise is, as our learned Master *Askam* doth most rightly affirme. *Commendation the Whetstone of the wit.*

To this purpose that sentence of *Tully* were worthy to be written in every Schoole, and to be set up in such places, where it might ever stand in the Masters eye, if it were possible; that so every teacher might at length be brought to the continuall practice of the good policy contained in it: to wit, to bend all his endevours to provoke all his Schollers, to strive incessantly, which of them shal carry away the worthiest praise and commendation. The sentence is this; *A sentence of Tully worthy to be ever before the Master's eye.*

Pueri efferuntur lætitia cùm vicerint, & pudet victos: vt tam se accusari nolunt, quàm cupiunt laudari: quos illi labores non perferunt vt æqualium principes fint. Cic. 1. de finib,

Be-

THE GRAMMAR SCHOOLE

This strife for Masteries is the most commendable play, and a chiefe meanes to make the Schoole Ludus literarius.

Besides this also, this same strift for these Masteries, and for rewards of learning, is the most commendable play, and the very highway to make the Schoole-house to bee *ludus literarius* indeed a Schoole of play and pleasure (as was said) and not of feare and bondage: although there must be alwaies a meet and loving feare, furthered by wise severitie, to maintaine authoritie, and to make it also *Ludus à non ludendo*, a place void of all fruitlesse play and loytering, the better to be able to effect all this good which we desire.

7. All to have their adversaries, and so to be matched and placed, that all may be done by strift.

7. To the end that every thing in the Schoole may bee thus done, by emulation and contention for praise; there would be a carefull sorting, and matching every one with him, who is next unto him in learning: for this is also a most true proverbe; *Marcet sine adversario virtus:* Vertue loveth the vigour and decayeth, where it hath no adversarie. So they would be placed as adversaries, that they may contend in all things, whether of them shall doe the better, and beare the bell away. Thus the whole fourmes through the Schoole should bee divided also into two equall parts; to strive alwayes, whether side of the fourme should get the victorie: like as it is in games, at shooting, or the like. Experience sheweth how this will provoke them, to be preparing and fitting for the victory. Even as Archers will prepare themselves by exercising, getting the best bowes & arrows; and then making first their choice so equall as they can, afterwards directing their fellows; thus striving by all means, whether side shall beat: so will it be here. But of this I shall have more fit occasion, to tell what I thinke, when we shall speake of the manner of dividing of the fourmes.

8. To use ever to appose the most negligent.

8. That we use ever to appose the worst and most negligent of each fourme above all the rest; though every one something, yet them principally. This will make them more carefull, and cause all to come on together in some good sort.

9. Continuall care of pronunciation.

9. That from the first entrance they be taught to pronounce every thing audibly, leasurely, distinctly, and naturally; sounding out specially the last syllable, that each word

THE GRAMMAR SCHOOLE

word may be fully understood. But of this we have spoken somewhat; and shall speake more in the due place, what a grace sweet pronunciation gives unto all learning, and how the want of it doth altogether mar, or much deforme the most excellent speech.

10. That they have daily some speciall exercise of the memory, by repeating somewhat without booke; as a part in their rules the foure first daies in the weeke, the Lectures of the weeke, or some part of them on the Friday, all the rules of the weeke on the Saturday: besides matters of reports, as Apologues or fables, theames, disputations, and the like.

10 To have some exercise of the memory daily.

The reason is, because the daily practice hereof, is the onely meanes to make excellent memories; so that the memory be not overloaden. But for this matter of saying without booke, how farre it is to be used, and what helpe may be had to prevent the overtoyling and terrifying of Schollers with it, and to supply some things better otherwise; I hope I shall take a fitter place to speake of it hereafter.

Reason of it for making excellent memories.

11. That for whatsoever exercises they are to learn, they have the best patternes to follow, which can be procured: as in writing, so for all kind of learning, how to do every thing; because all learning is principally gotten by a kinde of imitation, and Art doth imitate the most excellent nature. The patterns being singular, so shall their worke prove in time, either to expresse their pattern very lively, or happely to goe beyond it. Of this also we shall have occasion after to speake.

11 To have the best patternes of all sorts.

12. The Masters to be alwayes vigilant, as good leaders; to labour to a lively cheerefulnesse, to put life and spirit into the children; and to incourage themselves in well doing, by amending whatsoever is amisse, and supplying each thing, wherein they are defective (observing the daily growth of their Schollers) remembring still the worthy counsell, *Tu ne cede malis, sed contra audentior ito;* and also ever calling to minde whom they serve, and how their reward is with the Lord.

12 The Master continually to incourage themselves, and their Schollers.

13. Constancy in good orders, and exercises ought ever to be kept inviolable; with a continuall demonstration of love

13 Constancy in good orders with a continuall demonstration of love to the Schollers to doe all for their good.

in

THE GRAMMAR SCHOOLE

in the Masters towards the Schollers, and a desire to doe them the uttermost good. This shall overcome the most froward in time; and used with the rest, shall undoubtedly bring forth the fruit of their desires.

Though many moe directions might be added, yet wee will content our selves with these for the present; as being most generall, and belonging to all which follow. Others we shall adde, as we shall finde the fittest occasions.

Spoud. Certainly, Sir, these rules doe very much affect and delight me, at this hearing of them; neither can I easily discerne which of them is most to bee preferred. If you had given me so many crownes, you could not have gratified me more: I purpose to put them in practice presently, that I may finde that sweete and pleasant fruit of them, which I fully conceive may be attained by them.

Phil. If you take so much delight in the hearing of them, I trust you shall doe much more in the proofe: and therefore having finished these, we will now at length come unto the Accidence.

CHAP. VI.

How to make children perfect in the Accidence.

Spoud.

FOR the Accidence then, I pray you acquaint mee what you have learned, how children may get it most speedily; and how they may be made so very perfect in it, as to answer so readily to any question thereof, as you did affirme that they may; and to make the right use of it.

Phil. You must ever first let me heare of you, what course you

THE GRAMMAR SCHOOLE

you have taken, and what you thinke to bee ordinarie in Schooles, and then I will supply whatsoever I have learned; for that all shall be the better conceived.

Spoud. For reading over their Accedence, this is all that I have used; To let them reade it over every one by himselfe by lessons, as in reading other English: and so to heare them one by one, as they can say. In the harder lessons to reade it over before them. Thus I make them to reade over their Accedence once or twice within the booke, before they do get it without booke. *The usual maner of learning to reade the Accedence.*

Secondly, for getting it without booke, I cause them to doe likewise, and to say as oft as they can. To keepe that which they have learned, by weekely repetitions, and by saying parts. And for the meaning, to teach it after by practice. Now I pray you shew me your judgement, and vouchsafe me your helpe. *The ordinarie manner of getting the Accedence without booke.*

Phil. My judgement is, according to my experience, that though this be the ordinary course, yet it may be done with farre greater ease, in lesse time, and with much more profit, to effect your desire: yea, to teach ten or twelve as soone and readily as you shall teach one. Also to make them more full of understanding, that they shall be able to make right use of their rules, to enter into construction, and go forward readily together in construing, parsing and making Latine. Whereas otherwise they must be taught the understanding and use of it after: which shall be another labour, and bee as if they had not learned it at all before. Now the meanes how all this may be effected are these: *The wants in this course.*

1 For reading the Accedence.

So soone as they enter into the Accedence, put so many of them into a fourm as you can well, to enter together; as was shewed before. And therein first reade them over their lesson, telling them the meaning shortly, to make them a little to understand it: and so they will learn it much sooner. Then let them one helpe another, as they will doe learning together, and every one will draw on another; one of them ever reading over the lesson, that all the rest may heare, *The best meanes for learning to reade the Accedence.*

Ever one to be reading, all the rest marking and helping.

heare, and the rest telling where he misseth; and so never idle till all can reade it. When they come to say, cause every one of the fourme to reade his piece in order, in like manner the rest to helpe where he sticks.

By this meanes there will not be much more labour with twelve, then with one alone. Experience also wil shew that they will all goe forward more fast and surely then any other way. And although that they goe faster forward, and not so very perfectly as they thus read it first, yet they will soone reade most readily, when they come to get without booke.

Learning the Accedence without booke, to take but a little at once. This rule must be generall of all learning that seemeth hard, and of things to be gotten perfectly; but here specially.

When they have once gone through it within booke, let them begin to learne it without booke Or else if they can reade well before, you may let them learn to reade thus, as they get without booke, and so do both under one. But then some houre or two would be spent daily in the afternoon in reading, or some day of the weeke separate thereto: else they wil somwhat forget to reade, because they read but so little on a day; which must be carefully prevented. Therefore it will not be amisse to reade it over speedily once or twice before. When they learne without book, let them use this Caueat especially; That they take but little at a time, so as they may be able to get it quickly and well, and so goe on to a new lesson: for this will harten them exceedingly to take paines, in rejoicing how many lessons they have learned, and how soone they have learned each lesson; Whereas giving them overmuch, it will put them out of heart, so that they will either doe nothing at all, or with no life.

2. Before they goe in hand with a lesson, do what you can to make them to understand the summe of the lesson first, and the meaning of it: thus. 1. Reade them over their lesson. 2. Then shew them the plaine meaning of every thing so easily, shortly and familiarly, as possibly you can, and as you thinke that they can conceive. After propound all unto them in short questions, and aske the questions directly in order as they lie in the booke, answering them first your selfe. Then if you will, you may aske them

To make them first to understand their Lectures, and how.

THE GRAMMAR SCHOOLE

them the same questions, and let them answer them as you did before, still looking upon their bookes, when they answer. *To let them answer the questions upon their bookes.*

To require them to answer so, will much incourage them; because they shall find themselves able to do it. The moe the questions are, the shorter and plainer arising naturally out of the words of the booke, the sooner a great deale will your children understand them.

And therefore any long question is to be divided into as many short ones as you may, according to the parts of the question. Hereby the dullest capacities will come to conceive the hardest questions in time, and proceed with more facilitie; so that the masters doe enter them thus from the beginning, still causing them to understand as they learne.

Here the masters must not be ashamed, nor weary to doe as the nurse with the child, as it were stammering and playing with them, to seeke by all meanes to breed in the little ones a love of their masters, with delight in their bookes, and a joy that they can understand, and also to the end to nourish in them that emulation mentioned, to strive who shall doe best. Neither is the wise Master to stand with the children about amending the Accedence, if he thinke any thing faulty or defective; but only to make them to understand the rules, as they are set downe in the booke: for this they will keep. To make this plain by example. To begin at In Speech be, &c. First, reade them over the words: Then tell them for the meaning after this maner, or the like as you please. The meaning is this; That in Speech which men utter, there is nothing but words to call or know things by, and setting or joyning of words together. Like as it is in our English tongue, so in the Latine, & so in other tongues. And of these words which make this speech, are not many parts or kinds, but only eight parts of speech. For whatsoever can be spoken, belongeth to one of these eight parts. They are either Nownes, or Pronowns, or Verbs, or one of the rest. More shortly thus; There is not any word in any language whatsoever, but it is either a Nown or a Pronown, Verb, &c.

Admonition to Masters desirous to doe good, to be as the Nurses with little children.

Example how to make the child to understand, by shewing the meaning.

Also

THE GRAMMAR SCHOOLE

Also of these eight parts, the foure first onely are such as may be declined: That is, such as each of them may bee turned or framed divers wayes, and have divers endings; as *Magister, magistri, magistro. Amo, amas, amat.* The other foure last are undeclined; that is, such as cannot be so turned, and have but onely one ending: as, *Hodie, cras, &c.*

How by asking Questions.   Then aske them questions according to the same, following the words or the booke, in this manner or the like, as you thinke good.

Q. How many parts of speech have you? Or how many parts are there in speech?
A. Eight.
Q. Of these how many are declined, how many undeclined? So, which are declined, which undeclined?

Afterwards to aske the same questions backe againe, the last first. As which parts of speech are undeclined? Or how many are undeclined? So in the next.

Q. What is a Nowne?
A. A Nowne is the name of a thing.
Q. Of what thing?
A. Of such a thing as may be seene, felt, heard, or understood.
Q. Give me some good examples of some such things.
A. A hand, a house, goodnesse.
Q. What is the name of a hand in Latine? Or what is Latine for a hand? what is Latine for a house? and so forth.

Then aske the questions as it were backward thus:
Q. What part of speech is that which is the name of a thing, which may be felt, heard, or understood?
A A Nowne, &c.

Thus to goe forward in every rule. 1. Reading it over to the children. 2. Shewing the plaine meaning in as few words as you can. 3. Propounding every piece of it in a short question, following the words of the booke, and answering it your selfe out of the words of the booke. 4. Asking the same questions of them, and trying how themselves

THE GRAMMAR SCHOOLE

selves can answer them, still looking upon their books. Then let them goe in hand with getting it amongst themselves, untill they can say and answer the questions without booke readily; the highest of the fourmes poasing the rest untill they can say. By this meanes it will seem so easie to them, that they will go to it most cheerfully, and get it much sooner then you would imagine, both the understanding and the words: for the understanding of the matter will presently bring the words, as we said.

As they goe forward, strive to make them most perfect in these things specially:

1. In knowing a Nowne, and how to discerne the Substantive from the Adjective. After in the signes of the Cases.

Then in declining the Articles, *Hic, hæc, hoc*; every Article by it selfe: as *Nom. hic. Gen. huius. Dat. huic. Accus. hunc. Ablat. hoc*, &c. So in the Feminines. *Nom. hæc. Accus. hanc. Abl. hac*, &c.

By being perfect in these Articles thus, they shall both be able to decline any Nowne much sooner, and to know the right Gender for making Latine.

Also let them learne to decline both Latine and English together; I meane, Latine before English, and English before Latine, both in the Articles, and other examples of Nownes, Pronownes and Verbes. As in the Articles thus: *Hic* this Masculine, *hæc* this Feminine, *hoc* this Neuter. *Gen. huins* of this Masculine, Feminine, Neuter. *Dat. huic*, to this Masculine, Feminine, Neuter. *Accus. hunc* this Masculine, *hanc* this Feminine, *hoc* this Neuter, *Voc. caret Ablat. ab hōc* from this Masculine, *ab hac* from this Feminine, *ab hoc* from this Neuter. Or *hic* this Male, *hæc* this Female, *hoc* this Neuter, &c. or *hoc* this thing.

So the English before, if you will: Though in these Articles it may suffice to decline the Latine first, so as before, and in (*is*) and (*qui*) or the like. This kinde of declining in all examples following, will be found such a helpe, as it will hardly be thought, untill it be tryed, both to speedie construing,

In what points of the Accedence the chiefe labour would bee bestowed with the children to make them perfect in them.

Articles.

Declining English before Latine, Latine before English.

Benefit of this declining.

THE GRAMMAR SCHOOLE

struing, parsing, and making Latine, howsoever it may seem at first childish, or but a toy, and of no moment. The Latine before the English for construing. The English before the Latine, for making Latine true. Then make them as perfect in their Genders, forwards and backwards. As what Gender is *hic*, and *hic* what Gender? or what is the Article of the Masculine Gender? so in the rest.

Genders.

After these, make them as ready in their Declensions, not onely to know what Declension every word is of; but also the severall terminations of every case in every Declension, both as they learne them one by one, according to the booke, and after to give them together, when they have learned them all, and that in this manner as followeth.

Severall terminations of the Declensions.

The Genitive case singular of the first in æ dipthong: as, *musæ*, the second in *i*, as *Magistri*, the third in *is*, as *lapidis*, &c. so thorough: and backward; the Gen. of the fift in *ei*, as *meridiei*, of the fourth in *us*, as *manus*; the third in *is*, as *lapidis*, &c.

Then to decline perfectly every example in each Declension, in manner as the Articles: as for example;

Declining the examples in each Declension.

Musa, a song, *musæ* of a song, *musæ*, to a song, *musam* the song, ô *musa*, ô song, *ab hac musa* from a song, or from this song. So in the Plurall number, *musæ* songs, *musarum* of songs, &c.

After, English first. A song *musa*, of a song *musæ*, to a song *musæ*, &c. To give them these signes, because they signifie thus most commonly, though not alwaies. Then appose them untill they can give readily any case either English to Latine, or Latine to English: which they will soone doe. So in each Declension. After you may acquaint them to decline all the examples of the Declensions together, putting in *Regnum* also, because it differeth from *Magister*, as *Nominativo Musa, Magister, Regnum Lapis, Manus, Meridies: Gen. musæ, magistri, regni, lapidis, manus, meridiei*, &c. This will helpe them presently to joyne any Substantives, as they fall in the same case, or the Substantives and Adjectives together.

Declining all the examples of all the Declensions together.

So

THE GRAMMAR SCHOOLE

So if you please, you may cause them to decline them so with the English adjoined, either before the Latine or after. The moe waies they are thus declined, to make them each way perfect, the better they will be learned, if time will permit.

Of all other this is the shortest, and whereby they may be most easily kept by them, who have any understanding, to give the bare terminations alone together, as thus. Terminations of the Genitive singular, *æ. i. is. us. ei.* Dative, *æ. o. i. ui. ei. &c.* *Giving the bare terminations, the shortest way.*

And those usuall signes of the cases, as a, of, to, the, ô, from. Thus to ply continuall poasing, each day a little, untill they can give you any terminations, or case in these examples English to Latine, or Latine to English.

After to do the like in *bonus*; thus: *bonus* a good Masculine, *bona* a good Feminine, *bonum* a good Neuter, &c. We may English it after this manner, for the better understanding of the children: Or as we can finde any more easie way. *The like in bonus.*

After all these when they wax perfect in them; the declining of Substantives and Adjectives, of all sorts together, is of very great profit, either Latine alone together, or Latine and English both together if you will. *Declining of Substantives and Adjectives together.*

And first, the examples of the booke. As *musa bona* a good muse, *musæ bonæ* of a good muse, *musæ bonæ* to a good muse, &c.

So *Magister bonus, Magistri boni, &c.* So *Regnum bonum.* And *lapis bonus,* a good stone, *lapidis boni,* of a good stone; or *lapis durus, lapidis duri, &c.* So *manus fœlix, manus fœlicis, manui fœlici, manum fœlicem.*

Or *meridies tristis: meridiei tristis, meridiei tristi, meridiem tristem, &c.*

And in which you observe them to misse most, ply those untill all be perfect.

When they are very cunning in these, then they are to be acquainted with declining other words like their examples, still keeping them to those patterns, where they misse. And first, the words set downe in the margents of their bookes against each example. Then

THE GRAMMAR SCHOOLE

Then other Substantives and Adjectives together. As *sylua sonans, syluæ sonantis, syluæ sonanti, &c.*

Leo magnus, a great Lion, *Leonis magni* of a great Lion, *Leoni magno,* to a great Lion, &c.

Or English before. A great Lion, *Leo magnus,* of a great Lion, *Leonis magni,* &c.

Unto these adjoyne the daily forming of comparisons: as *Gratus, gratior, gratissimus. Bonus, melior, optimus.* So, *Fœlix, fœlicior, fœlicissimus*: first regular, then irregular or out of rule.

Chiefe examples in the Pronowns of most common use. Then doe the like in the Pronownes, to make them to be able to decline and give them readily, English to Latine: and Latine to English; like as the Nownes. As *Ego,* I. *mei* of me, &c. So backe againe. I, *Ego.* of me, *mei,* to me, *mihi. Tu* thou, *tui* of thee, and thou *tu,* of thee *tui, &c. Sui* of himselfe, or of themselves, *sibi* to himselfe, or to themselves, *se* himselfe or themselves. *Is* he, *ea* shee, *id* that thing, *eius* of that man, of that woman, of that thing, or that matter.

Qui which man, *quæ* which woman, *quod* which thing, *cuius* of which man, of which woman, of which thing; like as you may say, *hic* this man, *hæc* this woman, *hoc* this thing, &c., or *hic* this Masculine, &c.

In these two and (*hic*) it may suffice onely to decline Latine before, as we said.

Persons of the Pronownes. So to be very ready in the persons of the Pronowns, both to shew what person every one is of: and to give every one both English to Latine, and Latine to English. As when I say give your first person singular, Latine and English; The child answereth *Ego,* I. or I, *Ego, &c.* so what person every one is.

But in the Verbes above all, is your diligence to be shewed, in making them not onely perfect in declining every example to be able to decline any Verbe by them; but more specially in conjugating, and being ready to give you the Latine to the English, and English to the Latine in any Person, of any Moode, or Tense.

To

THE GRAMMAR SCHOOLE

To effect this most speedily, teach them to say first the first persons of one conjugation alone thorow the Active voice, both Latine before English, and English before Latine, thus: *Amo*, I love, *amabam*, I loved or did love, *amaui* I have loved; so thorow the Indicative mood. Then English first, thus: I love, *Amo*: I loved or did love, *amabam*, &c. *How to come most speedily to be perfect in the verbes, which are a meane foundation, and wherein the greatest difficulty lyeth.*

And after withall to be able to runne the terminations in every tense: as in *amo, o, as, at, amus, atis, ant*. In *amabam, bam, bas, bat, bamus, batis, bant*. And likewise the persons in English, I, thou, he, we, yee, they, according to the terminations; and then by apposing, they will presently answer any of them.

As thus; aske the childe, I love: he answereth *amo*: then aske, they love; he cannot tell. Bid him to runne the terminations of *Amo*; he answereth *o, as, at, amus, atis, ant*: then I say, give now, they love: he answereth *amant*: so ye love, or we love, &c.

So aske, I loved or did love; he answereth *Amabam*: then we loved or did love: if he cannot tell, bid him to runne his terminations, and he will answer, *bam, bas, bat, bamus, batis, bant*. Then aske, How say you, we loved or did love: he answereth *Amabamus*. Afterwards in *Doceo*: so in the rest.

When they come at the Passive, let them doe the like: and when they have learned it thorow, then let them practice to repeat Active and Passive together thus: I love, *Amo*: I am loved, *Amor*: I loved or did love, *Amabam*: I was loved, *Amabar*: I have loved, *Amaui*: I have been loved, *amatus sum vel fui*, &c.

Then by posing the first persons, and running the terminations, they will very soone give any of the verbs in any person.

They will by this meanes goe thorow all the Conjugations, and with this perfect readinesse, as soone as they will learne to say them without booke, without any understanding at all, if not sooner; so that they be well applyed. Yet if this prevaile not as you desire, you may exercise them

to

THE GRAMMAR SCHOOLE

These may be added if we will, to make them more ready. to repeat all the persons through every moode, and person, by themselves, but chiefly the first persons: as, *Amo, amabam, amaui, amaueram, amabo: Amem, amarem, amauerim, amauissem, amauero: amare, amauisse, amaturumesse: amandi, amando, amandum, &c.*

So in the second persons, *amas, amabas, &c.*

Or thus to conjugate those tenses together, which doe come one of another; as *Amo, amabam, amabo, amem, amarem, amare.*

So, *Amaui, amaueram, amauerim, amauero, amauissem, amauisse.*

The manner of apposing here. This is accounted the speediest way; in examining here, to appose the same tenses, of the severall moodes together: as the present tenses, I love, *Amo,* Grant I love, *Vtinam amem,* I may or can love, *amem:* when I love, *cùm amem.*

So in the Preterimperfect tenses.

Knowledge of the terminations. Comparing them together for memorie sake, though they come not one of another. To make them most perfect in this, practise them that they can give readily, the terminations of the first persons, first in the Indicative moode, in each tense; then how the same tenses differ in the rest of the moods, except the Imparative, together with the signes of the tenses in English. As for example: the termination *o,* in the Indicative moode present tense, is in the three other moodes turned into *em* or *am;* as *amo* is made *amem, doceo doceam, lego legam, audio audiam.* In the Preterimperfect tense, *bam* is turned into *rem:* Preterperfect tense, *i* into *rim:* Preterpluperfect tense, *ram* into *sem:* Future tense *bo,* or *am,* into *ro.*

So in the Indicative moode, the terminations are these: *o, bam, i, ram, bo* or *am.* In the other three are these answerable; *em* or *am, rem, rim, sem, ro.*

Though these be not one formed of another; yet comparing them thus together, will make the children to learne them sooner by much.

Generall signes of the five tenses active, are; Doe, Did, Have, Had, Shall or will.

Of the Passive present tense, Am, Is, Are or Art. Imperfect tense, Was, Were, Wert, Preterperfect tense, have beene.

Pre-

THE GRAMMAR SCHOOLE

Preterpluperfect tense, Had beene. Future tense, Shall or Will be.

Signes of the moodes are set downe in the booke; the Indicative having no signe: the other three having their severall signes in English.

This little Table well thought on, makes *all most easie.*

	Active voice.			Passive voice.		
	Signes of the tenses in English.	Terminations in Latine without a signe.	Terminations with a signe.	Signes of the tenses in English.	Terminations in Latine without a signe.	Terminations in Latine with a signe.
Present tense.	Do.	*o.*	*em* or *am.*	Am, is, are, art.	*or,*	*er,* (or) *ar.*
Preterimperfect tense.	Did.	*bam.*	*rem.*	Was, were, wert.	*bar.*	*rer.*
Preterperfect tense.	Have.	*i.*	*rim.*	Have beene.	*sum vel fui.*	*sim vel fuerim.*
Preterpluperfect tense.	Had.	*ram.*	*sem.*	Had been.	*eram vel fuer am.*	*essem vel fuissem.*
Future tense.	Shall or will.	*bo. am.*	*ro.*	Shall or will be.	*bor. ar.*	*ero vel fuero.*

For to make the childe to understand this Table, first shew him these things upon his booke, by comparing the Active voice, with the Passive, and the Indicative moode in both, with the other moodes. After pose thus: *For understanding this Table.*

Q. Do, without a signe of the moode, how must it end in Latine?
A. In *e.*
Q. Do, with a signe, how?
A. In *em* or *am.*
For example:

Q. I

THE GRAMMAR SCHOOLE

Q. I doe love, or I love?
A. Amo.
Q. Grant I love.
A. Vtinam Amem.
Q. I may or can love.
A. Amem.
Q. When I love?
A. Cùm amem.
So in the Preterimperfect tense.
Q. How say you Did, without a signe?
A. bam.
Q. With a signe.
A. rem, as *Amabam, amarem: Docebam, docerem.* Have, without a signe. *i.* With a signe, *rim*; as *Amaui, amauerim. Docui, docuerim,* &c.

☞ The shortest way of all, and most easie for all of under-
The shortest way standing, is, oft to repeat the bare signes and terminations,
of all to repeat specially at such times, as when the yonger sort are to make
and keepe these. Latine: and this daily then, untill they be perfect, or as shal be requisite, thus: Active signes, Doe, Did, Have, Had, Shall or will. Passive, Am, Is, Art, Was, Were, Wert, Have bin, Had bin, Shall or will be.

Terminations in Latine Indicat. or terminat. without a signe, *o, bam, i, ram, bo* and *am.*

Termin. with a signe. { *em.*
{ *rem, rim, sem, ro.*
{ *am.*

So Active and Passive together.

o, or. bam. bar. i, sum vel fui, ram, eram vel fueram { *bo, bor.*
{ *am, ar.*

{ *Em, er.*
{ *rem, rer, rim, sim vel fuerim, sem, essem vel fuissem.*
{ *Am, ar.* *ro, ero, vel fuero.*

These gotten, all will be plaine; if you use withal to cause them to runne the tenses, as was said, with the signes of the persons, thus: I, thou, he, we, ye, they: *o, as, at, amus, atis, ant,*

THE GRAMMAR SCHOOLE

ant, bam, bas, bat, bamus, batis bant: so in any. And withall to remember in what letters, or syllables every person ends, both in the Active and Passive: as the first persons Active, signifying (I) doe end commonly in *o, am, em, im,* or *i.* as *amo, amabam, amem, amaui, amauerim.* The second persons (or thou) in *as, es, is,* or *sti:* as *amas, doces, legis, amauisti.* (hee) in *at, et, it.* (wee) in *mus.* (yee) *in tis.* (they) in *ut.*

So in the Passive, (I) in *or, ar, er,* (thou) in *ris,* or like the Active. (he) in *tur.* (we) in *mur.* (ye) in *mini.* (they) in *ntur.*

By these the learners may have a great light: and though some of them bee both in the Active and Passive, and the Imperative moode doe differ so as no certaine rules can be given, yet they may be soone discerned and knowne. And the perfect knowledge of the terminations beeing the speediest way to the getting the full understanding, both of Nounes and Verbes in every tongue; these would be learned first, and ever kept most surely.

The benefite also of this exquisite perfection in Nounes and Verbes, is so singular, for the speedy attayning of the Latine tongue, as no paines in them can bee too great. *No paines can be too great for perfect getting Nounes and Verbes.*

First, the very difficulty of the Latine tongue, is in these.

Secondly, these examples set downe in the booke, are such lively patterns of all Nounes and Verbes; that Schollers being perfect in these, will soone be perfect in any other. And for the other parts of speech, the very words are most of them set downe in the Accedence; as Pronounes, Adverbes, Conjunctions, Prepositions, Participles, like the Adjectives.

So that these being gotten perfectly, the Latine tongue may soone be attained in good maner; even by the meanes following: whereas without this perfection it is very difficult. So that the learners shall goe still incertainly and fearefully.

Also by these meanes and helpes named, this readinesse in them may bee very speedily obtained; whereas onely

THE GRAMMAR SCHOOLE

onely to be able to say them without booke, without this understanding, is to little purpose: and to learne them by practice in construction, and in writing exercises alone, is most long, hard and wearisome, both to Master and Scholler.

My former toyle and griefe in these, above all other things in Grammar (though I tried all wayes which I could heare or devise) with the ease and benefit in this way, maketh me confident. For I have found more profit by this course in a moneth, then by all other in halfe a yeere. By this practice also, it is most soone recovered when it is lost, and most easily kept.

Yet children not to stay overlong in these. Yet my meaning is not to have Schollers to stay overlong, to be so exquisite in them, before they go any further; but to go on so fast as they can well, and to make them so ready by daily practice; spending each day a quarter of an houre, or more, in them, untill they come to perfection.

This were not amisse, to be practised sometimes also amongst the elder Schollers, which are not ready in them; as also those comming from other Schooles, till they grow perfect: here should be the beginning.

If yet a shorter way can be found out, we shall have more cause to rejoyce thereof.

Participles. In the Participles, the chiefe care would be to make them perfect, to know the severall tenses by their signes, and endings, English and Latine, as they are in the booke: for declining, they are the same with the Nounes.

Adverbes, Conjunctions, Prepositions, Interjections. In the Adverbs, Conjunctions, Prepositions and Interjections, they would be made so ready, as to give English to Latine, and Latine to English, and to tell of what kinds they are; and also to what cases each Preposition serveth: and these specially.

A want in the Adverbes to be supplied. Here it were to be wished (as I take it) that all the rest of the Adverbs, Conjunctions, and Interjections were also set downe in the Accedences; except onely such Adverbes as are derived of other words: by which words they may be knowne, or by their accents or terminations.

Also

THE GRAMMAR SCHOOLE

Also that some rules were set downe for framing of these derived Adverbes; and that all the rest of the Adverbes and Conjunctions, with all other words and sentences thorow the Accedence, were Englished, like as the Prepositions are. *Rules of deriving Adverbes necessary; and of the Latine in the Accedence Englished.*

Hereby all these Latine words would soone be learned perfectly, and proove a very great helpe when children come to construction: for then they should have but onely Nounes and Verbes to trouble them withall, as was said; and those most easie to be knowne, by the meanes above mentioned, and after.

For the English rules great care would bee had likewise, to make Schollers very ready in them: for these rules of themselves, with a few other, might serve for construction, or making Latine. The perfect knowledge of them also, will make the Latine rules easie, when your Schollers come at them. *English rules. Benefit of them well gotten.*

In teaching these rules, these two things would be observed generally: first, That the Schollers learne to construe each ensamples; and that without booke. Experience teacheth, that those which are apt, will construe almost as soone without the booke, as upon the booke, or as they will learne them construed: hereby they shall get so much Latine; beside that, it wil be a great help to the perfect understanding, and applying of them. The second is, to marke out with some speciall markes, those words in which the force of the examples doth lie; as the words agreeing, or the word governing, and the word governed, and to cause the children to be able to tell them: and so ever in saying their rules without booke, to repeate over those words againe, in all the longer examples. The rules or examples otherwise shall doe them little good, because they know not how to make use of them. *Generall observations in the English rules. 1. To construe the examples. 2. To tell in what words the force of the examples doth lie. See this more plainely, in examining the Syntax in Latine.*

But hereby they shall have perpetuall and sure patternes and warrants for parsing, making and trying Latine. I shall shew this more plainely, when we come to the Syntax in Latine.

These

THE GRAMMAR SCHOOLE

To make them most perfect in the rules of the principall Verb. Concords.

These two things being observed, have a chiefe regard in the rules, first, to make them perfect in the rule of finding out the principall Verbe; secondly, in the Concords, as being of continuall use; thirdly, in the rules of governement.

Relative Qui.

And amongst those, to looke specially to the two first rules, of the case of the Relative *Qui:* and namely, the latter of them, *viz.* But when there commeth a Nom, case; for in it Schollers most faile.

Governements. Manner of examining in them.

Also in all rules of governement, to make them able to tell you presently where any rule is, and what cases such words governe: as, Where beginnes the construction of Substantives? What cases they governe? How many rules there are of them? Or asking thus; What case must your latter of two Substantives be? What case will such a word governe? As *Opus* or *Vsus,* What cases doe they governe? Where is the rule? So in the rules of the Adjectives, and all the rest throughout.

In posing, remember that which was first directed: to marke carefully the drift of the whole rule, and so to propound your question; or else to propound the whole rule in a question. As thus: when two Substantives come together, betokening divers things; what case must the latter be? and why? or by what rule?

Other helpes to make Schollers ready in the Accedence.
1. Daily repetitions and examinations.

Furthermore, to the end to make your Schollers so very readie in the Accedence, and to keepe it perfectly; besides the learning all things so well as may be, there must be also, first, daily repetitions and examinations; because of the weakenesse of children's memories: that so by long custome all may be imprinted in them.

Herein cause your first enterers to repeate over every day, all that they have learned; as they proceede to learne more, to divide it into parts, to goe over all so oft as time will permit. For them that have learned all their Accedence, I hold it best (according to the manner of most Schooles) to devide it into foure equall parts, except the examples of the Verbes; and to

THE GRAMMAR SCHOOLE

to cause them to say a part every of the foure first dayes of the weeke, to say over the whole each weeke once: for the Verbes, how they specially would be parsed daily, I spake before.

In hearing parts, aske them first the chiefe question or questions of each rule in order; then make them every one say his rule or rules; and in all rules of construction, to answere you in what words the force of the example lyeth, both governour and governed; saying the governour first. Where helpe is wanting, to doe it onely in the hardest and most necessary rules and questions, or where we know them most defective: Or else onely to repeate the rules and examples in such sort as was shewed, without further examination. *Manner of hearing parts.*

Though, where there is helpe and time enough, it is far the surest, to cause them to repeate the whole part, and to examine each piece of it daily, though they say the lesse at a time. Secondly, the spending of one moneth or two, after they have first learned over their Accedence, to make them perfect thus every way, will be time as well bestowed as they can bestow any; to prevent both the griefe and anger of the Master after, and also the feare and punishment of the Scholler. Thirdly, every day some time would bee separate, to the examining Nounes and Verbes; chiefely the Verbes, untill they could not be set in declining, conjugating, giving any termination, case or person. *2. The spending of a moneth or two to make the Accedence perfect, after it is learned over.*
3. Some time separate daily to examine Nounes and Verbes.

This continuall practice of parsing, would bee constantly kept as neede shall require, untill by long use children grow to perfection and surenesse: because the Accedence thus gotten perfectly; and after in like maner the rules of Nounes and Verbes in *Propria quæ maribus*, Heteroclits, and in *As in præsenti;* the difficulty of learning is past: so that very children, with a little practice, will goe forward with much cheerefulnesse, in construing, parsing, making and prooving Latine, by the helpes following. *Constancy in poasing, till use bring surenesse.*

Thus have I set you downe so plainely as I can, how

THE GRAMMAR SCHOOLE

the Accedence may be gotten most speedily and profitably, to make all learning a play. Trie, and you will acknowledge God's blessing herein.

Spoud. I acknowledge your kindnesse : I can make no doubt of the courses ; because, besides your experience, I see so evident reason in every part.

Phil. Put them in use, and so you shall have more full assurance, and daily be helping to find out better, or to confirme the principall of these.

CHAP. VII.

How to make Schollers perfect in the Grammar.

Spoud.

I Intend to put them in practice forthwith: but in the meane time as you have thus lovingly gone with mee, to direct me, how to make the Accedence so plaine and easie to my little ones; so I entreat you to point me out the way, how they may proceede in the Grammar with like happy successe. As for mine owne selfe, I have onely used to cause my Schollers to learne it without booke, and a little to construe it; and after, to make it as perfect as I can, by oft saying Parts: Finally, in parsing their lectures to give the rules. This hath been all that I have done.

What is done ordinarily in Schooles in teaching Grammar.

Phil. I know that which you mention, to be the most that is done ordinarily: but to say without booke and construe a little, are finally availeable, unlesse your Scholler be able to shew the meaning and use of his rules. Yea, it is very requisite, that here also they should bee able to give the severall examples, and in what words the force of each example lyeth; and so to apply the examples to the rules, to the end that they may doe the like by them, in parsing, or making Latine. And moreover, in Nounes and Verbes, to

What things are requisite to bee done in learning Grammar.

be

THE GRAMMAR SCHOOLE

be able not onely to decline them, and to give English to the Latine words; but the Latine words also to the English. Grammar being made perfect in this manner, will make all other their learning more easie and delightsome, and be as a Dictionary in their heads, for many chiefe words: neither will there bee any losse of time in it; especially this beeing done as they learne it, and still gotten more perfectly by such continuall repetitions and examinations. I have had experience in both.

To the end that they may thus get the Grammar with most fruite and ease; *To get the Gramer with most ease and fruite.*

1. Let them learne every rule (I meane) those which are commonly read in Schooles, and that perfectly as they goe forward, together with the titles set before the rules, and the summes of the rules which are set in the margents. *To learne every ordinary rule perfectly. With titles and summes.*

The manner of it I finde to be most direct thus, for all the younger sort of enterers. *Manner for enterers.*

Where you have time enough, in giving them rules, doe as in the Accedence.

1. Reade them over their rule leasurely, and distinctly. *1. Reading their rules to them.*
2. Construe it, and then shew them the plaine meaning of it, by applying the examples, as teaching them to decline the words or the like. As I shall shew after. *2. Construing and shewing them the meaning.*

Or else for most ease and speedinesse in construing, and for lacke of leasure, cause every one of your Schollers to have a booke of the construing of *Lillies* rules, and each to reade over his rule, so oft upon that booke, untill he can construe without it; or else after a time, to trie how hee can beate it out of himselfe, and be helped by that booke where he sticketh. *How they may soonest learne to construe them. Each Scholler to have his construing booke, and learne to construe by that.*

By the helpe of these bookes, I finde that they will learne to construe their rules much sooner, then they can without, I take it by almost one halfe of the time; and thereby gaine so much time, to be imployed in other studies, because they shall have it ever before their eye without any asking or searching: whereas otherwise either their Master or some other, must tell them every word, which they *Benefit of the use of Lillies rules construed. 1. To gaine one halfe of time in construing them.*

THE GRAMMAR SCHOOLE

And free their Masters from much trouble, and the Scholler from much feare and toyle.
Also some recover their selves, having forgot.
Increase in reading English.
Masters freed from clamors.

they cannot tell, or else they must turne to it in their Dictionaries, untill they can construe: and that so oft as they forget: which, what a toyle and hinderance it is to the Master, and feare to the Scholler, every one knoweth. From all which they may bee freed hereby; and when they have forgot, they may soone recover themselves againe. Finally, they shall hereby increase daily in reading English, and be furthered to write true Orthography in English, as they grow in Latine. And so the Masters shall also be freed from feare of that mischiefe, of these little ones forgetting to read English, when they first learne Latine; and from the clamours and accusations of their Parents in this behalfe, spoken of before.

Wherein the construing bookes, under correctiō, may be much helped and made more profitable.
Thus I thinke is in hand or finished.
Necessary words to be Englished in their proper significations.

But here it were to be wished, that those books of construing *Lillies* rules were translated ever Grammatically; the manner of which translation I shall shew after, with the benefits of them: And also that not onely the Substantive and Adjective, Preposition and his case were ever construed and set together. wheresoever they are to be taken together; but withal that every word were Englished in the first, proper, naturall, and distinct signification. In which things they oft faile, as in the Verbes chiefely: though of all other things that be most necessary for Schollers, to know the first and naturall signification; for the other then will soone be learned, by reason and use: or else some of the other most usuall significations might be put in, in other letters, or with notes to know them.

Thus the child might goe surely forward, and have a certaine direction for the right and proper use of every word, to be more sure to him than any Dictionarie, all his life long, either for construing or making Latine: Whereas being set downe in generall significations not distinct, they shall ever goe doubtfully and abuse the words: as when *traho, promo, haurio,* are set downe every one of them to *draw,* without further distinction.

The benefit would be much more, if it were thus translated: for then they might learne thereby not onely to construe

THE GRAMMAR SCHOOLE

strue truly, to understand and goe surely; but also to make and speake the same Latine: I meane, to answer easily to all the rules, with the other benefits of Grammaticall translations.

When they can construe in some good sort, and understand (as was said) then let them get without booke perfectly. *Learning the rules without booke.*

In getting without book, when they can reade it perfectly, they may be much helped thus, in all things which they learn in verse; to reade them over in a kinde of singing voice, and after the manner of the running of the verse; oft tuning over one verse untill they can say that, then another; and so forward: which they will doe presently, if the Master do but reade them so before them. *Helps forgetting without booke all things which they learne in verse.*

Also, to say these rules at parts sometimes, after the same manner of scanning, or running as a verse, shall make them both more easily kept, and be a good helpe for right pronunciation of quantities, and to prepare them the more easily to make a verse, for authorities and the like. *So repeating the Rules in verse.*

When they can say perfectly without booke, then (if you please) you may cause all those who are any thing apt and pregnant, to learn to construe also without booke: which they will do very quickly, with a little reading over and over, upon the construing booke; and almost as soon as they will construe upon the booke. *Construing without booke.*

By this meanes they will be able presently to give not onely the English to the Latine, but also the Latine to the English, of any word in the rule, to be perfect thereby, and to keepe all more firmely. *Benefit of construing without booke.*

Or where leasure is wanting, among the elder sort, which are well entred in the rules; they may first learne without booke, then to construe, both upon the booke and without: Or to construe first. It is not very materiall: but, as themselves doe finde that they can get it most easily, at the Master's discretion. *Where leasure is wanting how to doe. And in the elder.*

Although for all the first enterers and younger sort, I finde it the surest way, where the Master's leasure will *The surest way for young beginners.*

THE GRAMMAR SCHOOLE

will serve, to cause them first to understand the rule and the meaning of it, by a short opening or expressing the summe of it, and then by questions in English, as I directed before: All of the learners looking upon their books as he readeth unto them; that they may see the questions and answers in their bookes, either wholly, or the most part thereof.

And when they can answer in English, looking upon their bookes, or to understand the rule, then to learne to construe it of themselves, and to get it without booke.

At saying of rules how to examine, to cause them to answer any question.

After, at the saying of their rules, when they have said without booke and construed; to labour especially to cause them to be able to answer, without booke, each part of the rule, and that both in English and Latine together, after they are a little entered; that with the meaning and English, you may beate the Latine into their heads also, to helpe to prepare them to speake and parse in Latine.

Manner of apposing.

Let the manner of the apposing be here, as in the Accedence, *viz.* by short questions, propounded unto them, arising directly out of the words of the booke, either out of the summe and title of the rule set before it, or set in the margent over against it, or out of the very words of the rule; and withall, the examples of the rule, and how to apply them to the severall rules.

Examples of making the rules plaine and apposing.
Propria quæ maribus.
Title of it.

I will set you downe an example or two more at large, that you or any may doe the like the more easily. To begin at *Propria quæ maribus:* first, you have the Title before; *Regulæ generales propriorum.* Out of which you may shew them thus; That according to the order of their Accedence, as the first part of speech is a Nowne, so here are rules first of Nownes: And as their Accedence hath first the Substantive, then the Adjective, so here begin rules first of the Substantives, after of the Adjectives. Againe, as the Substantive is either Proper or Cōmon; so here the rules of Proper Nowns are first set down, whereby to know the Genders of them; and after of the Common Nowns called Appellatives. You may also point them in their booke, where

each

THE GRAMMAR SCHOOLE

each of these begin: they will presently conceive of them, being first perfect in their Accedence.

Then that the rules of Proper names, are of Masculines, or Feminines: Or all proper Nownes are either of the Masculine or of the Feminine Gender, unlesse they be excepted.

Also all Proper Nownes which goe under the names of Males or Hees (as we call them) are the Masculine Gender. Then teach them according to the margent, that of those there are five kindes, which goe under the names of Males or Hees. As names of Gods, Men, Floods or Rivers, Moneths, Winds.

So all proper Nowns or names of Females, or Shees, are the Feminine Gender. And of those there are likewise five kinds: That is; names of Goddesses, Women, Cities, Regions or Countreys, Ilands, &c.

Then appose after the same manner, keeping strictly the words of the booke, as was said; onely putting in here or there, a word or two, to make the question; which by oft repeating, they will easily understand. As thus, out of the words set before the rule: Or in the like manner; *Apposing after the same maner, to helpe the weakest teacher, for whom I have set downe the more examples.*

Q. Where begin your generall rules of Proper Nowns? *Ubi incipiunt regulæ generales propriorum?*
A. Propria quæ maribus.
Q. How many generall rules are there of proper Nowns? *Quot sunt regulæ generales propriorum?*
A. Two: *Duæ.*
Q. What is your first rule? *Quæ est prima regula?*
A. Propria quæ maribus, &c.

This posing in Latine, if it be over-hard to the enterers at first, may be used after a time in examining their parts.

Then out of the margent thus:

Q. How many kinds of Proper names are there of the Masculine Gender? *Quot sunt genera propriorum nominum masculini generis?*
A. Quinq.; five: *Diuorum, virorum, fluuiorum, menfium, ventorum.* Or as they are set in the Margent. *Mascula sunt nomina Diuorum, virorum, fluuiorum, menfium, ventorum.* Names of Gods, Men, Floods or Rivers, Moneths, Winds.

Examining out of the margent.

After

THE GRAMMAR SCHOOLE

Examining out of the words of the rule.

After, out of the words of the rule, *Propria quæ maribus tribuuntur, &c.* you may propound your questions thus;

Q. *Cuius generis dicas, Propria quæ maribus tribuuntur?* What Gender are all Nownes, or names of Hees, or of the Male kinde. R. *Masculæ,* or *masculini generis.*

Q. *Cuius generis sunt nomina Diuorum?* R. *Masculini.*

Manner of apposing the examples of the rules.

Q. *Quomodo dicis Latinè?* The God of Battaile?
R. *Mars, hic Mars, Martis.*
Q. The god of Wine, *quomodo dicis?*
R. *Bacchus, hic Bacchus Bacchi, &c.*
Q. *Per quam regulam?* R. *Propria quæ maribus.*

Fewest words best.

In the fewer words you can do it, for brevitie, is the better, and that you may goe over the more. Or if you think it be too hard for children, to answer in Latine at first, and that it is best to doe it onely in English; you may doe it following the same order. As in the next rule, *Propria Fœmineum,* onely asking thus:

To oppose onely in English if children be too weake to answer in Latine. Manner of the questions in English, at Propria Fœmineum.

Q. What Gender are proper names of Females, or Shees? How many kindes are there of them? Where is the rule for them? What exceptions are there from that generall rule? Or how many Masculine Cities have you? How many Neuter Cities? How many Masculine and Neuter Cities?

So in the next rule. *Appellatiua Arborum,* to aske thus or the like;

Appell. Arborum.

Where begin your rules of Appellatives, or Common Nownes?

How many kinds of Appellatives have you? Or how many sorts of rules have you for Appellatives?

A. Three: of { Trees, Epicenes, The rest.

What Gender are names of trees? What exceptions? Or how many Masculine trees have you? How many Neuter trees? So of Epicenes.

Where is your rule of words of the Epicene Gender? How many kindes have you of words, or Names, of the Epicene Gender?

A. Three

THE GRAMMAR SCHOOLE

A. Three: of { Birds, Beasts, Fishes.

How know you the Gender in the Epicenes?
What Gender is every Nowne that endeth in *um*?
How know you the Gender in all Appellatives?
Then the speciall rules, thus, or the like: How many spe- *Examining of* ciall rules of Nownes Appellatives have you? *Ans.* Three: *the speciall rules.* The first, of Nownes not increasing; the second, of Nownes increasing acute, commonly called long; the third, of Nownes increasing, grave or short, as we call it.

What Genders each of these are of? Where are the rules for them? What examples have you of them? So to give the meaning, and apply the examples. How many exceptions there are from every one of these rules? As, how many rules of Masculines except; so of Feminines or Neuters except. Or thus: Of what Genders are all Nownes, not increasing in the Genitive case, as *Capra, capræ*: Or all Nowns like *Musa, musæ?* So what Genders are all Nownes of the second speciall rule? or all Nownes increasing acute, as *Pietas, pietatis*? What Gender are all Nownes increasing grave, or flat, or short? as *Sanguis, sanguinis.* And how many rules have you of Masculines except from the first speciall rule? or of Masculines not increasing in the Genitive case? How many rules have you of long Masculines, or Masculines increasing acute, excepted from the second speciall rule? Or of Feminines increasing short, except from the third speciall rule? Or yet more plainly thus: Where is your generall rule of all like *Capra, capræ:* or *musa, musæ:* Or of all like *Magister, magistri:* or *Dominus, domini: venter ventris.* Or of words ending in *er, os, us,* not increasing. Or where is your rule of all like *Virtus, virtutis?* Or like *Sanguis, sanguinis?* And of what Genders they are of?

For the exceptions, you may appose thus: Where is your *Examining the* rule of Neuters not increasing? Of Neuters increasing, a- *Exceptions.* cute or long? Of Neuters increasing, flat or short? Thus of Doubtfuls, Commons.

Or

THE GRAMMAR SCHOOLE

Posing by asking first the examples.
Or posing the examples, to aske what is Latine for any word, which is in any of the rules; and then to cause them to decline the word, the Nom. and Genit. case, and to tell the rule, as was shewed before: as,
What is Latine for a cloud?
A. *Nubes. hæc nubes, nubis, &c.*
Q. By what rule? What is the meaning of that rule?

☞ *The shortest course.*
Thus you shall receive divers benefit together.
Or thus only, when they have said any rule, to aske them what is the meaning of that rule, and to give the examples.
So in the Adjectives, to aske thus or the like:

Examining the Adjectives.
Where begin the rules of the Adjectives?
Where is the rule of all like *Fælix? Adjectiua unam.* So of all like *Tristis? Sub gemina, &c.* Of all like *Bonus? At si tres, &c.* Of Adjectives of two Articles like Substantives? *At sunt quæ flexu, &c.* Of Adjectives of a strange declining? *Hæc proprium quendam, &c.*

How to make Schollers perfect in the Genitive cases.
For all declining to make them very perfect in the Genitive case, you may practise them thus; sometimes to repeat the Nominative and the Gen. case together, as in *Propria quæ maribus* to run, thus: *Mars, Martis, Bacchus, Bacchi, Apollo, Apollinis, Cato, Catonis:* So in every rule when time will permit.

To appose the hardest ofttimes.
And chiefly appose them often in the most difficult, being noted with some marke: as, *Opus, Opuntis. Persis, Persidis. Barbiton, Barbiti. Senex, senis. Vir, Viri. Bes, bessis. Cres, Cretis. Pres, Predis. Semis, semissis,* and the like. The rest they will doe readily of themselves.

Examining in the Heteroclites.
In the Heteroclites to do the like, first to shew them what they are, *viz.* Nownes of another kinde of declining: and then the three severall kinds of them according to the titles.

{ *Variantia genus.*
{ *Defectiva.*
{ *Redundantia.*

Either such as change their Declension, or want something, or have too much. And so the severall rules of every one.

Then

THE GRAMMAR SCHOOLE

Then the severall rules to be examined particularly: like as in *Propria quæ maribus*: to understand every piece: and in them specially to looke to the Margents: to be able readily to give the rules to them.

And to make them able to repeat the Summes and Margents in order.

So to give any rule thereby: as when I aske, Where is your rule of *Aptots, Monoptots, Diptots, Triptots?* Of those which want the Vocative case: or *Defecta vocatiuo*, or *propria defecta pluralid?* or the like.

In the Verbes likewise shew them the order, that the rules are of Preterperfect tenses and Supines: and those first of simple Verbs in *o*. Then compounds after of Verbs in *or*. Last, of those that differ in their Preterperfect tenses, or Supines. *Making the Verbes plaine.*

In the simple Verbs, first are rules of the first Conjugation, then the second, so in order.

After cause them to tell by the summes and Margents, where every rule standeth: as where are verbes of the first Conjugation, so in the rest. *Examining in them.*

Practise them also to answer thus: The Present tense, Preterperfect tense, Infinitive moode and first Supine together. As if I aske, How say you To swim? He answereth, *No. No, naui, nare, natum*. So To wash, *Lauo, laui, lauare, lautum*. Because that these being knowne, all the rest are presently knowne; and to doe it also for brevitie sake: especially examine those Verbs often, which have two Preterperfect tenses, or two Supines, or moe; and would therefore have speciall marks: as *vello, velli, & vulsi, vellere, vulsum*.

- For the Syntax in Latine, though the English rules, with a few moe added to them, might serve for resolving any construction, or for making Latine; and so many do thinke them needlesse altogether; others do use to teach only the rules thereof, and one example onely in the rule; yet there may be very good use of them all, rightly understood, and specially of the severall examples rightly applied: that Schollers by them may goe surely, having severall exam- *Good use of the Syntax in Latine.*

ples

THE GRAMMAR SCHOOLE

Difficulty hereof, unlesse they be thus taught.

Though this may be thought an easie matter, and that every Scholler can doe it; yet trie it: and it will be found cleane contrary almost throughout, and to trouble many weake Masters to apply many of them aright. It is a matter most necessary: because the very life of the examples is in these; and the profit will doubly countervaile the paines.

With a little practice, they will almost as soone say their rules this way, applying each example, as without.

Spoud. I discerne evidently the great benefit and furtherance to Schollers, to be able to repeate the examples of every rule, in such sort as you have shewed, for continuall use both in parsing, and in making and writing Latine surely; as also to have the summes of the rules which are in the Margents, and before the rules, perfectly: but children cannot possibly get these, unlesse their bookes be marked so, as you directed.

The trouble and inconvenience in marking the bookes, chiefly by Schollers. The Grammars are procured to be thus printed, as to be most easie and profitable for Schooles, without inconvenience.

And for the Masters to marke all their Grammars so, it is an infinit toyle, and hinderance to him: to marke some one, and to cause the Schollers to marke theirs thereby; they will do them so falsely, as will oft more hinder then further, besides the trouble in it: also the summes of the Margents are very defective.

Phil. For the supplying of all this, and the avoyding of all these inconveniences, and other like, and for making our Grammar farre more easie and profitable to the Schollers, without any alteration; the Grammars are procured to be so printed, as to bee most plaine herein: all the words wherein the force of the examples doth lie, being printed in differing letters; that the least child may bee able to discerne them, and so to apply and repeate them: and also the Margents made more perfect. What is missed or defective herein, shall (as I hope) bee supplyed here after.

Spoud. Sir, all Schooles must needs hereby receive an exceeding benefit; as I see plainly by that which you have shewed for the use of them. But I pray you proceede, and let me

THE GRAMMAR SCHOOLE

me heare what other helpes you have for examining your Schollers, so as they may fully understand their rules.

Phil. Other helpes for the examination and understanding the rules, are these:

1. Where they cannot understand any question, or answer; remember that, to teach them to understand, by repeating English and Latine together, untill they fully understand it. For, as we said before, if they have the meaning in their heads, words, with oft repeating, will easily bee gotten to utter their minds, especially having them in their bookes. *Other helpest o examine and understand the rules. How to make them to understand and answer any question in Latine.*

2. Also this may further to understanding, to cause them to be able to give the English rules, answering to every Latine rule, of those which have English rules; to set markes upon those Latine rules, which have no English: and to answer to them that they have no rule, but to be able to give the meaning. *To give English rules to the Latine.*

3. These meanes may also much profit to the easie getting, full understanding, and perfect keeping of the rules; oft to reade over, and keepe perfectly the summes of the rules, which are either set before them, or in the Margents; as was noted, so to repeate them in order. Thus to be able to report all the summe; like as of the Accidence, so of the Grammar, as in a narration or continued speech, as thus: *Other helpes to get the rules easily, and to keepe them perfectly; repeating the Titles and Margents in a continued speech.*

Regulæ generales propriorum. Mascula sunt nominæ Divorum, Virorum, Fluviorum, Mensium, ventorum. Fœminina, Dearum, Mulierum, Urbium, Regionum, Insularum. Exceptio. Regulæ generales appellativorum. Arborum. Epicœna. Volucrum, ferarum, piscium, exceptio generalis. Usus trium regularum specialium. Prima regula specialis, &c.

So to know to give readily the beginning of every rule in order; as, *Propria quæ maribus. Propria fœmineum. Excipienda tamen quædam sunt, &c. Appellativa arborum erunt, &c.* *To repeate the beginnings of the rules in a continued speech.*

By these meanes they will be able both to answer the questions in Latine, with a very few other words: and also to give any rule presently, when but the summe is demanded or any word belonging unto it, to tell where the rule is, and to begin it. *Benefits of these.*

To

THE GRAMMAR SCHOOLE

Idæa.

To have an Idæa or generall notion of all in their heads, as if it were before their faces; which Idæa doth make any learning most easie, either to be gotten or kept.

Shorter examination and repetition.

Hereby also that shorter examination and repetition of parts, may sometime serve where time or helpe is wanting; and in parsing their Lectures, to rid twise so fast, when they can in a word signifie a rule, either by the word in the Margent, or before the rule, or by the beginning of the rule.

As to say in parsing, It is so, by the rule of the first concord: or *per concordantiam Nominatini & Verbi, &c. Per regulam Accusativi ante verbum infinitum, &c.* Or to repeate onely a word or two of the beginning of the rule; as *Verba infiniti modi, &c.* or the like.

Summes to be perfected. This is reported to have beene Master Brunswords order.

To this end it were to be wished, that the summes of the rules were set more perfectly in the Margents, in a word or two in all the Syntax, as they are in the Nounes, to have some speciall name to be called by: as *Adjectiva desiderij, verbalia in ax. Nomina partitiva;* and the like.

Helpe in hearing parts in straights of time.

In hearing parts in straights of time, thus we may examine onely in those places where we most suspect their negligence: asking first the summe of the rule, with an example in it; and then to cause him whom you examine, to say that rule. Or to aske onely an example of the rule, and cause them to apply it, and to give the rule.

To use the most profitable

I have set downe all these, that we may take and use which we find most profitable. The shorter the better, as was advised; so that we make sure that they doe fully understand the rule, and can make use of it.

The profit of rules thus learned.

One rule, so learned with understanding, is more profitable, then if they could say every word in a hundreth; and could but onely repeate them over as Parats, without any knowledge to make the right use of it.

Spoud. Sir, I do like very well of these things which you have said; yet for the helping of my memory and practice, tell me againe shortly, which you account to be the principall: wherein chiefe care would be had, to the end to make all easie; also to keepe all, and to make right use thereof.

Phil.

THE GRAMMAR SCHOOLE

Phil. This I account and find the chiefe; to have them perfect in the order both of the whole, and also of all the parts in Grammar, as I shewed; and also to be able to repeat the Titles, with those Margents which are necessary; the beginnings of the rules; and to have the understanding of them, and examples; and also to be able to apply the examples for the severall words wherein the force is: and so to give any rule of a sudden, either the beginning or the summe of it; and the words wherein the force of the rule is. *The summe of all: wherein chiefe care would be had.*

Spoud. Oh, but this is a matter, that is most accounted of with us; to have them very perfect in saying all their Grammar without booke, even every rule; and wherein I have found much griefe and vexation: because I have not beene able to cause my Schollers to get their rules so perfectly; and much lesse to keepe them: and hereby, ever the saying parts hath beene the greatest fretting to me, and feare to my Schollers, for the negligence of most, in them; so that doe I what I could, yet I have never beene able to bring most to any commendable readinesse in them.

Phil. To this I answere you; that this indeede is one principall thing, that makes our calling the more uncomfortable: and I doubt not, but that the griefe, which the best do find therein, is a meanes to humble them, and to keepe them that they be not too much lift up in the rest. And indeede it were to be wished that the rules were much shorter: but sith we see not how that may possibly be helped, without much greater inconvenience; we must in this, as in the rest of our inconveniences, use all the wisedome that we can, to make a benefit of necessity, and the burthen so light, as we may. And that, thus. 1. Making our Schollers to learne them so perfectly as we can. 2. To keepe chiefely the things last learned, by oft repetition. 3. Continuall care for parts; and so much as may be to let them have some little time over-night to reade them over, against morning. 4. To cause them at least where time will not serve, to repeate the summes of the rules: and by daily examining to make them able to give you the sum or beginning of any rule, with the meaning of it, and to apply the examples. *Difficulty of keeping the Grāmar rules perfectly without booke.*

How helped.

And

THE GRAMMAR SCHOOLE

Such a perfect saying every rule, not so absolutely necessarie.

And therein to content our selves, if we can but obtaine so much of many, as to be able to understand and make use of the rules, or to turne to them, though they cannot say them readily: for we see most Schollers, when they come to the Universities, to forget that perfectnesse in their Grammars, and most learned men cannot say the rules; yet so long as they have a full understanding and remembrance to make use, in resolving, writing, or speaking, this sufficeth.

Other helpe to have the Grammar perfect, to turne to each rule as they parse.
Note in examining Lectures.

Lastly, this shall much helpe, to cause them in preparing their Lectures in construction, to turne to every hard rule as they parse, and then to get these rules readily; and so ever to come to say, with their Grammars under their armes.

And also in examining Lectures, to cause them to tell you where they have learned the severall harder words, at least in their Grammars. For this I find, that the most ordinary words are in some part of their Grammar, or the words whereof they come, or some very neere unto them, whereby they may remember them.

Grammar to be made as a Dictionary.
Seldomer repeating rules in the higher fourmes may serve.

Thus may they become very exquisite in the Grammar, in time; and have it (as I said) as a Dictionary in their minds, not to neede to seeke here or there for every word.

In the higher fourmes, where daily repeating rules hindereth much other learning, if they repeate them but sometimes, and can answer in a word or two, giving the summe of each rule, it may suffice; although it is a great commendation to have the Grammar *ad unguem*, and to give an example of each thing belonging unto Grammar.

Readinesse of Schollers in Accedence and Grammar, will helpe to make the Schoolemaster's life most pleasant.

Thus have I shewed you what I have yet learned concerning making Schollers perfect in the Accedence, and Grammar: wherein as you see, I have beene much longer; because I find this by experience, and therefore dare constantly affirme it, that if this be once achieved in a Schoole, to have the Schollers thus made perfect in Accedence and Grammar as they proceede, the life of a Schoolemaster may bee made as ful of joy and contentment, without wearisomnesse, onely in observing the fruit of his labours, as I touched, as the life of any, in any other calling whatsoever: whereas of

the

THE GRAMMAR SCHOOLE

the other side, much of our fretting toile, ariseth onely for want of this.

Spoud. I would therefore thinke it a most profitable labour, to set downe this manner of examining the Accedence and Grammar, by Question and Answer particularly; that not onely the weakest Schoolemaster amongst us, but even our Schollers themselves might bee able so to oppose and whet one another. I my selfe have seene divers bookes of questions of our Accedence and Grammar, beeing gathered by learned men; yet in none of them have I observed (so farre as I remember) sundry of the principall of these points.

Besides, that no man can so well examine the Accedence and Grammar by them; because, first the words of their Question and Answer, do not arise so out of the words of the rules as you direct: neither do they alway keepe the order of the rules; and they have moreover sundry other hard questions intermixed, and sometimes many together, that my Schollers have not beene able to make use of them, nor my selfe very little, in regard of that which I might if they had beene so framed.

Phil. I myselfe have had experience of the same in them; insomuch as though I have greatly desired and tried to use some of them in my Schoole, in regard of the profit which I have conceived might come by them; yet I have not beene able without further inconvenience. And ever as new schollers have come to any Schoole, so they have beene alwayes to seeke in those new questions, as that I have beene inforced to leave them off utterly. In consideration whereof, and of the generall want herein; as also of the publique benefit, which I am certainely assured, may come by such a labour as you speake of; I have indeavoured by the helpe of all such bookes of Questions and Answers, of Accedence and Grammar, as are extant, which I could procure; as likewise of some written, to gather one in this sort, having all the Questions and Answers arising most directly out of the words of the rules. In which, I have chiefely followed the *order*

A most plaine manner of examining Accedence & Grammar, collected, to helpe to make all Schollers perfect therein; called, The posing of the parts.

THE GRAMMAR SCHOOLE

order of the Quest of that ancient Schoolemaster, Master *Brunsword*, of Maxfield in Cheshire, so much commended for his order and Schollers; who, of all other, commeth therein the neerest unto the marke. This I have studied to make so plaine, as every child may by it both presently understand the meaning of each rule; and, if he can say the rules, may as soone be able to answer these questions: and whereby they may also poase one another (as you wish) to make all rules and parts most familiar. I have in it tied myselfe strictly to the order and words of the rules, as it may serve for continuall poasing, and speedy examining Parts: and that from what Schoole soever they come, if they can say the Accedence, they may presently answer these questions. Other questions which I have thought needfull, I have set in the Margents, directly against the questions, to be learned after, if you will without troubling the learner, and that nothing may be wanting. But, for this booke, I referre you to the Epistle Dedicatorie before it, and the questions themselves.

Spoud. Sir, I see well you have spared no labour, to seeke to draw-on the little ones with ease and delight, and to make Schollers most perfect Grammarians; which all the learned do so highly commend. I trust I shall be partaker hereof.

Phil. It is and hath beene my desire, to hide no part of my talent; but to imploy all to the best, and communicate it to every one to whom it may doe good: and especially the little ones, in whom is the chiefest hope of most of our countrey Schooles, and of the age to come.

CHAP.

THE GRAMMAR SCHOOLE

CHAP. VIII.

Of Construction; how to make all the way thereof most easie and plaine.

Spoud.

WEll then (good Sir) now that you have thus farre forth directed me, how to lay so sure a foundation for my schollers to build upon; I doubt not but you can indeed guide me forward, how they may build upon it as speedily and happily, both for their construing, parsing, and making Latine.

To begin therefore with construction, which is the first thing that our children enter into, after their Accedence, and Rules: I desire greatly to heare of you those things which you affirme may be done by schollers; and whereby all the way of construction may be made so easie. As namely, that children should be able to take their lectures of themselves, truely and perfectly; and likewise with understanding upon sure grounds: or at least, to doe it with a very little helpe of their Masters, in such places where they doubt. So the rest which were mentioned in the note: as that they should be able to construe, both in propriety of words, and also according to the right sense and meaning. To doe this at any time, in all that which they have learned, to construe out of a translation in English, as out of the Latine it selfe. *Things seeming difficult in construction.*

These things doe justly seeme strange unto mee; because I am faine to give every lecture my selfe: or if I appoint the fourmes above to give them; yet I am compelled to heare the giving of them. And so I have as great trouble, *The ordinary toile of Masters about giving lectures, and to cause their schollers to construe.*

when

THE GRAMMAR SCHOOLE

when they construe false, to direct them right; That it were as much ease to me to give them, my selfe; and so I should be freed from the griefe that I have, when they cannot doe it, and from other inconveniences.

Difficulty in taking lectures in proprietie of words and sense.

Besides, to reade the lectures in proprietie of words, phrase, and sense also; this seemeth to mee a matter of some difficulty for many poore countrey Schoole-masters; and not onely for the yonger and weaker sort, but also for some of the more ancient and experienced; and requireth reading and judgement; that I doe not see how schollers can possibly doe it.

Hardnesse for schollers to remember how they were construed, and the trouble therein.

Moreover, when I have given my schollers their lectures, or have heard them given, unlesse they marke very well; yet they will commonly misse in some part of that which I have read. And if the chiefe of the fourme mistake or goe false, all the rest of the fourme likewise construe false, because they depend on them: and so oft as they doubt, I am faine to tell them, what businesse soever I have; which doth exceedingly trouble mee. They also are afraid to aske me so many things, and it may be the same things againe and againe: whereby it commeth to passe that when they come to say, few of them can construe, or hardly any of them perfectly: which increaseth oft my passion, and their feare.

Griefe of the Masters for their schollers forgetting of that which they have learned.

Finally, this I account the worst of all, that when I have taken a great deale of paines, and have made my schollers very ready in construing and parsing; yet come and examine them in those things a quarter of a yeere after, they will be many of them as though they had never learned them, and the best farre to seeke: whereby, when Gentlemen or others come in and examine them, or their friends try them at home, in the things which they learned a quarter or halfe a yeere before; they are ordinarily found so rawe, and to have so forgotten, that I doe receive great reproach, as though I had taken no paines with them, or as they had profited nothing.

And for that of being able to reade, construe, and parse

THE GRAMMAR SCHOOLE

parse lectures, or whatsoever they have learned, out of an English translation, I have not made triall; though I know they cannot doe it, being harder, then the construing and parsing of the Authors themselves: albeit it cannot be but a matter of exceeding profit, and must needs helpe to make schollers very soone.

Therefore, if you can direct me, how to do all these things, which you have mentioned in this behalfe, so to construe and parse of themselves, and that out of the bare English Translation, and also that they shall be able to goe certainly, and upon sure grounds; I must needs acknowledge my selfe to have received an incomparable and a perpetuall benefit: and you shall indeed even herein helpe to make my burden farre more light, and my whole life much more comfortable; besides, that my schollers shall be beholden unto you for ever, for delivering them from so much feare, and setting them to goe so fast forward with such alacritie, as should appeare.

Phil. Surely, Sir, all this may be done, by the perfect knowledge of their Accedence and Grammar rules first, and then the practice of that golden rule of construing, together with Grammaticall Translations of the first ordinary schoole Authours, framed according to the same rule, if they be translated rightly in propriety of words, phrase and sense.

All this may be done by the practice of the rule of construing, and of Grammaticall translations.

By these I dare be bold to affirme upon sure experience, and the trials of many very learned, that all these things may be effected amongst those who are apt, without any inconvenience at all, if they be rightly used, as I shall direct you the manner after. But without them, I cannot find how possibly the inconveniences, which you have recited, can be prevented, or these benefits can be attained in any like measure; chiefly in the greater schooles, where many schollers are.

Spoud. For the golden rule of construing, and the Grammaticall translations which you mention, I know not what you meane: Neither have I ever heard of any such. Have you

The rule of construing unheard of to the most.

THE GRAMMAR SCHOOLE

you any other rule of construing, then our Grammar teacheth? or any such translations made according to it, in this propriety which you speake of?

Phil. Yes indeed Sir, there is a speciall rule, and such translations also: by the constant practice whereof, not onely the former evils may be avoided, and the benefits mentioned may be obtained; but also the way to all construing, parsing, examining, making, writing, speaking, and also trying Latine, may be made most easie and plaine; So, as children may proceed upon sure grounds, and doe all things herein with understanding, and right reason, and farre more speedily, and with more delight, then usually.

And howsoever this rule be unknowne of most, who never heard of any such particular rule of construing, but only of such directions, as may be gathered here and there, out of our Accedence and Grammar, where they are dispersed thorow all, very hardly to be discerned; yet it is set downe by sundry learned Grammarians. As by *Susenbrotus, Crusius, Cosarsus,* and our ancient Schoolemaster Master *Leech,* in his little questions of the Accedence and others, as also lately by learned *Goclenius,* though in all of them imperfectly, and differing somewhat each from other, through the divers exceptions in the Grammar rules and variety of Grammars. *Crusius* hath also examples of the practice of the rule handled at large. It would be over-tedious to set them downe all, or what each of them hath written thereof.

This rule is set downe by sundry learned Grammarians.

Yet because the rule hath some difficulty, and that wee may consider the better of it, I will rehearse it briefly out of one or two of them. And seeing we are to deale for the first enterers into construction, I will set it downe first, as Master *Leech* hath it, who is the plainest.

The rule, as M. Leech hath it.

His words are these;

Q. What order will you observe in construing of a sentence?

A. If there be a Vocative case, I must take that first: then I must seek out the principall Verbe & his Nominative case
and

THE GRAMMAR SCHOOLE

and construe first the Nominative case : and if there be an Adjective or Participle with him, then I must English them next, and such words as they governe; then the Verbe: and if there follow an Infinitive moode, I must take that next; then the Adverbe; then the case which the Verbe properly governeth : and lastly, all the other cases in their order; first the Genitive, secondly the Dative, &c.

Q. What if there be not all these words?

A. Then I must take so many of them as be in the sentence, and in this order.

Q. Is this order ever to be observed?

A. No: it may be altered by Interrogatives, Relatives, Infinitives, Genitives of partition, and Conjunctions.

Q. What speciall things must bee observed in construing?

A. That the Nominative case be set before the Verbe, the Accusative case after the Verbe, the Infinitive moode after another moode : the Substantive and the Adjective must be construed together; except the Adjective do passe over his signification unto some other word, which it governeth.

The Accusative, before an Infinitive moode, must have the word (that) joyned with it.

The Preposition must be joyned with his case.

Afterwards he gives a short example hereof.

Crusius, from whom I received the first light hereof long agoe, he hath it something otherwise; though for the substance it be the same: whose words also, because he is but short, I will set downe; and the rather, for that there are so many learned, who have not so much as heard of the rule. The words of *Crusius* are these: *The rule according to Crusius.*

De ordine verborum in construendo & interpretando. Crusius *in his Latine Grammar, pag.* 382.

Q *Votuplex est ordo verborum?*
Duplex. Naturalis & Artificiosus.

Quid

THE GRAMMAR SCHOOLE

Quid est naturalis?
Est Grammaticus ordo, docens quid primo, secundo, aut postremo loco ponendum sit.
Quid artificiosus?
Quo Oratores, Historici, Poëtæ & Philosophi utuntur.
Quid est ordo verborum naturalis?
  1 *Sumitur Nominativus Substantivi nominis, qui dicitur subjectum, aut quicquid vim Nominativi habet.*
  Huic additur Adjectivum, aut quicquid Nominativum explicat. Sæpe sententiam inchoat Vocativus, aut particulæ Orationem connectentes, aut Ablativi absoluti, aut Relativa.
  2 *Verbum finitum personale, quod vocatur Prædicatum. Impersonalia constructionem sine Nominativo inchoant.*
  3 *Casus obliqui, inter quos dignior præcedat.*
  Sæpè infinitivus: quem antecedit Accusativus cùm adest.
  Sæpè Adverbium, aut Nominativi gestuum ac similes: quæ statim verbo subijciuntur.
  Interdum Gerundia, aut Ablativi absoluti.
  Præterea,
  Præpositiones cum suis casibus.
  Denique Conjunctiones quæ superioribus alia attexunt, in quibus idem ordo servandus est.
  Sic in quavis lingua.

Comprehende ista mihi regula quam
potes brevissima.

D*ictio regens præponenda est ei quæ regitur:*
Quæ declarant postponenda sunt ijs quæ declarantur.
Thus farre *Crusius,* of the rule.

☞
The rule expounded more at large.
The curious handling of it left to some other.

Spoud. I pray you expound it somewhat more at large, that I may conceive of it yet more fully.

Phil. I will endeavour to doe as you say; although for the more curious handling of it, I will leave it to some other, or else referre it to a farther time, because of the difficulty of it, through the manifold exceptions, as I noted, especially in the longer and more intricate sentences: wherein
I take

THE GRAMMAR SCHOOLE

I take it very hard, to set down any direct rule particularly.
    Therefore for the better understanding of the rule, we are to observe,

1 That the Scholler must reade the sentence, before he construe; and in reading, that he doe it distinctly, reading to a Period or full point, and there to stay.

2 To marke the sentence well, and to observe all the points in it, both Commaes and Colons; or else distinctions, and middle distinctions: that so he may see and consider both the beginning, middest, and end of the sentence together; and also each clause in it.

3 That if there be any words in the sentence, beginning with great letters, except the first words of all; to remember that those are proper names: and also if there be any words included within a Parenthesis, or two halfe Moones, as they are termed, that they are to be construed by themselves.

4 That he seeke to understand what the matter is about: and so in continued speeches, to marke what went before.

5 To observe if there be a Vocative case.

6 To seeke out carefully the principall Verbe, by the rule in the Grammar of finding out the principall Verb, viz. If there be moe Verbes then one in a sentence, the first is the principall, except it be an Infinitive moode; or have before it a Relative, or a Conjunction, as *ut, cùm, si, &c.* Which principall Verbe being found out, doth commonly point out the right Nominative case: which Nominative case is that, which agreeth with it in number and person; and it doth also direct all the sentence very much. So that this may be accounted as the load-star, guiding all.

7 To marke the clauses which have no Verbs in them, to fit them with their owne right Verbes, expressed or understood: for no clause can be without a Verbe.

8 To supply all such words as are wanting, to make perfect sense and construction.

9 To give every word his due signification and proper

THE GRAMMAR SCHOOLE

per signe, so farre as sense will beare.

10 To joyne Substantive and Adjective, also Preposition and case.
10 To joine the Substantive and Adjective together in construing, except the Adjective doe passe over his signification into some other word, which is governed of it. Also to joyne the Preposition with his case.

11 To marke if the sentence have not an Interrogative point.
11 To marke whether the sentence have not an Interrogative point: then to reade it as asking a question; and then the Nominative case is to come after the Verbe, according to the rule of the Accedence: or otherwise to be set directly before it, if our English phrase will beare it.

These things observed, then the order proceedeth thus usually:

The order of the the rule: to take 1 The Vocative case, or whatsoever is in place of it, or hangeth of it.
1 If there be a Vocative case, to take that first and whatsoever dependeth of it, that is, whatsoever agreeth with it, or is governed of it, to expresse it; or in stead of a Vocative case, an Interjection of Calling or Exclamation, or an Adverb of Calling, Wishing, Shewing, Exhorting or Swearing, Affirming, or the like; which have the nature of Interjections, if there be any such.

2 The Nominative case, or whatsoever is in place of it, or dependeth of it.
2 The Nominative of the principall Verbe, or whatsoever is put in stead of the Nominative case, and such words as depend on it; as namely, an Adjective or Participle, and such words as they governe: or a Substantive, being the latter of two Substantives.

3 The principall Verbe, and whatsoever dependeth on it.
3 The principall Verbe, and whatsoever hangeth or dependeth on it: as if there follow an Infinitive moode, to take that next, and the Adverbe, which is joyned commonly to the Verbes, to declare their signification.

4 The case which the Verb properly governeth.
4 The case which the Verb doth properly governe next unto it selfe, which is most commonly the Accusative case, and whatsoever hangeth on it; or an Accusative case before an Infinitive moode in stead hereof.

5 All the other cases in order.
5 Then follow all the other cases in order; first the Genitive, then the Dative or Ablative, with a Preposition, or without.

This is the summe of the rule, as it is most generall and naturall.

Yet

THE GRAMMAR SCHOOLE

Yet here these things must be remembred: *Other cautives in the rule.*

1. If all these words be not in the sentence which is to be construed, to take so many of them as there are, and in this order. *1 To take so many words as there are in the same order.*

2. That the order is changed by the Relative *Qui, quæ, quod:* also by Interrogatives, Indefinites, Partitives; because these (according to the Grammar rule) follow the rule of the Relative; going before the words whereof they are governed. So likewise Adverbs of likenesse (as, *Quemadmodum, vt, veluti, sicut*) when they have *sic* or *ita* answering to them in the second part of the sentence, do use to go before. As also Conjunctions, Copulatives, Rationals, Adversitives, having their Redditives following, answering unto them: so Expletives, and certaine others: *2 The order is changed by Relat. Interrog. Indef. Partit. words of dependance and Connexion.*

Finally, all such words as these mentioned (which wee may call words of dependence, because they depend on something going before or comming after in the same sentence) or else words of Connexion, serving to knit new sentences to the former (as these Conjunctions) are to be placed next the Vocative case: or in the first place where there is no Vocative case.

3. That instead of the Nominative case, we take whatsoever is in place thereof; as a whole sentence, a piece of a sentence, an Infinitive moode, an Adverbe with a Genitive case, two Nominative cases singular or moe, joyned with a Verbe plurall, or sometimes a letter set by it selfe, or moe, or any word put for it selfe; which we call a word of art: as *Amo est verbum. Amo* is here taken for the Nominative case: for all such words or sentences are supposed to be the Neuter Gender undeclined. *3 To take for the Nominat. case whatsoever is put in place of it, or includeth it.*

So whatsoever includeth the Nominative case; as, a Verbe Impersonall, an Ablative case absolute; Gerunds and Supines put absolutely with this Verbe *est:* as *Orandum est ut sit mens sana in corpore sano. Itum est in viscera terræ:* because these stand for Verbes Impersonals, and have the Nominative case included in them.

4. The

THE GRAMMAR SCHOOLE

4 Participles, Gerunds and Supines, follow the order of the Verbes.

4. The Participles with Gerunds and Supines follow the order of those Verbes whereof they come, in governing the same cases, as in the rules. Also that Gerunds and Supines are commonly put for the Infinitive moode.

5 New conjunctions & words of dependance serve to joyne new sentences.

5. Conjunctions or other words of dependance in new clauses of the sentences, serve to joyne together the later partes of the sentences to the former; wherein the same order must be kept againe as before.

6 Adverbs to be placed to the best sence.

6. That the Adverbs be placed before or after the Verb; as the sense will most conveniently beare.

7 To observe Latinissimes, and joyne phrases.

7. That the Latinismes be observed, to joyne the whole phrases together, so much as may be, and to expresse them by as elegant and fit phrases as we can in our tongue.

The reason of the rule.

The reason also of the rule, that every one may conceive each thing, is this:

1 The words to bee placed in naturall order.

1. That the words must bee placed in order, as they should stand, according to the plaine and proper nature of the speech, in which they are used to expresse any matter: which is the very order which Grammar teacheth, and as one governeth another.

2 Governours before the governed.

2. The word governing or directing, to be placed before those which it governeth or directeth.

3 Declarers to follow the declared.

3. Those words which do declare others, are to be set after those which they do declare or make plaine.

4 The principall words going before, direct the words following; except the Inter. Relat. Ind. Part.

So the principall word going before, doth commonly direct the words following; either in agreement or governement: that is, it causeth the word following to agree with it, or to be governed of it; except in oblique cases of Interrogatives, Relatives, Indefinits, Partitives, which doe commonly goe before together with the Substantives or Antecedents, with which they agree; and are governed or guided by the word following after: as, *Quem librum legis? Quarum rerum utram minus velim non facilè possum existimare.*

Spoud. I perceive the rule most plainely, and do see an evident reason of every thing; yet neverthelesse I desire you

THE GRAMMAR SCHOOLE

you further to give me a little briefe of it, as my Schollers may best remember it.

Phil. The summe is this; to reade over the sentence distinctly to a full point; observing carefully all the points and proper names, with the drift and meaning; but chiefely to marke the principall Verbe, because that pointeth out the right Nominative case, and directeth all the sentence: also to marke if there be any Vocative case. Then the order goeth thus: *The summe of the rule of construing.*

1. If there be a Vocative case, to construe that first, with whatsoever agreeth with it, or is governed of it, or whatsoever is put in the place of it; as an Interjection of Exclamation or calling, or an Adverbe of calling.

2. To take the Nominative case of the principall Verbe, or whatsoever is put in steade of it, and to adjoyne to it whatsoever hangeth of it: as the Adjective or Participle, and such words as they governe.

3. To take the principall Verbe, and whatsoever hangeth on it, each in the right order; as if there follow an Infinitive moode, to take that next: then the Adverbe; after, the case which the Verbe properly governeth (which is commonly the Accusative case) and whatsoever hangeth on that. Lastly, all the other cases in order: first the Genitive, secondly the Dative, and lastly the Ablative.

4. If there be not all these Verbes, to take so many of them as are in the sentence, and in this order.

5. That this order is changed by Interr. Relat. Indefinites, Partitives, and some Conjunctions with Adverbs of likenesse: as *Quemœdmodum, ut, sicut, &c.* having *sic*, or *ita*, to answer them in the second part of the sentence; because those words use to goe before.

Lastly, to take the Substantive and Adjective together, unlesse the Adjective passe over his signification unto some other word, which it governeth; and so likewise the Preposition with his case.

Most briefly thus: that the principall Verbe be first sought out; then

1. Take

THE GRAMMAR SCHOOLE

A briefe of the rule of construing, for every childe to be able to answer.

1. Take the Vocative case, or whatsoever is in stead of it, or hangs upon it, serving to make it plaine.
2. The Nom. case of the principall Verbe, or whatsoever is in stead of it, or depends of it to make it plaine.
3. Then the principall Verbe, and whatsoever hangs of it, serving to expound it: as an Adverbe, or an Infinitive moode.
4. Lastly, the case which the Verbe properly governes, and all the other cases after it, in order.

Note that the order is changed by Interrog. Relat. Partit. certaine Adverbs and Conjunctions: all which use to goe before.

Observe, specially for the enterers, to put them in minde of this often: the Nom. before the Verbe: the Accus. after the Verbe: the Substant. and Adject. to goe together; unlesse the Adject. pass his signification into some other word: the Preposition and his case together.

This is the briefest, plainest, and most generall forme, that (after long practice and considering of it) I can conceive, though it have some exceptions, as I said.

Spoud. I pray you give me an example hereof.

An example of construing, and of Grammaticall translations according to the rule.

Phil. I will take the very example which *Crusius* hath set downe out of *Tully de Senectute.*

1 The artificiall placing, according to Tully. Cicer de Senectute.

1. *Aptissima omninò sunt, Scipio & Læli, arma senectutis, artes exercitationésque virtutū: quæ in omni ætate cultæ, cùm multum diúque vixeris, mirificos afferunt fructus: non solùm quia nunquam deserunt, ne in extremo quidem tempore ætatis, quanquam id maximum est: verum etiam quia conscientia benè actæ vitæ, multorùmque benefactorum recordatio, iucundissima est.* This is *Tullies* order in placing this sentence.

2 The Grammaticall placing.

2. The naturall or Grammaticall order of it is this:

Scipio & Læli, artes exercitationésque, virtutum sunt omninò arma aptissima senectutis: quæ cultæ afferunt fructus mirificos in ætate omni, cùm vixeris multum diúque: non solùm quia deserunt nunquam, ne quidem in tempore extremo ætatis, quanquam id est maximum: verum etiam quia conscientia vitæ actæ benè, recordatióque benefactorum multorum est iucundissima. 3. The

THE GRAMMAR SCHOOLE

3. The Translation is after this Grammaticall order, thus:

O Scipio & Lelius, arts & exercises of vertues, [a] are altogether the *(verb)* fittest weapons of old age: which being *(verb)* exercised in *(verb)* every age do bring [b] marvellous fruites, when you have lived [c] much and long: not onely because they [d] forsake never, [e] no truely [f] in the extreme time of age, although that is [g] the greatest; but also because [h] the conscience of a life well done [or well passed over] and the remembrance of many good deeds, is most pleasant.

4. The construing is directly according to this translation. So that the translation leadeth the Scholler as by the hand, or in stead of his Master; so, as he cannot erre, if he be of any understanding: as thus;

Scipio ô Scipio, *&* and, *Lælî* ô Lelius, *artes* arts, *exercitationesque* and exercises, *virtutum* of vertues, *sunt* are, *omnino* altogether, *arma aptissima* the fittest weapons, *senectutis* of old age: *quæ* which, *cultæ* being exercised [or used] *in ætate omni* in every age, [or in all our life] *afferunt* do bring, *fructus mirificos* marvellous fruits, *cùm* when, *vixeris* you have lived, *multùm* much, *diúque* and long, *&c.*

5 This translation directeth to parse, chiefely for all the Syntax; Every principall word in the Latine, going before others, commonly governing, or directing and guiding some way that which followeth after. It helpeth very much for the Etymologie; that children well entred, shall go very neere to tell by the English alone, what part of speech every word is: of which I shall speake after.

The manner of parsing by it, is thus shortly for the Syntaxe:

Scipio] is the first word to be parsed, because it is the first in construing; for that we begin commonly of a Vocative case, if there be one. It is the Vocative case, knowne by speaking to, & by the Interjection *O* understood; governed of the Interjection *O*, by the rule *O Exclamantis Nominativo, Accusativo, & Vocativo ivugitur.* In English, Certaine a Vocative, *&c.*

Margin notes:
3 Translation according to the naturall or Grammaticall order.
a *Are the very fittest weapons.*
Verb *aptest.*
Verb *loved and adorned.*
Verb *in all age.*
b *Wonderfull fruits, or benefits.*
c *Very long.*
d *Never leave us.*
e *Not indeede.*
f *In our last age.*
g *The chiefe.*
h *The inward testimony.*
4 Construing according to the Grammaticall translation.
Or, quæ cultæ afferunt, &c.
5 Parsing according to this translation.

Scipio.

Et

THE GRAMMAR SCHOOLE

Et.   *Et*] the next word a Conjunction Copulative, serving to couple words or sentences; here coupling *Scipio* and *Læli* together.

Læli.   *Læli*] the next word, the Vocative case knowne also by speaking to, and put in the same case with *Scipio*, by reason of the Conjunction *&*; by the rule, Conjunctions, Copulatives and Disjunctives couple like cases, *&c.*

Artes.   *Artes*] is next, in construing according to my rule of construing. The Nominative case, comming before the principall Verbe *sunt*, by the rule of the first Concord.

Que.   *Que*] next, a Conjunction Copulative, coupling *artes* and *exercitationes* together.

Exercitationes.   *Exercitationes*] is the next, the Nominative case coupled with *artes*, by the Conjunction *Enclyticall, que,* which is set after *exercitationes* in the booke; by the rule of the Conjunctions Subjunctives, or which are put after.

Virtutum.   *Virtutum*] followeth next, the Genitive case, governed of the Substantive *exercitationes*: and is the latter of two Substantives; by the rule, When two Substantives come together.

Sunt.   *Sunt*] is next, agreeing with the Nominative case *artes exercitationésque*; by *Verbum personale cohæret cum Nominativo &c.* It is expressed to the one Nominative case, and understood to the other by the figure *Zeugma*.

Omninò.   *Omninò*] the next word, an Adverbe joyned to the Verbe, to declare the signification.

Arma.   *Arma*] the Nominative following the Verbe *sunt. Sum, forem, fio &c.*

Aptissima.   *Aptissima*] the Nominative case of the Noune Adjective, agreeing in all things with *arma*, by the rule of the second Concord. The Adjective, whether it bee Noune, &c. it agreeth with *arma*, because it expresseth the qualitie of *arma, &c.*

Senectutis.   *Senectutis*] next, the Genitive case governed of *arma*, because it expresseth *arma*, the weapon of old age, the later of two Substantives.

And

THE GRAMMAR SCHOOLE

And so forward, in all things giving the reason according to the rules of Grammar, and this rule of construing compared; the later word, still declaring the former. So much shortly for parsing by this rule.

6. This translation directeth the Scholler also for making Latine, to proceede easily; and likewise the Master to teach and guide the Scholler both to make true Latine and pure *Tully*, or what Author he will follow: so that he cannot misse so long as he followeth this and looketh on the Author: also, it guideth to give a reason of every thing, or to proove the Latine thus in the very same order as they parsed. *6 Making Latine according to this rule.*

As this Master to aske thus according to the order of the translation.

How say you, *Scipio*, or *ô Scipio?*
The Scholler answereth; *Scipio*, as it is in the booke. *Example.*
Aske why not *Scipionis* nor *Scipioni*, but *Scipio;* he answereth: because it must be the Vocative case, knowne by speaking to, and governed of *o* understood, as *ô Magister*, *ô Master*.

And] *&*.
Lælius] *Læli*. If it be asked, why not *Lælius*, nor *Lælij*, nor *Lælium*; he answereth, because it must be the Vocative case; and therefore *Læli*: because when the Nominative endeth in *ius*, the Vocative shall end in *i*. Also that it must be the Vocative case because *&* coupleth like cases.

So in all things, just as the child parsed; but onely asking the English first, and making the child to give it in Latine, and to give a reason of every thing more particularly.

: The causing the child to construe and to parse, looking upon the English onely; especially the parsing so, is continuall making Latine, and proving it.

So that we may see by this sentence, how this translation serveth to direct the younger Scholler: first, to resolve or cast each sentence in Latine, into the naturall or Grammaticall order: secondly, to construe directly according to the same: thirdly, to parse as it is construed, by marking the last chiefe word: fourthly, to make the same Latine as it *Use and benefit of Grammaticall translations, set downe in generall.*

was

THE GRAMMAR SCHOOLE

was parsed, and to prove it by reason and rule. Fiftly, by comparing the order of the translation and the order of the Author, to compose the Latine againe into the order of the Author. And so by daily practising these translations, young Schollers must needs come on very much, for that it makes all the way to learne so plaine.

Chiefe reason of the benefit of translations according to the rule, for the continuall use of Analysis and Genesis.

One principall reason is, for that this is nothing else but a continuall practice of *Analysis* and *Genesis*; that is, of resolving and unmaking the Latine of the Author, and then making it againe just after the same manner, as it was unmade. Or if we may so terme it, the unwinding, and winding it up againe; which is generally acknowledged to be the speediest way to all good learning. Now of either of these there may be three parts.

Three speciall parts both of Analysis and Genesis.

1. Of the *Analysis* or resolving a sentence; first, the resolving it out of the Rhetoricall order of the Author, into the first proper, naturall and Grammaticall order.

2. Construing, turning or translating it into English, according to the same order; giving the true sense and force of each word and phrase.

3. Parsing as we construe.

So of the *Genesis* or making up againe are three parts.

1. The making the same Latine againe, according to the order of the translation and the words of the Author; that they may goe surely.

2. To proove it to be true Latine, after the manner of parsing, by the same order.

3. To compose all againe for the Rhetoricall placing of the words, according to the order of the Author, by the helpe of a few rules, and by comparing with the Author; that a child may have a confident boldnesse, to stand against the most learned, to justifie that which hee hath done.

Spoud. This stands with all reason, that if the way of unmaking or resolving be so plaine thorow this rule; the way of making up againe must needs bee as plaine and readie: for there is the same way from Cambridge to London,

THE GRAMMAR SCHOOLE

don, which was from London to Cambridge.

Phil. You say as it is: Hence you shall finde by experience, that as children will soone learne to construe and parse their Authors thereby; so they will as soone learne to make them into Latine againe: yea they will come by daily practice, to reade the Latine almost as fast out of the English translation, as out of the Author it selfe, and prove that it must be so: and in short time to do the same in things which they have not learned; especially, where they shall have occasion to use the same phrase, to doe it readily whether they shall write or speake.

Particular benefits of the use of Grammaticall translations, and of the Rule.

Spoud.

IT is apparant by that which you have said, that you take the benefit to be very great, which may come by such translations rightly used. *Benefits of the translations, and the rule set down particularly.*

Phil. I doe indeed; and that for all these things following, which seeme most strange and hard to be done by children.

1. Teaching to resolve Latine Grammatically: which is the foundation of the rest. *1 Resolving Grammatically.*

2. In construing, to direct to doe it artificially by Rule, and also in propriety of words, and in true sense. *2 Construing.*

3. For parsing to do it of themselves: as reading a lecture without any question asked, unlesse some which they omit: which manner of parsing gaineth halfe the time which is spent therein commonly, when otherwise each question is asked and stood upon. *3 Parsing.*

4. For making Latine, to be able to make the very same Latine of their Authors upon sure grounds; and thereby to be incouraged to goe on boldly and certainly, with cheerefulnesse and confidence: when little children shall see, that they are able to make the same Latine which their Authors doe, as was said, and have also the Author to justifie that which they have done. *4 Making Latine.*

5 For

THE GRAMMAR SCHOOLE

5 Proving.
5 For proving Latine, specially for the Syntaxe, when each principall word going before, directs those which follow, except in some few.

6 Composing.
6 For composing artificially, by continuall comparing this Grammaticall order, to the order of the Author, and marking why the Author placed otherwise; and by being helped by a few rules, which I will shew after.

7 Understanding.
7 To helpe the yonger schollers to understand their lectures, so farre as need is; of the benefit of which understanding we have spoken before.

8 Taking Lectures of themselves.
8 Also to take their lectures for most part of themselves, as was said; to get and bring their lectures more surely and sooner then by the Masters teaching alone, as a little experience will shew.

9 Construing and parsing out of the English.
9 To construe and parse their lectures, out of the English as out of the Latine (which is a continuall making Latine, as we heard) and so to reade their lectures first in the naturall order, then as they are in their Authors.

10 Correcting their Authors.
10 To be able to correct their Authors of themselves, if they be false printed.

11 Keeping all learned in their Authors perfectly.
11 To keepe all which they have learned in their Authors so perfectly, as to be able in good sort to construe or parse at any time, in any place out of the bare Translation, onely by reading them oft over out of the translation.

12 Save getting Authors without booke.
12 To save all the labour of learning most Authours without booke, as all Authors in prose; which labour in many schooles, is one of the greatest tortures to the poor schollers, and cause of impatience and too much severity to the Masters, though with very little good for most part: to be able as it were by playing, onely reading their Authors out of the English over and over, at meet times, to have them much better for all true use and each good purpose, then by all saying without booke; to trouble the memory only with getting rules of Grammars and the like, and such other of most necessary use, as the Poets: which also are exceedingly furthered hereby.

13 To proceed in English, as in Latine.
13 To helpe to proceed as well in our English tongue as in

THE GRAMMAR SCHOOLE

in the Latine, for reading, and writing true orthography; to attaine variety and copy of English words, to expresse their mindes easily, and utter any matter belonging to their Authors. And so in time, to come to propriety, choise, and purity, as well in our English as in the Latine.

14 To learne the propriety of the Latine tongue, as they goe forward; to be able to justifie each phrase, and in time to remember words and phrases, for almost whatsoever they have learned, and where. Also by reading *Tully*, and other purer Authors constantly out of such translations, first Grammatically, then Rhetorically, to attaine to make a more easie entrance to that purity of the Latine tongue, whereof sundry great learned men have given precepts, then by precepts alone; and much more by joyning precepts and this practice together. *14 To learne the propriety of the Latine tongue, to justifie words and phrases, also to attaine the purity of the Latine tongue.*

15 By the translations of the Poets, as of *Ovid* and *Virgil*, to have a most plain way into the first entrance into versifying, to turne the prose of the Poets into the Poets owne verse, with delight, certainty and speed, without any bodging; and so by continuall practice to grow in this facilitie, for getting the phrase and veine of the Poet. *15 To enter and train up schollers in Poetry with ease & delight without bodging.*

16 To be (as was noted) not onely in stead of Masters, or Ushers, to give each lower lecture perfectly, for all the substance; but also to be after in stead of their owne presence, or of Dictionaries in every one of those fourmes continually, to direct them, untill every one of the fourme can construe, parse, make the same Latine, and prove it. Hereby both to free the children from that feare which they will have ordinarily, to go to their Masters for every word; and also to free the Masters from that trouble and hinderance to tell them every word, so oft as they forget, and the vexation and fretting to see the children's dulnesse and forgetfulnesse. For the helpe of the Master, or Usher, in the meane time what it ought to be, we shall see after in the use of these. *16 To be in stead of Master or Usher amongst the schollers for giving and preparing Lectures. To free children from feare of to oft asking, and the Masters from that trouble and hinderance.*

17 Hereby schollers having been well entered, and exercised in their lower Authors, shall be able to proceede to their higher Authors, *ex tempore;* and goe on with ease, by *17 To be able to proceed in other Authors of themselves*

the

THE GRAMMAR SCHOOLE

by some helpe of Master and Commentaries. the assistance of the Master, where they need, and by the helpe of Commentaries; that they may be thus inabled to construe any Author, and be fitted for the studies of the Universitie, at the first entrance thither.

18 A helpe to weaker Masters. 18 These will be also a helpe to many weaker Schoolemasters, for right and certaine construction, without so oft seeking Dictionaries for English, and proprietie of words; and so for parsing, and all sorts of the former directions.

19 To helpe weaker schollers to proceed in Latine in their privat studies in the Universities. 19 Also, weaker schollers in the Universities, who have not been so well grounded in the Grammar schooles, may proceed in their private studies, by the use of some of these translations, either one alone, or two or three together; and increase both for construing, understanding, and writing Latine. Also they may have continuall use of translating both into English, and Latine; whether reading out of the Author into the translation, or out of the translation into the Author, or doing it by pen; and ever a direction to try all by, and as a private helpe: which continuall translating both wayes is a most speedy way to learning, as M. *Askam* proveth at large.

20 So to helpe any who have lost their Latine or have but a taste. 20 Likewise, any who have lost the knowledge of the Latine tongue, may recover it hereby within a short time; and they who have had but a smattering, or some little beginning, may soone come to understand any ordinary Author, and proceed with pleasure and certainty.

21 To have daily much practice of Analysis and Genesis; which is all in all, in getting all learning. 21 Finally, hereby schollers may have daily much sure practice both of *Analysis* and *Genesis*; that is, resolving and making Latine· which as was noted, all the learned doe acknowledge to be almost all in all, in getting all learning, for all this practice by them is nothing else but *Analysis* and *Genesis*, as we shewed before.

Things

THE GRAMMAR SCHOOLE

Things more specially observed in the translating of the Schoole-Authors.

Spoud. THese benefits are indeed very great, and worthy the labour of every child, or other, who would attaine them, if it be as you say: yet by your favour, many of them cannot be obtained by bare Grammaticall Translations alone; as to get the propriety of both the tongues, both of Latine and English together, with variety of phrase, the sense, and the like. Therefore what course have you observed in your Translations, to make them to serve to all these purposes?

Phil. I have observed these things following, so neere as I have been able for the present: I shall amend them after, God willing. *Things observed in the Translations of the Schoole-Authors.*

1 This naturall or Grammaticall order throughout. *1 Naturall order.*

2 That the English Translation is set down alone, without the Latine adjoyning, to avoid the inconveniences of having the Latine and English together; as of making Truant, or the like: whereof I shall speake after. *2 English alone.*

3 The propriety of the English words, answering to the Latine, in the first and naturall signification, and expressing the force of the Latine words, so neere as I could, is set down in the first place. And where the Latine phrase is somewhat hard or obscure to be expressed in our English tongue, word for word; there I have also expressed that by a more plain phrase, sometimes included within two markes, almost like a Parenthesis, with [or] thus. Or else I have set it ever in the Margent: where also I have oft placed the meaning, with variety of other phrases over-against the word, and noted them with a character or letter, answering to the word in the Text. *3 The English answering the Latine in propriety. Where any phrase is somewhat hard, how it is expressed.*

Moreover, where any phrase is over-harsh in our English tongue, to expresse the Latine *verbatim*, *viz.* word for word, or in good propriety; that harsh phrase is also placed in the Margent, over-against the Latine phrase, with this marke, *Where any phrase seemes over-harsh in our English tongue.*

(*Verb*)

(*Verb*) or (*ver.*) or *v.* signifying *verbatim*, word by word, or word for word, and the more easie phrase set in the Text.

Where there may be two senses. Likewise where there may be two senses or constructions, I have commonly expressed both: the more likely and naturall in the Text, the other in the Margent. This I have done, to the end that the Scholler may see both construction and meaning together; with the propriety of the tongue, whereunto I have chiefly laboured.

No varying but on necessitie. So that there is no varying from the propriety, save where necessity inforced, for the impropernesse of the phrase in our speech, or in some few places, where the construction is easie and familiar; and there is set in the Margent (*Verb*) as was said before.

The order of some words changed. Lastly, where in the Grammaticall order in Latine, the Substantive goeth before the Adjective, the governour or guider first; in our English Dialect, the Adjective is most commonly set before: as *vir bonus*, a good man; not, a man good: unlesse the Adjective be divided from the Substantive; as where it passeth the signification into some other word governed of it: as *vir præstans ingenio*, a man excelling in wit.

So in the Adverbe *Non*: as *Non est*, It is not; we doe not say, Not it is. Also in the Enclyticall Conjunction *que*, and the like; as *idque*, and that.

Observation in the lowest Authors. In the first and lowest Authors is commonly translated Thou, Thee, Not you; because of the difficulty for children, to distinguish betweene Thou, and You.

Thus I place ordinarily the Accusative case before the Infinitive moode, in plaine words, for the ready and easie making the Latine out of it: as *Multum eum prævidisse dicimus* we say him to have foreseene much: and in the Margent usually thus; We say, that he foresaw much: according to our English phrase.

How

THE GRAMMAR SCHOOLE

How to use these Translations so, as to attaine the former benefits.

Spoud. Hese things diligently observed, must needs be very available to the purposes, which you have mentioned: the very propriety alone, I meane the knowledge of words, in their first and proper signification, is a singular helpe to learning. For reason will commonly teach, both the change of the signification by the circumstances of the place, and also the cause of the change. But I pray you, how might my Schollers use these Translations so, as that I might finde the benefits of them? *The manner of use of the Translations.*

Phil. You may cause them to use them after these directions following:

1 First, you are to see that every one who is to use them, can repeat the rule of construing, and answer the questions thereof, according to the briefest forme of it at least. And if your leisure will serve, to heare your selfe how they can take their Lectures of themselves, according to the same. *1 To see that every one can give the summe of the rule of construing.*

2 Where your leisure will not well permit you to see all Lectures given, you may appoint at the taking of the Lectures, that some one or two of the best of each fourme, doe looke upon the Translation; and in the lower fourmes doe first reade over the Translation once, only to give them some light, for the meaning and understanding of their Lectures; the rest looking on their Authors, or onely harkening to the meaning: although in the higher fourms which use them, they will not need so much as once reading over before, unlesse in some difficult places: only he who looketh on the Translation, may reade the Translation after, for their more full understanding of the Lecture, and more easie remembrance of it. *2 In the lower fourmes one to reade over the translation, to give some light, and looke on the Translation.*

3 After that, to appoint another, first, to reade over their Lecture in the Latine distinctly, as it is in the Author, and to try how he can construe, beating it out according *3 To construe according to the rule of themselves.*

to

THE GRAMMAR SCHOOLE

He who hath the Translation only, to direct where they goe false. to the rule. In the meane time cause him who hath the Translation, to be in stead of your selfe amongst the rest, to see that they goe right ; and where the construer sticketh, or goeth amisse, to call him backe to the rule, and wish the rest to helpe to finde it out by the same rule.

To do as the cunning Hunts-man. And when all the fourme are at a stand, and none of them can beat it out, then onely he who hath the booke, to doe it; as the cunning Hunts-man, to helpe a little at the default, to point and to direct them where to take it: and thus so many to construe over, or so oft, untill all of them can construe.

☞
The assistance of the Master or Usher herein. In the meane time your selfe or Usher, in the middest, both to have an eye to them, that they take this course; and also to helpe yet further, where need is: And after the taking of the Lecture, to note out unto them all the difficult or new words in their Lecture, to examine and direct them, for the parsing of them : and also to cause each of the fourme to marke out those words, to take speciall paines in them ; to make them perfect above all the rest: because they have learned the rest before, and have but so many new words to get in that Lecture.

☞
To construe and parse out of the Translation, is the surest & most profitable way. 4. According to the order as they construe, cause them to parse, as we shewed ; either looking upon the Author, or upon the Translation alone. But I finde it farre the surer and better, in all who are able, both to construe and parse out of the Translation : because thereby they are learning continually, both to make and prove their Latine ; and so do imprint both the matter and Latine, more firmely in their memory. So also all of ability, to construe and parse onely out of the Translation, when they come to say; and out of it to give the reason of every thing. This they will do most readily, with a little practice.

How to keepe all their Authors perfectly. 5. To the end that they may keepe all their Authors perfectly, which they have learned (which is thought of many almost impossible, and doth indeed so much incourage yong Schollers, and grace the Schooles when they can doe it) let them but use this practice : Every day

☞

after

THE GRAMMAR SCHOOLE

after that they have said their Lectures, cause each fourme which use these translations, to goe immediately to construing over all which they have learned, each day a piece, every one a side of a leafe, or the like in order, untill they have gone thorow all; construing it onely out of the translation: to spende an houre or more therein, as time will permit: one or two who sit next unto the Construer, to looke on the Translation with him, to helpe where hee sticketh; the rest to looke on their Authors. Appoint withall some of the Seniors of the fourme, to examine shortly the hard words of each page as they go; I meane those words, which they marked when they learned them. *To construe or reade oft all which they have learned, out of the Translations; to make and keepe all perfect, by oft repetitions. Manner hereo*

And when they become perfect in construing out of the English, cause them for more speedy dispatch, but onely to reade their Authors into Latine, forth of the Translation; first in the Grammaticall order: after as they are in the Author. They will thus soone runne over all which they have learned, without the least losse of time: for this will be found the best bestowed time, to keepe perfectly that which they have gotten. And what they can so construe or reade out of the English into Latine, they can also do it out of the Latine into English ordinarily.

Then, as they waxe perfect in that which they have learned, and grow a little to understanding; they may practise of themselves by the same meanes, to reade over the rest of their Author, which they learned not, or some easie Author, which they have not read; as first *Corderius*, or the like, by the help of the same Translations: first to construe *ex tēpore* amongst themselves, after to reade out of the Translations; according to the same manner as they did in that which they have learned: wherein they will do more then you will easily beleeve, untill you see experience. *To reade over other Authors after the same manner.*

After this, as they come to higher fourmes, and more judgement, they may be appointed likewise to reade *ex tempore* some other Author, whereof they have the Translation to direct them; and that both out of the Author into English: first, after the Grammatticall manner; and then in a *So in higher Authors translated. Practice will make them very prompt, both in English and Latine.*

good

THE GRAMMAR SCHOOLE

good English stile: afterwards out of the English into Latine, both wayes, both in Grammaticall order, and after in Composition, according to the Author. And within a time that they have beene thus exercised, they will be able to do this almost as easily and readily, as that which they have learned. I find *Tullies* sentences, and *Tully de natura Deorum*, with *Terentius Christianus*, to be singular books to this purpose for the best uses.

The fruit hereof. By this meanes it must come to passe by daily practice, that they shall attaine to the phrase, stile and Composition of any Author which they use to reade oft over, and to make it their owne; even of any piece of *Tully* himselfe (as was said) and much sooner then can be imagined, untill triall be made: though this must needes require meete time. For what thing of any worth can be obtained, but by time, industry, and continuall practice? much lesse such copy, choyse, propriety, and elegancy, as *Tully* doth affoord.

Objections against the use of Translations in Schooles answered.

Spoud. AS you have shewed me the benefits which may come by Grammaticall Translations; and also how to use them, that Schollers may attaine the same: so give me leave to propound what doubts I may suspect concerning the same for the present; and moe hereafter, as I shall make triall of them.

Phil. Very willingly; for I do desire to find out all the inconveniences that can be imagined, which may come by them: but for mine owne part, I can find none, if they be used according to the former direction; and yet I have done what I could, to finde out whatsoever evils might be to follow of them. Object whatsoever you can, I thinke I am able plainely to answer it, and to satisfie you fully in every point.

Spoud. I will therefore deale plainely with you, in what I can conceive for the present. *Object.*

THE GRAMMAR SCHOOLE

Object. 1. Translations in Schooles have not been found o bring any such benefit, but rather much hurt; and therefor the best and wisest Schoole-masters have not beene wont to suffer any of them amongst their Schollers.

Phil. I will first answer you for the benefits: That it is true indeede, that these uses and benefits cannot be made of any other Translation of any one of our Schoole-Authors. The reasons are evident: first, because none of the Translators, so farre as I know, have followed, nor so much as propounded to themselves to follow this Grammaticall rule in Translating: which you see is the meane foundation of all true construing, parsing, making and trying Latine: and of all these benefits, to keepe Schollers to goe surely. Secondly, none of them which I know, have laboured to expresse the propriety and force of the Latine, in the first and native signification; which this intendeth continually: and how much lieth upon the knowledge of the propriety of the words, for the certaine getting of any tongue, every Scholler knoweth. Thirdly, none of them have indeavoured by a double Translation to make all things plaine, as these do every where; labouring to expresse with the words, and Grammar, the sense and meaning also in all obscure places, with variety of English words or phrase: to the end to teach children thereby, Grammar, propriety, sense, with variety of phrase to expresse their minds in English, as well as in Latine: and all under one, that nothing bee wanting.

These uses and benefits cannot be made of any other Translation of the Schoole-Authors, but the Grammaticall, and why?

The Translators have seemed to ayme either onely or principally, at the meaning and drift of the Author; which benefit alone they do in some sort performe: but for the rest of the benefits and uses, or for the most of them (as for true construing, parsing, making and trying Latine, which are the chiefe things here mentioned) they either set the learner at a *nonplus*, or carry him ordinarily cleane amisse. And therefore there is no marvell, if in that respect they be utterly disliked. Triall in any of them, compared to the rule and the other limits, and especially how in construing, parsing,

What the Translators have aymed at. The Translations of our Schoole-Authors extant, do performe none of the benefits which these Grammaticall Translations do aime at chiefely.

parsing, and the like, they carry the learner utterly out of the way, will presently shew the truth hereof, and commonly in the very first sentence of them. I will set downe the words in one or two.

Esop's *Fables construed thus:*

Examples of the Translations extant, to manifest the truth hereof. *Dum* whilst, *Gallinaceus* the dunghill, *Gallus* Cocke, *Vertit* scratched, *Stercorarium* in the dunghill.

Tullies *Offices translated thus:*

| *Marci Tullii Ciceronis de officiis ad Marcum filium liber primus.* | *Marcus Tullius Ciceroes* first booke of duties to *Marcus* his sonne. |

Try all to construe by these. Trie in any one of these, whether a child can construe one sentence right and surely, according to the Grammar, or in any certainety of the propriety of the words, or be able to parse or make Latine, or the rest: though some of these Translators were learned, and gave the sense; yet you may perceive that they aimed not at these ends here mentioned, or few of them.

Thus you see what I have answered concerning the benefits: now let us heare what you say concerning the hurt comming by them.

Object. 2. *Spoud.* Besides that they leade Schollers amisse very ordinarily in construing, almost in every sentence; They are found also to make Schollers Truants, or to go by rote (as we commonly call it) which is worse.

A. Phil. For the first part, that they leade Schollers amisse, I have answered; that, that is onely in such Translations, which respect the sense alone, but do not respect the Grammar.

Secondly,

THE GRAMMAR SCHOOLE

Secondly, for making Truants, I answer; that these Grammaticall translations being thus meerely English, and separate from the Latine altogether, can never indanger any way to make Truants, if they be used according to the directions prescribed. For first, for construing Latine, there can be no likelihood hereof, if the Translation be onely used; first to give some light and understanding of the Lecture amongst the younger; after, to be only in place of the Master, where he cannot be himselfe. *Grammaticall translations separate from the Latine, cannot indanger any to make them Truants, if they be rightly used.*

Also, where all of the fourme cannot beat out the construing by the Grammaticall rule, there to direct and point it out how to take it. Likewise, to give propriety of English, and to guide the Schollers in place of the Master (who cannot be always with every one) to the end, that in all things they may go surely. Secondly, for construing and making the Latine out of the Translation, it chiefly consists upon understanding and conceit; and shall more stirre up the wit and memory to get propriety and copie of words and phrases, then all getting without booke can possibly do. In getting without booke alone, words and sentences may be learned, as by Parrats, without any understanding: hereby children must needs understand them: For, having nothing but the bare translation, they must be driven of necessitie to beate out the Latine, by learning and by reason, with diligence; and so stirre up their memories continually. Also, hereby whensoever they shall have againe the same English words or phrases to make in Latine, to write or to speake; the verie same Latine words and phrases, which they learned in their Authors, do come straightwayes to their memories to expresse their mindes. And in what things they can give Latine to the English, in that, as was said, they can ordinarily give English to the Latine.

Indeede, where the Translation is joyned with the Authour, and so they are set together answerably word for word, either as the Interlineall set over the head, or the English word or phrase set after the Latine; there the eye of the child *There is great difficulty to use an interlineall translation, or Latine joyned to the English.*

THE GRAMMAR SCHOOLE

child is no sooner upon the one, but it will be upon the other: and so the memory is not exercised, neither can this mischiefe be avoided. Yea, where the Author is of the one page, the translation is on the other overagainst it (like as it is in *Theognis*, and some other Greeke Poets) there must be much discretion for the right using of them; otherwise many inconveniences must needs follow amongst children. But in these bare translations so by themselves, these surmised dangers are prevented; if they be used as hath beene shewed. Although for them who are of full discretion to use them (as those who would study privately for the recovering their Latine, or increasing therein) it may be the most profitable of all, to have the translation over against the Latine, directly on the other page, after the manner as *Theognis* is printed; that folding the booke; they may looke upon the one when they would find out the other; and yet have the other ever at hand, as a Master, to helpe in an instant, where they need.

3. *Ob. Sp.* But the Schollers may be idle, when they seeme to be construing, when as one onely construeth, and the rest looke on their bookes.

How to prevent idlenesse or negligence in the use of the translations, so that one cannot bee idle, while they are in hand with these.

A. Phil. So they may be idle in whatsoever exercise they do amongst themselves, unlesse the Master be vigilant: but let the Master use any diligent circumspection, and they cannot possibly be idle in this, of all other: no not one in any fourme. For, let but the Master or Usher have an eye to all in generall, though they bee in hand in hearing any fourme; and where they do marke or but suspect any one of all the fourmes to be carelesse, or not to attend; there let them step to such a one of a suddaine, and bid him set his finger to the last word which was spoken: and so, if any be idle, he may be caught presently. Provided alwayes, that no one keepe his finger at the book, lest by them the Truants see where it is; but every one to use only his eye and his eare. Some of the most negligent and stubborne so overtaken now and then, and sharply corrected for ensample, will continually keepe all the rest in order and diligence, at this time

THE GRAMMAR SCHOOLE

time specially. This practice may serve for whatsoever they construe, parse, or examine together, to keepe them from loytering or carelesnesse.

4. *Ob. Spoud.* Well: you seeme to have answered the evils which I feared for the Schollers; I shall thinke further of them. But there may be greater inconveniences in them concerning the Masters: as 1. These may be a meanes to make the Masters idle, by freeing them from giving Lectures, and much other imployment about the same, which they are wont to be exercised in.

Phil. The best things may be abused some way: but otherwise there cannot be any such danger of idlenesse to the Master, who makes conscience of his dutie, or hath any desire to see his Schollers to profit; but an incouragement hereby to take all possible paines, by seeing the ease and fruit of his labours. Also, besides the continuall eye that he is to have, that every one bee painfully exercised by them in every fourme, and his marking out all the difficult words, that they may labour those above all, and helping in each fourme where neede is, the Master may bestow the more time with the higher fourms; and in poasing and examining, which is the life of all learning, as hath beene and shall be shewed further in due place. As before Lectures, he may spend more time continually in examining parts, and in more exquisite reading Lectures in the higher fourmes, or hearing them to reade their owne Lectures, which is farre the best of all; or taking paines with the first enterers for every tittle; so in examining and trying exercises and Lectures after.

These, no meanes to make Masters idle, but contrarily to incourage them to take all paines.

Spoud. You seeme to be marvellous confident in all things, for the use and benefit of these translations; and to make a principall reckoning of them.

Phil. I do indeed make a principall account of them very justly; and do acknowledge my selfe bound unto God chiefely for them, above all other things which he hath made knowne unto me in all my search and travell.

The account to be made justly of these translations.

For these are for me in stead of mine owne selfe, hearing and

THE GRAMMAR SCHOOLE

and directing in every other forme which I cannot be withall, or as so many helpers. And by the helpe and benefit of these, all my younger Schollers do seeme to attaine almost double learning to that, that by mine owne paines being farre greater, and my griefe much more, I was ever able to bring them unto before. For, before the time that I came to the knowledge and use of these, as I taught at one end, my children would forget at another; and be as raw in that which was learned a quarter or halfe a yeere before, as if they either had not learned it, or never learned it well; which was no small griefe unto me whensoever they were examined: but now take them where you will of a sodaine, in all the Authors which they have learned; and they shall be able in good sort, not onely to construe or parse, but also to reade out of the English into the Latine and prove it: at least so many of them as are apt, and the rest in better manner then I could have expected of them, unlesse the fault be in my selfe; and that without any losse of time: and to go faster forward in their Authors then ever they were wont to do; and without any such fretting or vexing to my selfe, though I have but some one written copie in a fourme. Now trie this amongst your Schollers, whether they be able to do the like at any time of a sodaine, by all your labour. For mine owne part, I could never by all meanes attaine unto it in any measure, especially having many fourmes: neither can I see how I could have done it, unlesse I had had so many bodies, or so many to have beene continually in my place, in each fourme one.

Triall to make all this evident.   A small triall will soone make this evident; prooving some Schollers with them, others learning the same things without them, in some quarter or halfe yeere's space, whether have learned more and the surelier. And therefore I dare be bold to commend this unto you upon most undoubted experience.

Spoud. I do not doubt then, but, upon this so happy an experience, you have thus translated many of our Schoole Authors.

Phil.

THE GRAMMAR SCHOOLE

Phil. I have indeed taken paines in translating so many of them, as I have had occasion for my schollers to use, since God made knowne unto me the benefit of them; and have either finished them wholly, or some part of each of them; and hope in time to goe thorow them wholly, if the Lord vouchsafe me life. As namely, to begin at the lowest: *Schoole-Authors translated Grammatically.*

Schoole-Authors translated, or in hand.
- *Pueriles confabulatiunculæ.*
- *Sententiæ pueriles.*
- *Cato.*
- *Corderius* Dialogues.
- *Esop's* Fables.
- *Tullies* Epistles gathered by *Sturmius.*
- *Tullies* Offices, with the books adjoyned to them; *de Amicitia, Senectute, Paradoxes.*
- *Ovid de Tristibus.*
- *Ovid's Metamorphosis.*
- *Virgil.*

Also these books following, whereof I find great benefit: *Other bookes also translated Grammatically for continuall helps in schooles.*

1. *Tullies* Sentences for entring schollers, to make Latine truely and purely in stead of giving vulgars, and for use of dayly translating into Latine, to furnish with variety of pure Latine and matter.

2. *Aphthonius* for easie entrance into Theames, for understanding, matter and order.

3. *Drax* his phrases, to help to furnish with copy of phrase both English & Latine, and to attaine to propriety in both.

4. *Flores poëtarum*, to prepare for versifying; to learne to versifie, *ex tempore*, of any ordinary Theame.

5. *Tully de Natura deorum*; for purity, easinesse, variety, to helpe to fit with a sweet stile for their disputations in the Universities.

6. *Terentius Christianus.*

Of the further uses of all of which I shall speake in their proper places: though this I must needs confesse unto you, that I know them all to be very imperfect, and to have many defects: which I every day observe, and am continually amending, hoping to bring them to much more perfection, *Translations as other things defective.*

as

THE GRAMMAR SCHOOLE

as either my selfe, or you, or any other good friend, to whose hands they shall come, shall observe the slips, & God vouchsafe life and his gracious assistance. In the meane time I intreat you to suspend your judgement, untill you have seene some triall, if you have any further doubt concerning the benefit of them; and then to let me heare plainly as you finde.

Of construing *ex tempore*.

Spoud. I Rest in these your answers, which you give upon your experience, for the doubts which may be made concerning the Grammaticall translations, and so for the use and benefits of them; and also for the construing of those lower Schoole-Authors, which are so translated. But when your Schollers have gone thorow these Authors; what helps may they use for the higher Schoole-Authors; as *Horace, Persius*, and the like; and so for all other things to be construed *ex tempore*?

What helps to be used for higher Authors.

Phil. By this time they will do very much in construing any ordinary Author of themselves, *ex tempore;* through their perfect knowledge and continuall practice of the rule of construing, and by that helpe of their reading in the lower Authors: I meane the help of the matter, words and phrase which they are well acquainted with, and of being able to cast the words into the naturall order.

Remembring ever to cast each sentence into the naturall order.

Yet, beside these, and the assistance of the Master where need is, they may use all these helpes following:

1. The best and easiest Commentaries of the hardest and most crabbed Schoole-Authors; as M. *Bond* upon *Horace*: who hath by his paines made that difficult Poet so easie, that a very child which hath been well entred, and hath read the former Schoole-Authors in any good manner, may goe thorough it with facility, except in very few places. Of him, it were to be wished, for his singular dexteritie, in making that difficult Poet plaine in so few words, that he would take the like paines in the rest of that kinde: as in *Persius* and *Juvenal*, for the great benefit of Schooles.

1 Commentaries of the hardest Authors. Bond upon Horace.

Or

THE GRAMMAR SCHOOLE

Or that some other would doe it, following his example.

Next unto him, of those which I have seene, are these: *Murmelius* and *Buschius* upon *Persius*, a double Commentarie; the one shortly expressing the matter, and beating out the sense and meaning, the other the words. *Lubin* also upon *Persius* and *Juvenal*, is much commended. For short Comments and Annotations of *Virgil*, there may be used *Ramus* upon the Eclogues and Georgicks. Also the *Virgils* printed with H. *Stephens* annotations; and with *Melancthons*.

2 Where they have no help but the bare Author, and that they must construe wholly of themselves, call upon them oft, to labour to understand and keepe in fresh memory the Argument, matter and drift of the place, which they are to construe: which matter they may either finde prefixed generally before the beginning of the Treatises, or Chapters, in the Arguments, or else they are to demand the understanding in generall, of the Master or Examiner, what the matter of the place is, or what it is about Otherwise many places may trouble the greatest schollers at the first sight.

3 To consider well of all the circumstances of each place, which are comprehended most of them in this plaine verse:

Quis, cui, causa, locus, quo tempore, prima sequela.

That is, who speakes in that place, what he speakes, to whom he speakes, upon what occasion he speakes, or to what end, where he spake, at what time it was, what went before in the sentences next, what followeth next after. This verse I would have every such scholler to have readily; and always to thinke of it in his construing. It is a very principall rule for the understanding of any Author or matter whatsoever.

4 In all hard words or phrases let them first call to remembrance where they have learned them, or the primitive word whereof they come, or some words neere unto them: or otherwise to search them out by inquiring of the Master, Usher, or some fellow; or of the Dictionaries, which they ought to have ever at hand.

And in construing their own Authors, let them remember that

Murmelius printed at Paris. 1531.
Lubin on Persius and Juvenal.
Helpes for Virg. with Melancht, annotations printed at Witeberg. 1598.

2 *Understanding the Argument, matter and drift in generall.*

3 *To consider the common circumstances of places. This verse comprehending the chiefe circumstances of places to be ever in minde. It is a principall rule for the understanding of Authors or matter.*

4 *To search out every hard word and phrase.*

THE GRAMMAR SCHOOLE

that generall precept, to marke the new words with a line under them, as was advised before; that they may oft go over them: or if they feare they cannot so remember them, to write them in their bookes over the word, or in the margents over against the words in a fine small hand, it will not hurt their bookes: or for saving their bookes, let every one have a little paper booke, and therein write only all the new and hard words as was observed generally, to be very perfect in those each way, by oft reading over; and so they shall come on very fast: having those (as I said) they have all. So that these things observed, shall accomplish your desire.

Or to have each a little paper booke to note all new and hard words in.

1 Consider and wey well the generall matter and argument.

2 Marke all the hard words in their proper significations.

3. Keepe in minde what verse of the circumstances of places; *Quis, cui, &c.*

4 Cast and dispose the words in the proper Grammaticall order.

The summe of all for construing without Commentarie or helpe.

5 See that nothing be against sense, nothing against Grammar: but if either the sense be absurd, or construction against Grammar, cast it, and try it another way untill you finde it out.

Finally, give me leave to adde this, before we end this matter of construing; That all these kinds of construing, or rather of expounding and expressing their minds, may be used by schollers of ripenesse, and with much profit.

Severall kinds of construing or expounding.

1 According to the bare words in their first signification, and in the naturall order plainly.

2 According to the sense to express the minde of the Author with understanding.

3 More elegantly, in finenesse of words and phrase.

4 Paraphrastically, by exposition of words and matter more at large, to make as it were a Paraphrase of it. And to do this last in good Latine, where they are of ability.

Spoud. Sir, you have satisfied me at large for all this matter of construing: now I pray you let us come to parsing, and
the

THE GRAMMAR SCHOOLE

the manner of it, which followeth next; that I may have your helpe therein. For this hath beene no lesse wearinesse and vexation unto me, then the construing hath beene.

Phil. Before we come to parsing, let me also tell you this one thing: That besides my Schollers ordinary Lectures, and repeating daily some part of that which they have learned in the lower fourmes; I finde very great good in causing them every day in each fourme to construe a piece of their Authors, where they have not learned; and that *ex tempore*, aside, or a leafe at a time, as leisure will permit: hearing them either my selfe, or by some other very sufficient, how they can doe it; and posing onely some hard things as they goe forward: noting also the harder words, and more difficult places, as was shewed. Also in those bookes, whereof they have translations, I cause them by course sometimes to construe or reade the same, out of the Translations: as at other times to reade out of the Author into English; according to the manner of the Translation.

A most profitable exercise, to cause the Schollers, dayly to construe some things ex tempore, besides their ordinarie Lectures.

Spoud. This must needs be exceeding profitable: I likewise will put it in practice forthwith, if God will; and doe heartily thank you for imparting it unto me. But now if you have done, to the matter of parsing.

Phil. Let me heare of you, what course you have used therein, and I will supply whatsoever I can.

CHAP. IX.

Of Parsing, and the kinds thereof; and how children may parse of themselves readily and surely.

Spoud.

FOr parsing, I have followed the common course; which is this, so farre as I have seene or heard: viz. To parse over, all my yongest, every word; and even in the same order as the words doe stand in their Authors: teaching them what part of speech every word is,

The usuall manner of parsing.

how

THE GRAMMAR SCHOOLE

how to decline them; and so all the questions belonging thereunto: and what each word is governed of; the rules for every thing, and the like.

How to teach children to parse of themselves most surely and readily.

Herein, after long and much labour, I have found very little fruit, through the hardnesse of it, and the weakenesse of the children's memories, to carrie away that which I told them: much lesse have I been able to make my little ones, no not in the second or third fourmes, so to parse of themselves, as to give a true reason of every word why it must be so; according to that which I saw in the note, what might be done in parsing. Now if you have seene the practice thereof, let me heare it of you, I intreat you; and that in so few words as you can.

Phil. Yes indeed, I have seene the practice hereof, and do knowe it, that children will do very much, to ease and delight both the Master and themselves exceedingly. Besides some of the best of those which you mention (as the shewing the youngest how to parse every word) I have learned to observe these things following, and find marvellous light, easinesse, surenesse, and helpe of memory by them:

The certaine direction for parsing.

1 To parse as they construe, ever marking the last word.

1. To cause the children ever to parse as they construe, according to the Grammaticall rule of construing, and the Translations; alwaies marking the last principall word which went before in construing: wherein (as I shortly shewed you before) the very child may see every principall word going before, governing or ordering that which followeth; and so he hath therein a guide leading him by the hand for all the Syntax at least: except in the exceptions mentioned in the Grammaticall rule; as of Interrogatives, Relatives, &c. which they will soone know: and where one word governes divers things; as in that example,

Dedit mihi vestem pignori, te præsente, propria manu.

Where the word *Dedit* governes most of the rest in a divers consideration.

2 To remember if they have not learned the words before.

2. To aske among them every word of any hardnesse, whether they have not learned it before? and if they have, to repeat where. As it was before, so it is there for the most part.

3 For

THE GRAMMAR SCHOOLE

3. For the Etymologie; all the difficulty is in these three parts of speech, Nowns, Verbs, and Participles; the rest being set down in the Accedence, or easily known as was shewed before. And in all words of these three parts, do but tell them what examples they are like in the Accedence: which examples being knowne, will presently bring to their understanding all the questions depending on them and their answers. As, of what part of speech the words are; of what declension or Conjugation: so the declining, Case, Gender, Number, Person, Mood, Tense, &c. Also with a little practice they will soon guesse at them, themselves; & that very right, to shew what examples they are like, either by the English, or Latine, or both. The same would be also for the Syntax, both in agreements and governments, ever to shew what examples they are like. The example makes the rule most plaine, and imprints all in the childe's memory.

3 To marke in Nowns, Verbs, Participles, what examples they are like. The rest are in the booke.

Paralleling by examples in the Syntax likewise.

To make this plaine to the capacity of the simplest, I will adde one onely example, particularly examined out of the two first verses of *Qui mihi discipulus, puer, es, &c.*

An example of parsing set down at large, to direct the rudest.

First, be sure that the child know the meaning of them, and can construe them perfectly, as thus:

First construe truely.

Puer Oh child, *qui* who, *es* art, *discipulus* a Scholler, *mihi* to me, *atque* and, *cupis* dost covet (or desire) *doceri* to bee taught; *ades* come, *huc* hither; *concipe* conceive (or consider well) *dicta hæc* these sayings, *animo tuo* in thy minde.

In this sentence, parse the child after the same manner; and examine him accordingly. As aske, where he must begin to parse? he answereth at *Puer*, Oh boy, because he began to construe there. And if you aske why he began to construe there? he answers by the rule of construing, which biddeth, If there be a Vocative case to begin commonly at it. Then aske what *Puer* is like? he answereth, like *Magister*: which being known of him, and he perfect in his examples, can tell you by *Magister*, what declension it is, how to decline it, and the number; and also by the increasing of it short in the Genitive case, he can tell you, it is the Masculine Gender by the third speciall rule.

Parse as they construe.
Examining in parsing.

Puer.

For

THE GRAMMAR SCHOOLE

For the case; that it is the Vocative, knowne by calling, or speaking to the child. And if you aske, why it may not be *pueri* nor *puero*, but *puer;* he answereth, because it is the Vocative case, which is like the Nominative.

Qui.   Afterwards, demanding what must be parsed next; he answereth *qui;* because *qui* is next in construing: and also that *qui* is a Pronoune Relative, set down in the Accedence, and there declined. Also that it is the Nominative case, comming before the Verb *es*, following it next, by the rule of the Relative; When there commeth no Nominative case: as, *Miser est* qui *nummos admiratur*, qui admiratur. So qui es. For the Gender likewise; that it is the Masculine Gender, because so is his Antecedent *puer* going next before in construing: with which the Relative agreeth, by the rule of the Relative: The Relative agreeth, &c. as *vir sapit qui pauca loquitur:* vir qui. So puer qui. Also he can shew it, to be the Masculine Gender, because in words of three terminations, the first is the Masculine, the second the Feminine, the third is the Neuter. Likewise he can tell why it must be *qui*, not *cuius*, nor *cui*, nor any other; because it must be the Nominative case to the Verbe, by the rule of the Relative; because no other Nominative case commeth betweene them. So all other questions. For person; it is made the second person here, by a Figure called Evocation, because it agreeth with *puer*, which is made of the second person; and by the same figure Evocation, as every Vocative case is, by reason of *Tu* understood.

Es.   Then followeth *es*, art: of which word the child can give you all the Questions; because he hath learned it in his Accedence, and is perfect in it. If you aske why it must be *es*, and not *est*, nor any other word; he answereth, because it is Thou art, not He is, nor I am: and also because in that place *qui* his Nominative case is of the second Person, as was said. If you then aske what is parsed next; he answereth

Discipulus.   *discipulus*, because he construed so: and *discipulus* is like *Magister*. Which being knowne, the child can tell the questions of declining, Gender, Case, Number, and the rest

apper-

THE GRAMMAR SCHOOLE

appertaining thereto. If you demand further, why it must be *Discipulus*, and not *Discipulum;* why it must be a Nominative case after the Verbe, and not an Accusative according to the rules, The Accusative followeth the Verbe; and also that rule, Verbes Transitives are all such, &c. He answereth, because this Verbe *Sum es*, is a Verbe Substantive intransitive, not a transitive; and therefore will have such case after it as it hath before it: as *Fama est malum*, est malum. And that other rule for the Accusative after the Verbe, is of Transitives, whose action passeth into another thing. So to proceede thorowout for shortnesse, thus:

Mihi] is parsed next, because it is next in construing. It is a Pronoune set downe in the booke. All the questions are plaine in it, except why it must be the Dative case: which is, because it is governed of *es*, the principall governour going before, by the rule of the Dative case after *sum*: Also *sum* with his compounds, except *possum*, &c. and for that, one word may governe divers cases; or it may be governed of *Discipulus*, the Substantive, by the rule of the later of two Substantives turned into a Dative: wherein the English rules are defective. The rule in Latine is, *Est etiam ubi in Datiuum vertitur*, &c. *Mihi.*

Atque] is next in construing; and therefore in parsing. It is a Conjunction Copulative, set downe in the booke. It is also a Compound Conjunction; compounded of *at* and *que*. It is put here to couple these members of the sentence together, viz. *Cupis doceri*, with that going before. *Atque.*

Cupis] is next: It is like *Legis*, Thou readest. Which being knowne, the child can tell you what Conjugation, Moode, Tense, Number, Person, the word *Cupis* is; and why it must be so, and not *cupiunt*, nor any other word; because *atque* couples like Moodes and Tenses: and it is, Thou covetest. Other questions which fall out in declining, the child can tell; as, why it is *Cupiui*, by the exception of the rule *Fit pio, pi*. And why *Cupitum*, by the rule *Cupis.*

rule of the ending of the Preterperfect Tense in *vi*. *Vi fi tum.*

Doceri.   *Doceri*] is parsed next, because it is construed next, it is in my booke, saith the child, and it signifieth to be taught. Thus hee can answer all the questions, why it must be *doceri*, not *docere*: also why it must come next; because an Infinitive Moode doth commonly follow another Moode.

Ades.   *Ades*] is next in order, and is in all things like *es* in *sum*, compounded of *ad* and *sum*: and it must be so, because it is Come thou, nor *adest* nor *adsunt.*

Huc.   *Huc*] is next in construing, because Adverbes are usually joyned to the Verbs, to declare their signification. It is an Adverbe of place, signifying hither, or to this place.

Concipe.   *Concipe*] is like *Lege*, Reade thou. This being knowne, the part of Speech, Moode, Tense, Number, Person, and most questions of it are knowne; except two or three of the compounding it with a Preposition, and of changing of the letters *a*, into *i*. Which are to be learned after by the rule in their booke.

Dicta.   *Dicta*] is next, because the Substantive, which is more principall, and to which the Adjective agreeth, must go before the Adjective in parsing; though in our English, Adjectives go before. It is like *Regna*. The Accusative case, Neuter Gender, Plurall Number, following the Verbe *Concipe*, by Verbes Transitives. And the Neuter Gender by my rule of all words like *Regnum. Omne quod exit in um.* And *Neutrum nomen* in *e*. It must also end in *a*, in the Accusative case, Plurall Number, because all Neuters do end so in three like cases. It is derived of the Supine *dictu*, by putting to *m*.

Hæc.   *Hæc*] is a Pronoune demonstrative, agreeing with *dicta*, by the rule of the Relative, and it must be so by that rule.

Animo.   *Animo*] followeth next. The Substantive to be set before the Adjective; it is like *Magistro* in all. The Ablative case, because it signifieth in the minde, and not into the minde: because, in, without this signe, to, serves to the Ablative case, and is a signe thereof. It is also by the rule, Sometime

this

THE GRAMMAR SCHOOLE

this Preposition *In*, is not expressed, but understood.   *Tuo.*

Tuo] A Pronoune possessive, like *bono* or *meo*, but that it wants the Vocative case. It is set downe in my booke, and doth agree in all things with *animo;* by the rule of, The Adjective, whether it be Noune, Pronoune, or Participle, agreeth with his Subst. &c. And so on for the rest.

In this first kinde of parsing, you may at the first entrance, aske them the English of each word, and cause them to give you the Latine, and so to parse, looking on their Latine bookes, to incourage them; just in the manner as is set downe. *Manner of hearing their Lectures.*

After a little time cause them to do it, looking onely upon the English Translation.

Then (which is the principall, and wherein you will take much delight) cause them amongst themselves to construe and parse out of the translation untill they can say, or out of their Authors, whether they can sooner: but when they come to say, cause them to say each sentence, first in English, then to construe and parse them; and all with their bookes under their armes: what they cannot repeate so, they will do it if you aske them questions of it. You shall find by experience, that with a little practice, all who are apt will do this as soone, readily, and perfectly, as looking upon their books (if so that they but understand the matter well before) and so they will make all their owne most surely. Thus I would have them to do in *Sententiæ, Confabulatiunculæ* and *Cato*, if you will. After in the middle fourmes, as in *Esop's* Fables, *Ovid de Tristibus*, or *Ovids Metamorphosis*, &c. (because either the matter is not so familiar and easie to remember, or the Lecture longer) I would have them to parse thus, looking upon their translation; but then to parse wholly in Latine: and I can assure you by some good experience, that through God's blessing, you will admire their profiting.

Spoud. Surely Sir, this way of parsing is most direct and plaine; and the benefits must needs be exceeding great: but give me leave yet to aske one thing of you, concerning this parsing amongst the younger. I have heard of some,
                                          who

THE GRAMMAR SCHOOLE

How to know by the words what part of Speech each word is.

who would teach their enterers to know by the very words, what part of Speech each word is. How may that be done?

Phil. This may very well be done, even according to this ensample above, when everything is examined at large. As for example, Cause your Scholler to do this:

1. To marke out all those words, which they have learned, being set downe in their Accedences; as Pronounes, Adverbes, Conjunctions, Interjections: that they know all those. Then have they nothing to trouble them with; but they may know that all the rest are either Nounes, Verbes, or Participles, or else Gerunds or Supines belonging to the Verbes, or some other Adverbes.

2. For those parts of Speech, when your Scholler can construe perfectly, they may be knowne by their Latine and English together, whether they be Nounes, Verbs, Participles, or such Adverbes; chiefly, when they are very cunning in their parts of Speech in their Accedence, and questions thereof.

Substantives, and how to know them.

1. The Noune Substantives, that they are names of things, to which you may put to *a* or *the*, as was said; as A boy, A Scholler, but cannot put to the word Thing, in any good sense. And more fully, when the Latine is put to the English; as *puer* A boy, like *Magister: discipulus* a Scholler, like *Magister*.

How Adjectives.

The Noune Adjectives contrarily, though they signifie a thing; yet they cannot stand by themselves in sense, unlesse you put to (Thing) or some other word expresly or understood; nor you cannot in proper speech put to *a*, or *the*. As we cannot say properly, A good, An evill: but we may say A good man, A good house, An evill thing. And when they are put Substantively, yet thing is properly understood: as *bonum* a good thing, *summum bonum* the chiefest good thing; though we call it the chiefest good.

By the Latine adjoyned. In us or er like bonus.

These Adjectives also may be more fully understood, by the Latine words: as if they end in *us* or *er*, they are like *bonus*; except those expressed like Nounes, and some few strange Adjectives, which are partly Substantives, partly Adjectives

THE GRAMMAR SCHOOLE

jectives set downe in the Rule, *At sunt quæ flexu, &c.* as *Pauper, puber, &c.* And in the Rule, *Hæc proprium &c.* as *Campester, &c.*

Adjectives ending in *ans* or *ens* (though they be Participles) and also in *x*, and *rs*, as *concors*, are declined like *fœlix*; and some in *or*, as *memor*. *In ans, ens, x, rs, like fœlix.*

Adjectives in *is, ior,* [or *jor,*] and *ius* signifying the Comparative degree, that is to say, more, are like *Tristis*: as *Dulcis, dulcior, major, dulcius.* *In is, ior, ius, like tristis.*

Finally, if the child but know his word to be like any of the examples of a Noune Substantive, as *Musa, Magister, Regnum, Lapis, Manus, Meridies,* he knoweth it to be a Noune Substantive. If like *bonus, unus, fœlix, tristis,* a Noune Adjective.

Verbes also may be knowne most plainely by the English and Latine together. As, the words signifying, doing, suffering or being, and like *Amo, doceo, lego, audio,* or *amor, doceor, legor, audior,* or any person comming of them in any Moode or Tense, and signifying like to them, are Verbs. So by the signes of the Tenses; do, did or didst, have, hast, hath, had or haddest, shall or will. By the signes of the Moods; Or signes of the Passive: as am, are, art, was, were, wert, be or beene: where any of these signes are, are commonly Verbes. *How Verbes may be knowne.*

And finally, this is generall for the Verbes, as for the Nounes; that if either the child can tell of himselfe, or you but shew him what person in a Verbe it is like, he can tell presently that it is a Verbe, and most questions belonging to it. As knowing that *cupis* thou covetest, is like *legis* thou readest, he knoweth presently, that it is a Verbe of the third Conjugation, and the Moode, Tense, &c.

The like may be said for Gerunds of Verbes, and Supines, in all things, as for the Verbe before. *Gerunds. Supines.*

Participles also may be plainely knowne by the very same manner; and chiefly by their endings in English and Latine both together. As the words that end in [ing] in English, and in Latine in *ans* or *ens*, are Participles *Participles*

of

THE GRAMMAR SCHOOLE

Present tense
Preter tense.

of the Present tense. Words in *d*, *t*, or *n*, and their Latine in *tus*, *sus*, *xus*, are Participles of the Preter tense. So those words ending in *rus* in Latine, and signifying to do or about to do, of the Future in *rus*. And in *dus*, signifying to be done like the Infinitive Moode Passive, are Participles of the Future in *dus*.

Future in rus.
Future in dus.

How to know other Adverbes besides those in the bookes.

Adverbes (besides those in the booke, or which should bee set downe in the English Adverbe as they are in the Latine) are but either Adverbes of Comparison or of Qualitie.

Of comparison.

Those of Comparison end in *us*, and signifie more; or in *e*, and signifie most.

Qualitie.

Those in Qualitie end in *è*, or in *er* commonly; and all of these have their English usually ending in ly: as *doctè* learnedly, *doctiùs* more learned, *doctissimè* most learnedly.

To conclude, they are also marked commonly in all bookes which are well printed, with grave accents over them, to distinguish them from other parts of Speech, and that they may be knowne to be Adverbes: as *doctè* learnedly, to be knowne from *docte* the Vocative case of the Adjective: so *doctiùs*. And thus are all Adverbes of like nature; as *quàm* then, to be distinguished from *quam* which, the Pronoune.

And also sundry Prepositions are so marked: as *ponè*, *propè*.

Spoud. I approve and see the reason of all this, that the parts of Speech may bee knowne or neerely guessed at: and do still go on with you, rejoycing in this our conference.

Notwithstanding, there is one thing I have heard, that a child may not only be taught to know what part of Speech each word is, but also of what Conjugation any Verbe is, if he heare but onely the first person of the Indicative Moode; that is, if he heare but onely the Verbe named. Now this seemeth to me unpossible; there being so many hundreth Verbes all ending in *o*, and they so like one another; and

THE GRAMMAR SCHOOLE

and especially those of the first and third Conjugation, so hard to be distinguished, that this may oft trouble a learned man, and much more a young Scholler. *A child may know of what Conjugation any Verbe is.*

Phil. This which seems to you so impossible, may bee likewise easily done by a child, by the helpe of this direction which I shall heere set downe before your face, and by one observation or two arising therefrom.

A direction how to know the Conjugation of any Simple Verbe (and so of the compounds which may be knowne by the Simples) although the learner never heard the Verbs before.

ALl Verbes in *ĕo*, as *doceo* are of the second Conjugation: except a few of the first Conjugation; and *eo, queo, veneo*, which are of the fourth. *A direction to know the Conjugations of Verbs.*

So Deponents also in *ĕor* are of the second: as *fateor, tueor, mereor, vereor, misereor, liceor*, with their Compounds.

And onely these sixe, so farre as I remember. So also Verbs in *ēo* alone. *Verbes of the second Conjugations easily knowne.*

All Verbes ending in *io* as *audio*, and in *ior*, as *audior*, and they onely, are of the fourth Conjugation, except a few which are of the third, and some of the first noted after. *Verbes of the 4. Conjugation.*

All the Verbes of the third Conjugation are set downe in the rules of the Verbs, at *Tertia præteritum formabit, &c.* Except these which follow in this Table, which are also of the third. *Verbes of the 3. Conjugation.*

acuo

THE GRAMMAR SCHOOLE

üo	*acuo, arguo, exuo, imbuo, induo, minuo, sternuo, suo, tribuo, delibuo, inde delibuens.*	po	*clepo, repo, scerpo, sculpo.*	These also of the first and third, in a diverse signification.
bo	*glubo.*	pso	*clepso, proclepo* to steale or take away.	*appello, as,* to call.
co	*ico.*		*depso,* to kneade.	*appello, is, appuli,* to bring to, to approach, to arrive, to apply.
do	*cudo, pando, pindo, idem quod pinso, prehendo, contractè prendo, accendo, succendo, incendo, à cando, obsoleto, defendo, offendo, infendo, à fendo obsoleto.*	to	*beto, quasi bene ito,* to go. *Varro.*	
		sco	All in *sco,* except *senisco, as,* to push with the head, as Rams do, *lucret.*	*caluo, as,* to make balde. *caluo, is,* to deceive.
go	*cingo, clango, fligo, frigo, mergo, mungo, plango, sugo, tego, tingo, ungo.*		These old words *clingo. cingo. cludo. claudo. lido. lædo. geno.* for *gigno. pago. pango. tago. tango. spicio. specio.*	*colo, as,* to straine. *colo, is,* to worship. *como, as,* to trim or lay out. *como, is,* to kembe.
guo	*distinguo, extinguo, restinguo, instinguo, à stinguo, obsoleto, inde instinctus, instinctor, consulo, molo,* to grinde: but *immolo, as: promello,* an old word, signifying to stir up strife, or to make delay.			*consterno, as,* to trouble in mind, *consterno, is,* to strew or scatter. *dico, as,* to vow, offer, dedicate. *dico, is,* to say.
lo			These following are of the first and third conjugation in the same signification. *lano, sono, tono, piso* to stampe out the huskes of corne.	*duco, as,* as *educo, as,* to bring up. *duco, is,* to leade. *euallo, as,* to cast out of the dores. *euallo, is,* to vanne or to make cleane corne.
mo	*remo, gemo, tremo.*			
no	*dispenno,* to stretch abroad. *vanno,* to vanne come.			*fundo,*

THE GRAMMAR SCHOOLE

fundo, as, to found, establish.
fundo, is, to poure out.
iugo, iugas, to yoake.
iugo, is, to cry like a Kite.
lego, as, to send Embassador, or to bequeath.
lego, is, to reade, to gather, steale, or to strike sayle.
mando, as, to command.
mando, is, to eate.
nicto, as, to winke often.
nicto, is, to open as a hound, or, quest as a spaniel
pedo, as, to prop.
pedo, is, to breake winde.
sero, as, to locke.
sero, is, to lay in order or to sowe.

These are of the second and third;
pendeo, pendo.
tergeo, tergo.

These old words,
fervo.	*ferveo.*
cavo.	*caveo.*
fulgo.	*fulgeo.*
olo. for	*oleo.*
cluo.	*clueo.*
frendo.	*frendeo.*

excello and *excelleo.*

Of the first Conjugation,
There are some in *eo, as, beo, meo, screo.*
And all other Verbs in *ĕo,* derived from Nounes in *ĕus,* & *ĕa,* as *calceo:* of which also is *calcio,* of *calceus; nauseo,* of *nausea.*
Some also in *īo,* as *frio, hio, pio* to please God by sacrifice.

Trauio.
gargaridio. } old.

And all other verbs in *īo* and *īor,* derived from Nounes in *īus, ia, ium,* and *ies:* as *nuncio,* of *nuncius.*

saucio,
ascio.
somnio,
calumnior.
auxilior.
glacio à glacies.
satio à saties.
meridior.
And so all other like; except these which are of the fourth Conjugation; as *ineptio,*
insanio,
vesanio,
lascinio,
balbutio,
fastidio,
munio à mænia.

Finally all other Verbes besides these, are of the first Conjugation; and are infinitely moe then of all the other three Conjugations jointly.

Spoud.

THE GRAMMAR SCHOOLE

Spoud. I see that to be true, which is said of a Parable; that before it be expounded, nothing seemes more hard and obscure; but when it is once made plaine, nothing is more cleare: so is it in this, and in the way of construing and parsing, by the helpe of the rule, and in divers other things, which you have shewed unto me.

Phil. It is most certaine which you say. I my selfe have so thought, this matter of knowing what Conjugation any Verbe is of, to be impossible: but you see what things, paine and diligence may finde out. As for this direction, I acknowledge it wholly to that painfull M. *Coot*, who writ the English Schoolemaster. And by this one, it may evidently appeare, what further benefit the Latine tongue might have hoped for by his labours, if God had vouchsafed him life to have brought them to perfection; or if others had bin carefull to have afforded him that helpe that they might have done.

This direction for finding out the Conjugation received from M. Coote.

Spoud. It is a great pitie that he, or any other, should want any helpe or meanes, in so profitable a worke; and a token of God's displeasure, that we should be deprived of such profitable labours. But, to returne againe to this matter of parsing; you have very well satisfied me concerning the yonger sort, and their parsing: yet there is one thing concerning this Grammaticall parsing amongst the yonger, which I must crave of you. That there is so much time spent in examining every thing; the Master asking each question particularly, and the scholler answering: which besides the losse of time, it is a very great wearinesse to the Master. I pray you shew me the very shortest and speediest way which you know.

Much time and toile in parsing through examining each word by the Master, how helped.

The surest, thortest & speediest way of parsing. Some account to be by pen and characters.

Phil. Some very learned would have this parsing to be by pen, and by characters for shortnesse: But howsoever this may be done among two or three schollers taught by themselves; yet this seemeth to require farre more time (both for writing to set every thing downe, and also for examining by the Master) then can be performed in the common Schooles.

But

THE GRAMMAR SCHOOLE

But the shortest, surest, most pleasant and easie way both to Master and Scholler, I touched before, if you marked it: and it is this. After that they have been entred, and trained up some twelve-moneth in the lowest fourme by questions, as the example was shewed out of *Qui mihi*; then, when they goe into the next fourme, as into *Cato*, to begin to parse every one of themselves, as reading a Lecture, each his piece: I meane chiefly, when they come to say their lectures. *But this will be found most short and easie.*

To parse every one his piece, as reading a lecture. Example.

For example: To take those two first verses of *Qui mihi*, because they are parsed before. First let them construe perfectly in the Grammaticall order, as was said: then let each parse his word or two, as they construed, ever marking the last word, and in all things just in the same manner, as is set downe before; but only to do it of themselves without any question asked for the saving of time: Onely the Master or he who heareth them, is to aske where they do omit any necessary question in any word, or where they misse.

As thus: The child having construed, begins of himselfe. *Example.*

Puer oh child. It is to be parsed first, because it is first in construing. *Puer*, is like *Magister*. A Nowne Substantive common of the second Declension; and so he declines it, so farre as the Master thinkes meet, at least giving the Genitive case; for if they be well entred in the Accedence, they will easily decline any regular word, when they know the example. After he shewes the rule when he hath declined any Nowne or Verbe. As *Puer pueri*, is a grave increaset; and therefore of the Masculine Gender. *Nomen crescentis penultima si Genitivi sit gravis, &c.* Also the Vocative case knowne by calling or speaking to, as *ô Magister*, ô Master. *Qui* is next, a Pronoune Relative, &c. So every thing in the same order as before.

To helpe your schollers to do this: Remember first when you have used for a time to parse them over every word so, before them, that by your example they may do the like; then for speedinesse, when they have taken their lectures of them-

To helpe to prepare the children for parsing, at taking lectures.

THE GRAMMAR SCHOOLE

themselves, that they can construe to cause only some one of them to reade over their lecture, to see that they pronounce it right, and to construe if you will, if time so permit, or to reade it over to them: And what words you observe to be hard, which you thinke they know not, you may aske them what those words are like, and how they are declined, or where they have learned them, as was said. Where they cannot tell any, or have any new word which they have not learned, to make that plaine unto them, and to cause every one of the fourm, as was directed in the third generall observation, to make a line under that word, or under that part of the word, that letter or syllable wherein the difficulty lyeth; for a little helpe will bring the whole remembrance. Or to note them with some marke or letter over the head of the word.

To marke out hard words.

See more of this marking before in the third generall observation.

As in the enterers, to note the Declension with a *d*, over the head, and a figure signifying which Declension.

The Conjugation with a *c*, and a figure.

Heteroclites with an h; lame Verbs with an *l*.

For example, to take that which was parsed before.

Example of marking hard words amongst the first enterers.

        2. *d.*   2. *d.*   3. *c.*
Qui mihi discipulus puer es cupis atq; doceri,

Huc ades hæc animo concipe dicta tuo.

Here *discipulus* and *puer* are noted for the second Declension, *cupis* the third Conjugation, *ades* for the Composition of *ad* and *sum*, *concipe* for changing *a* into *i*.

Or you may marke Declensions and Conjugations, by setting downe but onely the first letters of the examples,

        mag.   *mag.*   *leg.*
which they are like, as *discipulus, puer, cupis, &c.*

The former is the shorter, after they are acquainted with it, and can make their figures.

To cause them to turn to the rules.

And ever what rules they are not well acquainted with, turne them, or cause them to turne to the places in their Grammar, and to shew them to you.

                                                        As

THE GRAMMAR SCHOOLE

As they proceed to higher fourmes, and are more perfect, marke only those which have most difficulty, as Notations, Derivations, figurative Constructions, Tropes, Figures, and the like: and what they feare they cannot remember by a marke, cause them to write those in the Margent in a fine hand, or in some little booke. *Noting in the higher fourmes.*

In the lower fourmes, you marking one book your selfe, all the rest may marke theirs after it, untill they can doe it of themselves.

The ends of this marking, are, as I said, that they may take most paines in these; for the rest they can doe easily, and almost of themselves. And also that when they construe and repeat over their Authors, they may oft pose over those hard words. And thus they shall keepe their Authors, which they have learned, to the credit of the Schoole, with the profiting and incouragement of the Schollers, that they shall goe farre safer forward, then by any other meanes. *The ends of marking their books.*

Spoud. But this marking may indanger them, to make them Truants, and to trust their bookes more then their memories.

Phil. I answer no, not at all, but to performe a necessary supply unto the children. For children's memories are weak: and they are soone discouraged by the difficulty of learning, and by the hastinesse of their Masters. And therefore they had need of all helpes at the beginning. It is also the oft repeating over of any thing, which imprints it in their memory for ever. *Marking the hardest words for remebrance, is no meanes to make them Truants, but helpeth and preventeth many inconveniences.*

Of the contrary, try amongst children of the sharpest wits, and best memories, if they have not some helps, whether they will not be long in learning to parse a Lecture: and when they can parse it very perfectly, prove them within a moneth after, whether they will not have forgotten, at least, most of the hardest & chiefe matters. Then thinke what a vexation it is to the honest-minded Master that would be always ready to give an account of the profiting of his scholler; and withall when he must teach him every thing anew. *Evils of the want hereof.*

THE GRAMMAR SCHOOLE

new, which he hath forgotten: neither his leisure will any way serve; he having many fourmes, and being to goe forward daily with his Schollers in some new construction; besides many other like discommodities.

Spoud. But there is another kinde of apposing, which I remember in the note, and which you mentioned; how to teach children to make right use of their Authors, even of every sentence: which I conceive not of.

How to appose so as the children may get both the matter, words, and phrase of each Lecture.

Phil. Yes truely: and that which I account the very principall, and as it were the very picking out of the kernell, and the life of every Lecture; to get both the matter and also the Latine words and phrases, that they make them their owne, to use as need or occasion requireth.

Spoud. That must needs be of excellent use: for though it be commendable to construe and to parse perfectly; yet it is nothing in regard of this, if they shall not know how to make their use and benefit either of matter or phrase.

Phil. This is onely by apposing them, as I shewed you the manner in the *Propria quæ maribus*, to make them to understand; and that first in English, then in Latine: and to cause them to answer both wayes, both words and sentences, as time will permit.

Example.

For example; Take a sentence or two in the beginning of that little booke, called *Sententiæ Pueriles*: which is well worthy to be read first unto children, because it hath been gathered with much care and advice to enter yonger schollers, for Latine and matter every way meet for them: but of it and others, what I finde best to be read, I shall shew you my experience in another place. Out of it you may examine thus, for making use, as in these first sentences of it:

Amicis opitulare.
Alienis abstine.
Arcanum cela.
Affabilis esto, &c.

☞
Manner of propounding the questions.

1 If you will, you may aske them by a question of the contrary, Must you not helpe your friends? The child answereth, Yes. Then bid him give you a sentence

to

THE GRAMMAR SCHOOLE

to prove it; he answereth, *Amicis opitulare.*

Or aske by a distribution thus; Whether must you helpe or forsake your friends? The child answereth, I must helpe them. Then bid him to give you a sentence; he answereth, *Amicis opitulare.*

Or thus by Comparison; Whether ought you to helpe your friends, or others first? or friends or enemies, &c. When the child hath answered, ever bid him to give his sentence. So on in the rest.

The more plainly you can propound your question, that the child may understand it, and may answer in the very words of his Lecture, the better it is: so to examine the words severally: How say you Helpe? he answereth *Opitulare.* Friends, *Amicis.* But of this more after.

After the child hath been a while thus practised, then use to examine both in English and Latine together: I meane propounding the questions first in English, then in Latine; and so let him answer, that the matter and English may bring the Latine with them: which they will certainly doe. The manner I shewed in examining in the Latine rules: I will set down one other example, in the sentences of three words: *Amor vincit omnia.* *Example of examining English and Latine together.*

Out of this sentence I examine thus:

Q. What is that, that will overcome all things?
A. Love.

Then bid him give the sentence.
A. Amor vincit omnia.

Or thus: Is there any thing that can overcome all things?
A. Yes; Love.

Or thus more particularly, to put delight and understanding into them.

Q. What is that which wil overcome learning, and make it our owne?
A. Love of learning, or loving our bookes.
Q. Give me a sentence to prove it.
A. Amor vincit omnia, &c.

Then

THE GRAMMAR SCHOOLE

Then examine in Latine the very same things; but uttering them in Latine and English together, as thus:
Quid vincet omnia? what will overcome all things?
R. *Amor.*
Or thus: *Est ne aliquid quod potest omnia vincere?* Is there any thing that can overcome all things? R. *Imò.*
Q. *Quid est?* What is it?
R. *Amor.*
Q. *Da sententiam.*
R. *Amor vincit omnia.*
Q. Or thus: *Quid vincit amor?* What wil love overcome?
R. *Omnia,* All things.

Examining for the use in Cato.
So in *Cato,* to aske, as in the first verses,
Q. What thing ought to be chiefe unto us?
A. The worship of God.
Q. *Da sententiam.*
R. *Cultus Dei præcipuus.*
Q. *Da carmen.*
R. *Si Deus est animus nobis, &c.*

Then to examine the Verses by parts if you will: as *Si Deus est animus, &c.* Aske,
Qualis est Deus? What is God, or what a one?
A. *Animus,* A spirit, or spirituall nature or being.
Q. *Qui ita nobis dicunt? vel, Quæ nobis ita dicunt?* Who or what things tell us so?
R. *Carmina,* Verses, or Poets who write Verses.
Q. *Quomodo tum colendus est?* R. *Pura mente.*
Q. *Da carmen.*
R. *Si Deus est animus, &c.*

Thus throughout, onely where they understand not, to propound the question, as well in English, as in Latine, and so to answer.

Also you may examine thus: What Verses in *Cato* have you, to prove that the worship of God must be chiefly regarded?   A. *Si Deus est animus.*

What against sleepinesse and idlenesse?
A. *Plus vigila semper, &c.*

So

THE GRAMMAR SCHOOLE

So in *Esop's* Fables, besides the examining every piece of a sentence in the Lectures, as thus: *Gallus Gallinaceus, dum vertit stercorarium, offendit gemmam, &c.*

Q. Quid offendebat Gallus, dum vertit stercorarium?
R. Offendit gemmam, &c.

Cause the children to tell you, what every Fable is about or against, or what it teacheth, in a word or two. For example, thus:

Q. What Fable have you against the foolish contempt of learning and vertue, and preferring play or pleasure before it?
A. The Fable of the Cocke, scratching in the dung-hill.
O. after this manner:
Q. What Fable have you against the foolish neglect of learning?
A. The Fable of the Cocke, scratching in the dung-hill.

2. Cause them to make a good and pithy report of the Fable; first in English, then in Latine: and that either in the words of the Author, or of themselves as they can; and as they did in English. For, this practice in English to make a good report of a Fable, is of singular use, to cause them to utter their mindes well in English; and would never be omitted for that and like purposes.

In other bookes the use is according to the quality of them: as in *Confabulatiunculæ Pueriles*, the use is for the children to talke to one another in the same words.

In *Sturmius* Epistles, and others of *Tully*, the phrase principally is to be regarded: as also in the Poets, the Poeticall phrase.

For the further use of them for imitation both in Epistles and Verses, I shall speake after in their place.

But for the Latine and matter to make it our owne, I find the chiefe benefit to be in oft reading them out of the Grammaticall translations, over and over, untill the Latine be as familiar to the Scholler, as the English: as I noted in the benefits of the Translations. And also in saying and repeating of

Examining the Fables in Esop for the use.

Making a report of their Fables.

The use according to the quality of the books.

The surest way to make both Latine and matter our owne.

K

THE GRAMMAR SCHOOLE

of Lectures (I meane the weeke's worke) to construe without booke: and then repeate them in Verse, or as they are without booke.

Use in Tullies Offices, and Ovid's Metamorphosis.

For the use in *Tullies* Offices and *Ovid's Metamorphosis*, I have set in the Margents of the Translations, the summe of all the matter; which is very notable and full of delight.

☞ *Parsing in the higher fourmes.*

For parsing in the highest fourmes: to observe onely for brevity sake the difficulties of Grammar or Rhetoricke, speciall phrases, or the like; the Master onely to examine what things they omit, or wherein he suspects them negligent. In parsing they may use these or the like speeches:

Hæ sunt difficultates Grammaticæ. Hæ elegantiæ Rhetorices. Reliqua leviora, trita, puerilia, &c.

In Poetry also, *Phrases hæ: Epitheta ista.*

☞ *All in Latine in the higher fourmes.*

Let all this examination be onely in pure Latine, from the very lowest fourmes, except the first or second at the most. For they will do it with ease, if they be rightly entered from the beginning; and that the Master ever do it before them where they are not able: and to observe wherein they are most defective, therein to take the most paines.

Spoud. Although these things cannot but be very profitable; yet being so many, they can hardly be put in practice in the greater Schooles. I pray you rehearse me the summe of those which you take most necessary for daily use.

The summe of all, principally necessary for parsing.

Phil. These are they; Cause your Schollers to reade first their Lecture distinctly, and construe truly: to parse as they construe, ever marking the last principall word: to shew where they have learned every hard word: what example every hard word is like; so to give rules and examples of them, both for Etymologie and Syntax, as after for the Rhetoricke, as need is. To parse of themselves, as reading a Lecture, and that onely in Latine when they come to say, except, in the very lowest fourmes: to make some marke at every hard word, which you note unto them, to take the most paines in those: amongst the younger specially, to examine each Lecture for the use; whereby they may get matter, words, and phrases, all under one. In the highest, for speedinesse

speedinesse to examine onely the difficulties, as you see requisite, to let them name the rule in a word or two; to observe phrases and Epithets. In all repetitions amongst themselves, and construing over their Authors, to examine over all the noted words, as time permits.

CHAP. X.

Of making Latine; how to enter children therein with delight and certainty, without danger of false Latine, barbarous phrase, or any other like inconvenience.

Spoud.

Now that you have thus lovingly ledde me by the hand, thorow the way of laying a sure foundation amongst my children, for all the grounds both of Accedence and Grammar; and also of construing and parsing: let me still intreate you to goe on before me; and next to shew how I may enter my children for making of Latine: and then thorow the severall exercises thereof. This I have found extremely difficult. For although it hath beene a matter of continuall vexation and paine unto my selfe, and of feare unto my poore Schollers; yet have I found as little profiting therein, as in any other: but that my children will still write false Latine, barbarous phrase, and without any certainty, after a very long time of exercise. *To enter children to make Latine, a matter ordinarily extremely difficult, and full of toyle both to Master and Scholler.*

If therefore you can guide me the way, how I may do that which you spake of before, that I may enter my children with ease and delight, both to my selfe and to them; and also surely without danger of making false Latine or barbarous phrase; I shall further acknowledge my selfe, to have received yet a greater benefit then in all the former. And above all, if you can direct me how by that time

THE GRAMMAR SCHOOLE

time that they have beene not two yeeres onely, but three or foure yeeres in construction, they may be able to make true Latine, and pure *Tully* in ordinary morall matters. For I my selfe have hardly beene able to cause my children to do this at fourteene or fifteene yeeres of age; nor then to warrant that which they have done: neither do I thinke that it is much otherwise in our ordinary Schooles.

Phil. I shall willingly satisfie your request herein likewise, and shew you what I have found: onely let me see, as before, what course your selfe have taken, to enter your children.

<small>*The ordinary manner in countrey Schooles, to enter Schollers to make Latine.*</small>

Spoud. I have taken that course which I thinke is commonly practised in Schooles: I have given them *vulgars*, or Englishes, such as I have devised, to be made in Latine: and at the first entrance I have taught and heard them, how to make every word in Latine, word by word, according to their rules. After a while I have onely given them such vulgars, and appointed them a time, against which they should bring them made in Latine: and at the perusing and examining of them, I have beene wont to correct them sharply, for their faults in writing, and for their negligence; and so have given them new Englishes: and it may be I have told them the Latine to the hardest words. This is the course that I have followed.

<small>*The butcherly feare of making Latines.*</small>

Phil. Our learned Schoole-master M. *Askam*, doth not without cause tearme this the butcherly feare of making Latines. For to omit the trouble to the Master, and that it will require a ready wit, to give variety of such vulgars to the children; and also that it will aske good learning and judgement to direct them, to make not onely true Latine, but pure phrase withall; what a terrour must this needes be unto the young Scholler, who feares to be corrected for every fault, and hardly knoweth in any thing, what to make upon sure and certaine grounds? But for the way, this I find the shortest, surest, and easiest both to Master and Scholler; and which will certainely effect whatsoever hath been said: and that Master and Scholler may proceede cheerefully and

<small>*The shortest way to enter Schollers to make Latine easily and surely.*</small>

THE GRAMMAR SCHOOLE

and boldly, to justifie what they do.

1. See that your Scholler be very cunning in his Accedence, and Grammar as he goeth forward: and chiefely in Nounes and Verbs, to be able to give each case of a Noune, and every tense and person of a Verbe; both Latine to English, and English to Latine, as I wished you, and shewed the manner before; at least by the perfect knowledge of the terminations of them. *1. To be exceeding perfect in their rules; chiefly in Nounes and Verbes.*

2. Besides the construing and parsing their Lectures without booke, in the lowest fourmes, or out of the English translation, accustome yourselfe, in examining the Lectures of your first enterers, to do all after the manner of making Latine; as it were causing them every day to make the Latine of their lectures, and give a reason why each word must be so, and not otherwise, their bookes being shut. I set you downe the manner before, in the use of the Grammaticall rule for making Latine, in that example; *Aptissima omnino sunt, &c.* Yet to repeate you a word or two for your little ones; take that first sentence, *Amicis opitulare*: when you have made them to understand the meaning, and examined it, so as was shewed; aske but thus: *2. Each day to make the Latine of their lectures, and give a reason why each word must be so.*

How can you make this in Latine; Helpe friends? How say you, Helpe thou? *Examples repeated.*

A. *Opitulare.*
Q. *Opitulare* like what?
A. Like *Amare amator*, be thou loved.

So all the questions for parsing: then aske, why is it Helpe thou, and not, Be thou helped, as *Amare amator*, be thou loved. He answereth, Because it is a Verbe Deponent, and signifieth Actively, to helpe; and not, to be helped.

After aske the next word:
Q. Whom must you helpe?
A. Our friends.
Q. How say you friends?
A. *Amicis.*
Q. What is *Amicis* like?
A. *Magistris.*

So

THE GRAMMAR SCHOOLE

So the questions of declining and the like. Then aske, why not *amici* nor *amicos*, the Accusative case after the Verbe.

A. Because the Verb *Opitulor*, to help, will have a Dative case, by that rule of the Dative, To profit or disprofit, &c.

<small>These in stead of all vulgars.</small>
These may be in stead of all vulgars or Latines, both for ease, delight and certainty to your selfe and the child: and so you may ever have the Author to warrant both Latine, and phrase.

<small>3. Continuall reading lectures, and repeating what they have learned out of the Grammaticall translations, is continuall making Latine, to cause children to come on very fast.</small>
3. Next unto this, that continuall beating out and reading their Authors, both Lectures and repetitions, out of the translations, is continuall making Latine thus, (as I said, in the use of the translations) that children will come on very fast for propriety, choise, and variety of the best words, phrase, matter, and sentences of their Authors, to begin to have a store-house in themselves of all copie, as I have observed.

<small>4. Shewing fit sentences to turne into Latine out of the book which they learne, or others. The manner of their entrance to write Latine, to profit in English, Latine, Writing faire, and true, and all under one. Their bookes how ruled.</small>
4. After the former practised for a time, you may chuse some sentences which they have not learned, and cause them to make those, either some out of this booke of Sentences, or any other of like easie morall matter; and then let them beginne to write downe that which they make in Latine.

This manner I find to be most easie and speedy for children at their first entrance: whereby they may profit in English, Latine, Writing true and faire, and all under one labor.

Let them have their paper-books in *octavo*, of the one side to write the English which you give them; on the other to set the Latine directly overagainst it, and word for word.

To this end cause them to rule their bookes both sides at once, or at least the lines of one side directly against the other: their lines a good distance asunder, that they may interline any thing, if they misse any word; or for copie and varietie, to be set over the head if you will. On the first side toward the right hand, in which the English is to be set, to leave a lesse margent: on the other side for the Latine a greater margent; because the Latine may bee written in a

lesse

THE GRAMMAR SCHOOLE

lesse space then the English; and also to write all the hard words in the margent of the Latine, the Nominative case of the Noune, and the first person of the Verbe, if so you please. Then cause so many as are to write Latine together (having books, pen, inke, and copie before them, and every thing so fitted) to write as you speake, so faire as possibly they can.

Herein you are to dictate, or deliver unto them word by word, the English of the sentence, which you would have them to turne into Latin; and to do it according to the manner of the Grammaticall translation, every word in that order and in propriety of English, answering the Latine as neere as you can. Also, you are to utter each word leasurely and treatably; pronouncing every part of it, so as every one may write both as fast as you speake, and also faire and true together. *Manner of dictating the English which they are to turne into Latine.*

And to the end to helpe for writing true Orthographie, besides the former knowledge of spelling; as they are writing, cause every one in order to spell his 2. or 3. words together, speaking up, that all his fellowes may heare, and may goe on in writing, as fast as he spels and you speake. Those who can write faster, to take paines to write fairer; your selfe also to walke amongst them in the meane time, to see that every one of them write true and faire, and to shew them their faults by pointing them to their copies, and using like directions mentioned in the helpes of writing, of which I spake before. *A principall practice for writing true Orthography both in English and Latine.*

After; when they have thus set downe the English, cause every one in the like order to make his word or two in Latin after the manner which was shewed before for making latin, the very words of the Author in the naturall or Grāmaticall order: & cause them al to write the same words, as he speaks, unlesse any of them be able to make it before of themselves; who may correct, as they heare their fellowes to make it. Cause also every one to spell the words which he hath made in Latine, like as they did in English, so as all may heare, and go surely in writing true Orthography in Latine likewise.

And

THE GRAMMAR SCHOOLE

Repeating or construing without booke that which they have written.

And when they have done a sentence, or so much as you thinke good for a time, then cause them, to the end to commit it the better to memorie, to trie which of them can repeat the soonest without booke, that which they have made. First saying the English sentence; then giving it in Latine, or construing it without booke, which all of them who are apt, will do presently, or with a very little meditation. Or, which is shortest of all, appoint them folding their bookes, to looke onely on the English, and reade or construe it into Latine: or on the Latine, to reade or construe it into English. Thus as time will permit.

Benefit hereof for certaine directions to Master & Scholler, and to get Writing, English, Latine, all at once.

By this meanes you shall have a certaine direction in all things, both for your selfe and your Scholler, to goe truely and surely, both for propriety, Latine, phrase, and whatsoever you can desire. By this exercise also your Scholler shall get both Writing, English and Latine, all under one. And therefore an houre may be well imployed daily in this exercise.

To imprint it by repetition the next morning, together with their evening exercise.

And to imprint this, yet better; you may cause them the next morning at shewing their exercise made that night, to repeate together with it, that againe which they thus made the day before (if time permit:) Either some one to repeate all, or moe, every one a piece, or as time will permit; but all to be able to do it as they are called forth. Through this also they shall from the first entrance, get audacity and utterance, with good matter which will bring the Latine with it.

Spoud. But how shall they doe for composing, or right placing of their words? which you know is a principall matter in writing pure Latine.

Phil. I would have them first for a time exercised in this plaine naturall order; for this is that which Grammar teacheth: and then to compose or place finely; which belongeth to Rhetoricke, after. As first to write well in prose, before they beginne in verse: so in prose, to go upright and strongly, before they learne to go finely; and as M. *Askam* speaketh, first to go, before they learne to dance. But for entring them into composition, thus you may do.

How to enter young Schollers for composing, or right placing their Latine.

1. When

THE GRAMMAR SCHOOLE

1. When they have made it in the naturall order, onely reade unto them how *Tully*, or the Author, whom their sentence is taken of, doth place it, and some reason of his varying, and cause them to repeat both wayes, first as they have written, after in composition.

2. After that they have been practised a while in the former plaine manner, you may make them to doe thus: Cause their bookes to be ruled in three columnes; in the first to write the English, in the second the Latine *verbatim*, in the third to write in composition, to try who can come the neerest unto the Author.

Spoud. Although I take it that I do conceive your meaning in all, and do see an evident reason of everything: yet because examples do most lively demonstrate any matter; I pray you set me downe one example hereof, and shew me what Author you thinke most fit to gather the sentences forth of.

Phil. In stead of your Author, I thinke and finde *Tullies* sentences the fittest; and of those sentences, to make choise of such in every Chapter, as are most easie and familiar to the capacitie of the children. This booke I doe account of all other to be the principall; the Latine of *Tully* being the purest and best, by the generall applause of all the Learned: and because that booke is a most pleasant posie, composed of all the sweet smelling flowers, picked of purpose out of all his workes; that one booke, together with the bookes which the children have or do learne, shall also helpe to furnish them with some sentences, containing some of the choisest matter and words, belonging to all Morall matters whatsoever; whether to understand, write, or speake thereof; that they shall be able to goe forward with much ease and delight; first in it, and then in the other sentences adjoyned to it, or what exercise you shall thinke fit.

Tullies sentences the fittest to dictate sentences out of.

For an example: take these little sentences, which heere follow, as they are set downe in the first Chapter of *Tullies* sentences, *De Deo eiusque natura*, dictating the words to them plainely

THE GRAMMAR SCHOOLE

plainly, as the children may most readily make them in Latine. In their little paper-bookes they may write the English on the first side, with the hard Latine words in the Margent, the Latine on the other over against it, in two columns; the first plaine after the Grammar order, the latter placed after the order of the Author: your selfe may make the words or phrases plaine to them, as they are set in the Margent.

An example of Dictating in English, and setting downe both English and Latine; and the Latine both plainly and elegantly.

	Dictating according to the naturall order.	*Ordo Grammaticus.*	*Ordo Ciceronianus.*
a *Hath ever bin* b *At any time* (verb) *inspiration some divine* c *à* flatus, *breathing into.*	No man *a* hath been *b* ever great without (*verb*) some divine *c* inspiration.	*Nemo fuit unquam magnus sine afflatu aliquo Divino.*	*Nemo magnus; sine aliquo afflatu divino umquam fuit.* 2. *de Natura Deor.*
d *Bring to passe.*	There is nothing which God cannot *d* effect, and truely without any labour.	*Est nihil quod Deus non possit efficere, & quidem sine labore ullo.*	*Nihil est quod Deus efficere non possit, & quidem sine labore ullo.* 3. *de Nat. Deor.*
e *Ignoro.* f *In what mind, or with what minde.*	God cannot *e* be ignorant *f* of what minde every one is.	*Deus non potest ignorare, qua mente quisque, sit.*	*Ignorare Deus non potest, qua quisque mente sit.* 2. *de Divinatione.*

In these examples all is very plaine; except that in the first sentence we say, and so translate in our English tongue, some divine inspiration; according as it is more elegantly in Latine,

THE GRAMMAR SCHOOLE

Latine, the Adjectives usually before the Substantives; and not inspiration some divine, which would be very harsh; and so likewise after [without any labour] although in the Grammaticall order in the Latine, the Substantive is to be set before the Adjective ; as the child is to begin to make Substantive in Latine before the Adjective, and to make the Adjectives to agree unto, or to be framed according to the Substantives; as we have shewed in the rules observed in the Grammaticall translations.

If you thinke this course overtedious to write both wayes in Latine; then let them turn it only into the naturall order, thus *verbatim* by pen: and afterwards in the repeating that which they have made, aske of them how *Tully* would place each word, and to give you reasons thereof: and then to reade the sentence in the booke unto them; so by the booke and some rules to direct them how to proceede. *How to learne to compose the Latine otherwise.*

For further practice in translating amongst all the higher, after they grow in some good sort to write true Latine *verbatim*, according to the former kinde of translating; let them still write downe the English as you dictate it, or out of a translation; & try who can come neerest unto *Tully* of themselves, composing at the first; and then after examine their exercises, bringing them to the Author. *Translating into pure Latine, and composing it of themselves, trying who can come neerest unto Tully.*

For preventing of stealing, or any helpe by the Latine book, if you doubt thereof, you may both cause them to write in your presence, and also make choise of such places which they know not where to finde. *For preventing stealing.*

If you catch any one writing after another, and so deceiving both himselfe and you, correct him surely who suffereth him to steale. *And writing after one another.*

For going on faster, and dispatching more in translating; beside their writing so, you may onely aske them the words or phrases in English, how they can utter them in Latine; and then let them give them in Latine, every one his piece: first naturally, after, placing each sentence. Thus to goe thorow daily a side, or a leafe at a time, or as leisure will serve. *How to goe on faster, and dispatch more in making Latine.*

Besides

THE GRAMMAR SCHOOLE

Translating into English after M. Askam's maner. Use hereof.

Besides these, this may be a most profitable course as they proceed, to cause them to translate of themselves *Esop's* Fables, or *Tullies* Sentences, or the like, into plaine naturall English, so as was shewed; and to cause them the next day, for their exercise, to bring the same thus in English, and to be able without booke, first to make a report of it (striving in the Fables, who shall tell his tale in best words and manner) and then to reade it into the Latine of the Author out of the English, and be able to prove it, and where they have read the hard words. And after all these to try (if your leisure will serve) how they can report the same in Latine, either in the words of the Author, or otherwise, as they can of themselves; which all who are pregnant, and will take paines, will be able to doe very readily: by this you shall finde a great increase.

Here you must be sure that they have no translation to helpe them secretly.

The most speedy and profitable way of translating and composing.

Lastly, this is yet the more speedy and profitable way of all, as my experience doth assure me, to cause them to reade *extempore* some easie Author daily, out of the translation into the Latine of the Author, or out of the Author into English; first plainly, then artificially. And to this purpose I have translated, as I shewed, *Corderius* Dialogues, whose Latine you know to be most easie, familiar and pure; and also *Terentius Christianus;* with *Tullies* sentences to helpe hereunto.

For translating an Author into Latine.

For further translating, or turning any Author or piece of Author, or other matter into Latine; if it be difficult, direct your Schollers to resolve the speech into the naturall order of the words, so neere as they can. Secondly, if there be any phrase, which they cannot expresse; to resolve and expresse it by some other easier words and phrase of speech, with which they are better acquainted; and to doe it by Periphrasis, that is moe words, if need be. Besides, for such English words which they know not to give Latine unto; let them use the helpe of some Dictionary: as *Holyoke* or *Barret: Holyoke* is best, wherein the proper words and more pure, are first placed.

One good use of Holyoke's Dictionarie.

Things to be considered in translating.

In all such translating either English or Latine, this is carefully to be observed; ever to consider well the scope and

THE GRAMMAR SCHOOLE

and drift of the Author and the circumstances of the place; and to labour to expresse lively, not only the matter, but also the force of each phrase, so neere as the propriety of the tongue will permit.

But for all this matter of translating, that practice of reading the English out of the Authors, and the Authors backe againe out of the translations, shall fully teach it, so farre as it concerneth the scholler for propriety and getting of the tongues. For translating any Latine Author into English, only to expresse the sense and meaning of it; the sense and drift of the Latine Author is principally to be observed, and not the phrase nor propriety of the tongue to be so much sought to be expressed or stucken unto. The like may be said for the Latine. But this kind of translating into Latine, is onely for such schollers as are well grounded through long exercise and practice in the former kind of Grammaticall translation, and in *Tullies* or their Authors phrase.

Best direction for translating.

Translation for the sense and meaning.

This kinde of translating into Latine is for schollers well grounded.

Spoud. I hope I understand you right, and doe like very well of all, so farre as I conceive. Only let me intreat you, as in the former, to rehearse the principall heads briefly concerning this matter.

Phil. This is the summe of all, for this entrance in making and writing Latine. 1 Readinesse in their rules, chiefly in examples of Nownes and Verbes. 2 Making their owne Lectures into Latine daily. 3 Continuall reading or repeating Lectures and all their Authors which they have learned out of the Grammaticall translations, into the Latine of the Authors. 4 Translating into *Tullies* Latine, out of a perfect Grammaticall translation, or as the English is so dictated unto them, and reading or repeating the same out of the English into Latine. And lastly, out of the naturall order, into the order of *Tully.* 5 Translating into English Grammatically of themselves, and reading forth of the English into the Latine of the Author, or writing it downe.

Summe of all.

By these meanes constantly practised, they will soone be able to make, write, or utter any ordinary morall matter in pure and good phrase; especially if the matter be delivered

unto

unto them in the naturall order of the words. Make triall: and I doubt not but you will not onely confirme it, but still finde out more for the common good.

CHAP. XI.

Of the Artificiall order of composing or placing the words in prose, according to Tully *and the purest Latinists.*

Spoud.

BUt yet here is one thing wanting: namely, the rules which you spake of for composing or placing the words after the manner of the purest Latinists; I meane for turning them forth of this naturall order, into the Rhetoricall order, or order of *Tully*; without which, the truest and best Latine is little worth. This I have found very hard for my schollers to performe; neither have I had any certaine grounds that they might stand upon. Moreover, this I have knowne for certaine, that many young schollers, the more confusedly that they can transpose, or disorder the words of a sentence, the more excellent they thinke it to be, when as it is indeed most absurd to the learned eare.

Phil. Although this may seeme to belong to Declamations and Orations, because therein there is the greatest labour for curious composition & setting of words, as wherein schollers stand to shew most art, endevouring to perswade: yet it is in truth generall to all Latine, whether Translations, Epistles, Theames or whatsoever, and doth bring great grace and commendation to every part thereof; and contrarily being neglected, doth detract very much from the most excellent speech, be the matter and words never so choise. And because there is special use of it, in the practice

Composition a matter of difficulty.
The errour of young schollers in displacing sentences.

Composition generally belonging to all Latine.

THE GRAMMAR SCHOOLE

practice of all the translations: & in all this matter of making Latine for turning or composing out of the Grammaticall order, into the order of the Author, I will affoord you the best helpe I can. But for so much as neither *Tully* nor any of the purest Latinists do alwayes observe the same order, and therefore I take it that no certaine rules can be given as perpetuall; I will take those which *Macropedius* hath set down, as being the most easie of all that I know. He hath sundry generall precepts.

Precepts of Composition or placing the words in Latine, as they are set downe by Macropedius, *in the end of his method of making Epistles.*

The I. Precept.
Of placing the Nominative case, the Verbe, and the oblique case.

A Perfect sentence consisting most commonly of a Nominative case, a Verbe and an oblique case; this order is kept in placing ordinarily.

1 The oblique cases (that, is all besides the Nominative and the Vocative) are commonly placed in the beginning, the Nominative case in the midst, the Verbe in the end: For example; in the sentence following, the Grammaticall order is thus: *Oblique cases first. Nominative in the midst of the Verb in the end.*

Cæsar occupauit civitatem munitissimam hostium.

The Artificiall order is usually thus:

Munitissimam hostium civitatem Cæsar occupauit.

Yet if the oblique case be of a Nowne negative, or a Nowne of denying, it may be put elegantly in the end: as *Cæsare* *Except in ob- liques of denying.*

Cæsare fortunatiorem legimus neminem.

Yea, any Adjective or Participle may be put so, when the chiefe point of the matter or meaning resteth in it: as

Cæsarem in morte ferè omnes putant miserum.

The II. Precept.

Adjectives before.
Words placed betweene the Adjective and Substantive.
1. Genitive case.

THe Adjective is ordinarily to be placed before the Substantive. And betweene the Adjective and the Substantive may be fitly placed the Genitive case of the latter of two Substantives; as in this sentence the Grammaticall order is:

Severitas magna Cæsaris incussit terrorem hostibus.

The artificiall order thus;

Terrorem hostibus magna Cæsaris severitas incussit.

2 Word governing the Genitive.

Also betweene the Adjective and the Substantive of the Genitive case, the word governing the Genitive case, may be elegantly placed, as in this sentence:

Clementia Cæsariæ majestatis dedit pacem, & tranquillitatem provincijs.

The artificiall order may be thus:

Cæsariæ clementia majestatis pacem & tranquillitatem provincijs dedit.

The III. Precept.

Verbe.
Adverbe.
Conjunction.
Preposition.

BEtween the Adjective and the Substantive, *Tully* sometime placeth the Verbe in like manner; sometime the Adverbe, sometime the Conjunction, sometime the Preposition alone, or with his case; as,

Magnum profecto laborem Cæsar assumpsit, quem fermè ab ipsis ad nos venisse Gadibus aiunt, ut hostes suæ quidem maiestati rebelles, nostris autem supra modum rebus infestos armis subigeret. Quam ob causam, perpetuum illi amorem, & gratiam debemus immortalem.

The

THE GRAMMAR SCHOOLE

The IIII. Precept.
Of Adverbes and Prepositions.

ADverbs and Prepositions with their cases may be pla- *Adverbes and* ced any where, wheresoever they shall seeme to stand *Prepositions.* most fitly to please the eare: yet most elegantly before the Verbe or Participle which they declare. As,

Debitam, pro contemptu suis hostibus diuque dilatam severitatem, Cæsar tandem exhibuit, sed clementissimè mitigauit.

These are the principall of his rules which are necessarie.

To these may be added,

1. That this is to be observed very usually: That the word 1. *Observation.* governed is commonly placed before the words gover- *Word governed* ning, contrary to the Grammaticall order. As here: *first.*

Fortitudo Cæsaris potitur victoria.
The artificiall placing may be fitly.
Cæsaris fortitudo victoria potitur.

Also if in a sentence there be mention of two persons, 2. *Observation.* the one as it were an agent, the other a patient, they stand together most usually and elegantly; the agent commonly *Person doing* first: as, *first.*

Cæsar did great wrong to Pompey in this point.
Hac una in re magnam Cæsar Pompeio injuriam fecit.

These Precepts are set downe, to the end to direct young *The end of these* Schollers; yet so as we must not thinke, as I said, that these *precepts.* are ever to bee followed strictly; because neither *Tully*, nor *Cæsar* himselfe, nor any who have beene most curious, did ever observe the same: for that should be a fault rather, as we shall see after.

Notwithstanding, by practice in composing, and observation

THE GRAMMAR SCHOOLE

How to attaine to right composition.

vation in *Tully, Cæsar,* and the best Authors, and trying how neere we can come unto them in translating into Latine, by comparing ours with theirs; and finally weighing how every sentence may so fall as may best please the eare; Schollers may attaine much certainty and commendation herein.

More exquisite observation in placing and measuring sentences.

Observation in placing and measuring sentences in prose. Butler's Rhetor. Chap. 15.

FOr most exquisite observation of placing and measuring sentences, Rhetorically, in prose by Schollers of riper judgement, in their Theames, Declamations, Orations or the like, reade *Talæus'* Rhetoricke *de Numero Oratorio. Cap.* 17, 18.

Out of which Chapter, and out of the Commentaries of *Minos* upon them, these precepts may be further observed, which follow.

Prose must be unlike verse.

No verses to be made in prose.

1. That the placing and measuring of the sentences in prose, should be both unlike to the placing in Poetry, and also each sentence unlike other. And therefore that the Scholler make no verses in his prose, but that he shun them warily.

Verses cited in prose

Though in any exercise in prose, chiefly in Theames, he may cite verses out of other Authors either for authority or delight.

Beginning and ending of sentences most observed: endings chiefely, not to be like a verse.

2. That the beginning or ending of a sentence, in prose, be not the beginning or ending of a verse; although this be not so faulty in the beginning of a sentence, as in the end; where the fault is more observed.

Endings of sentences to be carefully weighed.

3. That the ending of sentences be specially weighed, which are chiefly marked of all, and therefore are to bee carefully varied, that they may not be displeasing.

This neede not be above sixe syllables.

4. That this curious Observation of the endings neede not be regarded above sixe syllables from the end; and those to stand on feete of two syllables, Trochees principally.

5. That

THE GRAMMAR SCHOOLE

5. That we do not continue the same feete in the ends; but dispose them diversly: not all long syllables, nor all short, unlesse more seldome; but commonly tempering long and short syllables together, as Trochees and Iambickes, sometimes Spondees and Perrichees, yet so as we bee not curious. *The same feete not to be continued in the ends. Tempering commonly long and short syllables.*

That sentence is accounted most sweete and excellent which endeth in two Trochees; *viz.* the first syllable long, the last short, as in this sentence: *The sweetest sentence ending in 2. Trochees.*

Deinde patris dictum sapiens temeritas filii cŏmprŏbāuĭt.

This endeth in an Iambicke and two Trochees.

Tully useth this most often. So as in that one Oration *pro Pompeio,* it is observed to be an hundreth and fourteene times. *Tullies ending.*

7. Yet the variety ought to be such, that this art of placing or setting the number of syllables, may not bee observed of every one, and so be made envious, nor the curiositie ridiculous; but to be laboured so as it may most delight and draw on others. *The art of placing to be hid.*

8. That the sounds of the very words and letters are the principall things to bee respected herein. For the elegant composition, is that which is made by a sweet sound of letters and words. *Sounds to be respected principally, in words or letters.*

9. Therefore words of the best sound are to be observed; and amongst them most elegant Adverbes and bonds of Conjunctions to be noted diligently. *Words of the best sound.*

Words sounding well are these:

1. Verbals: as, *Dominatrix, gubernatrix.*
2. Compounds: as, *pernoscere, excruciari.*
3. Superlatives: as, *Conspectus iucundissimus.*
   Ad dicendum paratissimus.
4. Words of moe syllables: as, *Moderatio animi.*
   Tempestas anni.

10. Words

THE GRAMMAR SCHOOLE

Insolent words to be avoided.

10. Words which are insolent, hard and out of use, are to be as warily avoided, as rockes for Mariners.

That all words may have an easie and distinct sound.

11. That in all sentences, the words have an easie and distinct sound: that is, neither harsh nor gaping; but that they fall and conclude aptly and sweetly, fitting best the utterance of the pronouncer, and as may most like the care of the hearer.

These are the summe of those rules as I remember. Although the excellency hereof is rather to be attained, by use and practice, then by any certaine precepts.

Spoud. Sir, these put in practice may bee very sufficient for whatsoever can be required in this behalfe, as it seemeth unto me.

Phil. These things concerne onely the placing and setting or measuring of sentences, which is one little part of Rhetorick; and there the rest is to be fully sought, and how to adorne all sentences with tropes and figures. The practice of these is to be used in their severall exercises.

Thus have I gone thorow all these at large, for making the Accedence and Grammar perfect, for construing, parsing, and making Latine; applying my selfe to the capacity of the rudest learner in so many words; because these things well performed, all other learning will be most pleasant, as was said before.

Spoud. But one other thing by the way, I cannot omit to demand that I did observe by your speech, that you would have your very enterers to make some exercise every night of themselves.

No Evening to be passed without some little exercise against Morning.

Phil. I would indeede have no Evening passed without some little exercise in Latine by all from the very lowest who begin to write Latine; I meane something to be shewed the next day about 9. of the clocke.

Spoud. But what exercise would you appoint to such little ones, that could be easie enough and meete for their capacitie?

Phil. I would appoint them to beginne even at, In Speech be these eight parts, &c. and so give them 2. or 3. lines

THE GRAMMAR SCHOOLE

lines of it for every one to turne into Latine. And for the examining what they have done where they are many, and time will not permit to examine what every one hath done; to cause some one or two whom you suspect to be most negligent, first to pronounce the English without booke, then to construe it into Latine without booke, or to repeat the Latine as they have made it: but to construe it without booke, is farre the surest, or to reade and construe it out of the English. And according to these as they pronounce, and are shewed their faults, for all the rest to correct theirs. If any be found not to correct so, or to have omitted his exercise, to have his due correction.

Though I have tried many wayes and exercises for these little ones, to do privately by themselves, yet I find none comparable to this: for this they will doe with much facilitie and contention, after a little that they are entered; being helped somewhat by their Latine rules, which they have learned.

Thus they may alwayes have a fit exercise, and know aforehand what they are to do. This also will further much towards their parsing in Latine, and better imprinting their rules.

CHAP. XII.

How to make Epistles, imitating Tully, *short, pithie, sweete Latine and familiar; and to indite Letters to our friends in English accordingly.*

Spoud.

I Am very glad I asked you this question: I rest fully satisfied in it, as also in all this matter of making and composing Latine, for the evidence of the meanes; and doe thanke you heartily for directing me so particularly.

Now

THE GRAMMAR SCHOOLE

Now let us come, I pray you, to the other severall exercises of Schollers, which are to be practised in Schooles continually, for the more full attaining of the knowledge of the Latine tongue.

Of making Epistles.

And first for the making of Epistles, in such sort as was mentioned before; that is, imitating *Tully*, short, pithy, full of variety of good matter, sweete Latine and familiar; and for inditing of like Letters in English:

Difficulty of making Epistles, purely and pithily.

I have found this exercise of making Epistles, no lesse difficult then the former toyle of making Latine. For although I have taken great paines: yet after long practice, I have hardly beene able to bring them to a shew of that which you speake of, I meane, so to imitate and resemble *Tully*; but that they will frame them of long sentences, matters unfit for an Epistle, flash and to little purpose; but very childish, and, more like unto a Theame or an Oration, then to an Epistle. Thus I see it to be also amongst the chiefe of the Schollers, of sundry of those who are much accounted of, and wherein the Schollers seeme to do the best.

Inditing English Letters little exercised in Schooles.

As for inditing Letters in English, I have not exercised my Schollers in them at all; neither have I knowne them to be used in Schooles: although they cannot but be exceeding necessary for Schollers; being of perpetuall use in all our whole life, and of very great commendation, when they are so performed. Therefore I still crave your helping hand to direct me, how to bring my Schollers to the attaining that faculty.

Phil. Let me first heare what way you have taken in these, like as you shewed me in the former kinds; and then I shall relate unto you how this may be done, so shortly as I can.

The ordinary meanes of directing Schollers to make Epistles.

Spoud. I have done this: I have read them some of *Tullies* Epistles, and also some part of *Macropedius* or *Hegendorphinus de conscribendis Epistolis*. I have directed them that they are to follow the rules set downe in the severall kindes of Epistles there mentioned, and made the ex-

THE GRAMMAR SCHOOLE

examples plaine unto them.

Moreover, I have used oft to put them in minde of this, that an Epistle is nothing but a Letter sent to a friend, to certifie him of some matter, or to signifie our minde plainely and fully unto him. And therefore looke how wee would write in English, so to do in Latine. These and the like are the helpes which I have used: and I take it to be the most that are done in ordinary Schooles.

Phil. I like well of your reading of *Tullies* Epistles, which indeed is the very foundation of all: but for *Macropedius* and *Hegendorphinus*, although their paines were great; yet I cannot see, but that they will rather require an ancient learned Master to understand, and to make use of them, then a younger Scholler, who is to be taught how to speake. Also for telling a child that he must invent variety of matter of his owne head, to write to his friend; this is a taske overhard to ordinary wits. For what can a child have in his understanding, to be able to conceive or write of, which he hath not read or some way knowne before? according to that Maxime: *Nihil est in intellectu quod non prius fuerat in sensu.* *Hard for children who have no reading to invent variety of matter of themselves.*

Therefore omitting these, wherein I myselfe have also found a great deale of toyle, with small fruit; I will set you downe plainely the very direct way, so neere as yet I have beene able to learne; and whereby I am out of doubt, that that same faculty may be easily gotten, of writing such Epistles; fully expressing *Tully*, as was said, and of inditing Letters like unto them, which are our usuall Epistles, as the Latine were of the Romanes.

The way may be this:

1. When your young Schollers have gone thorow *Sententiæ pueriles*, *Confab. Cato*, or the like; and can begin to make Latine in some such good sort as was shewed; let them then reade *Tullies* Epistles, gathered by *Sturmius*; as being of the choysest of his Epistles, and most fitte for children. This one booke rightly used, may sufficiently furnish for making Epistles, so far as shall be needfull *Helpes for making Epistles.* 1. *Reading Tullies Epistles.*

for

THE GRAMMAR SCHOOLE

for the Grammar Schooles. It would be read by them twise in the weeke at least, until they had gone thorow a good part thereof; unlesse they be able to reade it of themselves *ex tempore*, or be the helpe of the translation.

2. Making them very perfect in every Epistle.

2. As they reade every Epistle, or before they are to imitate any one, make them as perfect in it as you can, and as time will permit: not onely in construing, parsing, reading out of the Grammaticall translation into the Latine; but also to be able to give every phrase, both Latine to English, and English to Latine.

Also cause them to make you a report what the summe of the Epistle is; and this if you will, both in English and Latine also, as was said of the Fables.

3. To cause them to make another Epistle in imitation thereof.

3. Cause them for their exercise to make another Epistle in imitation of *Tullies* Epistles, using all the phrases and matter of that Epistle; onely applying and turning it to some friend, as if they had the very same occasion then presently: and also changing numbers, tenses, persons, places, times: yet so, as thereby to make all the matter and phrases, each way most familiar to them, and fully their owne.

To do this first in English, then in Latine.

And first let them do this in a good English stile, as was said; I meane, in making an English Letter first: setting it after the manner, as they did their English Translation; of that page of their booke towards the left hand, or on the first columne, the Latine on the other over against it, sentence for sentence.

To set the Epistles after the manner of the Translations.

Herein they are onely to differ from the Translations, that they do not in these Letters sticke so much to words, to answer word for word both English and Latine; as to write purely and sweetly, as well in English as in Latine; and to expresse their mindes most fully in both, and in most familiar manner.

4. Making answers to Epistles.

4. The next day to make another Epistle, as being sent from their friend to whom they writ, in answer to that which they writ the former day: and in that to answer every sentence from point to point, in as short manner as the former Epistle was, still retaining the same phrases as much

as

THE GRAMMAR SCHOOLE

as they can. I will take for example the first Epistle of *Stur-*   *Examples of imi-*
mius. The more easie it is for the children, the better it is.   *tating Epistles.*

M.C. Terentiæ *falutem plurimam dicit.*

SI vales, benè est: ego valeo. Nos quotidiè tabellarios vestros   Tullies *Epistles*
expectamus: qui si venerint, fortasse erimus certiores quid   *to be imitated.*
nobis faciendum sit: faciemusque te statim certiorem, vale-
tudinem tuam cura diligenter. Vale. Calendis Septembris.

    The summe of the Letter is; That *Tully* writes to his wife   *The manner of*
Terentia: signifying unto her, that he was in health: that he   *the report of the*
waited for the Letter-carriers daily: how by them he should   *summe of the*
know what to do; and that he would then certifie her of all   *Letter.*
things. And so concludeth, wishing her to looke well to her
health. The Letter bare date the Calends of September.

An English Letter in imitation of Tully.	*An Epistle in imitation of Tully.*
IF you be in health, it is well: I am in health. I have long looked for your * Messengers. When they shall come, I shal be more certaine what I am to do; and then I will forthwith certifie you of all things. See that you look very carefully to your health.	EPISTOLA. *SIvales benè est: ego quidē valeo: diu tabellarios vestros expectani. Cū venerint certior ero quid mihi faciendum sit. Tum autē te omnib de rebus certiorem faciam. Tuam diligentissimè valetudinem fac ut cures.* * *Letter carriers.*
The answer.	Responsio.
I Rejoyce greatly of your health. I am sorry that you have looked for the Carriers so long. They will be with you very shortly, and then indeed you shal be more certain what to do.	*TE valere maximè lætor. Doleo quòd tabellarios tam diu expectâsti. Statim vobiscum erunt, & tum re vera certior eris quid tibi agendum sit.* *Nos*

THE GRAMMAR SCHOOLE

| We shall forthwith looke to heare of all your matters. I will in the meane time looke to my health, as you advise. Farewell. | *Nos deindè vestra omnia audire sperabimus. Meam interim ut suades curabo valetudinem. Vale.* |

 Antonius Schorus in the end of his booke, *de ratione discendæ linguæ Latinæ*, hath sundry examples. I will set downe one Epistle, imitated two wayes: the first keeping almost the words and forme of *Tullies* Epistle; the other imitating onely the forme, but changing the words. *Tullies* Epistle is this:

Tullies Epistle. *Aulo Trebonio, qui in tua provincia magna negotia & ampla, & expedita habet, multos annos vtor valdè familiariter. Is cum antea semper & suo splendore & nostra cæterorumque amicorum commendatione gratissimus in prouincia fuit, tum hoc tempore propter tuum in me amorem, nostramque necessitudinem, vehementer confidit, his meis literis, se apud te gratiosum fore. Quæ ne spes eum fallat, vehementer te rogo: commendoque tibi eius omnia negotia, liberos, procuratores, familiam: inprimisque ut quæ T. Ampius de eius re decreuerit, ea comprobes, omnibusque rebus eum ita tractes, ut intelligat nostram commendationem non vulgarem fuisse.*

The first example of imitation of the former Epistle. The first imitation more following the words, is this:
 Petro *Fabro, qui in vestra vrbe & magna negotia, & multos amicos habet, multos annos vtor familiariter. Is cum antea semper & suo splendore, & nostra cæterorumque amicorum commendatione gratissimus in hac nostra Repub. fuit, tum hoc tempore propter tuum in me amorem nostram que necessitudinem vehementer confidit, his meis literis se apud te gratiosum fore. Quæ ne spes eum fallat, vehementer te rogo: commendoque tibi eius omnia negotia, amicos, cognatos, inprimisque vt quæ procuratori de eius rebus videbuntur, ea comprobes: omnibusque; rebus eum ita tractes, ut intelligat nostram commendationem non vulgarem fuisse.*

The second imitation. The second imitation, expressing the forme.
 Petrus Faber, *qui tibi notus est, & magnas res apud nos gessit, multos annos mihi valdè familiaris fuit. Is cum semper & sua dignitate, & beneficijs multis erga me, meis omnibus gratissimus*

THE GRAMMAR SCHOOLE

tissimus fuit: tum nunc ob tuum erga me animum, nostramque conjunctionem, non dubitat quin hac mea commendatione sit in maxima gratia apud te futurus. Quod vt fiat, summoperè te oro: committoque tuæ fidei & curæ omnes res eius, amicos, cognatos, parentes: præcipuè verò vt quæ procurator de rebus eius agat, ea consilio tuo iuues: & ita honorificè cum accipias, ut sentiat has nostras literas apud te pondus habuisse.

Thus practising and training up your scholler by little and little; first for imitation, more neerely following the words; afterwards only the forme, and such phrases as shall seeme fittest: and ever first writing their English Letters, and then their Latine answering thereunto; you shall see that they will come to a lively imitation of *Tully*: especially if you exercise them well in *Tully*, in such sort as is prescribed.

Spoud. Sir, this must needs be a most sure and ready way. But in imitation what things am I to direct them to observe? *The rule in imitation.*

Phil. That they take onely so much as is needfull, and fit for their purpose, leaving out all the rest; that they add what is wanting; alter and apply fitly to the occasions, according to the circumstances of times, persons, places, and the like; that nothing may appeare stolne, but all wittily imitated. Be sure that they know perfectly the matter and the phrase, of that which they should imitate: and then nothing will be hard, in imitation of Epistles, Verses, or whatsoever.

Spoud. What is then the summe of all, which you would have principally exercised, for the speedy attaining this faculty?

Phil. That your schollers have daily a piece of an Epistle, or a whole Epistle appointed them, matter and phrase made very familiar unto them; then one day to make an Epistle in imitation, and that both English and Latine; the next day to make an answer in like manner: thus to proceed, untill they come to some good perfection. And so much may serve for Epistles.

CHAP.

THE GRAMMAR SCHOOLE

CHAP. XIII.

Of making Theames full of good matter, in a pure stile, and with judgement.

Spoud.

Next after Epistles, Theames doe follow; wherein if you can direct me also, how these likewise may be composed by children, so as to be couched full of good matter, written in a pure stile, and with judgement, and with as much certainty and readinesse as you have shewed me for making their Epistles; I shall remaine more beholden, and returne home with greater hope to doe good.

For the Epistles, it cannot be otherwise, but that the course set downe must needs produce that effect, which you have affirmed; by reason of these singular patterns of *Tully* which children have to imitate. But what patterns or helpes can you have for Theames any way comparable to those?

Phil. What patternes Schollers may have, you shall heare after: but first relate unto me, as in the former, what way you have used, for the entring of your children in making their Theames.

Spoud. I have according to the custome in Schooles, read them some of *Apthonius'* rules, and so it may be, have begun with Apologues or Fables, or rather with a Chreia: & in their Chreia, I have first made the severall parts of it, or of their Theame so handled, very plaine unto them, with the manner of the proofes of it; and of gathering reasons to amplifie it, according to the same.

I have then given them a Theame to make, following the example in their booke, to prosecute the same parts of the Theame; as *Exordium, narratio, confirmatio, confutatio,*
con-

THE GRAMMAR SCHOOLE

conclusio, and also to follow the severall places, to amplifie each thing by. I have withall shewed them how to doe it: as to try what they could gather of themselves; and withall to seeke *Tullies* sentences what they could finde out of it, or out of other bookes to their purpose. But yet (alas!) that which my children have done hereby for a long time, they have done it with exceeding paines and feare, and yet too-too weakely, in harsh phrase, without any invention, or judgement; and ordinarily so rudely, as I have been ashamed that any one should see their exercises. So as it hath driven me into exceeding passions, causing me to deale over-rigorously with the poore boyes. Whereby some of them, whose Parents have been more tender, seeing their children heavy and unwilling to the Schoole, have suffered them to leave off the Schoole, and so to lose all which they had gotten before; others also have been made so fearefull, that they would rather desire to goe to any base trade or drudgery, then to be schollers, and hereby have very much reproached my schoole: Because, as they have over-rightly complained, they must be beaten for not doing that, which they knew not how to doe; so that this feare is worse to them then the first for making Latines. *The inconveniences of this course.*

And yet notwithstanding, in their entring to make Theames, and so likewise into versifying, I have not known how to avoid it, but I have been enforced to use so much sharpnesse, as to make them call all their wits together, and to stir them up to all diligence and paines; or otherwise I should have done no good at all.

Whereupon very great inconveniences have insued: and yet, as I said; I have seene very little fruit to answer unto my paines.

Phil. I doe not see how by this course, these evils could be avoided. As I said of *Macropedius* for Epistles, so I may here; that this way of entring your schollers is hard enough to many a Schoole-master, thus to follow every part of the Theame and those places of *Apthonius*, to invent matter and reasons to prove and illustrate every thing, *This way hard enough for many Schoolemasters.*

and

THE GRAMMAR SCHOOLE

Difficulty in making Theames, because schollers are not acquainted with the matter of them

and to doe it in a good stile. That which is said of Epistles, that children must be acquainted by reading, with matter and phrase fit for Epistles, before they can ever be fit to make such Epistles, is much more true concerning both Theames and Verses; inasmuch as the matter of them is harder, being of such things as they have never read of, nor been any way acquainted with, or at least very little. Besides, to follow the Logicke places in *Apthonius* in a Philosophicall discourse, doth require both some insight in Logick, and reading in such Authors as have written of such Morall mat-

The Master oft deserves to be beaten rather then the scholler.

ters. And therefore herein many a Master deserves rather to be beaten then the scholler, for driving the child by cruelty, to doe that which he himselfe can see no reason how the poore child should be able to doe it. It must of necessity either drive the scholler to use all devices to leave the schoole, or else cause him to live in a continuall horrour and hatred of learning; and to account the schoole, not *Ludus literarius*, but *carnificina*, or *pistrinum literarium*.

Spoud. I acknowledge it too true which you have said: I pray you therefore shew me your best advice and experience how to free my selfe and my children from these evils; that I may both so enter them in these, and also draw them on after, as not to discourage them in this manner, nor be driven to use the like sharpnesse any more.

Phil. Herein I my selfe am desirous to be a learner, as in all the rest. Although too much experience hath compelled me to seek out all meanes to redresse this; notwithstanding also that I have ever been afraid of using cruelty in my schoole. And the rather have I bin carefull to seek out the easiest and plainest way, that I might allure and draw on my schollers in this exercise, as in all other, to proceed as in a scholasticall play, with understanding, love and delight. So much as I have attained, I shall willingly impart unto you.

1 To consider the principall end of making Theams.

1 We are to consider, what is the end and purpose of their making Theams; and then to bethink ourselves, which way they may the soonest attaine unto the same. The principall end of making Theams, I take to be this, to furnish schollers with

THE GRAMMAR SCHOOLE

with all store of the choisest matter, that they may thereby learn to understand, speak or write of any ordinary Theame, Morall or Politicall, such as usually fall into discourse amongst men and in practice of life; and especially concerning vertues and vices. So as to worke in themselves a greater love of the vertue and hatred of the vice, and to be able with soundnesse of reason to draw others to their opinion. *The principall end of making Theames.*

The best meanes to effect this most soone and surely, are these, so farre as yet I know. *The meanes to furnish them.*

1 To see that by perfect learning, and oft repeating they be very ready in their first Authors, which they learned, of such Morall matters; as their *Sententiæ, Cato, Esop's* Fable: For some one or mo of these have the grounds of almost every Theame, which is meet to be propounded to schollers to write on. So that by these they shall be furnished with the judgements of many wise men, what is truth, what is false in most matters, with some words to express their minds, and also some reasons; as with the sentences or testimonies of the wisest, Similitudes, or Apologues in *Esop*, and some grave reasons out of *Cato*, which they may call to minde. All these may be done by the courses set downe before, and as soone as the bare learning of the construing and parsing alone. *1 Making them very perfect in all their first schoole-Authors. Reasons.*

2 Add to these the oft reading over of *Tullies* sentences out of the Gram. translations, and the sentences of the other Authors adjoined with the same. As also the reading them forth of Latine into a good English stile. Thus you shall find by experience, that after that children are perfect in their first schoole-Authors, they will also reade this booke of themselves, by the helpe of the translation alone, to goe over and over it, every day thus reading a piece of it amongst themselves, with little or no hindring any of their schoole-exercises. *2 Reading over and over Tullies sentences.*

3 To the end that they may have presidents and patterns for Theames, like as they had for their Epistles and for making Latine, some book is to be chosen which is written to this purpose, and such a one as is most easie, both for the sweetest Latine and choisest matter. *3 Presidents or examples.*

These

Theames.

THE GRAMMAR SCHOOLE

Presidents for matter.

These presidents are of two sorts: some are to furnish them still, with more variety of the best matter; others, for the whole forme and frame of the Theame.

☞ *Reusneri Symbola.*

Of the first sort, for singular matter notably compact together, *Reusneri Symbola* doth seeme to me most familiar and plaine: wherin the Poesies or sentences of the severall Emperors, both Italian, Greek, & Germane are handled: As these; *Artem quæuis terra alit. Apex Magistratus authoritas. Bonus dux, bonus comes. Bonis nocet, qui parcet malis. Cedendum multitudini. Festina lente:* and the like.

Reusner worthy to train up yong Gentlemen, and all of any good sort and condition.

This book I take to be a very worthy booke to traine up young Gentlemen, and all others whom we would have to become wise men, and good Common-wealths men. It is full of most singular precepts and instructions concerning duties and vertues; and for framing and ordering the whole course of our life, and managing all our affaires with wisedome, safety and commendations. So as any one may receive many wise directions, for all occasions of life, and withall much sweet delight in it. And for this matter of Theames it is fraughted full of the grave testimonies and sentences of many of the ancientest, wisest, and most experienced; all fitly applyed, without any matter to corrupt or offend, and in a most familiar, easie, and pleasing stile.

☞ *How Schollers may use Reusner's Symbola for Theames.* *The words or Mottoes.*

The manner of the use of it for the first enterers into Theames, where they have bookes, and the Teacher would specially apply them to Theames, and that they have time enough, may be this:

To take the *Poesies or Theames of it in order: or if any of them seeme over-hard for children's capacities, in regard of the matter of them, to make choise of the most easie and familiar, first: to reade unto them every night a piece of a Theame of it, as a side of a leafe, or more or lesse; according to the abilities of their Schollers. In reading, first to make the Theame or generall matter of it very plaine unto them. They are commonly expounded for the summe of them under the Poesie, in verse, or with some short glosse, or both. Afterwards, to shew your Schollers the chiefe

rea-

THE GRAMMAR SCHOOLE

reasons and sentences, as you do reade, and in what words the force of each Argument or reason lieth. Also to observe all the phrases which are either more difficult or pure, or most fit to that purpose in hand.

And thus to make every thing plaine unto them; first opening them, after examining the same, and so causing them to understand, and to be able to answer every point thereof in Latine, or to give the hard phrases to the English.

This poasing by short questions, with the other things mentioned, will make the obscurest pieces of it very evident, and cause both weaker Masters and schollers to profit greatly in understanding. After all this, if you will, cause them to construe it amongst themselves and to give the sense, and so make it as perfect as they can every way: Or if they be able, heare them to construe it themselves first, or to reade it out of the Latine into English, and then make it plaine to them. Then let each severally see how he can gather a short Theam out of that; choosing out all the principall sentences and reasons, and composing them in good order: following, if you thinke good, the parts of a Theame: *viz. Exordium, Narratio, Confirmatio, Confutatio, Conclusio,* though their Theame be not above 12. or 16. lines, according to their time and abilitie. To these they may adjoyne other reasons or sentences, as they can, either what they have learned, or what they can gather fitly to the same purpose.

To bring this Theame of theirs thus made, the next day at the time appointed for shewing their Theames each one to pronounce his Theame without booke; you in the meane time looking on that which is pronounced, and examining each fault, as they are uttering it or after, by asking them short questions of the faults, and causing them to answer them, and to shew how they should be amended; and so making a dash with a pen under every fault, or the letters where the fault is, to leave them to them to correct them after. Yet your selfe sometimes to peruse the exercises after againe, to see that they have corrected them; as I shall shew in another place. By this meanes the first enterers may have choice of

Pronouncing their Theames.

mat-

matter gathered to their hands, which otherwise they were to seeke in other Authors they knew not where nor how.

Benefit of Reusner so used, and of daily Theams out of it.

2. All the Theames of this Author being thus written of and pronounced by them *memoriter;* which may be done in a short time, keeping each night a Theame, must needs helpe to furnish them with variety of the best matter, and fit phrase. Besides that, this will be a great furtherance to audacity, memory, gesture, pronunciation: and by the continuall and diligent reading of that Author, with their other Authors, they shall have much helpe to construe and understand any other morall Author *ex tempore.*

☞ *These Theames to be limited according to leasure and oportunitie.*

Or if this course be over-tedious, by reason of the multitude of Schollers, or their other exercises; then to reade them the more at a time, and let them bring them once or twice in the weeke, made longer and more carefully.

Spoud. This way may be very good for entering young Schollers, and to store them, with the best matter and phrase: but might there not be some speciall rules and directions given, for writing their Theames according to the order of the chiefe Schooles, prosecuting the severall parts of the Theame?

The best and most easie direction for Theams to be written at large, with judgement according to the parts thereof. To take the Theames out of Apthonius, and how to make them to understand them fully, and prepare matter.

Phil. Yes: but these I thinke fittest to succeede in the second place, after that they have thus furnished themselves, with words and store of matter, by this helpe, or *Tullies* sentences, or the like; or in want of other bookes, to use *Apthonius.* Then to learne to flourish and adorne their Theames after.

For the surest and easiest direction for such Theames, to be done in more exquisite manner, where the Schollers may have leasure to them; I shall shew you my judgement, and what I can yet find or conceive to be the best.

1. Because I would not have my Schollers discouraged any way through the difficulty of this exercise, I would do as in their first Theames for matter: so in these. That is, I would take their Theames (at least for a time out of *Apthonius,*

THE GRAMMAR SCHOOLE

thonius, either in order as they stand, or choosing of the most familiar, and in all things reade and make it plaine unto them, with the severall parts and arguments, as I shewed you before in *Reusner*.

Then I would demand of them, first to give mee *Apthonius'* arguments: as, what reasons hee hath from the Cause, Effect, Contrarie, Similitude, Example, Testimonie.

Next, what reasons every one can give of his owne, to prove the same.

In the third place to shew, what any of them can object against it; or if it be true, what absurdities and inconveniences will follow of it; and also some of them to answer the objections and inconveniences: and lastly, my selfe to supply their wants and failings.

After this done, direct every one of them who are to write of it, to remember where they have read any thing of that Theame, or by the Indexes of their bookes of Common places: as *Tullies* sentences, *Reusner*, or the like, to seeke what they can find of that matter.

2. That they observe these parts, named
{ *Exordium.*
Narratio.
Confirmatio.
Confutatio.
Conclusio. } *Parts of the Theame.*

3. To make the *Exordium* very short, two or three lines, to gaine the approbation of the hearers, and their attention. *Exordium what one.*

If the Theame be of any person, in accusation or defence of them after the manner of declamations, then that their *Exordium* may be fitliest taken, from the partie himselfe who is accused or defended; from some description of him to his praise or dispraise; or else from the person of the adversarie, or of the auditors, or of the party himselfe who writeth. *If the Theame be of persons.*

For the persons whom they will defend, they must labor
to

to perswade their hearers of their vertues, or to remove from them all prejudicate opinion. And for the persons whom they will accuse, to dispraise them, by shewing their bad qualities; so to bring them into disgrace.

Theame of some matter.   But if the Theame bee of some matter to be proved or disproved; commended or discommended, which are most ordinarie; their *Exordium* may be taken from the matter, by commending it for the excellency thereof, or for the benefit which may redound to the hearers, by the knowledge of it; or discommending it by the contrary, or by some circumstance of time, persons, places, or the like.

Narration   In their Narration, to the end that the Auditors may fully understand the matter, and themselves may proceed more easily; let them set downe first the Theame or matter in as few and plaine words as they can.

Secondly, expound the doubtfull words or phrases, if there be any. If it concerne persons or facts of persons, then to set downe all the circumstances to expresse the nature and manner of it. Or if it concerne some speciall matter, to make some short division of it; if it be a generall, into his specials, or if a whole, into his members or parts: so to goe thorow every part in order, joyning each part together with fit transitions, to shew their passage from one part to another.

Confirmation.   In the Confirmation to the end, to be able to prove the matter the better;

1. To note in their Authors all the principall reasons which they can, to that end, and to gather them forth.

2. To trie what reasons they can invent of themselves according to the chiefe heads of Invention, following either *Apthonius*' order, or the ten chiefe heads of Invention: as Causes, Effects, Subjects, Adjuncts, &c, which are the same in effect, but farre more easie to prosecute, according to the Art of meditation, whereof we shal speake after. By considering wel either the thing it selfe, Causes and Effects of it: or if it be a Proposition, as in this (Children are to obey their Parents) by marking carefully both parts of the Composition or sentence, both Antecedent and consequent, as they are

are called; and the one part will surely afford some reasons.

As if we thinke first of the Parents what they have been, and are towards the children; and so what the children have and do receive from them (thus following the parts according to those places of meditation) any one of understanding shall be able to find out reasons why the children are to obey their Parents.

Then having found out reasons, before they set them downe in their Theame, as they will have them, to ranke them in their minde or in writing; so as they do purpose to set them in their Theame: setting some stronger in the first place, weaker in the midst, reserving some of the stronger to the last, crossing and leaving out the weake ones, whereof any one may discredit all the rest. *Confutation.*

In the Confutation to seeke out and set downe two or three good reasons, to overthrow or reprove the contrary opinion to the Theame: and also to consider what may be objected against it, and how to answer them, by way of Occupation and Subjection, or of preventing an objection. *Conclusion.*

Then to direct them, that the Conclusion is nothing but a collection gathered from all the former reasons: in which may be a short recapitulation, or rehearsall of the summe of the reasons, and an urging (if they will) of one or two of the principall and most forcible reasons somewhat more, to leave a deeper impression in the mindes of the hearers; and so out of them to conclude most firmly. And thus much may serve for the direction in generall for making the Theame.

Spoud. But this seemes still to me rather too obscure for young Grammar Schollers: I pray you let me heare, if you could not leade me yet unto more readie helpes.

Phil. The most excellent patterns, I take it to be the most speedy and ready helps for schollers to be acquainted with, and to learne to imitate them: for they in every thing doe most availe, to teach the soonest and sureliest.

As for variety of Exordiums and Conclusions, *Apthonius* his *Progymnasmata* may helpe to direct; and also Master *Stockwood* his Disputations of Grammar. *Imitation of Exordiums and Conclusions.*

For

THE GRAMMAR SCHOOLE

Authours for matter.

For furnishing with matter and substance, besides *Reusner's Symbola* mentioned, *Erasmus* Adages of the largest and last Edition, is a rich store-house. Also *Lycosthenes* his Apothegmata, printed at London by G. Bishoppe M.D.XCVI. is of good use.

Lycosthenes of the last Edition to be taken heed of, as it is augmented and corrupted by the Jesuites, printed Colonie, sumptibus Lazari Zetzneri An. M.D.C.III.

Lycosthenes of the last Edition (as I heare) is dangerously corrupted with Popery, and rayling against K. *Henry* the eighth, K. *Edward*, and our late blessed Queene; and therefore not to be permitted unto children. Many other I might name unto you, which have written of such morall matters; divers of them in English, and some of them very notable: as the French Academie, the morall part of its Characterry, Morall Philosophy Golden Grove, Wits common wealth, Civill conversation; and others.

So in Latine, *Zegedine* his *Philosophia Poetica*; The sentences fetched out of the best Authors, adjoyning to *Tullies* sentences; *Flores Poëtarum* for Verses to flourish withall.

But the former, viz. *Reusner, Erasmus* Adages, *Apthonius*, and *Lycosthenes*, may serve instead of many, for Schollers who are of understanding and judgement to use them aright; chusing out the summe of the most excellent matter, and making it their owne; composing every thing fitly, without apparent stealing out of any.

Helpes for invention of matter.

Spoud. But what helpe do you account the very best for invention of matter, to find it out as of their owne heads, which you know is principally esteemed of?

Phil. That which I named in the direction for the Theam, is the usuall manner in Schooles, as I take it; I meane the following the places of *Apthonius*: as *à Laudatiuo, Paraphrastico, Causa, Contrario, Parabola, Exemplo, Testimonio veterum, Breui Epilogo.*

So *à Manifesto, Credibili, Possibili, Consequente, Decoro, Vtili.* And *ab Obscuro, incredibili, Imposisbili, Inconsequenti, Indecoro, Inutili,* and the like.

Yet these do seeme to me also farre too hard for children's conceits, who have read no Logike, and over tedious. But

THE GRAMMAR SCHOOLE

But the following of those tenne first and chiefe heads of reasoning; to wit, from Causes, Effects, Subjects, Adjuncts, Disagreeable things, Comparisons, Notations, Distributions, Definitions, Testimonies (to one of which each of *Apthonius* or *Tullies* places do belong) is farre the easiest, surest, and plainest way.

The knowledge of the ten grounds of Invention, the readiest.

If that little booke called the Art of Meditation, were made somewhat more plaine for the definitions or descriptions, that children might see every thing evidently; and illustrated by a few moe examples; and so Schollers made perfect in it by examining; they would be able to invent plenty of good matter presently, after that they had beene exercised in *Reusner*, and the other Authors; in reading, and also in writing some variety of Theames, after the manner set downe before.

The art of meditation most profitable for invention.

Let them practise when they would invent matter, but to runne thorow those places cursorily in their mindes; and if one place do not offer fit matter, another will surely, and furnish them with store: so that by the helpe of that small Treatise, if it were so perfected, all this might bee accomplished; and that with a small meditation any Scholler of understanding might discourse very commendably of any such matter.

Spoud. It is great pitie it should not be made exact, if the use and benefit be such as you conceive of it to this purpose, besides the worthy end for which it is written.

But as you have given patternes for other exercises, so let me heare your judgement, where they may have the best patternes for Theames, for the whole frame thereof being handled according to all the parts severally.

Phil. Apthonius (out of whom these Theames may bee taken first, and the Schollers also to have liberty to gather out the principall matter; yet making it their owne, by seeking to better every sentence) hath sundry very good presidents for such Theames; and in sweete Latine, written by *Rhodulphus, Agricola, Cateneus, Lorichius,* or others: as the example of a Common-place, of the Thesis, and the like

Presidents for the manner of Theames, and out of which to take their Theames first; or out of Reusthner, or others as we will.

THE GRAMMAR SCHOOLE

Theames.

like. Though *Apthonius* his owne (I meane) those translated out of him, are of a more harsh stile in Latine; yet the order is good, as being written and set forth of purpose to this end.

☞ These very Theames may be written on, first for incouragement; after, others of like matter to be imitated, according to the same places.

Tullies *Paradoxes for more excellent patternes.*

Secondly, next unto those in *Apthonius*, which are more easie, *Tullies* Paradoxes are most singular patternes for true Rhetoricke, though the order of them seeme to be more obscure: they will be notable directions, if that the Schollers be of capacity and ripenesse, and have the severall parts rightly opened unto them, that they fully understand them.

Declamations and patternes for them.

Spoud. But for Declamations what examples or helpes would you use?

Phil. The Declamation being nothing else but a Theame of some matter, which may be controverted, and so handled by parts, when one taketh the Affirmative part, another the Negative, and it may be a third moderateth or determineth betweene both; we have very good Presidents in the *Thesis* in *Apthonius*: as in that question handled both Affirmative and Negative, viz. *Vxor est ducenda, Vxor non est ducenda.*

Examples of Invectives.

If it be in a more vehement invective against some vice, we have sundry examples in *Apthonius*, in *Loco communi*. As *In villarum incensores, In sacrilegum, In contumacem, In auarum.*

Examples of praise and dispraise.

Likewise the severall examples there set downe of praise and dispraise, of persons, cities, or the like. So the Presidents in *Apthonius* of paticular actions, in accusing or defence of them, may be great helpes to give much good direction.

For further patternes, see *Tully* his Orations; and specially the Invectives against *Catiline*.

In these kinde of Theames, we shall have farre more use of those figures of Sentences, which are the very life and strength of an Oration; as of Exclamations, Revocations

THE GRAMMAR SCHOOLE

tions, Apostrophees, Prosopopeis; and the rest of the figures in the *Dialogismo*.

I have heard of some good ensamples in English, viz. thirteene Declamations; but I have not beene able to finde them out.

But these kinde of exercises of Declaming are rather for the Universities; or at least for such Schollers in the Grammar-Schooles, as have been long exercised in the former kindes. *Declamations fit for the Universities, or for principall schollers in the Grammar schooles.*

For the manner of writing downe the Theames by schollers of judgement, it may not be amisse where leisure will serve, to cause the schollers to write them thus: In the first Margent towards the left hand, together with the severall parts of the Theame (as *Exord. Narratio, Confirmatio, Confutatio, Conclusio*, being set in great letters over against each part) to set also the heads of the severall arguments; chiefly against the Confirmation: as *Causa, Effectum*: like as *Apthonius* doth set his places, *à Causa, à Contrario*. And in the latter side of the page, towards the right hand, to set the severall tropes or figures, but in two or three letters. As for *Metonymia Efficientis*, no more but *Met. Effic.* or the like: making some line under the word in which they are; The shorter the better, if it can be understood. *Manner of writing downe the Theams by schollers of judgement.*

One Theame in the weeke well performed in this maner, besides all other exercises, may be sufficient; like as the order is in many of the chiefe schooles. *One Theame thus in the week may suffice, and to spend their odde times in making Verses, as more sharpning the wit.*

Spoud. Certainly Sir, these courses seeme to me as easie as the former, both for Masters and Schollers; that hereby they must needs labour, and goe on with delight; being thus plainly guided and directed from point to point.

Yet to proceed a little further herein, if you will give me leave: I have heard of some schollers marveilously praised for this, that they have been able to speake of a Theame *ex tempore* for a quarter of an houre, or more together, in good Latine, and to very good purpose. *Making Theams ex tempore, a matter of great commendations, if it be done scholler like.*

Now how doe you thinke that this may be done? for this

is

THE GRAMMAR SCHOOLE

is a matter of very high commendations to young schollers, even in the Universities; and much more in the Grammar Schooles, if it can be done.

The way to make Theames ex tempore.

Phil. This exercise must needs require much reading, and practice to do it, in such commendable manner; as indeed it may. The best way how to attaine it most soone and surely, is this, so farre as yet I can conceive:

1. They must practise constantly for a good space, the former or better course of making Theames; that they may become very ready in writing their Theames of any Morall matter with a little study.

A practice most easie and profitable to helpe to make Theames ex tempore.

2. I have seene this practice to be easie and profitable to this end: the very use of the Grammaticall translation of *Apthonius*, according to the manner of the use of the translations, for keeping the Schoole-Authors perfectly.

To follow a pattern of a Theam, made familiar unto them by the Grammaticall translations.

As first, causing them to reade a Theame out of the Latine into English; or where it is hard, first to reade it over in English to give some light; then out of the Latine into English, to understand it perfectly: afterwards to reade it out of the English translation into Latine, to have the phrase and Latine readily to expresse their mindes.

To see how each is able to better his Author, in uttering every part of themselves, both English and Latine.

Then every one in his course, to try how he is able to expresse or utter that Theame of himselfe; first in English, then in Latine, every part of the Theame in order.

For example: To begin first with the *Exordium*, to try how they can utter it in English, and whether they can better the Author. After the first, a second fellow to assay how he is able to better the first; so another after him to better them both: and so forward as you will.

After this, to make triall how they can utter the same in Latine; every one still bettering others: then to doe the like in the Narration; and so thorow every part, both in English and Latine; still contending to go beyond their patterns in purity of phrase and matter, contracting, adding or changing as they will.

☞ When they have for some good time used this practice, then trying how they are able to discourse of themselves in
a Theame

THE GRAMMAR SCHOOLE

a Theame given unto them, according to the order of medi-tation, or places of Invention, by continuall exercise they shall attaine hereunto.

To practise to discourse of themselves.

The practice in *Apthonius* will affoord them matter and words enow for imitation of *Exordiums*, manner of Confutations and Conclusions.

Where to be stored with matter, and words for all parts.

Their readinesse in their first Authors of morall matters, as also in *Tullies* Sentences, and *Flores Poëtarum*; and that their continued exercise in *Reusner*, with the helpe of the places of Invention, will commonly yeeld matter sufficient.

What phrase or word they cannot utter in Latine,

1. Let them bethinke themselves how they would first utter and vary it in English, and some of the English words will bring Latine words, or phrases to their remembrance; or else how they can expresse it by *Periphrasis*, or circumlocution in moe words, by some description, or by the generall, or the contrary, or by some property, or the like.

Helpe for supplying words or phrases.
1 To thinke how to utter it in other words in English.

2. Next to this, they may use the helpe of *Holyokes* Dictionarie; and for phrase, *Manutius* or Master *Drakes Calliepeia*: the phrases may be found more easily in the *Calliepeia*.

2 Helps of Dictionaries and words of phrases.

3. And to the end that they may be sure to have variety both of words and phrase, which doth much delight; it shall not be amisse to peruse before in the phrase-book, the principall words or phrases which concerne that Theame, and how many wayes they may be uttered: at least the Master, when he tryeth his Schollers in this *extemporall* faculty, if he be not a ready and perfect Latinist, may have the phrase-booke by him, to looke every hard phrase which they cannot utter well; and how they may vary it divers wayes.

To meditate the chiefe phrases before.

Helpe by the Master.

Spoud. But to the end that schollers may be sure ever to have store of matter, or to finde of a sudden where to turne to fit matter for every Theame; what doe you thinke of Common-place bookes of such Morall matters, that every Scholler should have his Common-place booke written?

Phil.

THE GRAMMAR SCHOOLE

Common-place books, a singular helpe.

Phil. I do account them a great helpe where the schollers have leisure and judgement to gather them; I meane, to gleane out all the choise sentences and matter in the most Authors. Or, because that that is over-great a toyle, and requires more judgement then can be looked for in so yong yeeres; if they had but only bookes of References, it would be exceeding profitable: to wit, such Common-place books as did but only containe the generall heads of matter, and then the Quotations of three or foure of the chiefe Authors; as *Reusner, Erasmus Adages, Tullies* sentences, or some other; setting downe the booke and the page, where to turne of a sudden to any such matter in them. This would ease them of much searching, and make schollers to doe such exercises much sooner, and with farre greater commendations: like as it is in Divinitie, Law, Physicke, and whatsoever other Arts. Thus they may use the matter of the best Authors, going farre beyond the matter which the wit of any child can conceive; sith that those bookes have in them the choisest sayings of the very wisest of all ages: although they are still to adde whatsoever they can invent of their owne braine, so it be wittily and pithily.

Such a booke of Reference well gathered, and made publike, would much further young schollers herein.

Spoud. I see well how they may be furnished for store of matter; yet for choise of good words and phrase, to have copie and variety ever ready at hand, I make some doubt how they may be furnished: for it is a toyle to goe ever to turne to phrase-bookes; neither can they have time when they are to speake *ex tempore.*

How to get store of phrases.

Phil. Take no care for that; store of matter being thus gotten, as I have shewed, will bring words: yet to have copie of *Synonymaes* and good phrase, besides their Authors made perfect, and other helps mentioned; *Calliepeia* translated in propriety, and read one while out of Latine into English, another while out of English into Latine, and after trying how to vary both in English and Latine; will helpe very much to furnish with copie both English and Latine.

Hereof

THE GRAMMAR SCHOOLE

Hereof I have knowne some experience. A little tryall will soone confirme this.

There may be also other helpes for varying: as the rules in *Erasmus de Copia*, in *Macropedius* and others; and more specially some select phrases to severall purposes noted in *Erasmus de Copia*. *Other helps.*

Spoud. But what say you concerning Orations? what course doe you thinke fittest to be able to performe them with commendations? *Orations.*

Phil. I take them to belong rather to the Universities, that there is more seldome use of them in Schooles, and then also to be performed by schollers growne to some maturitie. *Orations belong specially to the Universities. Examples of Orations.*

For examples or patterns of Orations, we can have no better than *Tullies* Orations; wherein are presidents of all sorts. In these is the scholler to be exercised to know the nature of them, and the manner of the loftinesse of stile used in them. Also *Turner's* Orations, *Muretus*, or others. Though for entrance into them we may follow the examples of praises in *Apthonius*. Chap. 8. Or some other select Orations.

Yet, because schooles of speciall note, and where there are ancient schollers, sometimes it may be expected amongst them, that some one of them should make an Oration to entertaine a Benefactor, or other person of note; and it may be, to doe it *ex tempore*, as their comming is of a sodaine; therefore certaine speciall heads of an Oration to that purpose might be ever in readinesse. As the commendations of a person for his descent, learning, love, and countenance of good learning and vertue, beneficence, courtesie, favour towards that place, and the like. Also for excusing themselves by their tender yeeres, want of experience and of practice in that kinde, bashfulnesse, timorousnesse; and yet their desire to answer the parties love and expectation, with presuming upon their patience, and such others. To be acquainted also with variety of choise phrases to the same purposes, to have them ever in fresh memory. *Orations ex tempore.*

Spoud.

Orations.

THE GRAMMAR SCHOOLE

Spoud. These courses are very plaine in my judgement: yet notwithstanding, sith they are of more seldome use, but Theames of daily practice, we are specially to looke unto them. Therefore for my weake memory, let me heare in two words, the summe of all concerning the Theames.

Phil. This is the summe;

Summe of all for Theames.
1 That they be acquainted with some matter for Theams and easie phrase, and so accustomed to write Theames in a plaine manner first, following *Reusner* principally.

2 That they learne to handle the Theame more curiously according to *Apthonius*, prosequuting and adorning the severall parts thereof, making choise of the most excellent patternes.

3 That they have the helps and grounds of inventing reasons of themselves, and do know where to finde more store of matter and phrase to expresse their mindes, and be furnished with helps of the best bookes.

4 Lastly, that as in all other exercises, they use continuall practice; which makes the hardest things easie and pleasant.

CHAP. XIIII.

How to enter to make Verses with delight and certainty, without bodging; and to traine up Schollers to imitate and expresse Ovid *or* Virgil, *both their phrase and stile.*

Spoud.

NOw that we have gone thorow all the whole course of writing Latine in prose, and the severall exercises thereof which are requisite in Grammar-Schooles, so farre forth as I remember; it remaineth that we come to verse: wherein I presume of your love as in all the former, not to conceale any thing from me, but to impart whatsoever may helpe to the attaining of that facultie.

Phil.

THE GRAMMAR SCHOOLE

Phil. Though Poetry be rather for ornament then for a- *Poetry rather*
ny necessary use; and the maine matter to be regarded in it, *for ornament*
is the purity of phrase and of stile: yet because there is very *then for any*
commendable use of it, sometimes in occasions of triumph *necessitie.*
and rejoycing, more ordinarily at the funerals of some wor- *Yet there may be*
thy personages, and sometimes for some other purposes; *commendable*
it is not amisse to traine up schollers even in this kinde also, *use of it.*
and the rather because it serveth very much for the sharpen-
ing of the wit, and is a matter of high commendation,
when a scholler is able to write a smooth and pure verse, and
to comprehend a great deale of choise matter in very little
roome.

Spoud. Surely (Sir) though it is, as you say, but an ornament, yet it is such a one, as doth highly grace those who
have attained it, in any such measure as you speake of; and
two such Verses are worth two thousand, of such flash and
bodge stuffe as are ordinarily in some schooles. But this I *The ordinarie*
have found also to be full of difficulty, both in the entring, *difficulty of this*
the progresse, and also in the end; that my schollers have *faculty.*
had more feare in this, then in all the former, and my selfe also
driven to more severity: which I have been inforced unto
or else I should have done no good at all with the greatest
part.

And yet when I have done my uttermost, I have not had
any to come to such perfection as you mention, to write *The folly of some*
so pithily or purely: yea, let me tell you this, that I have *in this kinde.*
knowne some Masters, who have thought themselves very
profound Poets, who would upon an occasion of a Funerall
have written you a sheete or two of Verses, as it were of a
sudden; yet amongst all those, you should hardly have
found one such a Verse as you speake of, unlesse it were
stolne; and most of them such, as a judicious Poet would
be ready to laugh at, or loath to reade. Therefore I intreat
you to guide me, how I may redresse this evill, and prevent
these inconveniences.

Phil. Though I be no Poet, yet I finde this course to be
found most easie and plaine to direct my schollers.

1 To

THE GRAMMAR SCHOOLE

The most plaine way how to enter to make a verse without bodging.
1 *To write true Latine.*
2 *To have read some Poetry.*

1 To looke that they be able in good manner to write true Latine, and a good phrase in prose, before they begin to meddle with making a verse.

2 That they have read some poetry first; as at least these bookes or the like, or some part of them: *viz. Ovid. de Tristibus,* or *de Ponto,* some piece of his Metamorphosis, or of *Virgil,* and be well acquainted with their Poeticall phrases.

3 Practice of turning them out of the Grammaticall translations into verse.

Giving Poeticall phrase.

3 I finde this a most easie and pleasant way to enter them; that for all the first books of Poetry which they learn in the beginning, they use to reade them dayly out of the Grammaticall translations: first resolving every verse into the Grammaticall order, like as it is in the translation; after into the Poeticall, turning it into verse, as the words are in the Poet: according as I shewed the manner before, in the benefit and use of the translations. For the making of a verse, is nothing but the turning of words forth of the Grammaticall order, into the Rhetoricall, in some kinde of metre; which we call verses. And withall, that in reading thus out of the translations, they use to give the Poeticall Phrases, to our English phrases, set in the Margents, and also the Epithetes.

For this practice of reading their Poetry, out of the translations into verse, a little triall will soone shew you, that very children will doe it as fast almost as into prose: and by the use of it, continually turning prose into verse, they will be in a good way towards the making a Verse, before they have learned any rules thereof.

4 To be very cunning in the rules of versifying.

4 Then when you would have them to go in hand with making a verse; that they be made very cunning in the rules of versifying, so as to be able to give you readily each rule, and the meaning thereof.

5 To be perfect in scanning.

5 That they be expert in scanning a verse, and in proving every quantity, according to their rules, and so use to practise in their Lectures daily.

6 To keepe from bodging in their entrance.

6 To keepe them that they shall never bodge in their entrance, neither for phrase nor otherwise, but to enter
with

THE GRAMMAR SCHOOLE

with ease, certainty and delight; this you shall finde to be a most speedy way.

Take *Flores Poëtarum*, and in every Common place make choise of *Ovid's* verses, or if you find any other which be pleasant and easie: and making sure, that your Schollers know not the verses aforesaid, use to dictate unto them as you did in prose. Cause also so many as you would have to learne together, to set downe the English as you dictate. *To use the like practice in Flores Poëtarum for verse, as in Tullies Sentences for prose.*

Secondly, to give you, and to write downe all the words in Latine *verbatim*, or Grammatically.

Thirdly, having just the same words, let them trie which of them can soonest turne them into the order of a verse: which they will presently do, being trained up in the use of the translations; which is the same in Effect.

And then lastly, reade them over the verses of *Ovid*, that they may see that themselves have made the very same; or wherein they missed: this shall much incourage and assure them.

After that they have practised this for a little time; if for speedinesse, and for saving paper (because they may soone runne over much) you do use but onely to reade the English Grammatically, and appoint some one of them to deliver it in Latine; then all to trie which of them can soonest turne those words into a verse, or how many waies they can turne them into a verse: you shall see them come on apace, and an earnest strife to be wrought amongst them. *To doe this without pen.*

This also may be done most easily, by the use of Grammaticall translations of all the choice verses in *Flores Poetarum*; practising as in *Tully* and other, to reade them *ex tempore* out of the English first into prose, after into verse. They will be as familiar and easie, as to reade prose, and to doe it with as much delight and contention or more, every day practising a little by course. For this is nothing (as I said) but the Poeticall composition. In the practice of this, likewise, use to note every new and hard word, and quantity, as also Epithetes; according to the generall rule before, and the manner in each Lecture, and oft to examine those. *The most easie way of turning verses out of Flores Poëtarum.*

To note hard words, quantities, Epithets.

7 To turne the verses of their Lectures.

7. Cause

THE GRAMMAR SCHOOLE

7. Cause them to turne the verses of their Lecture into other verses, either to the same purpose, which is easiest for young beginners, or turne to some other purpose, to expresse some other matter; yet ever to keepe the very phrase of the Poet, there or in other places, onely transposing the words or phrase, or changing some word or phrase, or the numbers or persons, or applying them to matters which are familiar, as they did in imitating Epistles. This may be practised, each to bring first a verse or two thus changed, either being given at eleven to be brought at one, or at evening to be brought in the morning, or both.

8. Contracting their Lectures.
8. As they proceed, to cause them to contract their Lectures, drawing seven or eight verses into foure or five, or fewer: yet still labouring to expresse the whole matter of their Author in their owne verse, and every circumstance, with all significant Metaphors, and other tropes and phrases, so much as they can.

The certaine benefit of this exercise.
Thus they may proceed if you will, from the lowest kind of verse in the Eclogues, to something a loftier in the Georgicks; and so to the stateliest kinds in the Æneids: wherein they may be tasked to go thorow some book of the Æneids, every day contracting a certaine number, as some 5. or 6. a day, for some of their exercises, striving who can expresse their Author most lively. By which daily contention you shall find, that those who take a delight in Poetry, and have

To expresse their Poet most lively.
sharpenesse & dexterity accordingly, will in a short time attaine to that ripenesse, as that they who know not the places which they imitate, shall hardly discerne in many verses, whether the verse be *Virgil's* verse or the Scholler's.

Caveat in contracting.
But therein there must be this care, that before they go in hand with this kind of contracting, they be both well exercised in the former kinds or the like; and also that they beare out the meaning of the place fully, marking what goeth before, and also what followeth after; and observing curiously every phrase, elegancy, and matter of any weight.

To make verses of any ordinary Theame.
Moreover, that your schollers may be able to write verses *ex tempore*, of any ordinary Theame, after they have bin well
practi-

THE GRAMMAR SCHOOLE

practised in turning the easy verses of *Flores Poëtarum*, forth of prose into verse, that they can do it readily; appoint them of the most familiar Theames of it, and the sweetest verses thereof in order, to see how they can turne the same *ex tempore* into other verses, to the very same purpose; either by imitation, or contraction, like as I shewed the practice in their lectures: or having but the light of those verses, how they can make other verses of their owne like unto them.

By this practice kept duely, to make some such verses twise in the day (as to give them Theames before their breaking up at noone, to bring them at one of the clocke, and at night to bring them in the morning, or nine, as before; only having this helpe and direction) or of a sodaine ever before they are to play, to versifie of some Theame not thought of: and secondly, by causing them to bring the summe of their Theames written under their Theames, comprized in a Disticke, or two moe, you shall finde that they will grow in so good sort, as shall be requisit to make you verses *ex tempore* of any usuall Theame, without hindering of their other studies. And hereby they will soone be acquainted with matter of all sorts according to those Common places, and also with variety of poeticall phrase of the best, with Epithetes and stile. This exercise is very commendable to satisfie such, as use to give Theames to versifie upon *ex tempore*; and also for that it is a very great sharpner of the wit, as was said, and a stirrer up of invention and of good wits to strift and emulation.

To verifie ex tempore.

Benefits of this practice.

The use of versifying ex tempore,

In this matter of versifying, as in all the former exercises, I take this Imitation of the most excellent patternes, to be the surest rule, both for phrase and whatsoever: And therefore I would have the chiefest labour to make these purest Authors our owne, as *Tully* for prose, so *Ovid* and *Virgil* for verse, so to speake and write in Latine for the phrase, as they did.

Imitation surest.

For them who desire to attaine to more exquisite perfection in this faculty of Poetry, these things may much further besides the former:

Further helpes for verifying

1 For

THE GRAMMAR SCHOOLE

<small>For store of matter to have Common place books, or books of reference to the most excellent places in Poets.</small>

1. For more store and variety of matter, to have Common place bookes (as I said for the Theames) therein at least to have reference whereby to turne of a sodaine to matters of all sorts, in the most exquisite and pure Poets: to have some direction both for matter and imitation; whether for Gratulatory verses, Triumphs, Funerals, or whatsoever. Or to referre all such principall places for imitation, to the heads in *Flores Poetarum*; which may serve in steade thereof.

<small>2. For variety of Poeticall phrase. Thesaurus poeticus.
Sylva Synonimorum</small>

2. For variety and copy of Poeticall phrases, the *Thesaurus Phrasium poeticarum* gathered by *Buchlerus* of the last Edition, *An. M.D. Cvij.* is a notable helpe.

Also both for words and phrases, *Sylva Synonimorum*, may stand in good steade, chiefely for Schollers of judgement able to make right choyce of the fittest.

<small>3. For Epithets, Textor's Epithets of the last and largest. Abbridgement of Textor.</small>

3. For store of Epithetes, which if they bee choyse, are a singular ornament, and meanes of speedinesse in this faculty, and so for all other matters belonging to Poetrie, Textor his *Epithetæ* of the largest and of the last Edition, printed at Lions, *M.D. Cij.* may be a great helpe.

The abbridgement of *Textors* Epithetes may serve in steade hereof to young Schollers: and namely to such who are not able to buy the large; though the large is more profitable.

<small>4 For Quantities and Authorities.
Smetij Prosodia syllabarum positione & dipthongis carentium.
Smetij Methodus.
M. Butler's Retoricke.</small>

4. For having of the best authorities for the quantities of all syllables, *Smetius* his *Prosodia* will furnish plentifully; all needfull words being set in it in the Alphabeticall order. For rules of quantities, though our owne Grammar may be sufficient; yet you may see also *Smetius* his *Methodus dignoscendarum Syllabarum ex Georg. Fabricio*, set before his *Prosodia*. And rules of the quantities of Syllables in M. *Butler's* Rhetoricke, short and very plaine. *Chap.* 14. *de Metro.*

<small>Virgil with E. Erythæus his Index.
5. For imitation of the best Poets, Sabine.</small>

Also the Virgils printed with *Erythræus Index*, for Authorities and uses of all words in *Virgil*.

5. For imitation of the best Poets, and further direction to attaine to more perfection in Poetry, see *Sabines* precepts

THE GRAMMAR SCHOOLE

cepts, *De carminibus ad veterum imitationem artificiosè componendis*, joyned with *Textor's* Epithets. Also *Buchlerus* his *Institutio Poëtica* in the end of his *Thesaurus phrasium poëticarum*.

6. For the Figures belonging to Poetrie, see *Butler's* Retoricke in his fourteenth Chapt. *De Metro*.

7. For turning of Verses divers waies, M. *Stockwood* his *Progymnasma scholasticum* is *instar omnium*, to direct and to incourage young Schollers. In which booke towards the end of it, you shall have one Disticke or couple of Verses, varied 450. wayes. The Verses are these:

1. *Linque Cupido iecur; cordi quoque, parcito: si vis*
   Figere, fige alio tela cruenta loco.
2. *Parce meo iecori; intactum mihi linquito pectus:*
   Omnia de reliquo corpore membra pete.
3. *Cæce puer, &c.*

And in the shutting up of all, this one Verse is turned by transposing the words 104. wayes; all the same words, and onely those words being kept: which might seeme impossible, but that there we may see it before our eyes, that nine words should serve to make a hundreth and foure Verses, all of the same matter. The Verse is this:

Est mea spes Christus solus, qui de cruce pendet.
Est Christus solus mea spes, qui de cruce pendet.
Est solus Christus mea spes, qui de cruce pendet.
Solus de cruce, &c.

A Scholler of any inclination and fitnesse for Poetry, cannot but receive notable incouragement, having these, or but the principall of these bookes: this exercise of Versifying will be found a most pleasant recreation unto him after a time.

8. Lastly, in this exercise, as in all the rest, I hold daily practice and diligence (following the best patterns) to be the surest and speediest guide; and which will bring in time much perfection, where there is aptnesse of nature concurring.

Spoud

THE GRAMMAR SCHOOLE

Spoud. But repeat me in a word, which exercises you would have daily put in practice.

Daily and easie exercises.

Phil. Turning the Verses of the Lectures, as was shewed; chiefely by contraction in *Virgil*, keeping strictly his phrase.

2. Before each breaking up at noones and nights, to have a Theame out of the easiest of *Flores Poëtarum* in order to bring Verses of it at their entrance againe, or as is appointed to them.

3. Writing Verses of their weekely Theames.

CHAP. XV.

The manner of examining and correcting Exercises.

Spoud.

Examining exercises never to be omitted.

Having thus gone thorow the principall exercises of writing; I pray you let me heare your judgement, for the examining of such exercises, and the best manner of performing it: for I finde it a matter very tedious and troublesome.

Though tedious yet profitable. Neglect of examining brings carelesnesse in Schollers.

Phil. Howsoever it be tedious, yet it is such a matter as would never be omitted, no more then the giving of exercises; not to be slightly passed over, so much as time and oportunity will permit. For when the Scholler knoweth that his exercise must be strictly examined, it will make him more carefull in performing thereof, and contrarily; and it will be a great helpe to bring him sooner to perfection.

For the manner of doing it;

1 Masters to observe generall faults.

1. The Master ought heedfully to observe those speciall faults, wherein his Schollers do most usually slip; and to acquaint every one, not onely with the generall, but also with his particular, to warne them of them.

For

THE GRAMMAR SCHOOLE

For example; I have found my schollers to misse most in these: through want of Dipthongs. In congruity in their Concords. In the use of the two chiefe rules of the Relative *Qui, quæ, quod*. Ablative case absolute. Apposition, Conjunctions to couple together like Cases, Moodes and Tenses. Nominative case after the Verbe, &c. The Accusative case before an Infinitive Moode. *Wherein schollers doe most commonly slip.*

Also that they will oft have a *Synchesis*, or a disordered confusion of their words; and sometimes they will use *hyperbaton*: which is a further fetching or carrying of some words, whereby a sentence is obscured; and the scholler forgets himselfe before he come to the end of his sentence, and so writes false Latine. Long Periods are therefore to be avoided as much as may be. *Synchesis, Hyperbaton to be avoided.*

2 The Schollers are to be called upon, to reade over their exercises in the naturall or Grammaticall order, so as they construe: and then they may see presently how the words doe hang together, both for agreement, government, and sense, and where the faults of Grammar are. *2 To reade over their exercises first in naturall order.*

3 That besides their rules, they be able presently to parallele or prove each phrase and construction, by the like example in Grammar, or by a like phrase out of *Tully*, or other Authors: and what they know not to seeke out; to the end that they may be able to justifie every word, even where they have readily read it, so much as may be. *3 To parallel each thing by examples.*

4 The higher schollers to looke to elegancie, and finenesse of phrase and Composition; and so to be reading their exercises over and over, still correcting and amending them, never thinking an exercise well enough, untill no fault can be found, in Latine, propriety, Composition; matter, no nor in the least tittle. The scholler is herein to imitate the curious Painter, who is still amending and bettering his picture, to draw all into admiration; that his Theames, Verses, Orations may be as the harpe of *Orpheus*, to draw all the hearers or readers after them. *4 To looke to elegancie and finenesse of Composition. Never to thinke any exercise laboured enough.*

5 To appoint adversaries to take one another's exercises, and

THE GRAMMAR SCHOOLE

5 Adversaries to note faults in one another's exercises. and to see whether of them can finde the moe faults: and if you will, to set underneath, how many faults either of them findes; and so to give them to the Master, or to themselves first to correct, then to the Master.

6 The manner of examining by the Master. 6 After all, the Master is carefully to reade over every one's exercise, so much as leisure will permit; and by questions to make themselves to finde where the errour is: as but asking; Doe we say thus or thus? and to cause them to amend it of themselves by giving a like example. And in the meane time, to make some little line under the phrase or word, or piece of the word or syllable wherein the errour is, that they may amend it after in their bookes. And for all correcting of translations in Latine, to do it by comparing their exercise with the Author; and so exercises of imitation, to see who cometh next to the example.

7 Speciall faults in the highest fourmes. 7 In examining exercises in the highest fourmes (as in Theames, Declamations, Verses, Orations, and the like) besides the faults against Grammar, the diligent Master should observe, first, all barbarous phrases, or Poeticall phrase in Prose, or contrary: secondly, Tautologies, or oft repetitions of the same thing or words: thirdly, want of transitions; that is, of fit bonds or phrases, whereby to passe elegantly from one point to another; so as they might be more easily understood: fourthly, harsh composition: fiftly, lacke of matter: sixtly, want of elegancy in Tropes and Figures; and so like elegancies noted in Grammar.

8 Care that they doe correct their exercises forthwith. 8 To have a diligent eye that the schollers do forthwith correct their exercises, so noted out unto them: and to this end he is oft to looke in their bookes, whether they have corrected their former exercises, and to use sharpe reprehension or correction for that carelesnesse, to make them to looke to that above all. For there is nothing wherein their negligence is more intolerable, nor for which the Master shall be more censured, when their parents, or others who be learned, shall looke into their bookes, and reade over their exercises, and thereto finde them uncorrected.

9 This to be done by others in straights of time. 9 If at any time the Master's occasions permit not so much time,

THE GRAMMAR SCHOOLE

time, yet to see that it be performed by the Usher or some of the highest schollers, and the number of faults noted.

Spoud. But what if there should be 30. or 40. in a fourme (as it may be in the greater schooles; especially amongst the lower fourmes) how would you do to examine all their exercises in a morning, but you shall hinder your selfe and them from many other things which you must of necessitie performe? *(marginal: How to doe for correcting where there are very many in a fourm; and where time will not permit to correct all.)*

Phil. In such cases we must yeeld to necessity, and use the best policy we can; as in that exercise of translating into Latine, to cause some three or foure whom you most feare, to pronounce their exercises, or to reade or construe them out of the translation; you to looke upon the exercises, as they are pronouncing, and cause them to shew how they must be amended: so all the rest to correct thiers, according as they heare those corrected: if any be found carelesse to correct so, that he be surely corrected: and this is the best helpe which I know in this behalfe. *(marginal: In exercises of translations.)*

So likewise where you give them a Theame to make verses *ex tempore*: or upon some small meditation, as those which are to be brought each morning, or at one of the clocke, when time will not permit to peruse the writing of every one; yet to cause every one to pronounce the Verses which he hath made: and as they pronounce, to shew them their faults, and then cause them to correct them after. Thus have I shewed you my judgment also for examining of exercises. *(marginal: Verses ex tempore.)*

CHAP. XVI.
How to answer any needful question of Grammar or Rhetoricke.

Spoud. WEll, good Sir, you see how bold I am to require your judgement in every matter, wherein I finde difficulty: now to returne to the briefe againe of those things which you affirmed might be done for learning.

This

THE GRAMMAR SCHOOLE

This I remember was another point, which cannot but greatly commend a scholler: to be able to answer any difficult question of Grammar, even beside those which are in the rules, which are commonly learned; and also how to oppose or dispute scholler-like in Latine, of any good Grammar question; as both what may be objected against *Lillies* rules, and how to defend them: I pray you let me heare of you how this may be done, and what is the most speedy way which you know hereunto.

Phil. The plainest, shortest, and surest way, I finde to be this:

1 See that they be very ready in all the usuall and ordinary Questions of Grammar, by daily examining at Parts.

2 For most of the rest fit for young schollers, I have gathered them for the use of mine owne schollers, and set them together after the end of the Accedence Questions; yet so, as I have sorted and referred every Question to the right place whither it appertaines: as to the Noune, Pronoune, Participle, and so to the severall heads thereof.

When as young schollers waxe perfect in all the former, which are in the Accedence; then a little paines in teaching them these, making them plaine unto them, and examining them some halfe side at a time (in stead of the time spent before in examining the former) will very soone make them as ready in these also.

3 After these, you may (if you please) goe through the questions of Grammatica, and make them plaine; examining them in Latine: and so through all the necessary questions which are scattered here and there, through the whole Grammar: directing them to marke out the questions, or the special words wherein the questions are, and how to be propounded; that they themselves may oppose one another, or one to oppose all as need is.

But this as you shall thinke necessary; and so as it do not hinder better studies.

4 You may runne through the questions in M. *Stockwood's* disputations of Grammar, as they are commonly noted

THE GRAMMAR SCHOOLE

ted in the Margents, but onely propounding the question in few words, both English and Latine, as need requires, and teaching them to answer in a word or two.

By going through these, they may be able to answer all, or most of those which are set together in the end of his disputations; wherein he hath with marvellous paines, and diligent observation, collected a very great part of the difficulties of all Classicall Authors, and in the last Edition noted the words in the Margents, in which the difficulty in each sentence is. What other are wanting in these, may be answered by them, being of like nature.

Most of the difficulties of the ancient Classicall Authors collected into one by M. Stockwood's last Edition printed Anno 1607.

5 To give a further light, and that nothing may be wanting for my children, I have adjoyned unto the latter end ot all the Accedence questions which I spake of, certaine generall figures: unto some of which, many of the difficulties of all ancient Authors (both those in *Stockwood* and others) may be referred, or else unto those figures set down in the Grammar and Rhetoricke.

5 Certaine generall Figures to answer many difficulties by.

For answering the questions of Rhetoricke, you may, if you please, make them perfect in *Talæus'* Rhetoricke, which I take to be most used in the best Schooles; onely to give each definition and distribution, and some one example or two at most in each Chapter; and those of the shortest sentences out of the Poets: so that they can give the word or words, wherein the force of the rule is. And so to proportion all other questions accordingly.

In Talæus' Rhetoricke to give definitions, divisions and one short example.

To this end, the words wherein the force of the examples consist, would be marked as in the Grammar; and that not onely in some one or two examples in every Chapter, which they are to have perfect without book, but also in every example through the booke, to be able to apply any.

Talæus' examples would be noted as Grāmar.

Claudius Minos Commentary may be a good helpe to make *Talæus'* Rhetoricke most plaine, both for precepts and examples.

Minos Commentary to helpe for understanding Talæus.

If your Scholler, after he hath read these, doe but use to be carefull to keepe a short Catalogue in his minde, of the names of the Tropes, and also Figures (and those both of

Grammar

Grammar and Rhetoricke) he shall with practice of examination and observation be able to tell any of them, but repeating the heads in his minde.

Butler's Rhetoricke, a notable abridgement of Talæus, and farre more easie and profitable.

Or instead of *Talæus*, you may use Master *Butler's* Rhetoricke, of *Magdalens* in Oxford, printed in Oxford; which I mentioned before being a notable abbridgement of *Talæus*, making it most plaine, and farre more easie to be learned of Schollers, and also supplying very many things wanting in *Talæus*. Both it and the Commentary together, are almost as small as *Talæus* alone, and not a much greater price, though the worth be double. It is a booke, which (as I take it) is yet very little knowne in Schooles, though it have bin forth sundry yeeres, set forth for the use of Schooles; and the use and benefit will be found to be farre above all that ever hath been written of the same.

Brasbridge's questions on Tullies Offices.

Finally, for answering the questions of *Tullies* Offices, M. *Brasbridge* his questions thereof, are as short and perspicuous as any of the former.

Spoud. Sir, I have not (in truth) so much as ever heard of either of those bookes: as neither of any almost of those singular helpes which you mentioned for Poetry; by which apt Schollers cannot choose but become excellent Poets.

Generall want in the ignorance of the best helps.

Phil. Thereby may appeare what a generall want here is amongst us; when God hath given so many worthy helpes, whereby we and our Schollers may attaine so readily the excellency of all learning meet for us, and make all our courses so full of all pleasant and alluring contentment, and yet we shall neglect to enquire after them.

CHAP.

THE GRAMMAR SCHOOLE

CHAP. XVII.

Of Grammaticall oppositions, how to dispute scholler-like of any Grammar question in good Latine.

Spoud.

IT seemeth to be very evident, that by these means they may be able to answer any necessary question, meet for them; but for those scholler-like oppositions in Grammar questions, I heare you to say nothing, although it cannot but be a marvellous profitable exercise.

Phil. It is indeed a profitable exercise: and I finde that it may be very easily attained thus;

1 About that time when they begin to reade *Virgil*, or before, as they are able, when they begin to make Theams, two of them may be appointed, in stead of their Theame or Verses to be made for that morning's exercise, to dispute every day by course. The manner of it thus: Let them take M. *Stockwood's* disputations, to direct them. And first for their greater ease and incouragement, to enter them; appoint them to dispute in the very words which M. *Stockwood* hath, and that of all the questions in order, about a side of a leafe at a time, or as they can well: so that following the words of the Author, there needeth no more labour, but committing it to memory and uttering; unlesse they can meditate to doe it more shortly of themselves. *Two to dispute each day in stead of their Theame or Verses.*

1 To follow M. Stockwood, and to use his very words.

2 After this, when they have thus gone over the booke or the greatest part of it, which they may doe in a short time, keeping a constant course: then cause them to practise to take a whole disputation at a time, or at least a whole question, and to bring only the substance of it as shortly as they can; yet still observing as much as may be, M. *Stockwood's* phrase, his order and witty conceits, which he useth both in objecting and answering. *2 After to take only the substance of his disputations, and goe thorow a whole question at a time.*

For

THE GRAMMAR SCHOOLE

Helpe for the understanding of the disputations amongst the enterers.

For their better understanding of their disputations, do as in their Theams: use at their entrance to reade them over unto them: shew them the plaine meaning of every thing, and by examining the summe of it all, first in English, after in Latine, cause them to understand so much as time will permit.

What they are not able to utter in Latine, remember to cause them first to utter in English, and then they will easily doe it in Latine, as we said.

When they have beene well exercised in these, that they are able thus to dispute with facilitie, and are acquainted well with *Stockwood's* phrase and order; they may have other questions given to handle wholly of themselves, if you will.

Benefits of such scholasticall oppositions.

By these meanes of continuall disputing, they shall reape these benefits:

1 They shall be much helped for the perfect understanding, and answering of any difficult Grammar question, as was said before.

2 They shall be very much furthered for delivering their minds easily in Latine.

3. They shall be notably fitted for disputations in the Universitie, or any like opposition, mooting, or pleading in the Innes of Court.

4 It shall bring audacity, helpe gesture, pronunciation, memory, and much provoke them to an ingenuous emulation and contention.

Spoud. But I have seene in a schoole, where the schollers have been able to dispute *ex tempore* of any ordinary Morall question, which you should propound unto them: which me thought did exceedingly grace them, & was a very rare commendation unto the schoole.

Disputations of Morall Philosophy belong rather to the Universitie.

Phil. Though I doe grant with you, that this deserved very great praise; yet this seemes to me rather to belong to the Universities then to the Grammar schooles. For I take it not onely meet, but also most equall and necessary, that every place have their owne Priviledges reserved unto them;

THE GRAMMAR SCHOOLE

them; and that one in no case should incroach upon another.

Above all, that there be a chiefe regard of the Universities, as unto which the Grammar schools are ordained principally, for training up young schollers to furnish them; and that they have all their honours and prerogatives reserved most carefully unto them. Of which sort these disputations in Logicke and other Philosophy are. *The priviledges and prerogatives of the Universities by all means to be preserved.*

Notwithstanding I shall shew you my judgement, how this may be performed also; and as I take it, in the most easie manner, and most surely, so farre as it may be. *How these may be done, and how farre.*

1 I would have my scholler well practised in these Grammaticall disputations, to have phrase and order of disputation in readinesse, and to keepe themselves within the compasse of that kinde of reasoning; leaving Logicall and strict concluding by Syllogismes, unto the Universitie. *1 By practice in the Grammaticall disputations.*

2 To have read over *Tullies* Offices, with understanding; which by the helpe of Master *Brasbridge's* questions, and the Grammaticall translations, they may the more speedily by farre. *2 To be acquainted with Tullies Offices and the questions of it.*

3 To choose out of the easiest of those questions, and to appoint the schollers instead of their disputations in Grammar, when they have gone thorow those, then to reply and answer an argument or two upon some of these questions daily. It were worthy the labour of some ingenuous and good Latinist, as M. *Stockwood*, to handle some of the questions of *Tullies* Offices, after the maner of his Grammaticall disputations, to fit schollers the more for such witty and pleasant disputations, against that they should come to the University. But I speake this as the rest, under better judgement, and so farre as these may be meet for the Grammar schoole. *3 To oppose of some of those questions instead of the Grammaticall. Some of Tullies Offices questions handled after the manner of M. Stockwood's Grammaticall disputations worthy the labour.*

4 For inventing reasons to reply, it may soone be performed, by the dullest capacitie, according to the manner of inventing reasons for Theames or Verses, following the chiefe heads of reasoning. If the replyer do but onely meditate, what may be said against the question or Position from *4 How to invent reasons, by the help of the places of Invention.*

some

THE GRAMMAR SCHOOLE

some one of those chiefe places of reasoning, discoursed in his minde in order; having the places ever in fresh memory (as I shewed before) by the practice of the Art of Meditation, or the like: For then if one place will not presently afford meet matter, another will. And commonly, the places from Causes, Effects, Contraries, Examples, Testimonies, are most pregnant to bring reasons to our minde.

Helps for the answerer.

Moreover, to helpe to answer the subtilties or fallacies; besides the perfect understanding of the question, and the matter of it, by reading or meditating of it diligently, the wise observing by the answerer from what place of reasoning the argument seemes to be taken, will usually answer the reason. For, the most ordinary fallacies or deceits in reasoning, are from a bare shew of Causes, Effects, Contraries, Testimonies, and the rest, mistaken or misalledged; yet urged as if they were true Causes, Effects, &c. when they are but fained or bare shews: Or else in wrangling about words, not disputing to the purpose, and to the point; but in some other sense mistaking the question.

All the chiefe schollers are necessarily to be acquainted with the heads of Invention For Inventing, Resolving, Remembring.

For those common places or heads of Invention, all schollers who come to any ripenesse, are necessarily to be acquainted with them, as was touched before. These will ever stand them in stead for making of all Epistles, Theames, Verses, Declamations, Oppositions.

Also to helpe them to resolve whatsoever they reade or heare in any continued speech; and to remember it, by gathering all the matter unto the severall heads of Invention. Thus to be able to remember, and confute a Position, or an Oration *ex tempore*, with much admiration.

Without these helps they shall never be able to doe these things; or at least not with that facilitie, and in so commenble a manner, though they have otherwise very singular gifts of nature and learning.

Continuall exercise, all in all.

But above all, as in all other exercise, so in this chiefly, continuall practice of disputing is all in all; when once you have directed them how to attaine good order, or Method, phrase, and matter.

If

THE GRAMMAR SCHOOLE

If you desire any more, concerning the difficult questions of Grammar, reade *Goclenius* his Problems in the end of his Observations of the Latine tongue.

Goclenius Problemes.

Spoud. I much approove of all that you have said in this matter; and principally that the Universities should be honoured by all meanes, and their dignities reserved inviolable; yet give me leave to tell you of one thing, which here may seeme to be blame-worthy, which is this: That you would have your enterers into this kinde of opposing, to bring the whole disputations of M. *Stockwood*, to dispute in his very words; this may helpe to make them Truants, to trust onely to their bookes and memory, and not to stirre up their owne wits and inventions.

Ob. That this may seeme to make them truants to dispute out of the words of the booke.

Phil. Nothing lesse: for you see how after that they have bin exercised this way for a time, then I would have them to trie their owne wits and inventions also; first abbridging their Author, then bringing their owne: But, for following this course, both experience and reason do shew it to be the surest; as in all other learning, so in this (like as we observed in generall before) to let them have first the most excellent patterns, and never to rest untill they have the very patterns in their heads, and as it were ever before their eyes; for then they will be able to go forwards of themselves with delight and commendations. Whereas, otherwise to inforce them by feare, to undertake such exercises, wherewith they are not acquainted, nor see the reason of them, it is a matter of overgreat rigor, that I say no more of it, and which must needs worke a marvellous distaste in the Scholler, as I have noted. Besides, to cause such young ones to dispute without hearing or seeing such presidents, is all one, as to teach them to write onely by precepts or some direction without copie. For even as therein they shall both write verie ilfavouredly, if any thing at all, and learne so bad a hand, as they shall be much troubled to forget, which they must doe before they can come to a good hand, so is it here. 1. They shall dispute very weakely and childishly, both for words and matter. if any thing at all, and 2. they shall get barbarous phrase, to make them to be scorned, & which they shal hardly forget againe.

Necessity of being well acquainted with the best examples.

The evils of inforcing Schollers to exercises, whereof they are not acquainted with the examples first.

But

THE GRAMMAR SCHOOLE

Benefits of the contrary; viz. of having the best patternes.

But of the other side, they being trained up thus, shall make not onely the matter of their learned Author their owne, but also his phrase; and be so furnished, that any man will take delight to heare them. And that which I say of this, the same I affirme of all excellent patterns, whether for making Theames, Verses or whatsoever; that the more absolute their Presidents are, and the more cunning they are in them, the more singular they shall undoubtedly prove.

This is the very maine reason, why all would have the children to learne each Author so perfectly, as to say every word without booke, as much as is possible, that the very phrase and matter of their Author may be their owne to use perpetually.

Triall by experience.

To conclude this point, triall and experience may teach us. Let two children be taken, one of a more pregnant and sharpe wit, the other of a slower and duller capacity: cause him of the sharpe wit, to do all onely by precept & his owne invention in making Epistles, Theames, Verses, disputing; but let the other of the duller capacitie be trained up, not onely by precept and his owne invention; but principally by being kept strictly to imitate the most excellent patternes in all things: then make the triall, whether he of the duller wit shall not expresse the sharpnesse, learning, gravitie, of the most learned and wise men, with certaine assurance to justifie what hee hath done: whereas in the other, shall bee found by a learned and a judicious examiner, nothing but froth, childishnesse and uncertaintie, in the greatest overweening of wit and learning; and whether the duller and harder wit shall not do it with farre lesse labour.

Sp. I must needs yeeld unto that which you say, for that evidence of truth which cannot be gainesaid. For this indeed all men doe see by common experience, that in all trades

Following constantly most excellent patterns, doth prevaile in every calling.

and sciences, they who get themselves most excellent patternes to follow, and are the curiousest in expressing them most lively, are ever found the most excellent workemen. And therefore I do content my selfe, as fully answered, intreating that we may still proceed.

CHAP.

THE GRAMMAR SCHOOLE

CHAP. XVIII.

Of pronouncing naturally and sweetly without vain affectation.

Phil.

What will you that we come unto next? I take it that we have gone thorow the most things, which concerne our function for teaching the Latine tongue.

Spoud. There remaine yet two other matters, and those of no lesse difficulty nor weight then most of the former; and without which, yet Schooles do lacke their principall ornaments, as I suppose; the one of them is pronouncing sweetly, the other speaking Latine purely and readily.

Phil. These 2 are endeed worthy of our best thoughts. The first of them, that is, Pronunciation, being that which either makes or mars the most excellent speech. For all speeches are usually esteemed even as they are uttered or pronounced: the finest Scholler without this is accounted no body: and a meane Scholler having attained this facultie, is ordinarily reputed and commended above the best. Whereupon you know how that famous Greeke Orator, when he was asked, what was the chiefe grace or excellency in Rhetoricke, what was the second and third; he still answered, To pronounce well. And for the second, that is speaking of Latine, as in examinations and disputations, so in all other things, there would be a perpetuall use of it amongst all Grammar Schooles of any yeeres. To the end, to fit them to answer any learned man in Latine, or to dispute *ex tēpore:* also to traine them up to be able to speake purely when they come in the Universities; as in some Colledges they are onely to speake Latine: or to fit them, if they shall go beyond the seas, as Gentlemen who go to travel, Factors for Marchants, and the like. The readinesse in which facultie, if it

The excellency of Pronunciation.

The necessity and estimation of being able to speake Latine readily and purely.

be

THE GRAMMAR SCHOOLE

be in a good phrase, how much it graceth a child in Universitie, Citie, or Countrey, we all of us know.

Spoud. Sir, you have spoken very truely of these: therefore let us come unto them in order, I intreate you; and first unto pronunciation. This I have found passing hard to acquaint my Schollers withall, to bring them to any ripenesse or commendable faculty, but still they will speake as a boy who is saying his lesson; though I have both directed them how to pronounce, uttering the sentences oft before them, and have very much called upon them for the same.

Phil. To bring your Schollers unto this sweetnesse of pronunciation, this is the plainest and surest way, so farre forth as yet I can find: and this I am assured will effect it in a commendable sort;

1. You must remember that which was generally premised in the beginning: To acquaint your young Scholler from the very first entrance, to pronounce every lesson and each word, audibly, leasurely, and distinctly, ever sounding out the last letter.

2. To pronounce every matter according to the nature of it, so much as you can; chiefely where persons or other things are fained to speake.

As for example: In the *Confabulatiunculæ pueriles*, cause them to utter every dialogue lively, as if they themselves were the persons which did speake in that dialogue, and so in every other speech, to imagine themselves to have occasion to utter the very same things.

3. What they cannot utter well in Latine, cause them first to do it naturally and lively in English, and shew them your selfe the absurdnesse of their pronunciation, by pronouncing foolishly or childishly, as they do: and then pronounce it rightly, and naturally before them likewise, that they may perceive the difference, to be ashamed of the one, and take a delight in the other.

So cause them to do it after you, untill that they can doe it in good sort, tuning their voices sweetly. When they can do

THE GRAMMAR SCHOOLE

do in English, then cause them to do it just in the same manner in Latine; and thus they will undoubtedly come unto it very easiely.

4. Also cause sundry of them to pronounce thus the very same sentence; disgracing the speech of those who pronounce absurdly, by imitation of it, and gracing as much the speech of those who do it most naturally and pleasantly: propounding such as patternes and markes to all their fellowes, for all to emulate and imitate them; as I have advised generally. *4. To cause sundry to pronounce the very same sentence in emulation.*

5. Cause them to doe the like in *Corderius*, *Esop's* Fables, or *Terrence* as they did in *Confabulatiunculæ*. For *Esop's* Fables, we have shewed before the manner, for making a report of each Fable first in English, after in Latine, and the benefit thereof. *5. In all Authors wherein persons are fained to speake to be carefull for this.*

So after when they shall come to *Virgil's* Eclogues, cause them yet still more lively, in saying without booke, to expresse the affections and persons of Sheepeheards; or whose speech soever else, which they are to imitate. Of which sort are the Prosopopeyes of *Jupiter*, *Apollo*, and others in *Ovid's* Metamorphosis, *Juno Neptune*, *Æolus*, *Æneas*, *Venus*, *Dido*, &c. *Virgil's* Æneids.

So in all Poetry, for the pronuntiation, it is to bee uttered as prose; observing distinctions and the nature of the matter; not to be tuned foolishly or childishly after the manner of scanning a Verse as the use of some is. Onely to tune it so in scanning, or getting it without booke, unlesse you would have them to pronounce some speciall booke, for getting authorities for quantities; or others, onely to that same purpose. *Poetry to bee pronounced as prose, except in scanning.*

6. To helpe hereunto yet more, and that they may doe everything according to the very nature; acquaint them to pronounce some speciall examples, set downe in *Talæus'* Rhetoricke as pathetically as they can: as examples of Ironies, Exclamations, Revocations, Prosopopeyes, and those which are in his rules of pronouncing. *6. Further helpes as they proceede. Practice of oft pronouncing pathetically, some speciall example in Talæus.*

Let them also be taught carefully, in what word the Empha-

THE GRAMMAR SCHOOLE

To marke in each sentence in what word the Emphasis is.

phasis lieth; and therefore which is to be elevated in the pronunciation. As namely those words in which the chiefe Trope or Figure is.

☞ Butler's *Rhet.* li. 2 cap. 2. de voce in singulis verbis.

Thus let them take speciall paines to pronounce Theames or Declamations, striving who shall do best: and in all their oppositions to dispute, as if *ex animo* in good earnest, with all contention and vehemencie.

Care in pronouncing all exercises.
The curious pronouncing some of Tullies *Orations or the like.*

Finally, the practice of pnonouncing emphatically, of some of *Tullies* Orations, which are most flowing in these Figures of sentences (especially in Exclamations, Prosopopeyes, Apostrophees, and the like: as some against *Catiline*) must needes much acquaint them with great variety of pronunciation to be fitted for all sorts.

More exquisite knowledge hereof left to the Universities.
Butleri *Rhet.* li. 2. de pronunt.

For more exquisite knowledge and practice hereof, I leave it to the Universities, which are to perfect all those faculties which are but begun in the Grammar Schooles; & do referre you for precepts, to the second booke of *Talæus* Rhetoricke *de pronunciatione*, or rather of Master *Butler's* Rhetoricke, as I said before.

CHAP. XIX.

Of speaking Latine purely and readily.

Spoud.

I Pray you Sir, go on to the last point: in the which you have said for the manner of pronunciation, I have heard nothing which I can justly except against, it doth all sound so pleasing and likely in mine eare. When I have more triall, I shall be able to say more.

In the meane time let me crave the like, for the manner of learning to speake Latine. If you can shew me so plaine a way of it, as this seemeth to be, surely you shall make me much more to rejoyce.

For

THE GRAMMAR SCHOOLE

For of this I may complaine yet more, then of most of the rest; that though I have laboured and striven by *Ferula*, and all meanes of severity, yet I have not beene able to make my Schollers to utter their mindes in any tolerable manner, of ordinary things, but in very barbarous phrase, nor so much as to put it in practice amongst themselves; much lesse to utter their mindes in Latine easily, purely, and freely as it were to be wished, and as you have shewed the necessity and commendation thereof. *Complaint of the trouble and difficulty to traine up Schollers to speake Latine.*

Phil. I myselfe have had long experience of the truth and griefe of this complaint likewise, though I also have done what I could continually: and yet of late time I grow to this certaine assurance, that Schollers might be brought to talke of any ordinary matter which can be required of them, both in good Latine, and also most readily and easily.

Herein hath beene a great part of my errour and hinderance, that I ever thought as most do, that children were not to be exercised to speake Latine, for feare of Barbarisme, untill they came into the highest fourmes; as at least untill they were in the third, fourth, or fift fourmes: and hereupon I could never attaine to that which I desired. *The generall errour for the time when Schollers are to begin to speake Latine.*

But now I find evidently, that this must be begunne from the very first entrance into construction; their first bookes being principally appointed, and read to them to this end, to enter and traine them up in speaking of Latine of ordinary matters: *To learne to speake Latine, must be begun from the first entrance into construction.*

As *Confabulatiunculæ, Pueriles, Corderius*, and other like Colloquiums. And therefore they should then begin to practise to use those phrases which there they learne.

Also for the Grammar, I see no reason but it might have beene all as well set downe in the English, like as the Accedence is, and learned in one halfe of the time, and with much more delight; but onely or chiefly to traine up Schollers to deliver all their Grammar rules, and matters concerning Grammar in Latine.

Spoud. It standeth with very great reason, that it should
be

THE GRAMMAR SCHOOLE

be as you say, that in the learning of those bookes, the right foundation of speaking Latine familiarly should bee laied; and the practice begunne; and that indeede there is a generall mistaking about this: but I desire you to set downe the whole course and proceeding in it, how to bring it to perfection; and then I shall bee much better able to judge.

Phil. For the manner of effecting it, I find it to be most easie thus:

The surest course for entring young Schollers to speake Latine.
1. Examining and answering every piece of a rule or sentence in Latine, to make them their owne. So in their Authors.

1. You must remember that which I said, concerning the manner of the examining both of their Grammar rules and Lectures; to pose every piece of a rule, and every part of a sentence both in English and Latine, as leasure will permit; and to cause them to answer both in English and Latine, untill they be able to understand and answer in Latine alone. And so both the examining in the words of their Authors, and causing them to answer likewise in the very same words of the Authors, they will enter into it with great delight. For the particular manner, I referre you to the Chapter of examining in Latine, which I shewed you before at large, and set downe examples of it.

2. To utter before them what they cannot. How the Master himselfe may do it easily before them.

2. What they are not able to utter in Latine, utter you it ever before them; that as the child learneth of the Mother or of the Nurse, to begin to speake, so they may of you and of their Author.

If you were not able so to utter every thing before them, as very many are to seeke this way, amongst others (I meane in this, to speake in Latine easily and purely, even in ordinary matters;) yet this continuall practice of daily examining and teaching your Schollers to answer out of the words of the Author (as the manner was set downe before) and watchfulnesse to use to speake Latine, onely amongst all whom you would have to learne it, shall bring you unto it; and much more by the meanes following.

3. The daily practice of Grammaticall translations; chiefly reading bookes of Dialogues out of English into Latine, which is nothing but such talking.

3. I do find the daily practise also of those Grammaticall translations, which I have so oft mentioned in reading the Latine of the Author out of the translation, to be a

mar-

THE GRAMMAR SCHOOLE

marvellous helpe hereunto; especially the reading of books of Dialogues: as of *Confabulatiunculæ pueriles, Corderius, &c.* For if there they can presently expresse their mindes in Latine, of any such matter as is there handled; why shall they not be able to doe it likewise, of any such thing falling nto their common talke.

4 As they learne these Dialogues, when they have construed and parsed, cause them to talke together; uttering every sentence pathetically one to another (as was shewed in our former speech of pronouncing) and first to utter every sentence in English, as neede is, then in Latine. So you shall be sure that they shall not goe by rote (as we tearme it) and as they may do soone, if they only repeate the Latine so talking together. And moreover, ever thus with the English, the Latine will easily come to their remembrance, so often as they have occasion to use the same.

4. To talke together in the words of the Dialogues, each sentence first in English, then Latine.

5 The practice mentioned of turning every morning a piece of their Accedence into Latine, for their exercise, shall much prepare them to parse and speake in Latine.

5. Translating and uttering every morning a piece of their Accedence in Latine.

6 Accustome them to parse wholly in Latine, by that time that they have been a yeere or two at the most, in construction, and are well acquainted with the manner of parsing in English, as we advised before. This they will do very readily, if you traine them up well in their Accedence, and in the former kindes of examining and exercises, which I spake of even now; and more specially by the right and continuall apposing of their Grammar rules in Latine. Moreover, the Dialogues in the end of the first booke of *Corderius* Dialogues, wil much further them in this parsing, because they are principally written to this purpose; as all his foure bookes are very sweet and pleasant for all ordinary schollers talke.

6. Custome to parse wholly in Latine, and how to doe it.

Corderius li. 1. Colloq. 69. 70, 71, 72, 73, 74. 75.

7 Next unto these I finde the daily practice of disputing or opposing in Latine (following the order, and using the helpe of M. *Stockwood*) to be marveilously profitable, for witty and sweet speech.

7. Daily practice of disputing.

8 Unto

Speaking 218 *Latine.*

THE GRAMMAR SCHOOLE

8. Practice of varying a phrase into divers formes.

8 Unto these you may adde the practice of varying of a phrase, according to the manner of *Erasmus, Rivius,* or *Macropedius, de copia verborum:* as the wayes of varying the first Supine, of the Imperative mood, the future tense, the Superlative degree, and the like. But these onely as leisure wil suffer, not hindering the most necessary exercises.

9. Copie of Synonimaes, and the purest phrases, and how to get them. This noted before.

9 So also for copie of the purest phrases and Synonimaes, besides the daily helpes of all their Authors, *Manutius* or Master *Draxe* his phrases, to see how many waies they can utter any thing in good phrase; and so to turne any phrase when they have occasion. And more specially for that practice of the reading them out of the Grammaticall Translations in propriety (as was shewed before of the Dialogues) any shall finde to be most easie, to furnish with store of the purest phrase for any purpose.

10. Exercising the schollers oft to give variety for every difficult matter.

10 Besides, for the Master to use oft, at taking or saying Lectures or exercises, or at their pronouncing or shewing exercises, to cause them to give variety for any thing; who is able to give a better word or phrase, or to give the greatest copy to expresse their minds, and where they have read the words or phrase.

11. Holyoke's Dictionary, describing things by Periphrasis or circumlocution.

11 Where none can give a fit word, there to turne their Dictionaries, as to *Holyoke's* Dictionary, and then to furnish them, or to describe the thing by some Periphrasis or circumlocution of words or the phrases mentioned.

12. To give daily certaine proper words, and where they have read them.

12 But to the end to have copie of proper words, besides all other helpes spoken of, it were not unprofitable to have daily some few words to be repeated first in the morning; as out of *Adrianus Junius* his Nomenclator; or out of the Latine Primitives, or the Greek Radices; the use whereof I shall shew hereafter: and ever for those words which they have learned (any one who can soonest) to name where they have learned them.

Thus by all meanes they should be furnished with propriety and copie of the best words; which is a wonderfull helpe to all kinde of learning, especially to the knowledge of the tongues.

13 To

THE GRAMMAR SCHOOLE

13 To all these may be added for them who have leisure enough, the reading over and over of *Erasmus'* Colloquium, *Castalion's* Dialogues, or the like.

13. Reading over Erasmus' Colloquium.

14 Lastly, when you have laid a sound foundation, that they may be sure to have warrantable and pure phrase, by these meanes or the best of them, and all other their schoole exercises; then continuall practice of speaking shall undoubtedly accomplish your desire, to cause them to speake truely, purely, properly, and readily; Practice in a good way being here, as in all the rest, that which doth all.

14. Continuall practice, when they have learned a pure phrase

Spoud. These things, or but the best of them, being constantly practised, cannot but effect marvellous much, and very surely; chiefly, if we could bring them to speake Latine continually, from that time that they begin to parse in Latine: but this I have had too much experience of, that without great severity they will not be brought unto: but they will speake English, and one will winke at another, if they be out of the Master's hearing.

Difficulty to cause schollers to practise speaking Latine amongst themselves.

Phil. It is indeed exceeding hard, to cause this to be practised constantly amongst schollers. That is a usuall custome in Schooles to appoint *Custodes*, or *Asini* (as they are tearmed in some places) to observe and catch them who speake English in each fourme, or whom they see idle, to give them the Ferula, and to make them *Custodes*, if they cannot answer a question which they aske.

Inconveniences of Custodes.

But I have observed so much inconvenience in it, as I cannot tell what to say in this case: for oft-times, he who is the *Custos*, will hardly attend his owne worke, for harkening to heare others to speake English.

Also there falleth out amongst them oft-times so much wrangling about the questions, or defending themselves, that they did not speak English, or were not idle, that all the whole fourme is troubled. So likewise when the *Custodes* are called for, before breaking up at dinner and at night, there will be so much contention amongst them, as is a disquieting and trouble to the Master. Moreover, this I have observed, that ever if there be any one simple in a fourme,

or

THE GRAMMAR SCHOOLE

or harder of learning then the rest, they will make him a right *Asinus*, causing such to be the *Custodes* continually, or for the most part, if they cannot answer: and to this end will be always watching them; whereby many such are not onely notably abused, but very much discouraged for being schollers, when they see themselves so baited at by all: some others are made over malapert thereby.

☞ *Of one scholler smiting another with the Ferula.*

Besides all these, I doe not see any great fitnesse, that one scholler should smite another with the Ferula; because much malicing one another, with grudges and quarrels doe arise thereupon. So that the discommodities that follow the *Custodes* seeme to me to be many moe then the benefits can be; chiefly in losse of time, and hindering more in other learning, then can be gotten in that.

Spoud. I my selfe have had experience of most of these inconveniences: but what way will ye take then, to cause your schollers to speake Latine continually?

The best meanes.
☞ 1. *Seniors of each fourme to looke to the whole.*

Phil. This is the best way that yet I can find, and to avoid the former inconveniences; First, to appoint the two Seniors in each fourme (of whom we shall speake after) as to looke to all other matters in the fourme, so to this more specially, that none speake English nor barbarous Latine: and if they be found partiall or negligent, then to preferre others into their places; besides the other censures to be inflicted upon them which I shall mention to you, when we shall come to speake of punishments; and so to have their due rewards, being found carefull. Secondly, the Master's owne eye and eare in the Schoole, to be continuall *Custodes* so much as may be, both for Monitors and others. Thirdly, if they doe use to parse in Latine (and therefore must needs exercise themselves in that against that time that their Master doth come to heare them) and secondly, if they be kept in their places, and strictly looked unto for performing all exercises; I doe not see but they may be made to speake Latine in the schoole at schoole-times; neither that they shal have any great occasions of the contrary. Fourthly, for speaking Latine in all other places, it must only be by Monitors appointed

☞ 2. *The Master's eye and eare.*
☞ 3. *Parsing in Latine.*

4. *Weekely Monitors abroad.*

THE GRAMMAR SCHOOLE

appointed weekely, as we shall have occasion to speak more after, and some severely corrected who are found most carelesse herein.

Spoud. But if any one alone, who hath some understanding of Latine, would learne to speake of familiar matters, to be able to talke with others, what course doe you thinke the speediest? *[How any one may by himselfe alone attaine to speake Latine of ordinary matters.]*

Phil. Even the same which I would use to helpe a whole Schoole: which if I should take a course for a wager, amongst others, I would use specially, to cause them daily to spend some quarter, or halfe an houre, each in his order, reading *Corderius* first out of Latine into English, after out of English into Latine, every one a little piece; where one failes, another to helpe; and the booke or Master, where all faile: and also the Master to cause them to vary each hard phrase (and chiefly all which are of most common use) so many wayes as they can, trying who can do best; himselfe to adde moe where they faile. After *Corderius* gone over, to doe the like in other easie Authors, as *Terence*, or *Terentius Christianus*, and the like. So I would have the private learner to practise daily the same, reading *Corderius* first out of Latine into English, by helpe of the translation; after trying how he can read it out of English into Latine, and ever where he failes, to use the helpe of the Latine book lying by him. The continuall exercise in this, if they labour to be perfect in the examples of Nounes and Verbs, and somewhat in knowing the Rules of the Accedence, as was shewed, shall most speedily effect this desire. For thus may any one soone learne to utter all that booke: And in it is the substance of most things falling out in ordinary speech. After this, he may do the like in another easie booke by the same helpe of translations. And lastly, practising to translate other bookes of Dialogues (as, *Erasmus Colloquium*, or the like) and afterwards reading them forth of English into Latine againe, any one may come on very fast.

Spoud. This stands upon the former grounds. These severall points which you have gone thorow, for training up schollers

THE GRAMMAR SCHOOLE

schollers to attaine to so good perfection in the Latine tongue, seem to me very sufficient, and to need no addition.

Phil. These are but an entrance, meet for the Grammar schooles; but to attaine to the perfection of the Latine tongue, for propriety, choise, elegancy, puritie, will require much and long reading, and exercise in the Universities.

<small>Goclenius his observations for them who seeke to come to purity and ripenesse in the Latine tongue.</small>

For further direction thereunto, I refer you to *Goclenius* his observations of the Latine tongue: whom I take to be worthy the diligent reading of all schollers who are of judgement, and who doe desire to come to the purity and ripenesse of the Latine.

CHAP. XX.

How to attaine most speedily unto the knowledge of the Greeke Tongue.

Spoud.

Now that we have gone thorow all the principall points of learning, which belong to the knowledge of the Latine tongue, so much as can be required in schooles, as farre forth as I can conceive or remember for the present; let me (I intreat you) require your like helpe for the Greeke: for I desire now, to be directed in every matter, which may concerne our calling and facultie. I doe perceive by our former speeches, that you likewise have travelled and found much experience and assurance herein.

<small>The Greeke may be gotten with farre lesse labour than the Latine.</small>

Phil. Although I am onely a learner in the Greeke, as in the Latine, and my hope is chiefly for the time to come; yet this I have found by experience, that the Latine once obtained, the Greeke may be gotten with farre lesse labour, and every thing as certainly. And this also in a little time, so much as it shall be requisite for the Grammar schooles.

Spoud.

THE GRAMMAR SCHOOLE

Spoud. Surely Sir, if but that one thing that I saw in the note, may be attained, concerning the tongues, the Greeke and Hebrew, I do not see what can be more required for the Grammar schooles: that is; That schollers may be able as they proceed, to reade the Greeke of the New Testament, and the Hebrew of the old, first into Latine, or English exactly, out of the bare text, and after, out of a translation to reade them into the text, that is, into their owne words againe: and also to give the reason of every word, why it must be so, and to be able to proceed thus of themselves in the Universitie. *One benefit worth all our labour in the Greeke.*

The continuall practice thereof, must needs make them worthy Linguists, as was there said, and notable text men. I pray you therefore let me heare of you, how this may be effected, and I shall thinke my selfe sufficiently satisfied for all my travell, though it were but in this one thing alone besides all the former.

Phil. Nay rather, let us goe thorow the whole course still, so farre as we can, how the exact knowledge of this famous tongue may be gotten most speedily. For when I do remember the worthy testimony, which our learnedest Schoolemaster doth give, concerning this Greeke tongue, I cannot thinke any paines over-much, for the finding out the ready way to the perfect knowledge of it. He in one place having mentioned sundry of the renowned Greeke Authors, as *Plato, Aristotle, Xenophon, Demosthenes, Isocrates,* and others, whom he names there (the matchlesse masters in all manner of learning) adds these words in praise of the Greek tongue, and the learning in it: *To goe thorow the whole course of the Greeke.* *M. Askam's testimony concerning the Greeke tongue. Schoolemaster p. 17. 2,*

Now let Italian, saith he, and Latine it selfe, Spanish, French, Dutch, and English bring forth their learning, and recite their Authors, *Cicero* onely excepted, and one or two more in Latine; they be all patched clouts and ragges in comparison of faire woven broad cloathes. And truely, saith he, if there be any good in them, it is either learned, borrowed, or stolne from some one of those worthy wits of Athens. Thus farre M. *Askam.*

Spoud.

THE GRAMMAR SCHOOLE

Spoud. This is a high commendation indeed, to be given by a man of such reading and estimation for learning, as M. *Askam* was; and which must needs incite all students to the reading of the principall Greeke Authors, to desire to heare these peerelesse Masters to speake in their owne tongue.

Wherefore, I pray you let us heare from you, how you thinke that the way may be made so ready unto it.

The way to the Greeke, the same with the Latine.

Phil. The way may be most short and easie to him, who is acquainted with the maner of getting the Latine tongue, so as hath been mentioned; because it is the very same with it in effect.

Getting first the chiefe rules.

1. If your schollers who are to enter into it, be such as have time enough before them; let them get the Grammar very perfectly, especially all the chiefe rules, by continuall saying and poasing, as in the Latine. Most exceptions or Anomalies may be learned after, or turned unto presently, as they learne their Authors, Because *Rectum* is *Index sui, & obliqui*. And knowing the rule perfectly, they will soone know the reason of the change.

To be very perfect in Nounes and Verbs.

More specially, make them very perfect in declining Nouns and Verbs, and giving all the Terminations of them: I meane the severall Terminations of each Declension, and every case in them; and so likewise the Terminations of every Conjugation, and each Tense therein.

Terminating Nounes. Conjugating and terminating Verbs.

In the Conjugations, to give the first person of every Mood and Tense, in each voice together (whereby they are the soonest learned, one directing another) and also to be able to runne the Terminations as in the Latine.

To give the first person in every Mood and Tense in each voice together.

For example, in the first Declension. The terminations of the Declension are ας and ης. Terminations of the cases are ας, ου, ᾳ αν, α, &c.

So declining the example.

Αἰνείας, αἰνείου, αἰνείᾳ, αἰνείαν, ὦ αἰνεία.

So in the rest: The Terminations gotten first perfectly, the words are declined presently, as I said.

In the Verbs also, besides the Terminations, to use to give the

Greeke. 225

THE GRAMMAR SCHOOLE

the first persons together in every voice. Onely let them be perfect in the Active voice, giving all the first persons in order; then the passive and middle voice, by comparing them to the Active: As *Indicatiuus præsens,* τυπτω *verbero,* τύπτομαι τυπτομαι. *Imperfectum,* ἔτυπτον *verberabam,* ἐτυπτόμην, ἐτυπτόμην. *Futurum prius,* τύψω *verberabo,* τυφθήσομαι τύψομαι.

So the Terminations of them, if you will: As ω, ομαι, ομαι, ον, ομην, ομην, &c.

To this end, make them very perfect in the tables of the *cognata tempora.* And also cause them to run the Terminations in each voice thus; ω, εις, ει, ετον, ετον, ομεν ετε, ετε, ουσι ον, ες, ε, ετον ετην, ομεν, ετε, ον.

You shall find they will be learned not onely very soone and surely this way, but also most profitably for use.

After these to be perfect in Pronounes, Adverbs, Conjunctions, and Prepositions; giving (if you will) Latine to Greeke, and Greeke to Latine, as I shewed before in the Latine. Because then all the labour is with the Nounes and Verbes onely. *To be very perfect in Pronouns, Adverbs, Conjunctions, Prepositions.*

If your schollers who begin Greeke, be of good yeeres and judgement; it may suffice to have them perfect in the examples of the Nounes and Verbes, and some fewe principall rules, in such sort as I have shewed: and to be well acquainted with the order of the Grammar, by shewing how and where every part of it stands; that so they may learne the Rules or the meaning of them, by turning to them; as they shall have occasion in every lecture. *How schollers of understanding and judgement, may take yet a shorter course.*

Spoud. But what Grammar would you have them to use?

Phil. Master Camdens Grammar, notwithstanding the faults in the print (as indeede there are very many; which thing would bee carefully amended in all our Schoole-Authors) and what other exceptions can be taken: because, as it is one of the shortest as yet, so it is most answerable to our Latine Grammar, for the order of it. Whereby schollers wel acquainted with our common Grammar, wil be much
helped

THE GRAMMAR SCHOOLE

helped both for speedy understanding and learning it. Also the words of Art set downe in it in Greeke, as well as Latine, will bee a great helpe for reading Commentaries in Greeke: as upon *Hesiode*, and *Homer*.

To make it plaine: Grammatica Græca pro Schola Argentinensi per Theophilum Golium.

To the end to make that Grammar most plaine, and to supply and helpe whatsoever is defective; I take it, that the *Strasburge* Greeke Grammar, set forth lately by *Golius* (which seemes to me to have beene made in an imitation of *Camden*) may be as a good Commentarie, though the order be not ever directly kept. The first part of it serving for a brief summe of the Etymologie, the second for an exposition at large.

Spoud. But with what Author would you begin, to enter them into Construction.

☞ *To begin Construction with the Greeke Testament.*
Reasons.
1. For the familiarnesse of it.
2. Because that booke with the Hebrew of the Old Testament, are the Booke of bookes.
Being onely written by the Lord.
Having life in them.

Phil. I hold the Greeke Testament to bee most fit; and that for these reasons:

1. Because, that through the familiarnesse of the matter, (in that children are so well acquainted with it, by daily hearing or reading of it) the Greeke thereof which is easie of itselfe, will be made yet farre more easie to the learner; for that the matter will bring the words, as I have oft said.

2. Because all Schollers who can have meanes to come to any knowledge of the Greeke, should indeavour above all other Authors, to be well acquainted with this. First, for that this booke together with the Hebrew of the Old Testament, were written by the Lord himselfe; not onely the matter, but also even the very words of them.

Secondly, for that eternall life is onely in these bookes, being truly understood and beleeved. So that wee may rightly tearme these the Bible, or Book of books; because all other bookes are but as servants unto these, and all other are nothing without these, for any true good, but onely to condemnation by leaving men more without excuse.

All who may, are to labour to see with their owne eyes, and why.

Yea, every one who can have opportunitie, should labour to see with his owne eyes, for the fulnesse of his assurance, rather then to rest on others. And much more because there are so many and such malicious slanders against all

our

THE GRAMMAR SCHOOLE

our translations; as that those shameless calumniations have beene a principall meanes to turne many thousand soules, after Satan and Antichrist, by causing them to reject the sacred Scriptures utterly, to their endlesse perdition, and have beene enough to shake the faith of God's Elect. Under this very pretence of false translations, and obscuritie of the Scriptures, hath Antichrist principally holden up his kingdome; keeping all in palpable ignorance to be drawne to dumb Idols, to murther Princes, to lying and all abominations which himselfe listeth.

And therefore in these respects it were to bee wished, that all schollers who have any leasure, and may come to these studies of Greeke and Hebrew (especially they who purpose in time to become teachers of others) would do their indeavours to be as perfect in these two bookes, and to have them as familiarly as ever the ancient Jewes had the Hebrew. This cunning in the Text should make them to speake as the words of God indeed, with facility, authority, and power. *To strive to have these bookes as familiarly as the Jewes had the Hebrew*

Those also, who have but a little time to bestow in the Greeke, would bestow it here, for the former reasons; and because they may have good occasion and helpe to increase in this continually, by the daily use which they have of the Scriptures: whereas they, having but a smattring in some other Greeke Authors, and contenting themselves therewith, do come in a short time utterly to forget all; and so all that labour which was taken therein, is altogether lost. *If any purpose to have but a smattering in the Greeke, to have it here, and why.*

If any do preferre some other Greeke Author, for the sweetnesse and purity of the Greeke, and so will spend their little time in that; *Luke* is inferior to none therein, by the judgement of the learned. If they looke to the excellencie or all wisdome, what light is there to the light of the Sunne? Also, for them who have a desire to travell further, amongst all the famous Greeke writers, for the surpassing humane wisedome to bee found therein; this booke once perfectly knowne, will make the passage thorow all of them both very direct and plaine, and also full of all delight and contentment, *The Testament compared to other Greeke writers. This is a notable entrance to reade all other Greek Authors.*

THE GRAMMAR SCHOOLE

tentment, and to reade all other Authors without any danger.

In the Testament to begin at the Gospell of John.

In the Greeke Testament, to begin at the Gospell of *John*, as being most easie; and next unto that, to go thorow the Gospell of *Luke*, if you please. In which two Evangelists most of the History of the Gospell is contained: that by them the Evangelists may bee sooner runne thorow; And also the Acts: Then all the Epistles may be read with speed.

Spoud. I cannot but allow and like of all these things; and principally of reading the Greeke Testament, in the first place, making it the entrance, and another foundation to all the Greeke studies. But if that could be brought

How schollers may be made most perfect in the Greeke Testament

to passe, that Schollers, as they proceeded herein, might grow as perfect in the Greeke Testament, as it is said of the learned Jewes, that they were in the bookes of the Old Testament; what a blessing might it be to the Church of God, and what a happinesse to all posterity?

Phil. Surely, I am fully perswaded of it, that very much may be done in it; and after also, in the Hebrew of the Old to come neere unto them: except that, that was their native language. This perswasion I ground, partly from that little experience which I have had in mine owne triall; yet sufficient to confirm me by proportion. More especially, by that which is well knowne in a worthy Schoole in London, (to which I acknowledge my selfe much beholden for that which I have seene in this behalfe, and some other) where some of the Schollers have beene able in very good sort to construe and resolve the Greeke Testament out of the Latin into Greek, wheresoever you would set them, and to go very neere to tell you, where they had read any speciall word or phrase in it, to turne to them. And lastly, for the evident reasons thereof, and the agreement of it with some former courses in the Latine, whereof I have a full assurance.

Spoud. I pray you shew me the meanes how.

Meanes particularly.

Phil. The meanes are these, most easie and plaine, for every one to teach who hath any Greeke, and for others to learne:

1. That they have so much knowledge in the Grammar,

mar, as I shewed chiefely in Nounes and Verbes.

2. Besides the Greeke Testament, I would have every one to have his English Testament, or Latine, or both; and ever in the entrance before they learne a lesson, to have read it over in the translation, and to bee able either to say it without booke, or make a report of it in English or Latine: but better to say it without booke, even in the English; which with a little reading over, especially before bedde time, those who are of good memories will get quickly. This same done with understanding, will exceedingly bring the Greeke with it: besides, that thus they shall have much opportunity and furtherance, to get the English text almost by heart, as we tearme it.

3. In reading a Lecture to them, ever tell them what example each Noune and Verbe is like unto, and for Pronounes, Adverbes, and the like: if they bee not perfect in Grammar, tell them in a word, or point them where they are in the Grammar; just after the manner as in the Latine.

4. Shew them carefully all the hard words, and those which they have not learned; & for those which you thinke they cannot remember otherwise, or wherein there is neede of speciall labour, cause every one to write them in a little paper-bookè, made for that purpose, with sundry columnes in each page, to write at least the Greeke word and Latine or English in, in each Chapter, and the Verse against them: to the end to take most paines in those, and to run oft over them: and so ever to see after where they have had those words before. And thereby also to account how many new words they have in every Lecture: for all the rest learned before in any place, or which are very easie, are not to be accounted for any new words.

Thus shall you provoke and encourage them to more paines, when they have not over five or sixe new words in a doozen or twenty Verses, and in time happely not two in a Chapter. So that they will have the most of the hard words in a short time, and be able easily to proceed of themselves,
without

THE GRAMMAR SCHOOLE

without any reading through these and other helpes following.

5. When they learne to construe, let them doe it by the helpe of the translation; observing wherein the translation seemes to differ from the words of the Greeke, and marking the reason thereof; and after to trie of themselves how they can construe, looking onely upon the translation, beating the Greeke out of it, as formerly they did the Latine. Those who are of any aptnesse, will do it presently.

And thus by practice, every day going a piece, and oft reading over and over, they will grow very much, to your great joy.

Spoud. But give me leave to aske of you two or three doubts.

1. Why to have the hard words written downe. 1. Why you would have them to write downe their hard words in a book: will not making some markes at the words serve as in their Latine Authours, according to the generall observation?

Phil. This was observed before, as I remember, to marke their hard words either in their bookes, or setting them downe in a paper. But here I thinke it to be better, thus to write downe the principall; First, because Schollers now will be carefull to keepe their Greeke Testaments faire from blotting or scrauling, although a booke were well bestowed to make them perfect in it, though it were never so marked. Secondly, because when they are fit to reade Greeke, they have commonly good discretion to keepe their notes, and to make use of them; going oft over them.

Spoud. But might there not be some other meanes for the getting of the hard words aforesaid? for this must needes be some labour, and aske care and diligence thus to write them downe.

Phil. Yes verily, if it be looked to in time; all these may be so prepared aforehand, that most of this labour now may be spared, and onely speciall difficulties to be observed.

☞ The manner of it is thus. That whereas there is nothing in getting any tongue, but to get words, and Grammar for framing

THE GRAMMAR SCHOOLE

framing and setting those words together, and afterwards practice; I hold it to be farre the speediest course, to have the Schollers to have learned the Greeke *Radices* or Primitive words, before that they go to construction; or at least to be well acquainted with them. *The speediest way, to get the Greeke Radices first.*

This course some famous Grecians have taken: we may do it most easily, and without any losse of time, or very little, if any; as I have made triall: First, having gathered the Greek *Radices* out of *Scapula*, after the manner of that abbridgement, called *voces primogeniæ*, I have heretofore caused such as I have thought fit, to write it out, and to bring me a side (or so much as I thought good) every morning at my entrance into the Schoole, or presently after; and so have used to examine those words amongst them all, once or twice over, and where they have learned the principall Latine words. (Of late I have seene the Greeke *Nomenclator* used, not without fruit; though it be unperfectly gathered.) *How it may be done easily, without losse of time.*

The manner of getting the words may bee most easie, thus: *Manner of learning them.*

Having these in this manner with the English adjoyned: if you would make triall herein; when you have examined a side, reade them over as much more against the next day; reading first the English word, then the Latine, and Greeke last: shewing them some helpe how to remember, by comparing the Greeke with the Latine, or English; and so the English will bring the Latine to remembrance, and both of them the Greeke.

And in examining them, to aske them the English word; and to cause them to give both Latine and Greeke together, both backeward and forward againe. *Manner of examining them for speed and memory.*

As, posing thus: How say you, I love? He answereth, *Amo*, ἀγαπάω; ἀγαπάω, *amo* I love: so they will be perfect each way. Thus within the space of a twelvemoneth they may go thorow the whole; spending not much above a quarter of an houre in a day, or halfe an houre at most of Schoole time. Those who are diligent may get them in good sort, onely

THE GRAMMAR SCHOOLE

onely (as I have oft admonished) making some little pricks or markes at the hardest to runne oft over them: and when they have once gone over them, you may cause them to bring you a leafe at a time, or more; as those who are apt will doe readily.

Benefit hereof. By this means besides that they shall learne very many Latine words, chiefly most of the Primitives to further them greatly in the Latine, and to countervaile all the time and labour bestowed in them: they may also, when they come to construction, either have every *Radix* in their head, or turne to it with a wet finger, and make it perfect in an instant; and thereby have such a light to all other words comming of these, as presently by them, to conceive of and remember any word.

And thus by them and their readinesse in the Grammar, to goe on in reading by the helpes mentioned, faster then you would imagine.

Having Scapula in the Schoole to runne to, they shall presently have any thing For having these *Radices* perfect, they will conceive presently by a little observing, of what roote every word commeth, and ghesse neere at the significations of them.

Spoud. But how shall I teach my fourmes which have not learned the Greeke Grammar, to reade these *Radices*?

☞
How children may soon learne to reade the Greeke, before they learne the Greek Grammar.
Phil. Nothing more easily: for I finde by experience that they will learne that presently, by knowing but the value and power of the Greeke letters; I meane what every letter signifieth, or soundeth in the Latine: and so calling them by their names, as *A. b. g. d.* or giving them their sounds. Although if you will, the names of the Greeke characters are soone learned: but that former course, with continuall reading over to them before-hand, so much as you would have them to learne at once, will sufficiently effect it, until they learne the Grammar.

In learning the Radices to observe right pronunciation for accents and spirits. In learning these *Radices*, call upon them oft to marke carefully the accents of each word, with the spirits: for that will further them exceedingly to accent right, when they come

THE GRAMMAR SCHOOLE

come to write in Greeke, by knowing but the accent of the Primitive word, and a few other rules. Right pronouncing of them, will make both their accents and spirits remembred.

By some experience of the fruit of this booke, for the speedy getting of the Greeke, I have endevoured to make it more perfect, by placing so neere as I can, *This booke laboured in for the common good.*

First the most proper significations in the first place; and only one word in each signification, lest the volume should prove over-great: though (if the volume would beare it) variety under every one, being rightly placed, were the better, to use as need required; and thereby also helpe to furnish with copy of *Synonimaes*.

Secondly, by setting downe also the English in one proper word, or just as the Latine; onely to expresse it, and without variety: except in some special things which have divers names in our owne tongue, not commonly knowne.

Thirdly, setting downe also the Articles in the Nounes, at least in all which are hard to distinguish. The Future and Preterperfect tenses of the Verbes may be knowne by their figurative letters: Anomalyes are set down in the Grammar for most part.

I also intend (God willing) to set in the Margent of it all the Hebrew *Radices*, against every *Radix* in Greeke; at least so many as can be found: which I presume upon good ground will be found a speedy introduction to the Hebrew.

Thus young schollers, and all others who are desirous to get the tongues, may make a most easie entrance into them, and goe forward with much pleasure in all together: for having these, they shall lacke nothing in effect, but some precepts of Grammar, with practice in reading.

Spoud. But I would thinke, these *Radices* should be very hard to remember.

Phil. Not so: for there is such an agreement and harmony betweene all the foure tongues, or some of them in

many

THE GRAMMAR SCHOOLE

Helpe for committing words to memory.

many words, as will make the learners to take a delight in them, and much quicken and confirme the memory of the weakest; if it be but by the very sounding of one word like another.

Those words which they cannot remember thus, direct them to remember them by some other name or thing which we know well; being of a like sound: which so soone as they but conceive, the Greeke or Hebrew words may come to their minde, or the significations of them.

Caveat in remembring.

Here must be remembered that *Maxime* in the Arte of Memory, that the more we doe animate or give life unto the object, or thing whereby we would remember the more presently will the word which we would remember come to our minde. But yet withall, we must alwayes looke to that divine Caveat, that we never helpe the minde by any filthy object, or whatsoever may any way corrupt it, or offend the Lord: because we must never doe the least evill, that we may obtaine the greatest good. If we get any thing so, the more the worse; for it cannot prosper, but to bring a curse with it.

But for this point of the agreement of the tongues, it may be I shall have more occasion yet after, and how to remember the words.

And thus much shortly for remembering the *Radices*.

The Greeke Radices contrived into continued speeches.

Yet besides these, there might yet be a shorter way for committing all the *Radices* to memory, or exceedingly helping thereunto;

If all the principall of them were contrived into continued speeches, and divided into certaine *Classes* or chiefe heads; and they translated *verbatim* into Latine or English, or both: and the translation to be made in a booke separate, or in several pages; as in the one page the Greeke, in the other over against it in the Latine or English, line for line, and so many words in a line, like as is the translation of *Theognis*, and the other small Poets adjoyned, with *Sylburgius* annotations; that so looking only on the Greek, they might learne first to construe into Latine, and after

looking

THE GRAMMAR SCHOOLE

looking onely on the translation, they might beate out the Greeke (as I shewed before in the use of the translations) and onely use the helpe of the Greeke text where they could not finde it out otherwise.

By this meanes, when they were able to reade these both wayes, both the Greeke into the translation, and the translation into the Greeke readily (as they might soone doe, by oft reading over, and by understanding the matter of them well) it must needs make all other Greeke very easie, being but the same words in effect.

This worke also is done in part: it perfected and adjoyned as a *praxis* in the end of the *Radices*, being so framed (as was shewed) the one might soone be learned by the helpe of the other.

And finally for this matter of thus getting all the *Radices*, or principall words in the tongues, if all the hard Latine words, and specially whereof they may have use in good Authours, and which they have not learned in their former Authours (as namely in *Virgil*, or the rest under him, or which were not to be found in this *Nomenclator*) were set downe after all these *Radices*, in a few leaves in the end, the schollers should be withall furnished for ordinary Latine words. *Strange Latine words.*

As for such words as are peculiar to some speciall Arts, as to Physicke or the like, they are to be studied and learned onely of them who apply themselves to those Arts.

Spoud. Well Sir, to returne unto the point againe for making your schollers so perfect in the Testament, by helpe of reading it out of the Translation; I would thinke that it must needs be hard to learne to construe or reade it out of our translation, or doe it with judgement on sure grounds; because ours so oft doe expresse the sense and force of the words, for the better understanding of the matter, according to the phrase in our owne tongue; and not the words particularly. *Learning the Greeke out of our translations.*

Phil.

Greeke.

THE GRAMMAR SCHOOLE

☞
The readiest and surest way by a perfect verball translation, or the verball set in the Margent, where it differeth from that we use.

Phil. Indeed it is oft-times the more hard and uncertaine: and therefore the Scholler must take the more paines to remember it.

But to this purpose, for the exact getting of the Greeke Testament, if there were a perfect verball Translation, according to the manner of the interlineall (that so out of that the scholler might daily practise to reade the Greeke) this must needs make him exceeding ready, without danger of any missing, either of the phrase, or misplacing the words: or instead of such a perfect verball Translation, if you take the ordinarie interlineall Translation; and where it doth not sufficiently expresse the force of the Greeke words, there setting downe the different words in the Margent, as they are in the best Translations, you shall finde it very profitable. Or if you will, you may take *Bezaes* Translation, and set the verball in the Margent, where *Beza* differeth from it. The difficult *Radices* would also be set in the Margent.

Spoud. It is very like that this would make them very perfect in the words of the Text: but yet this verball translation would not serve for the manner of construction, or the parsing of it; like as the Grammaticall translations did in the Latine.

How to cast the Greeke into the Grammaticall order.

Phil. By this time, when they know the words, and the meaning, they will be able to cast them into the Grammaticall order of themselves; and so all that labour is supplyed for construing and parsing: for even as they cast and dispose the Latine into the naturall order; so they may the Greeke.

☞
How any who have but a smattering, may proceed of themselves in the Greeke Testament.

Spoud. Then that must needs follow which you affirme; that by daily practice of reading the Greeke out of such a translation, they may be exceeding perfect in the Testament; and that after that they are a little entred, they may goe on of themselves in it: and so likewise all others by the same reason, who have any smattering in the Greeke, as all such Ministers who are desirous hereof, may grow to

great

THE GRAMMAR SCHOOLE

great readinesse and perfection in it by themselves, through such a Translation.

Phil. It is most certaine: for there is the very same reason in it that is in the Latine; and this I finde that a child of nine or ten yeere old, being well entred, shall be able only by the helpe of the translation, to reade of himselfe an easie Author, as *Corderius*, or *Tullies* sentences, as fast out of Latine into the English, or the English into the Latine, as the Latine is ordinarily read alone, after he hath read it over once or twice: to be able to reade you thus, in the space of an houre, a side of a leafe or more, of that which he never saw before: And by oft reading it over, to have it almost without book, if he understand the matter of it.

Spoud. But if they should use the very Interlineall of *Arias Montanus*, as it is: I meane the Greeke and Latine together; might they not as well learne by that, as having them so severally, the Greeke in one booke, the Latine in another? *This cannot be so well done, by the Interlineall, or having the Greeke and Latine together, as by having them separate. Experience.*

Phil. No in no wise. This will appeare most evidently to any who shall make triall, how much sooner and more surely they will learne, and keep that which they learne, by this meanes of having the bookes separate.

The reason also is evident; because when the bookes are so severed, the minde beates out the words, and makes them its owne: yea, and also imprints them; and doth use the Translation but onely as a Schoolemaster, or a Dictionary, where it is not able to finde out the words of it selfe; and also to try after, that it hath gone surely. But when both are joyned together, as in the Interlineall the eye is as soone upon the one as the other: I meane, as soone upon the Latine as upon the Greeke; and so likewise upon the Greeke as upon the Latine, because they are so close joyned one unto the other. So that the book, instead of being a Master to helpe onely where it should, where the mind cannot study it out, it becommeth a continuall prompter, and maketh the minde a truant, that it will not take the paines, which it should. *The Interlineall is continually a prompter to the schoiler, and a deceiver of the minde in stead of a Master, unlesse it be used with great wisdome.*

How

THE GRAMMAR SCHOOLE

This evill cannot be prevented amongst schollers.

How this evill can be prevented amongst schollers, having both together, I doe not possibly see. For, whether they be to get it themselves, or to be examined; yet still will their eye be upon the helpe, where it should not be.

How men of understanding may use the Interlineall.

Indeed this I grant, that the Interlineall translation may be a worthy helpe for a man of judgement or understanding; who can so moderate his eye, as to keepe it fixed upon either Greek or Latine alone, when he would beat the other out of it; as upon the Greeke onely, when he would construe, or reade it into Latine; or on the Latine only, when he would reade it into Greeke, and so can use them as was said, without hindring the minde to study and beat out, or to remember: Though the wisest shall find it very hard to use it in this sort, but the eye will be where it should not; unlesse he use this course, to lay a knife, or a ruler, or the like, on the line which he would not see, and so remove it as neede is. Thus he may use it both for the Greeke and Hebrew.

Spoud. It stands with great reason. Well then, the way being so ready and plaine, they are utterly unworthy so great a benefit, who will not take paines in so easie a course.

How the schollers may proceed in other Authors.

But if I would have my schollers to proceed in other Greeke Authors, what courses should I then take: though I cannot doubt, but being onely thus entred in the Testament, that they will be well accepted in the Universitie, and goe forward speedily?

Phil. If you traine them up thus first in the Testament, they will goe forwards in others with the smaller helpes. But if you would have them to begin in other Greeke Authors; I take the very same helpe of translations, either verball or Grammaticall, to be the most speedy furtherances, so that there be a diligent care of propriety in translating, and of variety set in the Margents; to use them in all things as in the Greeke Testament, and in the Latine Authors mentioned.

Spoud. But how shall we do for such translations of those Greeke Authors?

Phil.

THE GRAMMAR SCHOOLE

Phil. In stead of reading lectures to them, you may thus translate them their Lectures daily, either in Latine or English; and cause them then either to seeke them out of themselves by their translations, Grammars and Lexicons: Or reading them first unto them, cause them to make them perfect thereby.

By this labour of translating, you shall finde your selfe to profit very much in this knowledge of the Greeke, and be greatly eased in your paines.

Spoud. But be it so, that I am not able to translate thus; as he had need to be a good Grecian who should translate in such manner: what then should I do?

Phil. If you be able to read the Author truely unto them, and profitably; then may you also translate it thus: you may have helpe by such Translations as are extant, to give you much light. But it were much to be wished, that to this purpose, some skilfull Grecians would translate some of the purest Authors in this manner. As namely, *Isocrates, Xenophon, Plato,* or *Demosthenes,* or some parts of them, which might seeme most fit for schollers; only to be for this purpose of getting the Greeke. To begin with the easiest of them first. All painfull students would be found to profit exceedingly, and to become rare Grecians in a little time. *[The benefit of such translations of some of the purest Authors performed by skilful Grecians.]*

Thus they might goe on, untill they were able to reade any Greeke Author of themselves, with such helpes as are extant.

In the meane time, you may use such Authors as are so translated, or which come the neerest unto them; of which sort are those Fables of *Æsop* translated in the Argentine Grammar, and others which I shall shew you in the manner of parsing. *[As the Fables translated in the Strasburge Grammar.]*

Spoud. For the parsing then, what way may I use? *[Parsing in Greeke.]*

Phil. I have shewed you this in part: as the noting and causing your Schollers to write every hard word, shewing what examples they are like, the speciall rule, and so the other helpes as they are in the Latine, by casting
words

THE GRAMMAR SCHOOLE

words into the Grammaticall order.

More speciall helpes for them, who are not acquainted with *Camden's* Grammar.

Helps for construing and parsing.
Praxis præceptorum Grammatices Antesignani.

1 They may use the *Praxis Præceptorum Grammatices* of *Antesignanus*, set downe in the end of *Cleonard's* Greeke Grammar; wherein is both an Interlineall verball translation, such as I spake of; and also a parsing of every word familiarly and plainely, much according to the manner of parsing of Latine, which I shewed you; which may be a good direction for parsing.

Barket on Stephens Catech. printed by Wechelus, an. 1604.

2 *Berket's* Commentary upon *Stephens'* Catechisme, parsing every word according to *Cleonard* in *folio*, is found to be a speedy helpe.

M. Stockwoods Progymnasma scholasticum ex Anthologia Henrici Stephani

3 M. *Stockwood* his *Progymnasma scholasticum*: wherein is also a Grammaticall practice of sundry Greeke Epigrams gathered by *H. Stephens*, having a double translation in Latine (the one *ad verbum*, the other in verse) and also a varying of each Epigram in Latine verse by divers Authors. And lastly, an explanation or parsing of every hard word set in the Margent, or under each Epigram in manner of a Commentary. In it also the Greeke Text is set downe both in Greeke Characters, and also in Latine letters interlineally, directly over the head of the Greeke words; of purpose for the easie entering and better directing of the ignorant.

The Commentary in it for parsing, may be also a good direction, for parsing in the shortest manner by pen or reading.

The best and fittest Authors for Poetry, and most easie.
Theognis.
Phocilides.
Hesiode with Ceporine and Melancthon.

Besides these, for Poetry, we may take these Authors, which are easie and plaine by their helpes mentioned:

1 *Theognis* his sentences with the other Poets joyned with him: as namely, *Phocilides* with the Latine translation and notes, set forth by *Sylburgius*; which is very notable to enter young Schollers into Poetry, for making a verse.

2 *Hesiode* his *Opera* and *Dies*, with *Ceropine* and *Melancthon's* Commentaries set forth by *Johannes Frisius Tigurinus*,

THE GRAMMAR SCHOOLE

gurinus, and the new translation of it, *ad verbum*, by *Erasmus Schemidt*, Greeke professour at Wittenberge, printed 1601.

3. *Homer* with *Eustathius* Greeke Commentairie may easily be read after these (especially after the Commentarie on *Hesiode*; which may be as an introduction to it) by the helpe of the verball Latine translation of *Homer*: and the words of Art, belonging to Grammar set downe in Greeke, in M. *Camden's* Grammar. *Homer with Eustathius.*

Moreover, these directions following will be most speedie helpes for all the Poets:

To have in readinesse some briefe rules of the chiefe figures, and dialects: as those which are in Master *Camden's* Grammar; so to be able to referre all Anomalies in Greeke unto them. Those with the *verba anomala*, and the particular dialects, according to each part of speech, set downe in the end of *Camden*, may resolve most doubts: for Anomalies and special difficulties which you cannot find otherwise, you may find many of them set Alphabetically together in the end of *Scapula* his Lexicon, where they are expressed fully, and particularly: which you shall prove to be a marvellous readinesse to you. *To have in readinesse a short briefe of all the dialects and figures, a speedy help for the knowledge of the Poets. A principall help for all Anomalies and difficulties in Greeke.*

Spoud. Here are indeed very many and singular helpes: most of which, I may truly say as before, that I have not so much as heard of. But if I would have my Scholler to write in Greeke, what meanes should I use then?

Phil. If you meane for the tongue, to be able to write true and pure Greeke, the sure meanes are even the same as for writing Latine. *How to write purely in Greek.*

1. The continuall practice of construing, parsing, and reading forth of the translation into the Authors, is making the Greeke continually.

2. To come to the stile and composition, and so for Orthography, to do as for the Latine. As I directed you to give them sentences in English, translated Grammatically out of *Tullies* sentences, to turne into *Tullies* Latine, whereby both your selfe and they may have a certaine guide for

them

Q

THE GRAMMAR SCHOOLE

them to goe surely; so here to give them sentences or pieces out of the Testament, or out of *Isocrates*, as *ad Demonicum*, or out of *Xenophon* to translate into Greeke, and so to see how neere they can come unto the Author. Or else, to aske them onely the Latine or English of the Greeke, and to trie how they can turne it into Greeke first Grammatically, after in composition: or sometimes one way, sometimes the other. And to this purpose also, the translations of some excellent parts of the purest Greeke Authors were most necessary.

By these meanes they might come in time, to be as accurate in writing Greeke for the stile and composition, as in the Latine. For all other exercises in Greeke, I referre you to that which hath beene said concerning the Latine, the reason and meanes being the like.

How to write faire. Or if you meant for writing the Greek hand faire, most exquisite copies constantly followed, as in the Latine and English, and practice, shall bring them unto it. But for this, I likewise referre you to that which was said concerning the way of writing faire.

Versifying in Greeke. *Spoud.* But what say you for versifying in Greek, for that you know to commend the chiefe Schooles greatly?

Phil. As I answered you before, so I take the meanes to be in all things the same, as for versifying in Latine; except that this is more easie, because of the long and short vowels so certainely knowne. To be very perfect in the rules of versifying; in scanning a verse. To learne *Theognis*, that pleasant and easie Poet without booke, to have store of Poeticall phrase and authorities: which is the speediest and surest way: And so to enter by turning or imitating his verses, as in Latine. But herein as in all the rest, I do still desire the helpe of the learned, who can better shew by experience the shortest, surest, and most plaine wayes.

☞ *Theognis may be easily learned without booke by the helpe of the translation.*

☞ *A Caveat for the time bestowed in such exercises of writing in Greeke.* Notwithstanding, let me heere admonish you of this (which for our curiositie wee had neede to bee often put in minde of) that, seeing we have so little practice of any exercises to be written in Greeke, we do not bestow too much

THE GRAMMAR SCHOOLE

much time in that, whereof we happely shall have no use; and which therefore we shall also forget againe : but that we still imploy our precious time to the best advantage in the most profitable studies, which may after do most good to God's Church or our countrey.

Spoud. Your counsell is good : yet repeate me againe a briefe of the principall of these helpes for my memorie sake.

Phil. That was it;

1. To make your Schollers very perfect in the Grammar, chiefely Nounes and verbes; that they may be able to prove and parallel every thing by a like example, or at least to turne to them readily. *Summe of all.*

2. To have the Greeke *Radices* by the meanes mentioned.

3. Continuall use of most accurate verball or Grammaticall translations; and in the meane time to make them perfect in the Testament, by daily use of our ordinarie translations, so as was shewed, by reading the Greeke out of them over and over.

4. Helpe of the best Commentaries and Grammaticall practices in the booke mentioned.

5. To be ready in the dialects and the common figures for the Poetry.

6. Noting all the difficulties, and running oft over them as in the Latine; and so all other helpes of understanding the matter first, and the rest mentioned generally.

CHAP.

CHAP. XXI.

How to get most speedily the knowledge and understanding of the Hebrew.

Spoud.

But what say you, for that most sacred tongue, the Hebrew? How, I pray you, do you think, that that may be attained, which you mentioned, that students may come so soone to the understanding of it?

The knowledge of the Hebrew may be the soonest gotten and why.

Phil. This may be obtained the sooner, because we have it all comprised, so farre as is necessarie for us to know, in that one sacred volume of the old Testament. Also because the principall rootes of it are so few, the matter so familiar, as which everie one of us ought to be acquainted with. The Nounes have so little varying or turning in them.

And finally, for that we have such singular helpes for the understanding of it (as the Interlineall verball translation, and the translations and labours of others, which beat out the propriety, force and sense of every word and phrase) like as in the Greeke Testament, that nothing can be difficult in it, to the good heart, who will use the meanes which the Lord hath vouchsafed, and will seeke this blessing, from his Majesty.

Spoud. Surely, he is utterly unworthy of this heavenly treasure, who will not seeke and beg it from the Lord, and dig deepe for it: I meane, who will not use any holy meanes, for the obtaining of it; and much more the course being so short, plaine and direct, as you say. But I intreat you to trace me out the shortest way.

Phil. The way, so farre as yet I have beene able to learne, is wholly set downe already in the manner of getting the Latine and the Greeke. But to make a briefe rehearsall,
1. For

THE GRAMMAR SCHOOLE

1. For them who would be more accurate Hebricians for the beating out of every tittle, they are to have the Grammar very accurately, and that by the like meanes even as the Greeke and the Latine.

But for those who onely desire the understanding of it, and to be skilful in the text, the chief care must be, that they be made perfect in some few principall rules of Grammar of most use. Also in declining and conjugating the examples set downe in the booke, and in the severall terminations of Declensions, Numbers, Moodes, Tenses, Persons, to be able in them in some good manner to give Hebrew to Latine, and Latine to Hebrew, and to run the terminations in each; at least to give the Latine to the Hebrew perfectly. And so in the severall Pronounes, Adverbes, Conjunctions to do the like; I meane, to give Latine to the Hebrew, to have them very readily, seeing they are but few, and sundry of them of continuall use.

Spoud. But what Grammar would you use?

Phil. Martinius of the last Edition, with the *Technologia* adjoyned to it, I take to be most used of all the learned, as most methodicall and perfect; although *Blebelius* is farre more easie to the young beginner, as much more answering to our Latine Grammar; and made so plaine of purpose by questions and answers, that any one of judgement may better understand it, and goe forward with delight: so as it may be a notable introduction or Commentary to *Martinius*, who had need of a good Reader, to learne to understand him perfectly.

Both read together, must needs be most profitable; *Martinius* for method & shortnesse, *Blebileus* for resolving and expounding every obscuritie: yet every one who hath learned a Grammar, may best use the same, because that is most familiar to him.

But for them who are to begin, or to teach others, they may take the easiest first, that the learner may no way be discouraged; and after, others as they shall thinke meete, or which shall be found most profitable, by the judgement of the

margin:
1. The Grammar to be gotten most exquisitely of them who desire to come to perfection in the Hebrew.
Some chiefe parts for others who only desire the understanding.

Grammars to be used.
Martinius with his Technologia.
Blebelius accounted most plaine and easie.

The several points in Martinius you may find in Blebelius by the Table in the end of Blebelius.

THE GRAMMAR SCHOOLE

the greatest Hebricians. This I think to be the surest advice; and by comparing of Grammars together, ever to beate out the sense and meaning.

Spoud. What is your next meanes?

The second principall means, the perfect getting of the Radices.
Phil. The getting of the Hebrew roots, together with the Grammar, every day a certaine number. Hereunto the *Nomenclator Anglolatinus-Græcus-Hæbraicus*, mentioned before, if it were so finished, might be a notable introduction.

Manner of committing the Radices to memory.
For the manner of committing the *Radices* to memory, I shewed it before: yet here to speake of it a little more fully, first to helpe our remembrance by some of the chiefe helpes of memory; as by comparing in our meditation the severall words in the Hebrew, with what words they are like unto, either in the English, Latine, or Greeke, which words either doe come of them, or sound like unto them, or with some other root in the Hebrew, wherewith they have affinity: That so soone as we see the Hebrew roote, the other word which we would remember it by, comming to our minde; the understanding or meaning of the Hebrew roote may also come to minde with it.

Examples of helping memory to the Hebrew.
As for example, to begin in the first *Radices*, & to give some light in two or three; אבב & אב *puber*, or *pubertas*, may be remembered by ἥβη, *pubertas*, and by *ephebe*, or *ephebus*, in Latine comming of it, signifying the same: as *Postquam excessit ex ephebis Terent.* Also אבב may be remembred by the moneth *Abib* in the Scriptures, which was amongst the Jewes *mensis pubertatis, in quo seges terræ Canaan protrudebat spicas*, אבר *Perijt*, may be remembred by *Abaddon* in the *Apocalyps*, called in Greeke *Apollion*, the destroyer, or destruction; the angell of the bottomless pit. אבל *voluit, acquieuit*, or *bene affectus est in aliquid, ut pater in filios*: It may fully be remembred by *Abba* Father, comming of אב *pater*: and so the word αββα in Greeke, as *Abbas*, an Abbot, *quia Abbas erat pater totius societatis.* And *Avus* seemes to come of the same. By any of these we may remember the roote.

Thus we may remember very many of them by the helpe of *Auenar's* Dictionary (as I shewed) or by our own meditation;

THE GRAMMAR SCHOOLE

tion; even from the words comming of them indeed, or in shew, observed according to certaine rules which *Auenarius* giveth in the beginning of his Lexicon.

The reason hereof also is most evident; for that this is the mother tongue of all tongues, and was the only tongue, until the cōfounding of the tongues at *Babel*: in which confusion, some words were changed altogether, in others, the significations were altered, & many have bin depraved and corrupted by continuance and succession of time. Therefore as this tongue is to be honored, so this diligence in comparing and deriving other tongues, must needs be of exceeding great profit many wayes: and amongst other, for this very purpose of conceiving or committing to memory, and retaining the Hebrew more surely, by other words better knowne to us. *The Hebrew the mother tongue most ancient and worthy. Others derived from it. The benefit of diligence in comparing the tongues.*

Other words which cannot be remembred thus, yet may be remembred by the learned, by some thing which they found like unto, in one of the three tongues; So that we forget not to animate that which we remember by: that is, to conceive of it in our minde, as being lively and stirring; like as we noted before in the Greeke. *How other words may be remembred, which cannot be so derived.*

The rest of the roots besides these, will be but few: and being noted with a line with a blacke lead pen (as was said) or any marke, and oft run over, they may soon be gotten. *The hardest rootes which seeme to have no affinitie.*

Besides these, some marke would be given under every derivative, in each roote, which doth differ much in signification from the *Radix*, and cannot be remembred well by the *Radix*, nor how it may be derived from it. *To marke out also the harder derivations in the Hebrew.*

Spoud. Such a *Nomenclator* as you speake of, must needs be a rare and speedy helpe to all the tongues, if it were well gathered by some very learned and judicious Hebrician. But in the meane time, what abbridgement would you use for getting these *Radices* of the Hebrew?

Phil. The Epitome of *Pagnine* I take to be most common: but *Buxtorphius* his abbridgement (going under the name of *Polanus*) must needs be the best in all likelihood; as having had the helpe of that and all other, and gathered by great judgement. *The best Epitome for getting the Radices.*

I

THE GRAMMAR SCHOOLE

This is not fully finished.

I have seene a draught of another, much shorter then them both, collected by comparing *Pagnine*, *Auenar*, and others; shewing also for most part how the Hebrew derivatives, which are more obscure are derived from the *Radices*, giving at least a probable reason for them: and also in sundry, shewing the agreement and manner of the derivation of the tongues, one from another, and the affinity of many of them; to help the memory with the speedy and sure getting of all.

Spoud. It were great pitie, but that that should be perfected; for the benefit of it must needs be very great. But might there not be such a device, of contriving all the Hebrew roots into continued speeches; and so learning them by studying them out of verball translations, as you shewed for the Greeke?

The way might be more compendious by the rootes reduced to Classes. By the Dictionarie alone they might be gotten in a short time.

Phil. Yes undoubtedly, it might easily be accomplished by some exquisit and painfull Hebrician, to make this labour yet much more compendious: Although I do not doubt, but any indifferent memory might, in the space of a twelve moneth or lesse, get all the Hebrew *Radices* very perfectly, by the former meanes of *Buxtorphius* or *Pagnine's* abbridgement alone; spending but every day one houre therein. And when they were once gotten, they were easily kept by oft repetition, running over the hardest, being marked out; and by daily practice in reading some Chapters; though much more easily, by having the heads reduced to such classes, and the oft running over them.

I have heard moreover of all the *Radices*, with their Primitive significations alone, drawne into a very little space; which being well performed, must needs be a notable furtherance.

Spoud. What is your third helpe?

The third helpe, perfect verball translations, and continuall practice of them.

Phil. The perfect verball Translations written out of *Arias Montanus*, by conferring with *Junius* and our owne Bible, specially our new translation, and setting the divers readings in the margents with a letter, to signifie whose the translations are, and also every hard *Radix* noted in the margent,

THE GRAMMAR SCHOOLE

margent, as now sundry of them are; with references to them by letters or figures, as I shewed for the Greeke: these being used as the English translations, for getting the Latine, and as the Latine or English for the Greeke, will be found above all that we would imagine:

And that after this manner,

First, as I said for the others, by reading over the translations, to understand the matter.

Secondly, learning to construe the Hebrew into the Latine exactly, and backe againe out of the translation into Hebrew; looking onely on the translation, to meditate and beate out the Hebrew. This helpes understanding, apprehension, memory, and all (as I said) to have the text most absolutely. *The manner of using these repeated.*

Lastly, beginning with the easiest first (as in the other tongues) as either some part of the History (as namely *Genesis*, the books of *Samuel*) or else the *Psalmes*; and therein specially the hundred and nineteene Psalme, as most plaine of all other: or rather to begin with the *Praxis* upon the Psalmes, the first, the five and twentieth, and the threescore and eighth, set down in the end of *Martinius* Gramar printed by *Raphalengius*, Anno 1607, which will both acquaint the learner with the understanding of *Martinius*, and set him in a most direct and ready way, by the other helpes.

For the certainty of this, besides that the reason is the very same with the Latine, and like as I said for the Greeke also, I have moreover knowne this experience in a childe under fifteene yeeres of age; who besides all kinde of studies and exercises, both in Latine and Greeke, as those mentioned before, and his daily progresse in them, had within the space of lesse than a yeere, gotten sundry of the principall and most necessary rules of Grammar: Also a great part of the *Radices* in *Buxtorphius*, though he spent not therein above two houres in a day. And besides all this, he had learned about fourteene or fifteene Psalmes: wherein he was so ready, as that he was able not onely to construe or reade the Hebrew into the Latine; but also out of the bare *Experience of this for assurance.*

bare translation, to reade the Hebrew backe againe, to shew every *Radix*, and to give a reason in good sort for each word, why it was so. Of this hath been tryall by learned and sufficient witnesses.

The which experience with the daily trials of reading the Latine so exactly and readily out of the English, and getting it (as it were without booke) by that practice, do fully assure me, that by this daily exercise the very originals of the Hebrew may be made as easie and familiar as the Latine is; yea, in time with continuall practice, to be able to say very much of it without booke: as I shewed before for the Greeke. And what Student, especially of Divinity, can ever bestowe some part of his time in a more pleasant, easie and happy study? when there will be no more but reading over and over with meditation, and still to be reading the words and wisedome of the Highest; in whose presence he hopes to dwell, and to heare the same sweet voice in the Temple in heaven eternally.

A student cannot be better imployed then in thus imprinting the originals in his heart, if he have leisure.

Spoud. By these means, it seemeth to me that any tongue may be gotten speedily.

Phil. Yea verily, I doe so perswade myselfe. For seeing (as I said) that there is no more in any tongue, but words and joyning of those words together; therefore the words being first gotten, chiefly by being contrived into continued speeches, and those so learned out of such verball translations: secondly, some few rules of them being knowne: thirdly, continuall use of such translations; would make any tongue to be understood and learned very soone, so farre as I can conceive.

It seemeth that any tongue may be gotten thus.

Spoud. Howsoever this be, which seemeth indeed most probable; yet I take it, there can be no doubt of this, but that in every countrey of the world, the Latine, Greeke, and Hebrew may be attained by the same meanes: which three are enough (yea the two last alone sufficient) to know God and Jesus Christ to eternall life: and that so by the knowledge of the Originals, men may have a certaine knowledge of the eternall Word of the Lord.

These tongues, Latine, Greeke, and Hebrew may be gotten in each Nation, by these meanes of translations in their owne tongues.

Phil.

THE GRAMMAR SCHOOLE

Phil. I can see no reason at all to the contrary, but that these our Latine Classicall Authors being translated Grammatically into other tongues, by some who are learned amongst them, the Latine may as well be learned thereby by them out of their translations, in their own tongues, by such helps of rules as have been mentioned, or the like, as out of translations in our English tongue. Secondly, the Latine tongue being once gotten, the getting of the Greeke and Hebrew are the very same unto them which they are to us.

Or otherwise, the Greeke and Hebrew but translated so alone; into the severall tongues of each Nation (I meane verbally) they might as easily, if not more easily, be learned in each countrey out of them, as out of the English or Latine; and the sense or meaning also, if in every difficult place, or where the words seemed to be out of order, it were set in the Margents over against them. *Greeke or Hebrew most easily learned by perfect translations in each tongue.*

The same I say for our English; into which the Hebrew, in most places translated *verbatim*, doth keepe a perfect sense, and might be learned out of it. Also the most absolute fulnesse of understanding of the matter in our heads, doth bring words, most readily to expresse it; which I have oft told you of.

But remember this that I have said; that the verball translations, for these originals, shall make the learners most cunning in the Text, & in the very order of the words of the Holy Ghost, without danger of any way depraving, corrupting or inverting one jot or tittle: though for the Latine, the Grammaticall translations be farre more profitable, as we have shewed. *Of the use of perfect verball translations for getting the originals.*

Spoud. Are these all the directions that you would give me herein?

Phil. These are all which yet I know.

Spoud. By these then it seemeth that you are fully perswaded that this holy tongue may be obtained.

Phil. Yea undoubtedly, so much as shall be requisit for us, by observing withall those generall rules set downe for

the

THE GRAMMAR SCHOOLE

Observation repeated how much and what to learne in every booke.

the getting of the Latine; and chiefly that, of making markes under every hard word in each page, without marring our bookes; and to runne oft over those.

But herein it is necessary that I put you in minde againe, of that which I admonished you of in the Greeke; that your scholler learne so much onely, as either the present time requires: I meane, whereof he may have good use presently, or else when he shall proceed to higher studies in the Universities, or to other imployments. And for other speculative or more curious knowledge in Quiddities, either to cut them off altogether, from hindring better and more needfull studies, or to reserve them to their due time and place; or to leave them onely to them who shall give themselves wholly to these studies, to be readers in the Universities or for like purposes; as, the learning of the musicke and Rhetorica accents: the *Prosodia metrica*, and the like.

Spoud. What is then the summe of all?

Phil. For them who desire to be exact Hebricians, to be very perfect in the Grammar; for them who desire but only the understanding, to have,

1 Some necessary rules, and principally examples of Nounes and Verbes very readily.

2 The *Radices*.

3 Continuall use of verball translations, or others; as in the Greeke.

4 Oft running over the hardest words.

But these, as all other things, I write under correction, and with submission and desire of better judgement.

CHAP.

THE GRAMMAR SCHOOLE

CHAP. XXII.

Of knowledge of the grounds of Religion and training up the schollers therein.

Spoud.

Ow that we have thus gone thorow all the way of learning, for whatsoever can be required in the Grammar schooles; and how to lay a sure foundation, both for the Greeke and the Hebrew, that they may be able to go on of themselves in all these by their own studies: it remaineth that we come yet to one further point, and which is as it were the end of all these. That is, how schollers may be seasoned and trained up in God's true Religion and in grace; without which all other learning is meerely vaine, or to increase a greater condemnation. This one alone doth make them truely blessed, and sanctifie all other their studies. *Schollers to be trained up in Religion.*

Moreover, they being taught herein in their youth, shall not depart from it when they are old. I entreat you therefore to shew me so shortly as you can, how schollers may be taught all those things which were contained in the note: As,

1 To be acquainted with all the grounds of religion and chiefe Histories of the Bible.

2 So to take the Sermons, at least for all the substance both for doctrines, proofes, uses; and after to make a rehearsall of them.

3 Every one to begin to conceive and answer the severall points of the Sermons, even from the lowest fourmes.

These are matters that I thinke are least thought of in most schooles, though of all other they must needs be most necessary, and which our lawes and injunctions doe take *This most neglected in schooles.*

prin-

THE GRAMMAR SCHOOLE

principall care for; and that the schoolemasters, to these ends, be of sincere religion.

Phil. I feare indeed that it is as you say, that this is over-generally neglected. And herein shall the popish Schoole-masters rise up in judgement against us, who make this the very chiefe marke at which they aime, in all their teaching; to powre in superstition at the beginning, first to corrupt and deceive the tender minds.

The popish Schoolemasters shall rise up against us.

But to returne unto the matter, how they may be thus trained up in the feare of the Lord; I shall set you downe the best manner, so neere as I my selfe have yet learned, following the order of these particulars mentioned.

1 For being acquainted with the grounds of Religion and the principles of the Catechisme; Every Saturday before their breaking up the schoole (for a finishing their weeke's labours, and a preparative to the Sabbath) let them spend halfe an houre or more in learning and answering the Catechisme.

How to teach them the Catechisme, and when.

To this end, cause every one to have his Catechisme, to get halfe a side of a leafe or more at a time; each to be able to repeate the whole. The more they say at a time and the ofter they runne over the whole, the sooner they will come to understanding. This must be as their parts in their Accedence.

In examining, first your Usher or Seniors of each fourme may heare that every one can say. Afterwards, you having all set before you, may poase whom you suspect most carelesse.

Manner of examining Catechisme.

1 Whether they can answer the questions.

2 In demanding every question againe, to stand a little on it, to make it so plaine and easie, as the least child amongst them may understand every word which hath any hardnesse in it, and the force of it.

Let the manner of the poasing be as I shewed for the Accedence. The more plainly the question is drawne out of the very words of the booke, and into the more short questions it is divided, and also examined backward and forward, the

sooner

THE GRAMMAR SCHOOLE

sooner a great deale they will understand it, and better remember it.

Herein also to use all diligence to apply every piece unto them, to whet it upon them, to work holy affections in them; that each may learne to feare the Lord and walke in all his commandements. For, being in their hearts and practice, it will be more firmely kept. This also must be remembred for all that followeth.

2 For the Sabbaths and other dayes when there is any Sermon, cause every one to learne something at the Sermons. *Taking notes, or writing sermons.*

1 The very lowest to bring some notes, at least three or foure. If they can, to learne them by their owne marking; if not, to get other of their fellowes, to teach them some short lessons after. As thus: Without God we can doe nothing. All good gifts are from God: or the like short sentences; not to over-load them at the first.

To this end, that the Monitours see, 1 That all be most attentive to the Preacher.

2 That all those who can write any thing, or do but begin to write joyning hand, doe every one write some such notes, or at least to get them written, some five or sixe or moe as they can, as I said, to be able to repeat them without book, as their other little fellowes. *2 All who can write to take notes.*

But herein there must be great care by the Monitours, that they trouble not their fellowes, nor the congregation, in asking notes, or stirring out of their places to seeke of one another, or any other disorder; but to aske them after they are come forth of the Church, and get them written then. *Caveat of any noise or disorder in gathering notes.*

3 For those who have been longer practised herein, to set downe, 1 The Text, or a part of it. 2 To marke as neere as they can, and set downe every doctrine, and what proofes they can, the reasons and the uses of them. *3 The higher to set downe parts of the Sermon more orderly.*

4 In the highest fourmes, cause them to set downe all the Sermons. As Text, division, exposition, or meaning, doctrines, and how the severall doctrines were gathered, all the proofes, reasons, uses, applications. I meane all the substance *4 In all the highest fourmes to set down all the substance exactly.*

and

THE GRAMMAR SCHOOLE

and effect of the Sermons: for learning is not so much seen, in setting downe the words, as the substance.

Manner of noting, for helping understanding and memory.

And also for further directing them, and better helping their understanding and memories, for the repetition thereof; cause them to leave spaces betweene every part, and where need is, to divide them with lines. So also to distinguish the severall parts by letters or figures, and setting the summe of every thing in the Margent over-against each matter in a word or two. As Text, Division, Summe.

Helps for memory in the Margent, and for understanding.

First Observation, or first Doctrine, Proofes, Reasons 1. 2. 3. Uses 1. 2. 3. So the second observation or Doctrine, Proofes, Reasons, &c. so throughout. Or what method soever the Preacher doth use, to follow the parts after the same manner, so well as they can.

To leave good Margents. To set downe quotations as they are spoken. To set downe the heads of all in the Margents after. Benefit of this

Direct them to leave good Margents for these purposes: and so soone as ever the Preacher quotes any Scripture, as he nameth it, to set it in the Margent against the place, lest it slip out of memory.

And presently after the Sermon is done, to runne over all againe, correcting it, and setting downe the summe of every chiefe head, faire and distinctly in the Margent over against the place, if his leisure will suffer.

By this helpe they will be able to understand, and make a repetition of the Sermon, with a very little meditation; yea to doe it with admiration for children.

To turne it after into Latine for the next dayes exercise.

After all these, you may (if you thinke good) cause them the next morning, to translate it into a good Latine stile, in stead of their exercise the next day (I meane, so many of them as write Latine) or some little piece of it according to their ability.

Or to reade it into Latine ex tempore.

Or rather, (because of the lacke of time, to examine what every one hath written) to see how they are able out of the English, to reade that which they have written, into Latine, *ex tempore*, each of them reading his piece in order and helping others to give better phrase and more variety, for every difficult word; and so to runne thorow the whole.

This

THE GRAMMAR SCHOOLE

    This I finde that they will begin to do, after that they have been exercised in making Latine a twelvemoneth or two, if they have bin rightly entred, and well exercised in *Sententiæ Pueriles*; especially in the divine sentences in the end thereof, and in *Corderius* with other books & exercises noted before, chiefly by the practice of reading out of the translations. *Experience how soone they will doe this.*

    Spoud. But when would you examine these?

    Phil. For the reading into Latine, I would have it done the next day at nine of the clocke, for their exercise, or at their entrance after dinner; that so they might have some meete time to meditate of it before: and for examining of it in English, to doe it at night before their breaking up, amongst them all shortly, or before dinner. *Examining the Sermons.*

    Herein also some one of the higher fourmes might be appointed in order to make a repetition of the whole Sermon without book, according as I shewed the manner of setting it down; rehearsing the severall parts so distinctly & briefly, as the rest attending may the better conceive of the whole, and not exceed the space of a quarter of an houre. *One to make a short rehearsall of the whole first.*

    After the repetition of it, if leisure serve, the Master may aske amongst the highest some few questions, of whatsoever points might seeme difficult in the Sermon: for by questions, as I have said, they will come to understand anything. *To aske questions of all things difficult.*

    Next to appose amongst the lowest, where he thinkes good, what notes they took of the Sermons, and cause them to pronounce them; and in appoasing to cause them to understand, by applying all things to them in a word or two. Thus to goe thorow as time shall permit. *To cause the least and all sorts to repeat their notes.*

    Spoud. This strict examining will be a good meanes to make them attentive.

    Phil. It will indeed; so as you shall see them to increase in knowledge and understanding above your expectation: And besides it will keepe them from playing, talking, sleeping, and all other disorders in the Church. To this end therefore poase diligently, all those whom you observe or suspect most negligent, as I have advised: then you shall have them to attend heedfully. *Benefit of this strict examining.*

Spoud

THE GRAMMAR SCHOOLE

Spoud. But how will you cause them to be able so to repeat the Sermon? Me thinkes that should be very difficult.

How they may be able to repeate the whole sermons without booke.

Phil. The schollers will do it very readily, where the Preachers keep any good order; when they have so noted every thing as I directed before, and set downe the summe in the margent. For then, first meditating the text to have it perfect: secondly, meditating the margents to get the summe of all into their heads, and the manner how it stands: thirdly, observing how many doctrines were gathered, and how, what proofes, how many reasons and uses of every doctrine; they will soone both conceive it, and be able to deliver it with much facilitie after a little practice.

Principall helpes for it.

But herein the principall helpes are understanding, by getting the summes, and margents; observing the order, and constant practice. Understanding will bring words: practice perfection.

Helpe of notes for assurance.

If those who are weaker or more timorous, have their notes lying open before them, to cast their eye upon them here or there where they stick, it shall much embolden them, and fit them after to make use of short notes of any thing; I meane of the briefe summe of that which they shall deliver.

Spoud. These are surely very good exercises for the Saturday for catechizing, and the dayes after the Sermons for repeating of the Sermons: but would you have no exercises of religion at all in the other dayes of the weeke?

Phil. Yes. As there is no day but it is the Lord's, and therefore it & all our labours to be consecrated to him by a morning and evening sacrifice, I meane prayer and thanksgiving morning and evening; so there would no day be suffered to passe over, wherein there should not be some short exercise or lesson of religion: which is both the chiefe end of all other our studies, and also that, whereby all the rest are sanctified. And to this end, one quarter of an houre or more might be taken every evening before prayer, though they were kept so much the longer, that it might not hinder

THE GRAMMAR SCHOOLE

der any other of their daily studies: Although in this, no losse will ever be found, to any other study, but the Lord will blesse so much the more; That also to be in such a course as none could any way dislike, and which of all other might be both most sure and profitable.

Spoud. What such a course can you find which is so profitable, and which all must needs so approve of, which might be so short?

Phil. To goe thorow the History of the Bible, every day a historie, or some piece of a historie: I meane, some few questions of it in order, as the time will permit.

To this purpose, there is a little booke called the History of the Bible, gathered by M. *Paget*: wherein if you cause them to provide against every night a side of a leafe, or as you shall think meet, of the most easie and plaine questions; and to examinine them after the manner of examining the Catechisme; you shall see them to profit much, both for the easinesse of the history, and the delight which children will take therein. *Every night to goe thorow a piece of the history of the Bible. Manner of examining the History.*

Wherein also if first you shall shew them, or aske them what vertues are commended in that History; what vices are condemned; or what generals they could gather out of that particular; or what examples they have against such vices, or for such vertues; and thus examine them after the same maner, so going over and over as the time permits, you shall see them come on according to your desire.

Spoud. But me thinks that you would not have them to take every question in that booke before them.

Phil. No: I would have onely those Histories which are most familiar for children to understand, and most to edification; and so those questions only to be chosen. There are sundry concerning the Leviticall lawes, which are beyond their conceit, and so in divers other parts. For that should ever be kept in memory, that things well understood are ever most soon learned and most firmly kept; and we should ever be afraid to discourage our children by the difficulty of any thing. *Not to trouble them with every question.*

Spoud

THE GRAMMAR SCHOOLE

Spoud. It is true indeed. And moreover, howsoever it is most certaine that all holy Scripture is profitable, and all to be knowne: yet some parts are more easie, and as milke, meet for the weakest and youngest children to be taught, and which they may understand and conceive of easily; others are as stronger meate, and more obscure, wherewith they are to be acquainted after. But as in all other learning, so it is here, everything is to be learned in the right place. The more plaine and easie questions and places will still be expounders and masters to the more hard and obscure.

Objection, concerning them who would not have their children taught any religion.

But yet, howsoever I like very well of all this, you know that there are some who would not have their children to be taught any religion, nor to meddle with it at all.

Phil. There cannot be any such who either love or know the Gospel of Christ, or regard their owne salvation, or the saving of their children.

The rest are to be pittied and prayed for, rather then to be answered.

The Popish sort know the necessitie hereof: and therefore they labour principally to corrupt the youth, and offer their paines freely to that end. They shall be the Judges of all such.

Spoud. But it will take up over-much time from their other learning.

How to deale that this may not hinder any other learning.

Phil. I directed you how to cut off all such exceptions: I would take the time to that purpose over and beside their ordinarie. It is but mine owne labour, for a quarter or halfe an houre in the day at the most, keeping them a little longer; although if it should be part of the schoole time, there would never be found any losse therein.

Spoud. But how will you teach your children civility and good manners? which is principally required in Schollers.

How to teach the schollers civility.

Phil. Religion will teach them manners: As they grow in it, so they will also in all civill and good behaviour. The Word of the Lord is the rule and ground of all, to frame their manners by; that is therefore the first and principall meanes.

Secondly,

Civilitie.

THE GRAMMAR SCHOOLE

Secondly, out of their Authors which they reade, you may still take occasion to teach them manners; some of their Treatises being written of purpose to that end: as *Qui mihi, Sententiæ pueriles, Cato, Tullies*·Offices, &c.

For the carriage of Youth, according to the civility used in our time, and for the whole course of framing their manners in the most commendable sort, there is a little booke translated out of French, called The Schoole of good manners, or The new Schoole of Vertue, teaching Youth how they ought to behave themselves in all companies, times, and places. It is a booke most easie and plaine, meet both for Masters and Schollers to be acquainted with, to frame all according unto it; unlesse in any particular the custome of the place require otherwise. *The Schoole of good manners, or The new Schoole of vertue for civilitie.*

Spoud. How would you have the children acquainted with this?

Phil. The Master sometimes in stead of the History, or if he will (at some other times) might reade it over unto them all, a leafe or two at a time, and after to examine it amongst them. It is so plaine, that they will easily understand it.

Spoud. But if I could thus teach them Religion, and Latine all under one; it were a most happy thing, and I should cut off all quarrell and exception.

Phil. I will shew you how you may doe it. Cause your Schollers to reade you a Chapter of the New Testament, or a piece of a Chapter, as time will permit, about twenty verses at a time, in stead of the History mentioned. One night to reade it out of the Latine into English; reading first a verse or a sentence in Latine to a Comma, or a full point, as they can: then English that, not as construing it, but as reading it into good English; so throughout: the next night to reade the same over againe forth of an English Testament, into the same Latine backe againe. *How to teach Religion and Latine all under one, by reading each night a piece of a Chapter. Practise this constantly and carefully, and try the experience of God's blessing in it.*

Thus every one of those who are able, to read in order, each night; all the rest to looke on their owne Testaments, English, Latine, or Greeke, or to harken. Let them beginne at the Gospell of *John*, as was advised

for

THE GRAMMAR SCHOOLE

for the Greeke, as being most easie; or as *Matthew*, if you please; and you shall soone finde that through the familiarnesse of the matter, they will so come on both wayes (both in reading the Latine into English, and English into Latine) as your selfe will marvell at, and their parents will rejoyce in; and acknowledge themselves bound unto you for to see their little ones to be able to reade the Testament into Latine.

Besides that, it will be also a notable preparative to learne the Greeke Testament, when they are so well acquainted with the English and Latine before.

Spoud. But what Latine translation would you use?

Phil. Such as my Schollers have: *Erasmus* or *Beza*; but chiefly *Beza*, as the more pure phrase, and more fully expressing the sense and drift of the Holy Ghost. Therein your selfe, or your Schollers marking the peculiar Latine phrases, when they reade first forth of the Latine into the English, they will be able of themselves (when they reade them the second time forth of the English into Latine) to give the same phrases againe, and to imprint them for ever.

Spoud. But what time should I have then for the History of the Bible, that little booke which you mentioned; whereof must needs be very singular use? would you have me to omit it?

Phil. No, in no case: one quarter of an houre spent in examining it before prayers in the forenoone, a side or a leafe at a time (as I said) may serve for that; and another quarter or not much more, before prayers at the breaking up at evening for this; and so neither to lose time, nor to omit any thing necessary for their happy growth herein. In this reading of the Chapters so, you shall finde that they will get as much Latine, and goe on as fast as in any other exercise whatsoever; and also will do it with ease, when they have beene first well trained up in the Grammaticall translations, and that each knoweth his night, to looke to it aforehand.

Spoud.

When the History to be repeated.

Religion.

THE GRAMMAR SCHOOLE

Spoud. But at this kinde of reading the Chapter, the lesser sort which understand no Latine, will get no good.

Phil. Yes very much. If after that the Chapter is read, you use but to examine some two or three, as time will permit; asking them what they remember of that which was read, or how much they can repeat without booke of it: you shall see that in short time they will so marke, or so looke to it afore-hand, as they will (almost any of them) repeate you a verse or two apiece. If you use to appose ordinarily for example, some one whom you know can repeate a great deale, it will much provoke the rest, to marke and take paines: and especially if (as in other things) you use to appose adversaries, whether can repeate the more. And thus much for that, how they may get Religion and Latine together. *How all the least may profit by reading of the Chapters.*

CHAP. XXIII.

How to understand and remember any Morall matter.

Spoud.

YEt one other point remaineth, which is of great use, and very fit to be asked here; how children may be made to understand, and conceive of any ordinary matter meete for them? as the points of the Sermons, the History of the Bible: for even most of these things may seeme to be above children's capacities; and I see understanding to be the life and substance of all.

Phil. This point hath beene taught throughout in part: but this I say unto you againe, and you shall finde it most true; that for any one who would conceive of any long sentence and remember it, let him divide it into as many short questions as he can, and answer them (though closely) in his minde; it shall give a great light. So do with your *A principall help of understanding how to make children to understand any thing, and remember.*

schol-

THE GRAMMAR SCHOOLE

schollers in any thing which you would have them to understand: divide the long question or sentence into many short ones; by the short, they will understand and conceive of the long. I shewed the manner in examining young schollers, at *In Speech*, and in *Sententiæ Pueriles*.

For other helpes; as for marking the summe and drift of every thing, and also for observing what goeth before, what followeth after, the propriety of words, those circumstances of examining and understanding, casting the words into the naturall order, and the like : I referre you to the Chapter of construing *ex tempore*; where these things are handled at large.

Spoud. Yet for my further direction, give me one ensample in a sentence, in the story of the Bible, because we were speaking of that last, and how to teach children to understand that. I take it there is the like reason in the Latine, and in all things.

Phil. There is indeed the same reason. I will give you an instance in a sentence or two in the first Chapter in *Genesis*: and the rather, because this is used by many, to cause children to reade a Chapter of the Bible, and then to aske some questions out of that. For example:

Examples of asking questions, to helpe understanding.

1 In the beginning God created the heaven and the earth.

2 And the earth was without forme and voide, and darknesse was upon the face of the deepe, and the Spirit of God moved upon the Waters.

3 Then God said; Let there be light, and there was light, &c.

I would propound my questions thus, sundry wayes, out of the words, and that they may answer directly in the very words:

Q. What did God in the beginning?
A. He created heaven and earth.
Q. When did God create heaven and earth?
A. In the beginning.
Q. Were not heaven and earth alwayes?
A. No;

THE GRAMMAR SCHOOLE

A. No; God created them.
Q. What a one was the earth?
A. The earth was without forme or fashion.
Q. Had it any thing in it?
A. No; it was voide or waste.
Q. Was there nothing upon it?
A. Yes; darknesse was upon the deepe.
Q. Was there nothing else moving?
A. Yes; the Spirit of God moved on the Waters.
Q. What said God then?
A. Let there be light.
Q. Was there light as he commanded?
A. Yes; there was light.
Q. Was there no light before?
A. No; God commanding created it: there was nothing but darknesse before: darknesse was upon the deepe.

These questions and answers arise directly out of the words; and are the same in effect with those in the little booke, called the History.

Spoud. These verily give a great light, and are marvellous easie, and do cause that a child may conceive and carry away most of them; whereas reading them over, he marked little in them. But yet there are some things darke, and over-hard for children to understand: as, what is meant by created, by the deep, and the moving of the Spirit upon the waters, &c.

Phil. It is true; but yet by this meanes a childe shall have a great light and helpe for understanding, conceit and memory in most. And for those things which remaine obscure, the learner is to marke them out, and inquire them of others, or of the notes and short Commentaries upon them, and so by the other helpes mentioned: and especially considering the drift of the Holy Ghost, and comparing with more plaine places where like phrases are used. But here it shall be the safest, in poasing to aske those things which arise clearely and naturally out of the words, and may be fully understood; to omit the rest untill God shall make them as evident. The easiest being first learned perfectly, the

These short questions give a great light to harder points, how they are to be understood.

rest

THE GRAMMAR SCHOOLE

rest will come in their time, and the fruit according to your desire.

Helpe in private reading. And let me tell you this for your owne benefit: In your private reading Scriptures, or other bookes, where you would fully understand and lay up, use thus to resolve by questions and answers in your minde; and then tell me what you do finde. The benefit which I doe conceive of it, makes me bold thus to advise you: but this by the way.

Spoud. Thus you will binde me unto you for ever, in directing me in every thing, so plainly and so easily; and not only for my children, and how to do them all this good, but even for mine owne private. Though I cannot require you, yet the high God, who hath given you this heart, and who never forgets the least part of the labour or love which any of his servants shall shew to his name, he will certainly reward it.

Thus have we gone thorow all the maine and principall matters concerning this our function, for all parts and exercises of learning, which I do remember; so farre as doe belong to our calling: so that now I should leave off from hindering or troubling you any further. Yet neverthelesse, whereas I remember that you said, that God might direct, this our conference, not only to our own private benefit, but also to the benefit of many thousand other; and verily I see that he may turne it to a perpetuall blessing: give me leave to propound some other doubts, to the very same purpose, to remove whatsoever may hinder or bring scruple to any, and so supply what yet may seeme wanting or hard to be effected.

Phil. Goe on, I pray you: I shall resolve you in all, according to my poore abilitie, as I have in the rest. Now indeede we have a fit time: and God knoweth whether ever we shall have the like opportunity againe. Therefore propound whatsoever may tend hereunto.

CHAP.

THE GRAMMAR SCHOOLE

CHAP. XXIIII.

Some things necessary to be knowne, for the better attaining of all the parts of Learning mentioned.

1 *How the Schoolemaster should be qualified.*

Spoud.

MY first question shall be this: How you would have your Schoolemaster qualified, to be able to doe all these in this manner: he had not neede to be every ordinary man. *How the Schoolmaster should be qualified.*

Phil. I will answer you, how I thinke it necessary, that the Schoolemaster should be qualified.

1 To be such a one as is sufficient to direct his Schollers in the things mentioned, or in better; according as the learning of his Schollers shall require: or at least such a one as is tractable, and not conceited, though his ability be the meaner; and who will willingly use any helpe or direction, to fit him hereunto. Neither is there any thing here, but that any one meete to be admitted to that place, may by his labour and diligence (following but even this direction) attaine unto in short time, through the blessing of God. *1 Sufficient to direct his Schollers. Or, tractable.*

2 He must resolve to be painfull and constant in the best courses; of conscience, to doe a speciall service to God in his place: to be alwayes upon his worke, during schoole times; never absent from his place or office more then upon urgent necessitie. *2 Painfull and constant of conscience to God.*

To cast aside all other studies for the time of his schoole, I meane in the greater Grammar schooles: his eye to be on every one and their behaviours, and that nothing bee wanting *To cast off all other studies for school times.*

THE GRAMMAR SCHOOLE

Not to poste o'ver the trust to others.

wanting to them: his minde upon their taskes and profiting; not posting over the trust to others, for hearing parts or Lectures, or examining exercises, so farre as his owne leisure will serve. For he shall sensibly discerne a neglect, even in the best, where they have any hope to escape the Master's owne view. One day omitted shall make them worse two dayes after. The Master's eye must feede the horse: therefore where he is compelled to use the help of some schollers, he is to see that they deale faithfully, and to take some short tryall of them after.

3 Of a loving disposition to incourage all by praise and rewards.

3 He should be of a loving and gentle disposition with gravitie; or such a one as will frame himselfe unto it; and to incourage his schollers by due praise, rewards, and an honest emulation; who also dislikes utterly all severity, more then for necessity: yet so, as that he be quicke and cheerefull to put life into all, and who cannot indure to see sluggishnesse or idlenesse in any, much lesse any ungraciousnesse; and therefore can use also not onely sharpenesse, but even severity with discretion where neede is.

4 A godly man and of good carriage. To seek to gaine and maintaine his authority, and how.

4 He ought to be a godly man, of a good carriage in all his conversation, to gaine love and reverence thereby. And therefore to avoide carefully all lightnesse, and overmuch familiarity with boyes, or whatsoever may diminish his estimation and authority. And also to the end that God may grace him with authoritie, to aime in all his labour, not at his owne private gaine or credit; but how he may most honour God in his place, doe the best service to his Church, and most profit the children committed to him. To expect the blessing of his labours onely from the Lord, and to ascribe all the praise unto him alone. Thus to serve forth his time, so long as he remaines therein, that he may be ever acceptable unto the Lord, looking (as was said) for his chiefe reward from him.

Spoud. Indeed Sir, such a man cannot doubt of a blessing, and a reward from the Lord: yet neverthelesse he had neede of good helpe, and also to be well rewarded and incouraged from men, at least by them with whose children

THE GRAMMAR SCHOOLE

dren he takes these paines. You thinke it then necessarie that he should have an Usher: I pray you let me heare your judgement of this, and what a one you would have his Usher to be.

CHAP XXV.

Of the Usher and his Office.

Phil.

TO answer your questions, and first for an Usher. I thinke it most necessarie, that in all greater schooles, where an Usher can be had, there be provision for one Usher or moe, according to the number of the schollers; that the burden may be divided equally amongst them. As *Jethro* exhorted *Moses* concerning the Magistracie; wherein he was overtoiled, and the judgement of the people much hindered for lacke of helpe; that therefore there should be provision of helpers made: so is it as requisite here.

An Usher necessary in all greater schooles.

To divide the burden.

That so the Master may imploy his paines principally amongst the chiefe; as the Usher doth amongst the lower. For otherwise, when the Master is compelled to divide his paines both amongst little and great, he may much overweary himselfe, and yet not be able to doe that good with any, which he might have done having helpe.

Evill of lacke of an Usher.

Hence also it shall come to passe, that another Schoolemaster who hath but two or three of the chiefe fourmes only under him, shall have his schollers farre to excell his, who is troubled with all; though the other neither take halfe the paines, nor observe so good orders. Besides, that he who hath the care of all, can have no leisure nor opportunity to furnish himselfe more and more for the better profiting and growth of the highest, nor for any other study to answer the expectation

THE GRAMMAR SCHOOLE

The Master burdened with all, is as the husbandman o'ercharged with more then he can compasse. — expectation of his place. In this case as we see in husbandry; where the meanest and most unskilfull husband having but a little husbandry to follow, which he is able to compasse throughly, goeth ordinarily beyond the most skilfull being overcharged, though he toyle never so hard, and weary himselfe never so much.

Supply by schollers not sufficient. — And howsoever wise order and policy may much helpe, to the supply of the want of an Usher, by meanes of some of the Schollers: yet it shall not be comparable to that good which may be done by a sufficient Usher, because of his stayednesse and authority; neither without some hinderance to those schollers, who are so imployed.

Besides this, in the absence of the Master (which sometimes will necessarily fall out) how hard a thing it is to keepe children in any awe without an Usher (when boyes are to be governed by boyes) every man knoweth; what inconveniences also come of it, and specially what discredit to the schoole. And thus much for the necessitie of an Usher.

Sufficiencie of the Usher. — Now for the sufficiency of the Usher, it would be such, as that he should be able in some good sort to supply the Master's absence; or that he be such a one, as who will willingly take any paines, and follow any good direction to fit himselfe for his place.

To be at the Master's command. — For his submission, he should be alwayes at the Master's command, in all things in the schoole, ever to supply the Master's absence, as need shall require; and to see that there be no intermission, or loytering in any fourme, if the Master be away: but that every one doe goe on in his place. Yet a wary care must be had, that he be used with respect by the Master, and also the schollers, to maintaine and increase his authoritie, to avoid all disgrace and contempt.

To be used with respect.

☞ *Not to meddle with correcting the highest.* — Also, for the avoiding of all repining and malice against him, there would be this caveat; that he doe not take upon him the correction of those which are under the Master; without a speciall charge, or some extraordinary occasion.

And

THE GRAMMAR SCHOOLE

And to speake further what I thinke in this case; That although I would have the Usher to have authority to correct any under him, or others, also, need so requiring in the Master's absence, and all the Schollers to know so much: Yet he should not use that authoritie, no not in correcting those under himselfe, unlesse very sparingly, but rather of himselfe, and in his own discretion, to referre or to put them up to the Master; so to keepe the schollers from that stomaking and complaints which will be made against him to the Parents, and otherwise, doe he what he can to prevent it: unlesse it be where the Usher teacheth in a place separate from the Master; there he is of necessity to use correction, though with great discretion, and so seldome as may be. Experience also sheweth, that the schollers will much more willingly and submisly take correction of the Master without the least repining. Neither need this correction to be so great, as to trouble the Master very much, if right government be used. *It were the best if the Usher medled with no correction at all, unlesse in the Master's absence.*

All this must be ordered by the discretion of the wise Master, so as they may stand in awe of the Usher: otherwise little good will be done.

The principall office and imploiment of the Usher where there is but one, should be, for all under construction, and the enterers into it, to prepare and fit them for the Master, to lay a most sure foundation amongst them; to traine them up to the Master's hand; and so to make them exceeding perfect in all the first grounds, that they may goe on with ease and cheerefulnesse, when they come under the Master. *The Usher's principall imployment with the younger, to train them up for the Master.*

Also to the end that the Usher be not a meanes of the negligence of the Master, but to prevent that, and a number of inconveniences, and also to tye both Usher and Schollers, to perpetuall diligence and care; and withal, that the Master may have an assured comfort in the profiting of his Schollers, and boldnesse against the accusations of any malicious party: this shall be very requisite, that the Master goe over all once in the day (if he can possibly) to see what they have done, *To prevent all inconveniences by the Usher.*

THE GRAMMAR SCHOOLE

done, and to examine some questions in each fourme of them under the Usher, to make triall in some part of that which they have learned that day, how well they have done it; or at least amongst some of them where there are many. This account will inforce all, both Usher and Schollers, to a very heedfull care. It may be shorter or longer, as time and occasions permit.

CHAP. XXVI.

Helps in the Schoole.

Spoud.

Helpes besides the Usher.

BUt be it so, that you be destitute of an Usher; or having an Usher, yet your number is so many, as you are not able to goe thorow them all, in that sort that were meete: what helpe would you use then?

Phil. My helpes are of two sorts; generall or particular. My generall helps which are common to all schooles, even where there are Ushers, are these:

1 Helpe in schooles, fewnesse of the fourmes.

1 That which was noted amongst the generall observations; to have all my schoole sorted into fourmes or *Classes,* and those so few as may be: though twenty in a fourme or moe, the better, as was said; and my fourmes divided into equall parts. This shall gaine one halfe of time, for the reasons there mentioned.

2 Seniors in each fourme.

2 In every fourme this may be a notable helpe, that the two or foure Seniors in each fourme, be as Ushers in that fourme, for overseeing, directing, examining, and fitting the rest every way before they come to say; and so for over-seeing the exercises.

Also in straight of time, to stand forth before the rest, and to heare them. The Master to have an eye and see carefully that they deale faithfully, and make some short examination

THE GRAMMAR SCHOOLE

mination after. And in all lectures those two Seniors to be blamed principally for the negligence of their sides, and contrarily to be commended for their diligence. This may be a second and a very great helpe: like as it is in an army, where they have their under-officers for hundreths or for tens; as *Decuriones, Centuriones, &c.* for the speciall government of all under them. These who thus take most pains with the rest, shall still ever keep to be the best of the fourmes.

A third might be added: which is Authority and good Government, which indeed is above all. But of that it will be fitter to speake by it selfe. *3 Authority.*

The particular helpe where either an Usher is wanting, or else is not sufficient, is by a Subdoctor, one or moe, according to the number of the schollers. The Subdoctor is to be appointed out of all your highest fourmes, every one to be his day in stead of an Usher, to doe those things which the Usher should, according to their abilities; and so to observe the behaviour of all under them. *Particular help, Subdoctor in place of the Usher, or where the Usher is not sufficient.*

Spoud. These cannot but be very worthy helpes. But here I pray you resolve me a doubt or two, arising hereon.

1 How will you divide your schoole thus, and especially your fourmes, for the appointing of your Seniors, that every one in a fourme may be placed according to his learning? which I take to be very necessary; so as they shall not think, that any are preferred by the favour of the Master: also that all may sit as Adversaries and fit matches, and so to have sides equally divided, to doe all by that emulation, and honest strift and contention, which you speake of.

Phil. For my fourmes, I would put so many in a fourme, as possibly can goe together, as was noted: the better will be continuall helpers to the other, and much draw on the worse. *Sorting the fourmes so many together as may be.*

Secondly, for the division of my fourmes, and election of Seniors, I finde this the onely way to cut off all quarrelling, and to provoke all to a continuall contention;

1 By voyces; all of a fourme to name who is the best

of

S

THE GRAMMAR SCHOOLE

Choise and matching each fourme. of their fourme, and so who is the best next him. Those who have the most voices, to be the two Seniours of the fourme. These they will choose very certainly. Then to the end to make equall sides; let the second or Junior of those two so chosen, call unto himselfe the best which he can, to make his side.

After that, let the first choose the best next; then after, the second & his fellow, to choose the best next to them againe: And thus to goe thorow choosing, untill they have chosen all the fourme. The two Seniours, I say, to be chosen by election of the whole fourme: then they two to choose, or call the rest of the fourme by equall election; the Junior choosing first, and so to goe by course: If the Senior should choose first, then his side would ever be the better; which by the Junior choosing first is prevented.

Benefits of this election. By this meanes you shall find that they will choose very equally, and without partiality, to the end that each may have the best fellowes; even as gamesters will do at matches in shooting, bowling, or the like: and every match shall be very equall, or small difference amongst them.

Also hereby all mutterings shall be cut off, whereby some kinde boyes will be whispering to their Parents, that their Master doth not regard nor love them, but prefers others before them. Thus also the painfull shall be incouraged, when they finde themselves preferred by the judgement of all their fellowes; and each made to strive daily to be as good as his match or adversarie, and for the credit of their side: and finally, they will labour that they may be preferred at the next election; or at least, not be put downe with disgrace. This election would be made oftener amongst the younger, as once in a moneth at least; because their diligence and quicknesse will much alter: Amongst the Senior fourmes once in a quarter may suffice; yet at the Master's discretion.

Spoud. This election surely is most equall, and the benefits of it must needs be very great according to that which you have said; and chiefly to helpe as much as any one
thing

THE GRAMMAR SCHOOLE

thing to make the schoole to be indeed a pleasant place of honest, scholler-like, sweet and earnest contention. But you spake of a third generall help, which might be added, which you said was above all; to wit, good government: of this I doe desire to heare.

This a chiefe meanes to make the schoole Ludus literarius.

CHAP. XXVII.

Of government and authoritie in Schooles.

Phil.

Concerning the government of the schoole, of which you so desire my sentence; I doe indeede account it the helpe of helpes: as it is in all kinde of societies; so principally in the schoole: out of which, all other good and civill societies should first proceed: To the end, that out of the schooles, and from the first yeeres, children may learne the benefit and blessing of good government, and how every one ought to doe his dutie in his place: and so from thence this good order and government may be derived into all places in some manner. *Government the helpe of helpes.*

This government ought to be, 1. By maintaining authoritie, which is the very top of all government; and is indeed a speciall gift of God. *Authority the top of government.*

This authoritie must be maintained, as in the Magistrate, by his so carrying himselfe, as being a certaine living law, or rather as in the place of God amongst them; I meane, as one appointed of God, to see the most profitable courses to be put in practice painfully, and constantly, for the speediest furnishing his schollers with the best learning & manners, to the greatest good of the Schollers, God's Church and their Countrey. *Authority how to be maintained. 1 By being a living law.*

2. It must be maintained by a most strict execution of justice, *2 By most strict executi-*

THE GRAMMAR SCHOOLE

on of justice in præmio pœna. justice, in rewards and punishments. As *Solon* said, that the Common-wealth was upholden by two things; *præmio & pœna*. That the painfull and obedient be by all means countenanced, incouraged and preferred: the negligent and any way disobedient, be disgraced, and discouraged in all their evill manners, untill they frame themselves to the diligence and obedience of the best.

Incouraging vertue. Discouraging vice. The evils of the contrary, or of partialitie.

Observe this, and be warned.

Thus by the incouragement and commendation of vertue, and discountenancing of vice; you shall in time overcome the most froward nature, and bring all into a cheerefull submission: Whereas of the contrary, dealing partially, or making no difference betweene the good and the bad, and much more discountenancing the painfull and toward, and countenancing or favouring the idle and ungracious, you shall see all overturned: for who will not frame himselfe to the lewdest, when it is all one unto them, whatsoever they be? our corrupt natures being so prone unto the worst things.

3 By a demonstration of conscience and love in all.

3 That in all their government there be a true demonstration of conscience and love, to doe all as of conscience to God, and of love to the children, for the perpetuall good of every one; and in an indevour and study to draw them on by love, in an honest emulation, with due praise and rewards; abhorring cruelty, and avoiding severitie (as was said) more then of necessitie.

4 By being presidents to the children, of all vertue.

4 By being Presidents of all vertue to their children; and being as carefull in their owne places first, before the children's eyes to do their duties, as they would have their children to be in theirs. And so finally, by their holy and faithful carriage, to seeke that God may rule, and that the children may obey God: For then he will both blesse all their labors, and maintaine their authoritie.

Spoud. Surely, Sir, these are worthy meanes to maintaine authoritie: which unlesse it be preserved inviolable, all government goeth downe. But I perceive, you utterly dislike that extreme severitie whereby all things are done in very many schooles, and the whole government maintained on-

ly

THE GRAMMAR SCHOOLE

ly by continuall and terrible whipping; because you have so oft mentioned it as with griefe.

Phil. You shall finde that M. *Askam* doth as oft and more vehemently inveigh against it. For mine owne part I doe indeed altogether dislike it, more then necessity inforceth: and I take it that I have better grounds for my dislike, then any one can have to the contrary, even from those things which cannot be contradicted. *Extreme severitie and whipping to be avoided in schooles, and all meanes used to prevent it.*

1 Wee are to imitate the Lord himselfe; who though he be justice it selfe, yet is evermore inclined unto mercy, and doth not execute the severity and rigour of his justice, when any other meanes can serve: who if he should smite us, even the most vigilant of us all, so oft as we offend, as many doe the children; which of us could live? *1 By the example of God.*

2 What father is there; nay which of us is there who is a father, who would not have our own children rather trained up by all loving meanes of gentle incouragement, praise and faire dealing, then with buffeting and blowes, or continuall and cruell whipping, scorning and reviling? Or which of us could but indure to see that indignitie done to our owne children, before our faces? *2 By the general desire of all wise parents, having naturall affections.*

Now our government and correction ought to be such, as which the very parent being present (I meane the wise parent) might approove; and for which we may ever have comfort and boldnesse, even before the holy God. To this we are to strive and contend alwayes, untill at length we attaine unto it.

3 Which of us is there that would willingly live under such a government of any sort, that our state should be as the people, under their Taske-Masters in Egypt, that wee should be smitten continually for every little fault? and labour we never so much to doe our duties, yet still we should be beaten. *3 By that which every one of us would have done unto our selves.*

4 Let every man's experience teach whether extremitie or excesse of feare (which must needs follow upon such cruell and continuall beating and dulling) doth not deprive and robbe the minde of all the helpes which reason offers. *4 For the mischiefes which follow excesse of feare, taking away all understanding and sense from the wisest.*

THE GRAMMAR SCHOOLE

offers. So as that the minde running about that which it feares so much, forgets that which it should wholly intend; whereby in timorous natures, you shall see some to stand as very sotts, and senselesse, through an apprehension of some extreme evill, or by extremity of feare: whereas they are otherwise as wise and learned as the best. Insomuch as all devices are to be used to rid children of that kind of overwhelming feare; and sometimes correction for it, when this feare is without cause, and cannot be helped otherwise.

5 For the schollers to worke in them a love of learning.

5 For the schollers themselves; because all things should be done in the Schoole, so as to worke in the children a love of learning; and also of their teachers: for that this love is welknowne to be the most effectuall meanes, to increase and nourish learning in them the fastest; and also that government which consists in love, is ever the firmest.

Now this extreme whipping, all men know what a dislike it breedeth in the children, both of the schoole, and of all learning, as that they will think themselves very happy, if the parents will set them to any servile or toiling businesse, so that they may keep from schoole: And also it workes in them a secret hatred of their Masters; according to the sayings, *Quem metudunt, oderunt:* and, *Quem quisque odit, perijsse expetit;* whom men do feare with a slavish feare, them they hate, and wish in their hearts to see their death.

6 In regard of the Masters to gaine hearts of children and parents.

6 In regard of the Masters themselves; because by this milde and loving government, they shall both have the hearts and commendations of the children presently, when they see in the Masters the affections of fathers towards them; and also they will ever keep a sweet and thankfull remembrance of them, all their life long: that ever when they have occasion to speake of their Schoolemasters, they will do it with reverence, and praise God that ever they fell into the hands of such Masters: wheras of the contrary, they shall be sure of the secret hate and complaints of the poore children presently, where they dare speake: and ever after when they come at their own liberty, they will then report as they have found, and it may be, farre worse: So that they can never

THE GRAMMAR SCHOOLE

ver speake of their Master, but as of a thing which they abhorre: his name is as a curse in their mouthes: many wishing they had never knowne him: For that then they had beene Schollers, if they had not falne into the hands of so cruell Masters.

7 And finally, because in this loving, equall, milde and tender government, the Masters shall ever have boldnesse and comfort before the children, their parents, in their owne consciences, and before God himselfe: whereas in the cruell and unmercifull tyrannie, they shall have nothing but feare; feare of the children, feare of their parents, feare in their own consciences, feare for the Lord who hath said, that there shal be judgement mercilesse for them who shew no mercy; and so the conscience being awaked, to have nothing but feare round about, except the Lord doe grant unfained repentance to escape thereby. *7 That Masters may ever have boldnesse and comfort.*

Spoud. I know not how to answer that which you say. The Lord be mercifull unto us all who are in this calling, even for this sinne: for it is no small matter to moderate our passion, and our correction. When the parents and others looke for great things at our hands, and we find little good, and oft-times those the worst, whom we would fainest have to do the best: which of us can herein justify our selves? But I pray you Sir, how would you have our authority maintained, and justice executed, which you so commend? You would have correction used, and sometimes sharpnesse too; as I observed in your speech for your Schoolemaster. How would you have the justice, *in præmio & pæna* in rewards and punishments? Set me downe shortly the meanes: and first for rewards and incouragements; after for punishments. *It is hard for the Master striving to doe good, to moderate his passion.*

CHAP.

CHAP. XXVIII.

Of preferments and incouragements.

Phil.

Incouragements to be by these meanes:
1 Often elections and preferments therein.

FOr the rewards of learning by preferments and incouragements; thus I finde best to doe it:
1 By often elections of every fourme, in such manner as was shewed; and so ever preferring the best thereby, to higher places as they grow in learning.

2 Countenancing and gracing the Seniours, and all the best and most painfull.

2. By gracing all the Seniours, and best in each fourme, both to incourage them, and to provoke their fellowes to emulate them, to strive in all things to be like unto them: and also to cause all their fellowes in all things to reverence, and preferre them, both by giving place to them and otherwise.

3 Putting up into higher fourms.

3. By preferring or putting up those into higher fourmes, who profit extraordinarily.

Giving places.

Also daily (if you see good) to give higher places to them who doe better, untill the other recover their places againe, by the election of the whole fourme, or by their diligence.

4 Commending every thing well done.

4 To use to commend every thing in their exercises, which is well or painfully done; passing over the lesser faults onely with a word shewing our dislike: and that which is absurd, with some pretty speech; sharpely reproving or disgracing their absurditie, without further correction, if there doe not appeare in them extreme negligence.

Caveat in praising.

Yet in praising them, you are to beware of making any of them wantonly proud, or letting them to be any way overbold or malepart, or of using them over-familiarly: for

fami-

THE GRAMMAR SCHOOLE

familiaritie will certainly breed contempt, and sundry inconveniences; wheras a reverend awe and loving feare, with these incouragements, shall continually nourish all vertue and diligence.

5 This might be used also with much fruit, to incourage and provoke: but this as shall be found meet; to have a disputation for the victorship once every quarter of the yeere: as the last Wednesday or Friday of each quarter in the afternoone; the manner thus: *5 Disputation for the victorship.*

Cause the two Seniours of the two highest fourmes to sit together in the upper end of the Schoole; and all the Schollers from the lowest which take construction, unto the highest, to aske of either of them, each two questions in order; of the best questions, which they have learned in their Grammar or Authours; first the two Senior adversaries of the highest fourme to answer, then two of the next. And then let those two of them foure, who answered best (that is, one of either fourme who answered most questions) be the Victors for that Quarter. Two other of their next fellowes, or moe, to take note, and set downe to how many questions each answered; and so the victorship to be decided. *Manner of the Disputation.*

After this, some use to cause the schollers every of them, to give something for a *Præmium* to the Victours: as each one a point or a counter, or moe; or else better gifts if they be well able, of such things as they may without their hurt, or the offence of their parents, and as every one will himselfe. These to be divided equally betweene the two Victors, as a reward of their diligence and learning; to incourage them and all the rest of them by their ensample to strive at length to come unto the Victorship; because then besides the honour of it, each may come to receive againe more then ever they gave before. *Præmia given to the two Victors.*

The practice of this disputation must needs be very profitable; though some good Schoolemasters doe doubt of the expediency for Schollers to give any thing, but to honour them otherwise.

The

THE GRAMMAR SCHOOLE

Office of the Victours for their Præmia.

The two victors, in regard of this dignity, and the applause from their fellowes, should use to make some exercises of Verses or the like, to get leave to play on every Thursday, when there was no play-day in the weeke before. And so they two continually to have that day for their fellowes, as a further reward and honour of their learning; I meane onely in such weekes when they had no play before, or at the Master's discretion. But this (as was advised) as Masters shall finde it most expedient.

Solemne examination to be made once every yeere.

6 Above all these, this may be used as a notable incouragement and provocation, both to Masters and schollers, and very necessarie; That every yeere, at least once in the yeere, there be a solemne examination by the Governours of the schoole, or some especially appointed thereunto.

Exercises to be provided against that time.

Against which time, all of any ability should provide some Exercises faire written; as either Translations, Epistles, Theames, or Verses, according to the dayly exercises of every fourm: and withall some declamations where there are ancient schollers, an Oration by the highest, to give the visitours intertainment. That in these their exercises, all may see their profiting, at least in writing, and receive some other contentment.

To keepe their daily exercises faire written in bookes, for tryall then by comparing.

Also all to keepe their chiefe exercises faire written in bookes, to be shewed then; that by comparing them together with the former yeeres, both the Master's diligence and their profiting may appeare, and have due commendation.

A course of examination to be appointed, and to be performed first by the Masters and Ushers.

Besides these also, for the full examination of the schollers in all their learning, the Schoolemasters and Ushers are to be appointed an order and course in their examination; and themselves first to make a demonstration before the Visitours, what the children can doe in every fourme, both in their Grammar and Authors, and each kinde, as shall be fit. It would be done first by themselves, because the schollers are best acquainted with their maner of examining, and will be most bold to answer them. After them, the Visitours and

After by others not satisfied.

THE GRAMMAR SCHOOLE

and others, who are not satisfied, to examine where, and as they please.

Then when all is done, as the Visitours are to incourage all who doe well, with praise; so those who doe best, would be graced with some *Præmium* from them: as some little booke, or money; to every one something: or at least with some speciall commendation. *All who do well to be praised.*

The best specially graced.

It were to be wished that in great Schooles, there were somthing given to this end, to be so bestowed; five shillings or ten shillings. It would exceedingly incourage and incite all to take paines. *Some Præmia given.*

This set solemne publike examination, will more inforce all, both Masters, Ushers and Schollers, to take paines, and tye them to make conscience of their duties, and to seeke to profit and increase daily in knowledge, that they may then answer the expectation of all men, and give up a good account; then any augmentation of maintenance, or statutes, or whatsoever device can possibly doe: *Benefit of set and solemne examination.*

Although all necessarie provision is to be made, both for the best Statutes and Orders; and chiefly for sufficient maintenance, and rewards to give all kinde of hartening and incouragement both to Masters, Ushers, and Schollers.

Also if at such examinations, something were given by the Visitours or other Benefactors, to be allowed upon some poore scholler of the schoole, who is of speciall painfulnesse and towardlinesse; to the end he might be assistant to the Usher: it would much help both Usher & the yonger schollers, and animate all such to take paines; striving who should have that preferment. *Something given to some painefull poore scholler to helpe the Usher.*

Before such publique examinations, all the parents of the children should have notice given them: that all of them may know certainly, the hopes of their children, and contrarily; and all who will, may take tryall: *All parents to have notice before such examination.*

That so neither the parents may be abused, neither schooles, nor schollers discredited, nor any lose their time, nor be wearied out, in that to which they are not fitted by nature;

THE GRAMMAR SCHOOLE

nature; but every one to be imployed to that in due time, to which he is most apt.

Spoud. These meanes constantly observed, together with that strift & contention by adversaries, must needs provoke to a vehement study and emulation; unlesse in such who are of a very servile nature, and bad disposition: but how will you deale with them? you must needs use extreme severitie towards them, who regard neither preferment, nor credit, nor feare ought but stripes.

Phil. For these and all the rest (besides the former preferments) to the end to avoid this cruelty, which is so odious to all, we are to strive to this one thing following:

7 To labour ever to worke conscience in all, to do all of conscience to God.

7 Above all, to labour to worke in them some conscience of their duties, by planting grace in them, and the feare of the Lord; with childelike affections towards the Lord, as towards their heavenly Father:

By calling on them to remember these things.

And that also, besides all other meanes of Religion, spoken of before, by calling oft upon all, to remember these things:

1 That in their calling they are God's servants.

1 That in their calling they serve not men, but God; that they are God's children and servants. As the very drudge is God's servant: so they are much more, being imployed in so holy a calling, as to get knowledge and good nurture, for the good of the Church of God, and their owne salvation; and principally that they may be most serviceable to God in all their lives after, in what calling soever:

His eyes upon them.

And therfore ever to bethinke themselves that God's eye is upon them, and he markes all their labour, and of what conscience to him they do it; and so will accept and reward them according to their faithfulnesse: so to be painfull and obedient, not for feare of their Master, nor of the rod; but for the feare and love of God, because hee hath appointed them so. And so herein to make a full demonstration, who they are amongst them that are truely wise, who feare and love God indeed; and who otherwise.

2 To call on them oft, to aime at this, to use all their wit, their labour, time, and all their gifts, which are God's,

to

THE GRAMMAR SCHOOLE

to get the best learning that they can; to doe the Lord the greatest honor which they are able, whilst they shal remaine in the earth, and the best service to his Church; and thereby to walke towards eternall life. Because, thus they shall be sure that God will honour them seeking to honour him; and will cast learning upon them so farre as shall be good. *2 To study to get learning to honor God with, and doe service to his Church.*

3 To put them oft in mind of the reward of their learning, which they may looke for even in this life. As those rewards which accompany great learned men; namely, riches, honours, dignities, favour, pleasures, and whatsoever their hearts can desire; and much more that reward which shall be eternall; that if men should be unthankfull, yet God will reward all our labour and study aboundantly, even every thought and meditation that ever we had for his name. *3 To put them in minde of the rewards which follow learning.*

To this end, to inculcate oft unto them some of *Salomon's* Proverbs, concerning the excellency of learning and wisedome. *Excellent sentences to be oft inculcated, to worke in the schollers a love of learning. Prov. 3.13.*

As Pro. 3.13. Blessed is the man that findeth wisdom, and the man that getteth understanding.

14. For the merchandize thereof is better then the merchandize of silver, and the gaine thereof is better then gold.

15. It is more precious then pearles; and all things that thou canst desire, are not to be compared unto her.

And so forth, the 16, 17, & 18. verses. Also Prov. 4, 7, 8. & 8. 14, 15, 16, 17, 18, 19, 20, &c. & 33, 34, &c. These and the like, being indeed chiefly meant of the divine wisdome, comprehend also this learning, which is the way and means unto that divine and heavenly wisedome.

By these meanes, and remembring well the generall observations to put them in practice (as, to make all grounds exceeding perfect as they go, chiefly their Accedence and Grammar, and to keepe them by continuall repetitions and examinations, that they may goe with ease, and feeling a sweetnesse of learning, and keeping a constant course in your government; observing wisely the nature and disposition of every one, and framing your selfe thereto accordingly) you shall undoubtedly see the Lord so *To keep grounds perfect. To observe the nature of each wisely, & frame our selves thereto accordingly.*

bringing

THE GRAMMAR SCHOOLE

bringing them in obedience by your prayers, as a very small punishment shall serve.

Spoud. It cannot be, but if we can plant the feare of the Lord in them, to worke in them a conscience of their duties, it must needs be most availeable; and much more all these: but yet feeling that punishments also must needs be inflicted on some oft times, and on all sometimes (because otherwise as you said, justice cannot be executed, nor any government or authority maintained) I pray you let me heare, how you would proceed in the same.

CHAP. XXIX.

Of execution of justice in Schooles, by punishments.

Phil.

FOr inflicting punishments, we ought to come thereunto unwillingly, and even inforced; and therefore to proceed by degrees: that who cannot be moved by any of the former meanes of preferments, nor incouragements, nor any gentle exhortation nor admonition, may be brought into order and obedience by punishment.

To punish unwillingly.

And therefore, first to begin with the lesser kindes of punishments; and also by degrees to the highest and severest, after this manner observing carefully the natures of every one, as was said.

To proceed by degrees in punishing.

1 To use reproofes; and those sometimes more sharpe according to the nature of the offender, and his fault.

1 Reproofes.

2 To punish by losse of place to him who doth better according to our discretion.

2 Losse of place.

3 To punish by a note, which may be called, the blacke Bill. This I would have the principall punishment, I meane most

3 Blacke Bill of principal use, and most availeable.

THE GRAMMAR SCHOOLE

most of use: for you shall finde by experience, that it being rightly used, it is more availeable then all other, to keepe all in obedience; and specially for any notoriously idle or stubborne, or which are of evill behaviour any way.

The manner of it may be thus:

To keepe a note in writing: or which may more easily be done; to keepe a remembrance of all whom you observe very negligent, stubborne, lewd, or any way disobedient, to restraine them from all liberty of play. *Manner of the blacke Bill to deprive them of the play dayes.*

And therefore, to give them all to know so much beforehand, that whosoever asketh leave to play, or upon what occasion soever, yet we intend alwaies to except all such; and that the liberty is granted onely for the painfull and obedient, which are worthy to have the priviledges of schollers, and of the schoole, because they are such, and are an ornament to the schoole: not for them who are a disgrace unto it. *To make them all to know what to looke for.*

So alwayes at such playing times, before the *Exeatis*, the Master and Ushers to view every fourme thorow; and then to cause all them to sit still, whom they remember to have been negligent, or faulty in any special sort worthy that punishment, and to doe some exercises in writing besides; either those which they have omitted before, or such as wherein they cannot be idle. *To view the fourmes before play, and to separate all the disobedient and unworthy to be left to their tasks.*

But herein there must be a speciall care, when they are thus restrained from play, that either Master or Usher, if it can be conveniently, have an eye to them, that they cannot loyter; or some one specially appointed, to see that they do their taskes. *Care for their taskes to be performed faithfully in their restraint.*

Also that they be called to an account the next morning, whether they have done the taskes injoyned, under paine of sixe jerkes to be surely paid.

Moreover, for all those who are notoriously stubborne, or negligent, or have done any grosse fault, or cause them to sit thus, not onely one day, but every play-day continually untill they shew themselves truely sorry for their faults, and doe amend; becomming as dutiful, and submisse as any other, *Notorious offenders to sit, untill they shew good tokens of amendment.*

THE GRAMMAR SCHOOLE

other, and until they do declare by good signes, their desire and purpose to please and obey their Master; unlesse they be released at very great suite, or upon sufficient sureties of their fellowes, to incurre otherwise their penalty if they amend not.

Benefit of this punishment strictly observ'ed, and why.

This course straightly observed, partly through the shame of being noted in the rank of disordered fellowes, and also lest their Parents should know it; and partly through depriving them of play, and more also through this strict account to be given of their taskes, and severity of correction otherwise, will more tame the stubbornest and proudest, through God's blessing, then any correction by rod: and this without danger to the scholler, or offence to their friends.

To looke to this strictly.

And therefore, when rod and all other meanes faile, let us looke carefully to this, not to leave one stubborne boy untill he be brought as submisse and dutifull as any of the rest. For, those being brought into obedience, the rest may easily be kept in order, with very little correction, whereas one stubborne boy suffered, will spoile, or at leastwise indanger all the rest.

4. Correction with rod more seldom, and chiefly for terrour.

Sometimes in greater faults, to give three or foure jerkes with a birch, or with a small red willow where birch cannot be had. Or for terror in some notorious fault, halfe a doozen stripes or moe, soundly laid on, according to the discretion of the Master.

Custome of some in the use of the blacke Bill.

Some do only keep a bill, and more carefully their severall principall disorders; and now and then, shew them their names and faults mildly, how oft they have been admonished; and when they take them in hand, pay them soundly, and by this policy keepe them in great obedience.

Caveats in correction.

In this correction with the rod, speciall provision must be had for sundry things

1. Manner of correction of the stubborne and unbroken.

1 That when you are to correct any stubborne or unbroken boy, you make sure with him to hold him fast; as they are inforced to do, who are to shoo or to tame an unbroken colt.

To

THE GRAMMAR SCHOOLE

To this end to appoint 3. or 4. of your Schollers, whom you know to be honest, and strong inough, or moe if neede be, to lay hands upon him together, to hold him fast, over some fourme, so that he cannot stirre hand nor foot; or else if no other remedy will serve, to hold him to some post (which is farre the safest and free from inconvenience) so as he cannot any way hurt himselfe or others, be he never so peevish. Neither that he can have hope by any device or turning, or by his apparell, or any other meanes to escape. Nor yet that any one be left in his stubbornnesse to go away murmuring, powting, or blowing and puffing untill he shew as much submission as any, & that he will lie stil of himselfe without any holding; yet so as ever a wise moderation be kept. Although this must of necessitie be looked into; because besides the evill ensample to others, there is no hope to do any good to count of, with any untill their stomacks be first broken: and then they once thorowly brought under, you may have great hope to worke all good according to their capacity; so that it may be, you shall have little occasion to correct them after. *To hold them fast. Not to let any to go away in their stubbornnesse.*

Moreover, a very child suffered in his stubbornnesse, to scape for his struggling, will in a short time come to trouble two or three men to take him up, and to correct him without danger of hurting himselfe or others.

2. To be very wary for smiting them over the backes, in any case, or in such sort as in any way to hurt or indanger them: To the end to prevent all mischiefes, for our owne comfort; and to cut off all occasions from quarrelling parents or evill reports of the Schoole. And withall, to avoid for these causes, all smiting them upon the head, with hand, rod, or ferula. Also to the end that we may avoid all danger and feare for desperate boyes hurting themselves, not to use to threaten them afore, and when they have done any notorious fault, nor to let them know when they shall be beaten; but when they commit a new fault, or that we see the Schoole most full, or opportunity most fit, to take them of a sodaine. *To be wary to avoid all smiting or hurting the children. Caveat of threatning.*

3. That

T

THE GRAMMAR SCHOOLE

That the Master do not abase himselfe to struggle with any Scholler.

3. That the Master do not in any case abase himselfe, to strive or struggle with any boy to take him up: but to appoint other of the strongest to do it, where such need is, in such sort as was shewed before; and the rather for feare of hurting them in his anger, and for the evils which may come thereof, & which some Schoolemasters have lamented after.

To avoid all furious anger.

4. That the Masters and Ushers also do by all meanes avoid all furious anger, threatning, chafing, fretting, reviling: for these things will diminish authoritie, and may do much hurt, and much indanger many waies.

How correction ought ever to be given.

And therefore of the contrary, that all their correction be done with authority, and with a wise and sober moderation, in a demonstration of duty to God, and love to the children, for their amendment, and the reformation of their evill manners.

Sparing the rod where necessitie requireth, is to undoe the children.

Finally, as God hath sanctified the rod and correction, to cure the evils of their conditions, to drive out that folly which is bound up in their hearts, to save their soules from hell, and to give them wisedome; so it is to be used as God's instrument to these purposes: To spare them in these cases,

Assurance of safety in correction when it is done aright. Such correction is no cruelty.

is to hate them: To love them, is to correct them betime. Do it under God, and for him to these ends and with these cautions, and you shall never hurt them: you have the Lord for your warrant. Correction in such manner, for stubbornnesse, negligence and carefulnesse, is not to be accounted over-great severitie, much lesse crueltie.

Spoud. But how hard a matter is it to keepe this moderation in correcting, and thus to temper our anger! Surely, it must be a greater worke then of flesh and blood: how may wee attaine unto it? It is a matter which hath oftentimes troubled me, but I have not beene able to overcome it.

Anger necessary in Schoole-masters, so it be tempered aright.

Phil. I do not condemne all anger in us: nay, anger in the Schoole-master is as necessary as in any other, to be angry at the negligence and other vices of the children; for God hath ordained this to be a meanes, to whet us on to do our duties, and for the reformation & good of our schollers,

to

THE GRAMMAR SCHOOLE

to keepe them ever in a holy awe by the feare of it. Yea, sometimes in more grievous offences, God is wonderfully pleased with it, though it be mere vehement; as we may see in the anger of *Moses* and *Phineas*, so that we temper it in such sort, as that we sinne not in it. That it doe not cause us to breake out to reviling, fretting, chafing, blowes on the head, or otherwise to any cruell or unmercifull dealing with the children, to use them worse, then we would use a dogge, as we say:

But that we ever remember, that they are children, God's children, heires of his kingdome; wee are to nurture them, onely under him, to traine them up for him, and for his Church; nor to correct nature, but vice; to do all to the end to make them men.

Now the helpes of repressing this our anger, are the wise consideration of those things which I have mentioned, or the like: As to keepe a continuall memory, whose the children are; what they are; for whom we bring them up; under whom, and in whose place; whether we would have God angry at us, and to smite us as we doe the children, for every fault which we do: how wee would have our owne children dealt withall: and also God's justice to measure to us or ours, with what measure we mete to others. Besides, to remember, that anger will blind our minds, that we cannot see to correct or use any right moderation. *Meanes to represse furious and raging anger.*

Moreover, to have ever in mind, the mischiefes that come of anger; but it will diminish our authoritie, and disgrace us extremely in the eyes of the children, when it is immoderate, and without just cause. Also that in our anger, wee may doe that evill in a moment, which we shall repent all our lives long: And the rather, because Satan watcheth to get advantage against us, to bring us to some notable evils in our anger. Into whose hand, it is just with God to leave us, because we would not watch over this passion to keepe it in temper; when we know that of all other our affections wee most lye open to his malice in this, by reason of our continuall occasions of anger.

There-

THE GRAMMAR SCHOOLE

Therefore to conclude this point, as we are to use all wisdome to prevent these evils; so principally, a constant course in observing all orders, shall prevaile marvellously, by cutting off most occasions of anger.

And finally, when all other meanes faile of conquering this unruly passion: let us call to minde the meanes, which the Lord hath sanctified to bring every thought into obedience; to wit, his heavenly Word and Prayer. To this end it shall be necessarie, to have ever in minde, some speciall places of holy Scripture against anger; as these and the like;

Places of Scripture to be ever in our minds for repressing and moderating our anger.

Ephes. 4. 26, 27. *Be angry, but sinne not, let not the Sunne goe down upon your wrath: neither give place to the divell.*

Jam. 1. 20. Be slow to wrath: For, *The wrath of man doth not accomplish the righteousnesse of God.*

Psal. 37. 8. Cease from anger, leave off wrath: *Fret not thy selfe also to doe evill.*

A foole in a day is knowne by his anger.

Be not of a hastie spirit, to be angry: for anger resteth in the bosome of fooles.

The angry man is said to exalt folly, to set up his folly to be seene by all.

Prov. 19. 19. *A man of much anger shall suffer punishment: and though thou deliver him, yet will his anger come againe.*

In a word, that severe denunciation of our Saviour for this undiscreet anger, breaking out into evill speeches, may humble us continually, and make us afraid of this sinne:

Math. 5. 22. Danger of rash anger when it exceedes. *That whosoever is angry with his brother unadvisedly, shall be culpable of judgement* [or subject to punishment.] *And whosoever shall say unto his brother, Racha, shall be worthy to be punished by the Councell; And whosoever shall say, Foole, shall be worthy to be punished with hell fire.*

By all which words it is most evident, that our undiscreet and hasty anger which overtakes us too oft in our places, making us to breake out (unlesse wee be more watchfull) not onely into reviling speeches, but also to blowes, and to great severitie, is highly displeasing to the

THE GRAMMAR SCHOOLE

the Lord; and it doth exceedingly indanger us for his wrath and vengeance, unlesse we be daily humbled by unfained repentance for it: and yet so, that as we cannot looke to escape some like measure from him, that we or ours shall surely feele his hand, unlesse we prevent and amend it.

Spoud. These are worthy places of holy Scriptures; and able to stay us, if we could keepe them in memory. But yet even in the most moderate, the very desire to do good, and to answer our places, moved by the untowardnes and carelesnesse of many of our children, doth cause us sometimes to forget our selves, and to breake out over-much.

Phil. God hath left this to our calling, as a meanes to trie us, and to humble us continually; and also to have matter wherein to exercise us to strive against, and to make us more watchfull in our places. But if wee could learne but these three lessons, wee should wonderfully prevent Satan in these occasions of our anger, wherein we are so overtaken. *Occasions of anger left to our calling to humble and exercise us. Three lessons for preventing of anger.*

1 So much as ever we are able, to have our eye continually round about the Schoole upon every one; and namely the most unruly, to keepe them in awe: and that we keepe order strictly in every thing at all times; as specially in all examinations and taskes, and our times for every thing most precisely, that they may looke for it: for omitting them sometimes, makes the best too carelesse, and some bold to offend, in hope that they shall not be seene, or not called to an account: whereas by the contrary they grow into a habit of painfulnesse and obedience. *1 Constancy in observing order, and our eye ever on all.*

2 Studying to put on a fatherly affection, and to deale so with them as a good father amongst his children. This shall also bring them or many of them to the affections and dutifulnesse of loving children, to doe all of conscience. *2 Fatherly affections.*

3. Labouring to be *Enochs*, to walke in our places with God, as ever in his presence, his eye alwayes on us, that he observes all our wayes, and will reward and blesse us according to our conscience herein: thus to walke before him, *3 To walke in our places with God, as Enoch.*

untill

untill he translate us hence, being as little absent from our place and charge, as possible may be; cutting off wisely all unnecessary occasions. Oft absence of the Master is a principall cause of the schollers negligence and not profiting, with the griefe and vexing of the Master, arising thereon; unlesse he have very good supply.

Spoud. Happy men were we, if we could attaine to this. But I pray you Sir, what thinke you of this, to have ever the rodde or Ferula in our hand, at lesser faultes to give them a blow or a jerke on the hand; and so when we see any of them idle?

Phil. If we will strive earnestly, according to the former meanes, we shall by little and little attaine to that ability, to cut off those occasions, and come to this good governement, so farre as the Lord shall be well pleased with us; and that he will passe by our weakenesses. But for having the rodde or Ferula alwayes in our hands, if we be of hastie natures, I take it to be, as for a furious man to carrie ever a naked sword in his hand. It will make us to strike many a time, when wee will bee sorry for it after, if it fall not out worse. For these lighter faults, proceeding from lacke of time, yeeres, capacity, discretion, or the like, would rather be corrected by words, and reformed lovingly, then by this continuall whipping and striking; neither will any good and wise father smite his child for every fault.

The danger of having the rod or ferula ever in our hand.

I would therefore have neither of these to be continually holden up; but rather some little twigge, if you will needes: I meane a small twigge, something more then a foote long; that if you a little rap them on the heads, you can no way hurt them, neither their head, eyes, nor face.

Rather a little twigge, if any thing at all.

But I account this farre the best, for a Schoolemaster by his grave and wise carriage, and his faithfulnesse in his place; and also by carefully observing, and surely and soundly correcting the negligent and disobedient, when other meanes faile, to strive to come to this, that his owne presence, or at least his eye and speech, may sufficiently prevaile

For the surest, to have nothing ordinarily, but gravity and authority.

THE GRAMMAR SCHOOLE

vaile to keepe all in a submisse obedience; and that he may use the rodde very sparingly, but onely in greater faults, and on the principall offenders for example and terrour. This shall be a fatherly and worthy governement indeede, when the children thus obey of conscience; striving who shall be the best, and each way most dutifull. And thus in a short time, when your Schollers are so inured to your governement, that they know what to looke for, you shall find, that very seldome correction will serve.

Spoud. I like your advice wonderfull well herein: but when would you have the time of common punishment to be inflicted; as namely that for their misdemeanours in the Church, or other grosse faults noted by the Monitours? *The time of inflicting common punishments.*

Phil. I would have this done commonly at the giving up of the Monitours' Bils, some day before prayer; sometime one day, sometimes another: and when the Master findes the greatest company present, then to call for the Monitours of that weeke; lest keeping a set time, any absent themselves by fained excuses or otherwise, or cry unto their parents, that they dare not go to the Schoole, because they must be beaten. But for extreme negligence, or other faults in the Schoole, the very fittest time is immediately before the breaking up, upon the play-dayes; then if neede so require, first to whip all the stubborne and notoriously negligent, as also those who have done any grosse fault: and after to cause them to sit, and do some exercises whereof they are to give a strict account, as I said. This will surely by God's blessing tame the proudest of them in time, and bring them to be as submisse as the least child; as experience will manifest.

Spoud. But what if you have any, whom you cannot yet reforme of their ungraciousnesse or loytering, and whom you can do no good withall, no not by all these meanes? As some there are ever in all Schooles extremely untoward. *Such as of whom is no hope of reformation, to be sent from Schoole in time.*

Phil. These I would have some way removed from the Schoole; at least by giving the parents notice, and intreating

ting them to imploy them some other way; that neither other be hurt by their example, nor they be a reproach to the Schoole, nor yet we be inforced to use that severity with them which they will deserve. But keepe these courses strictly, and you shall see that they will either amend, or get away of themselves, by one meanes or other; I meane by some device to their parents, to leave the Schoole, and to goe to some other imployment.

CHAP. XXX.

Of Schoole-times, intermissions and recreations.

Spoud.

NOw that you have thus courteously gone thorow this point concerning the Schoole-government, by rewards and punishments (which being rightly put in practice, must needs bring a great blessing with them) let me crave your judgement also for the times of Schoole and intermissions; with recreations to be used therein.

Phil. To give you my judgement in all these briefely, according to that which by tryall I finde best:

Schoole-time to begin at sixe.

1 The Schoole-time should begin at sixe: all who write Latine, to make their exercises which were given overnight, in that houre before seven, unlesse they did them the night before, to get parts or the like.

Spoud. Would you then have the Master and Usher present so early?

The Usher to be present at sixe, only to oversee all.

Phil. The Usher should necessarily be there, to be present amongst them; though he follow his owne private study that houre, yet to see that all the Schollers doe their duties appointed, and that there be no disorder: which will

THE GRAMMAR SCHOOLE

will be, unlesse he or some other of authoritie be amongst them. For otherwise the best children, left to their owne liberty, will shew themselves children. If the Master be present at seven, it may suffice, where there is any in his place, whose presence they stand in awe of.

Spoud. But it is hard for the little children to rise so early, and in some families all lye long: how would you have them come so soone then? You would have them beaten every time that they come over-late, as the custome is in some schooles.

Phil. That I take farre too great severity, and whereby many a poore child is driven into wonderfull feare, and either to play the truant, or make some device to leave the schoole; at least to come with a marvellous ill will, and oft to be dragged to the Schoole, to the reproach of the Master and the Schoole.

The best meanes that ever I could finde to make them to rise early, to prevent all this feare of whipping, is this; by letting the little ones to have their places in their fourmes daily, according to their comming after sixe of the clocke: so many as are there at sixe, to have their places as they had them by election or the day before: all who come after six, every one to sit as he commeth, and so to continue that day, and untill he recover his place againe by the election of the fourme, or otherwise. Thus deale with them at all times, after every intermission, when they are to be in their places againe, and you shall have them ever attending who to be first in his place; so greatly even children are provoked by the credit of their places. *How to make all children to strive who shall be first at schoole without any correction.*

If any cannot be brought by this, then to be noted in the blacke Bill by a speciall marke, and feele the punishment thereof: and sometimes present correction to be used for terrour; though this (as I said) to be more seldome, for making them to feare comming to the Schoole.

The higher Schollers must of necessity rest to doe their exercises, if their exercises be strictly called for. *Intermission at nine and three, for a quarter of an houre, or more.*

Thus they are to continue untill nine, signified by Monitours,

THE GRAMMAR SCHOOLE

tours, Subdoctour, or otherwise. Then at nine I finde that order which is in Westminster to be farre the best; to let them to have a quarter of an houre at least, or more for intermission, either for breakefast, for all who are neere unto the Schoole, that can be there within the time limitted, or else for the necessity of every one, or their honest recreation, or to prepare their exercises against the Masters comming in.

After, each of them to be in his place in an instant upon the knocking of the doore, or some other signe given by the Subdoctor or Monitors, in paine of losse of his place, or further punishment, as was noted before; so to continue untill eleven of the clocke, or somewhat after, to countervaile the time of the intermission at nine.

To be againe all ready, and in their places at one, in an instant; to continue untill three, or halfe an houre after: then to have another quarter of an houre or more, as at nine for drinking and necessities; so to continue till halfe an houre after five; thereby in that halfe houre to countervaile the time at three; then to end so as was shewed, with reading a piece of a Chapter, and with singing two staves of a Psalme: lastly, with prayer to be used by the Master.

To sing part of a Psalm before breaking up at night: and each to begin in order, and give the tune.

For the Psalmes, every scholler should begin to give the Psalme and the tune in order, and to reade every verse before them; or every one to have his booke (if it can be) and reade it as they doe sing it: where any one cannot begin the tune, his next fellow beneath is to helpe him, and take his place.

By this they will all learn to give the tunes sweetly, which is a thing very commendable; and also it will help both reading, voice and audacitie in the younger.

Spoud. But these intermissions at nine and three, may be offensive: they who know not the manner of them, may reproche the schoole, thinking that they do nothing but play.

Intermissions at nine and three a clocke, not offensive.

Phil. Wee are so much as may be in all things to avoid offence: but when by long custome the order is once made knowne, it will be no more offensive then it is at Westminster,

THE GRAMMAR SCHOOLE

ster, or then it is at noone and night; so that it be done in a decent manner.

The benefits of such intermissions will be found very great, and to prevent many inconveniences. *Benefits of intermissions.*

1 By this meanes neither Masters nor Schollers shall bee over-toiled, but have fit times of refreshing. For there is none (no not almost of the least) but being used to it a while, they will sit very well in their places, for two houres together, or two houres and a halfe; without any wearinesse or necessitie, observing duely those times. *1 None overtoiled, but with ever fresh. The least will soone learne to sit two houres together.*

2 By this meanes also the Schollers may be kept ever in their places, and hard to their labours, without that running out to the Campo (as they terme it) at schoole times, and the manifold disorders thereof; as watching and striving for the clubbe, and loytering then in the fields, some hindred that they cannot goe forth at all. *2 Kept ever in their places at Schoole-time.*

But hereby all may have their free liberty in due time; and none can abuse their liberty in that sort, nor have their minds drawne away, nor stirre abroad all the day at schoole times: except upon some urgent necessity, to be signified to the Master or Usher; and so leave to be gotten privately, to returne presently againe: And also in those cases to lose their places for that day, unlesse the case be approved very necessary and sure; to the end to cut off occasions from such as will pretend necessities. If any one be caught abusing his Master or his liberty, without necessity only, upon desire of idlenesse or play, he is to be corrected sharpely, for ensample. By this meanes you shall bring them to that order and obedience in a short time, as they will not think of stirring all the day, but at their times appointed, or upon very urgent and almost extraordinary necessity. *Leave to be granted upon urgent occasions besides.*

3 Besides these benefits, this will also gaine so much time every day, as is lost in those intermissions; because there is no day but they will all looke for so much time or more, to the Campo: especially the shrewdest boyes, who use to waite for the club, and watch their times; these will be sure to have much more then that. Besides all *3 The time may be gained daily, and sundry inconveniences prevented.*

the

THE GRAMMAR SCHOOLE

the time which they lose in waiting for that idle fit; and that they will, if they can, be away at Lectures, and shewing exercises: and likewise they will exceedingly trouble the Master in asking three or foure sometimes together, what businesse soever he be about.

Spoud. I have been well acquainted with these disorders of the Campo, and vexed with them many a time: I shall be most glad, if I may thus reforme them, and finde these benefits in stead thereof. But what say you for their recreations? Let me also heare your judgement in them: for I see that you would have in like manner a speciall regard to be kept thereof.

Phil. I would indeed have their recreations as well looked unto, as their learning; as you may perceive plainely, by their intermission, at nine and at three.

Weekely recreations. Besides those, and all other their intermissions, it is very requisite also, that they should have weekely one part of an afternoone for recreation, as a reward of their diligence, obedience and profiting: and that to be appointed at the Master's discretion, either the Thursday, after the usuall custome; or according to the best opportunitie of the place. That also to be procured by some Verses, made by the Victors, as was shewed: and then onely, when there hath beene already no play-day in the weeke before, nor holy day in all the weeke.

Before breaking up to play, to make verses ex tempore. Before their breaking up also, it shall not be amisse to give them a Theame to make some verses of, *ex tempore*, in the highest fourmes, after they have beene for a time exercised therein: or if time permit, sometime to cap verses.

Or cap verses. The best manner of capping verses. In capping verses, the way to provoke them the most, and to have most variety of good verses, is, to appoint some one or two of the best, to challenge their fellowes to come one after another; and ever as any one but sticketh or misseth in a syllable, the other to tell him, and another to come in his place: or else to try adversaries or fourmes together.

Benefit of capping verses. This exercise will much helpe capacitie and audacitie, memory, right pronunciation, to furnish with store of authorities

THE GRAMMAR SCHOOLE

ties for Poetry, and the like; so as that they may be very cunning in their Poets by it.

Therefore it may also be used in regard of the benefits at some other fit times besides, in stead of some other examination.

Hee that brings the most sweet verses, out of *Ovid* and *Virgil* or *Cato* amongst the yongest, and so out of other most approved Poets, is to have ever the greatest commendations. *The greatest commendation in these.*

Absurd Verses, such as most are of those called *Carmina Proverbialia*, are to be hissed forth: Namely, those which are termed *versus Leonini*. As that first verse,

Si canis ex hilla religatur mordet in illa.

And so all other of the same mould. Though even amongst those of that book there are some tolerable verses, if good choice be made.

This exercise may well goe before play: for it is nothing but a pleasant schoole-recreation, and will exceedingly whet on the schollers to an ingenuous contention.

All recreations and sports of Schollers, would be meet for Gentlemen. Clownish sports, or perilous, or yet playing for money, are no way to be admitted. *Manner of their recreations.*

The recreations of the studious are as well to be looked unto, as the study of the rest: That none take hurt by his studie, either for minde or body, or any way else. *The recreations of the studious to be regarded.*

Yet here of the other side, very great care is to be had, in the moderating of their recreation. For schooles, generally, doe not take more hinderance by any one thing, then by over-often leave to play. Experience teacheth, that this draweth their mindes utterly away from their bookes, that they cannot take paines, for longing after play, and talking of it; as also devising meanes to procure others to get leave to play: so that ordinarily when they are but in hope thereof, they will doe things very negligently; and after the most play, they are evermore farre the worst. *Overmuch play to be carefully avoided.*

And contrarily, when they are most holden to it, without looking for any play, in such a course, as wherein they may take

THE GRAMMAR SCHOOLE

take delight, and goe on with ease; then will they doe farre the best, without any danger of taking hurt thereby; for that then their learning is for most part as a play to them who are ingenuous.

Therefore Masters are to use great wisdome in avoiding this, and answering with mildnesse, all those who are ever importunate in asking leave.

And whereas such suiters are wont to be instant thus: That the Schollers will learne the better after; we may say truely, that they will learne far the worse after. Also, whereas they think that they do them good; they doe both them, their friends and the schoole very great hurt, for the reasons mentioned. It is continuall applying which brings learning, and the credit of a schoole. And for this cause it were not amisse, nor inconvenient (neither for the schoole, nor the Master himselfe who hath a regard of the profiting of his schollers) if in such places where both Master and schollers are hindred hereby, that there were some statute for the helpe of the Master, that he could not give leave of himselfe above once in the weeke, without consent of the Minister, or some man of authority in the towne; unlesse very seldome, and unto some chiefe parties to be yeelded unto of necessity, in regard of some speciall dignity or desert.

Spoud. Many Masters would count this a bondage.

Phil. They should yet finde it a profitable bondage, and which would bring no small freedom and comfort to themselves, or benefit and credit to their schooles in the end.

CHAP.

THE GRAMMAR SCHOOLE

CHAP. XXXI.

Inconvenience growing by diversitie of teaching, and of Grammars.

Spoud.

But what thinke you of diversities of Grammars, and of divers courses in teaching? do you not take them to be very inconvenient? *Inconvenience by diversity of Grammars and courses of teaching.*

Phil. Yes indeed: for by this meanes the younger schollers comming at new schooles, or under new Masters, are new to begin; or are hindered, and do lose much time, when they must after a sort begin againe. Many of great towardnesse and hope are thought to have nothing in them, because they are not acquainted with the new courses.

Also their former Masters are discredited, which happely had taken the best and most profitable paines with them: the children are utterly or very much discouraged. Besides that many schoolemasters are extremely ignorant, and insufficient, not knowing any good course of teaching at all.

Spoud. But how might these be helped?

Phil. Only thus: The best courses being once found out by search, conference, and tryall, with directions and helpes for the practice thereof, and the same universally received, or at least knowne; these inconveniences should be for most part prevented, and both Masters and Schollers goe on with cheerefulnesse in every place. In the meane time this is the safest course; To make them perfect in our ordinarie Grammar, by the use whereof alone so many excellent Schollers have beene: then they shall be sure to goe forward in any schoole or course, and to be well liked by every one. *How helped.*

CHAP.

CHAP. XXXII.

Evils by ordinarie absence of Schollers.

Spoud.

Evils by absence of Schollers.

Although I have beene troubled by that diversitie, yet much more by the absence of many of my Schollers, when some of them are away, two or three dayes in a weeke, and sometimes happely a moneth together, or almost a quarter of a yeere, as in the harvest time, and it may be they have no bookes neither; and yet the Parents will expect, that they should profit as much as if they were there daily, and as if they had all necessary bookes.

Also they will be ready to raile upon me that their children doe no good: whereby both my selfe and my schoole are much traduced; when the fault is wholly in themselves or principally, neither can I tell how to helpe it.

Phil. I know this to be a common grievance. The best way to redresse it, is this, so farre as I know:

1 Parents are to be admonished, either to keepe their children to schoole daily, or to keepe them away continually. For by such absence, though it be but now and then, the mindes of the best and most studious will be much drawne away, or they discouraged, and made unable to goe with their fellows.

Other their fellowes also, are often much hindred for them; Schooles and Masters discredited by them: Besides that in their absence they commonly learne much evill; and chiefly stubbornnesse to corrupt themselves and others.

THE GRAMMAR SCHOOLE

Therefore this would bee looked unto, specially to be a-voided so much as may be: And order to be taken by the governours and overseers of Schooles, that all such should be sent home againe, who are kept away above a certaine number of dayes; as thirteene in a Quarter (as the statute is in some Schooles) or a like number: unlesse in case of sicknesse, or such necessary occasion to be approved by the Master or overseers. *How redressed.*

Those most seldome absences, to be punished by losse of their places, and correction too, if the fault be found to be any way in themselves; or at least to sit still on the play-daies to learne, when their fellowes play, to recover that time againe, and to make them more carefull to come; or by all these meanes together. This will make the Parents to amend it.

CHAP. XXXIII.

Discouragements of Schoolemasters by unthankfulnesse of Parents.

Spoud.

THis is good counsell, if I could get our overseers to put it in execution; I my selfe will trie what I can doe to redresse it by these helpes: Yet there is one other discouragement, whereby I have beene very much troubled in my selfe, many times; that is, the great unthankfulnesse that I finde, and have ever found in many whose children I have had; That some, if they thinke they have any little priviledge by the place, they will not so much as give me thanks for all my labours, nor (it may be) afford me a good word, though their children do never so well under me. *Discouragement of Schoole-masters by un-thankefulnesse of Parents.*

Others

THE GRAMMAR SCHOOLE

Others who have no priviledge in the place, will give little or nothing, in regard of my paines, or to my meete maintenance, according to my place, to incourage mee to take paines: and besides, they will run behind with me two or three Quarters, and then they will seeke some occasion to take away their children, to set them to other Schooles, finding some quarrell that their children did not profit, or the like; and thus not onely defraud me of my due, but also raise such slanders against me, for the recompence of all my paines.

Thankes to bee expected at God's hands. Remedies against discouragements by unthankfulnesse of Parents.

Phil. We must looke for thankes, and the rewards of our labours from God, where the world is unthankefull. But for the helpe of this, my advice is, that first we labour to bee faithfull in our places, in the best courses and kindes; chiefly to make our Schollers good Grammarians: and when wee may be bold to cause them who are of abilitie to pay accordingly, in some sort, for the instruction of their children. They will better esteeme the worth of learning, and of the service we performe to them (in those in whom they are to live after their time) and also to the Church and Commonwealth. And if God do blesse us, that our Schollers profit indeede, we shall in time have Schollers enow; such as will be willing to pay well, how basely soever learning be esteemed of.

Moreover, to prevent all such shifting and detraction, it is wisedome ever to call for our due at the Quarter's end; and to see that our cariage and government be such in our place, as that we may stand in the face of any such unthankefull detractour. Also, that God's blessing on our labours, may ever answer for us; which following but these directions, we may certainely expect.

Finally, that in our places we labour to serve the Lord faithfully; and then wee may be sure to receive the full reward of all our labour, from him; let men, as I said, be never so unthankefull.

CHAP.

THE GRAMMAR SCHOOLE

CHAP. XXXIIII.

What Children are to be kept to learning.

Spoud.

Sir, if I should not take heart and courage to set to my calling afresh, I were much to be blamed, having all my doubts thus answered, and being thus heartened in every part. But yet, that I may both returne unto it cheerefully; and also goe forward, and continue happily to the end: I pray you let me have your judgement in these two points:
   1. What children you would have set to learning, and incouraged to go on in the same.
   2. Which you would have sent to the University, and how qualified.

Phil. To both these I shall answer you what I hold.

To the first: I would have those who after good time of triall shall be found the fittest amongst a man's children, to be applied unto learning; as being the meetest to be offered to God in a more speciall manner, to the publike service of his Church or their Countries.

And so those onely of them, to be incouraged to goe on in the same, whom you find most ingenious, and especially whom you perceive to love learning the best; which also do witnesse the same by their painfulnesse and delight in their bookes. The rest to be fitted so farre as may be conveniently, for trades, or some other calling, or to be removed speedily.

   2. To the second I answer: that such onely should be sent to the Universities, who prove most ingenious and towardly, and who, in a love of learning, will begin to take paines

1. What Schollers to be set to learning. Most apt and of greatest hope.

2. What Schollers to be sent to the Universities.

THE GRAMMAR SCHOOLE

Ingenuous and lovers of learning.
Good Grammarians.
Of discretion.

paines of themselves, having attained in some sort the former parts of learning; being good Grammarians at least, able to understand, write and speake Latine in good sort.

2 Such as have good discretion how to governe themselves there, and to moderate their expenses, which is seldome times before 15. yeeres of age; which is also the youngest age admitted by the statutes of the University, as I take it.

Some of chiefe note for learning and governement, and of long experience in the Universitie (as namely, some worthy heads of Colledges) would have none sent nor admitted into the Universitie, before they be full fifteene yeeres old at least; for these reasons specially amongst others:

None to be sent to the Universities, before 15 yeeres of age at least.

1 Because, before that time, they will commonly require more bodily helpe, then can be there afforded.

2. The Universitie statute forbiddeth to admit any under this age.

3 Because that daily experience doth teach how inconvenient it is in divers respects.

Finally, all generally of whom I can heare in the Universitie, do assent hereunto. Many would have them 17. or 18. yeeres old before; because then commonly they have discretion to sticke to their studies and to governe themselves.

Spoud. I do much approve their judgement. I would have them good Schollers, before they goe to the Universitie; and namely sound Grammarians, that the Tutors need not to be troubled with teaching them to make or to construe Latine; but that they may go forward in Logick or other studies meet for the Universities. For such a Scholler as is able to understand well what he reades, or what is read unto him there (I meane in regard of the Latine) shall do more good in a yeere, then a weake Scholler shall do in two or three; chiefely, if he have discretion to governe himselfe, and abide close to his booke.

For when as the Scholler is faine to turne his Dictionary for

THE GRAMMAR SCHOOLE

for every word, or hearing a Lecture read, doth come away as he went; unlesse he be placed under a most painefull Tutor, how is it possible that he should profit any thing, in respect of him who goeth a good Scholler thither? How many evils do come upon the sending of Schollers so rawly thither, both University and Countrey doe fully know and rue.

Now you have so lovingly and fully answered me in every doubt, and so largely laid open your minde unto mee, as indeede I cannot desire any more of you: Onely let me tell you this, that the points are so many, as I feare that I shall never be able to put them in practice.

Phil. You may make triall of all, or the most likely of them; and constantly practise those which you find most profitable: the shorter that you can be in every thing, the better shall you do; so that all be done with understanding, as I said before. *To practise the most profitable.*

Spoud. I trust you wil give me a copie of them: for otherwise I shall never be able to remember them; besides that they will require to be oft read over and over, untill I shall grow perfect in them. I do not doubt, but you have set them downe.

Phil. I have; though as yet very imperfectly, for lacke of meete leasure. Such as I have, I shall impart (feeling your earnest desire to doe good) and more as God shall adde more helpe and experience by your selfe, and by others.

CHAP.

THE GRAMMAR SCHOOLE

CHAP XXXV.

A briefe rehearsall of the chiefe points and helpes mentioned in this booke.

Spoud.

How much shall you make me more indebted by that favour, above all your other kindnesse hitherto! Yet in the meane time before we depart, to the end to helpe my weake memory, and to cause me to go on more cheerefully, let me request onely these two things of you further:

A briefe rehearsall of the chiefe points mentioned in this book. A rehearsall of the bookes and helpes mentioned.

1 To repeate the principall heads of those things which should be as it were in the Master's remembrance alwayes, to be continually put in practice.

2 To set me downe a short Catalogue of the bookes and helpes which you have mentioned belonging hereunto, for the better accomplishing of all these severall parts of learning.

Phil. For those principall heads, though most of them were named in the observations; yet sith such little briefes do much helpe memory, I will rehearse them so neere as I can.

These were of the chiefe:

The principall heads of those things which would be kept ever in memory, to be put in practice by the Master continually.

1 To cause all to be done with understanding.

2 To cut off all needlesse matters, so much as may be, and passe by that which is unprofitable.

3 To note all hard and new words: to observe matter and phrase carefully.

4 To learne and keepe all things most perfectly, as they goe.

5 To have few fourmes.

6 To discourage none, but to draw on all by a desire of commendation.

7 To stirre up to emulation of adversaries, and to use all good policy for one to provoke another.   8. Con-

THE GRAMMAR SCHOOLE

8 Continuall examining (which is the life of all) and chiefely posing of the most negligent.

9 Right pronunciation.

10 Some exercise of memory daily.

11 To have the best patternes for every thing; and to do all by imitation.

12 The Master to stirre up both himselfe and his Schollers to continuall cheerefulnesse.

13 Constancy in order.

These were generally premised. To these we may adde;

14 To get an Idea or short summe and generall notation of every Treatise or Chapter.

15 To parallel all by examples, or to give like examples for each thing, and where they have learned them.

16 To see that they have continually all necessaries.

17 To countenance and preferre the best, to be markes for the rest to aime at, and that all may be incouraged by their example.

18 Maintaining authority, by carefull execution of justice in rewards and punishments, with demonstration of love, faithfulnesse and painefulnesse in our place, with gravitie: working by all meanes a love of learning in the Schollers, and a strift who shall excell most therein, of a conscience to do most honour and service unto the Lord, both presently, and chiefely in time to come.

19 In a word; Serving the Lord with constant cheerefulnesse, in the best courses which he shall make knowne unto us, we shall undoubtedly see his blessings, according to our hearts.

M. *Askam* hath these steps to learning: First, Aptnesse of nature: Secondly, Love of learning: Thirdly, Diligence in right order: Fourthly, Constancy with pleasant moderation: Fiftly, Alwayes to learne of the most learned; pointing and aiming at the best, to match or go beyond them. *Master Askam his steps to learning.*

Philip Melanchton also, in his Preface before *Hesiod*, adviseth after this manner; To strive to make Schollers exceeding cunning in every Authour which they reade. To *Philip Melanchton's direction.*

do

THE GRAMMAR SCHOOLE

do this by oft reading and construing over their Authors; causing them to note every thing worthy observation, with some marke, to run ofter over those: not regarding how many the Authours are, but how exactly they learne them; chiefely all their sentences and speciall phrases, that the speech of the children may ever savor of them: for thus hee saith; *Ut quisque author optimus, ita sæpissimè relegendus ad imitationem:* And that thereby they may alwayes have of a sudden a patterne or president in their minde, whereunto to run, as the Painter hath. And so much for the chiefe points: for the severall bookes and helpes, I referre you rather to the severall Chapters; where you may soone see them together, as you shall have occasion to use them for their severall purposes.

Spoud. But it is a great charge to poore men, to provide so many bookes as may seeme necessary.

Phil. It is true indeede; yet one yeere gained in their children's learning, will recompence abundantly all charge in bookes which they shall neede: and much more, if by them they shall gaine sundry yeeres, and be furnished with all kind of excellent learning meet for their yeeres; which without the best bookes, it is no more likely to do, then for any to prove exquisite in other trades and sciences, without the most fine instruments serving thereunto.

And this one certaine assurance of the obtaining this treasure of learning, by following the right meanes and courses, may counterpoize all labour and charges whatsoever can be furnished, for attaining of the same.

Spoud. Sir, I rest fully satisfied; praying the Lord, and acknowledging my perpetuall debt for this our conference.

Phil. Let us give God all the glory; to whom of due it appertaines; and let us ever intreate him, that as he hath thus begun, so he will perfect his own worke, for the everlasting praise of his owne name, and the perpetuall good of all his people, untill Christ Jesus shall come. Αμὴν, ναὶ, ἔρχου κύριε Ιησοῦ.

Μόνῳ Τῷ Θεῷ δόξα

THE SEVERALL
CHAPTERS, WITH THE
particular Contents of them.

CHAP. I. [1–8]

A Discourse betweene two School masters, concerning their function: in the end ,determining a conference about the best way of teaching, and the manner of proceeding in the same.

Herein these particulars:

The Schoolemaster's place, ordinarily, wearisome, and thankelesse.

They who have felt the evils of labouring without fruit, will neither spare travell nor cost to help the same.

Many honest-hearted and painfull Schoolmasters utterly discouraged, and living in continuall discontentment, through lacke of knowledge of a right course of teaching.

Some few God much blesseth in this calling, though rare.

More true contentment to be found in this calling, rightly followed, then in any recreation.

The fruits of this, most sweet in the remembrance.

Knowledge and practice of the best courses will much augment the blessing of our labour, and fill our lives with contentment.

How the way of all good learning may be made more easie, then ever in former ages.

Many worthy helps lye hid from the greatest part, onely through neglect.

A

THE CONTENTS.

A briefe rehearsall of the chiefe contents, for the better entring into the conference, and for giving more light and life to all that followeth.

The manner of proceeding in this conference

[8-12]
CHAP. 2.

2. When the scholler should first be set to the schoole. Branches.

The time of the first entrance in countrey schooles, at seven or eight yeere old.

The child of any ordinary towardlinesse, to begin to learne about five yeere old, Reasons and benefit of it.

Two or three yeeres may be gained hereby, to fit them sooner for the Universitie.

Parents ought to labour to see their children's good education before their eyes, so soone as may be.

Objections against setting children so young to the schoole, answered.

[12-27]
CHAP. 3.

3. How the scholler may be taught to reade English well and speedily, to fit him the sooner and better for the Grammar schoole.

Herein these things handled;

The inconveniences of having the Grammar Schooles troubled with teaching *A. B. C.*

How this might be remedied by some other schooles in each towne for that purpose.

The redresse hereof to be sought.

To be borne with patience, where it cannot be avoided, and the burden of it to be made so light as may be.

The first entring of children to be looked to heedily.

To teach to reade well, a matter of good commendation.

Griefe and discredit to the Schoolemaster for want of this.

To teach to call and pronounce each letter right.

How,

THE CONTENTS.

How to know their letters the soonest.
To spell, and take a delight therein.
Some of the hardest syllables and words set downe, for the practising children in spelling of them; to help by them to spell any other speedily, & for writing true orthography.
Of joyning syllables together.
Bookes to be first learned of children.
In what time children well applyed, may learne to reade English.
Dividing and distinguishing syllables.
The pleasantest way to teach the little ones, to pronounce their letters, and to spell before they know a letter: and how to doe it.
Any one who can reade, may thus enter children, if they will follow the directions; and so a poore body make an honest living of it, and free the Grammar schooles.
Complaints for children forgetting to reade English, when they first enter into Latine; and how to avoid them.
The just complaint of want of care in our schooles, for proceeding in our owne tongue, as in the Latine or Greeke; whereas our chiefe care should be for our own language: and reasons for it.
How schollers may increase continually, as fast in our owne tongue, as in the Latine.
The chiefe fault of children going backe in English, when they begin to learne Latine, is in the Parents.
An ordinarie fault, that schollers are to seeke in matters of common numbers; and how to redresse it.

CHAP. 4. [27–40]

OF writing. How the Master may direct his schollers to write faire, though himselfe be no good pen-man.
Herein these particulars:
Faire writing, a great benefit and ornament to schooles.
The opinion is fond, that a good scholler cannot be a good writer

The

THE CONTENTS.

The trouble of Schoolemasters, for want of this skill to teach their schollers how to write.
When the schollers should begin to write.
To have all necessaries thereunto, and bookes kept faire.
Each to learne to make his owne pen, and how.
Holding the pen, and carrying it lightly.
In stead of setting copies, to have little copie-bookes fastened to the tops of their bookes; and those of the best which can be procured.
Manner of their copy-bookes and copies.
Inconvenience of following divers hands.
Evils of the want of such copie-bookes.
Faire writing to be practised by all the schollers once every day.
Generall rule in writing, to make all like the copie.
How to keepe even compasse in writing, not over-high, nor too low.
Benefit of ruling-pens for each, and what ones.
The bookes of the young beginners to be ruled with crosse lines.
The compasse in greatnesse and neerenesse of the letters.
Joyning the letters in writing.
Writing straight without lines.
Speciall furtherances for the first enterers, when they cannot frame any letter.
Leisurely drawing the letters as the Painter, a chiefe helpe.
To observe ornaments of writing.
To make all the letters most plaine.
Mischiefes of getting a bad hand first.
What the Master is to doe, to the end that he may learne to teach his schollers to write faire.
To walk amongst the schollers, to see that they observe their directions, and to marke all faults in writing.
This skill is to be gotten, to avoid the evils by wandring Scriveners.
The use of Scriveners in Grammar Schooles, what.
The summe of the principall directions for writing, to be ever in memory. CHAP.

THE CONTENTS.

Chap. 5. [41–52]

CErtaine generall observations to be knowne of Schoolmasters, and practised carefully; chiefly in all Grammar learning.

1 That schollers be taught to doe all things with understanding, and to have a generall knowledge of the matter before.

To doe all things by reason with understanding, brings almost double learning, besides ease and delight.

Reading without understanding, is a neglect of learning.

Triall of difference betweene learning with understanding and without.

Verses of *Horace* to this end, worthy to be written in letters of gold, to be imprinted in the memories of all.

How some Writers have so farre gone beyond others in eloquence, through their ripenesse and understanding.

How to teach all to be done by understanding.

2 To learne onely such things as whereof they may have good and perpetuall use.

3 To note all hard words or matters worthy of observation, and the manner of marking them.

4 To learne all things so perfectly, as the former may be in stead of a Schoolemaster to the latter.

5 That the whole schoole be divided into so few fourmes, as may be; with reasons for the same.

6 To have a great care that none be discouraged, but all to be provoked by emulation, and desire of praise.

A sentence of *Tully* to this purpose worthy to be ever before the Master's eye.

Strift for victories the most commendable play, and a chiefe meanes to make the schoole *Ludus Literarius*.

7 Each to have his adversarie: and they to be so matched and placed as all may be done by equall strift.

8 To

THE CONTENTS.

8 To use ever to examine the most negligent.
9 Continuall care of pronouncing.
10 To have some exercise of memory daily, for making excellent memories.
11 To have the best patternes of all sorts that can be gotten.
12 The Masters to incourage themselves and their schollers continually.
13 Constancie in good orders, with continuall demonstration of love, to doe all for the greatest good of the Schollers.

[52-70] CHAP. 6.

How to make children perfect in the Accedence. Herein these particulars:
The usuall manner of learning to reade the Accedence.
The ordinarie manner of getting the Accedence without booke.
The best meanes, for learning to reade the Accedence.
Generall rule in learning without booke, or getting whatsoever seemeth hard: To take but a little at a time.
To cause them first to understand their lectures, and how.
Admonition to Masters, desirous to do good; To be as the Nurses with little children.
Example how to make children to understand, by shewing the meaning, and by asking questions.
In what points of the Accedence, the chiefe labour would be bestowed to make young Schollers very perfect: *vis.* in all kinde of declining.
How to be most speedily perfect in the Verbs; which are a meane foundation, and wherein the greatest difficultie lyeth.
No paines can be too great in Nounes and Verbes, untill they be exceeding perfect.
Two generall observations in the English rules: what parts

THE CONTENTS.

parts of the English rules, to be made most perfect in.

Helpe for examination of the Accedence : *viz.* The questions of the Accedence, called the Poasing of the English parts. Other needfull questions adjoyned to the end of the same.

CHAP. 7. [70–88]

HOw to make Schollers perfect in the Grammar.
What is done ordinarily in schooles in teaching Grammar.
What things are requisite in learning Grammar.
How to get the Grammar with most ease and fruit.
Benefit of *Lillies* rules construed.
Learning the rules without booke.
Construing the rules without booke.
How to doe where leisure is wanting.
How to examine so as to make your scholler to answer any question of his Grammar ; with an example thereof.
To appose onely in English; where children are too weake to answer in Latine.
Examining in the Latine Nounes and Verbes.
Examining the *Syntaxis*, and helpes thereunto.
Repeating Titles and Margents, or the beginning of the rules, in a continued speech, to keepe the rules perfectly.
Helpe for hearing part in straights of time.
Helpes for further understanding the rules.
The summe of all, wherein chiefe care would be had.
A perfect saying every rule, not so absolutely necessarie.
To turne to each hard rule in parsing, a helpe to make Schollers perfect in the Grammar.
Grammar to be made as a Dictionary to the Schollers.

CHAP.

THE CONTENTS.

[89–125]   Chap. 8.

OF construction, or of construing Authors, how to make all the way thereof most easie and plaine.
Herein these particulars:
Things seeming difficult in construction.
The ordinarie toile of Masters about giving lectures, and making their schollers able to construe.
Difficultie in taking Lectures, in proprietie of words and sense.
Griefe of the Masters for their Schollers forgetting that which they have learned.
The way of construing most plaine, by practice of the Rule of construing, and of Grammaticall translations.
The rule of construing unheard of to the most.
The rule set downe by sundry learned Grammarians.
The rule according as Master *Leech* hath set it downe.
The rule according to *Crusius*.
The rule expounded more at large, though the curious handling of it be left to some others.
The summe of the rule briefly.
An example of construing, and of Grammaticall translations, according to the rule: wherein may be seene the generall benefits thereof, for resolving Latine into the Grammaticall order, construing, parsing, making Latine and trying it.
The chiefe reason of the benefits.
Benefits of translations according to the rule, set downe more particularly.
Things specially observed in the translations of the School-Authors.
How to use the translations, so as to attaine the former benefits.
Objections against the use of translations in Schooles, answered.
                                                         The

THE CONTENTS.

The uses and benefits mentioned, cannot be made of any other translations of the Schoole-Authors, except of the Grammaticall: and the reason of it.

Some examples of other translations, to manifest the truth hereof.

Grammaticall translations separate from the Latine, cannot indanger any to make them Truants.

How to prevent idlenesse or negligence in the use of the translations.

These no meanes to make Masters idle, but contrarily to incourage them to take all paines.

The account to be justly made of such translations.

Schoole-Authors translated Grammatically.

Other bookes also translated Grammatically for continuall helpes in Schooles.

What helpes to be used for construing higher Authors, and so for construing *ex tempore*.

The higher fourmes to practise to go over so much as they can, construing *ex tempore*.

CHAP. 9.   [125–147]

OF Parsing and the severall kindes thereof. How children may parse of themselves, readily and surely.

The particular branches are these;

The usuall manner of teaching to parse.

The certaine direction for parsing.

To parse as they construe, marking the last word.

To observe carefully, where they have learned each word, what example every word is like; so to parallel by examples, each thing which they have not learned in their rules.

An example of parsing, set downe at large for the rudest.

Manner of hearing Lectures amongst the lower.

How to know by the words what part of Speech each word is.

How

THE CONTENTS.

How a child may know, of what Conjugation any Verbe is.

Much time and toyle in parsing, thorow examining each word by the Master, how helped.

The surest, shortest and speediest way of parsing, to parse as reading a Lecture.

How to helpe to prepare the children for parsing at taking Lectures, by shewing them onely the hard words, that they may take most paines in them.

Example of marking the hard words amongst the first enterers.

Marking the hard words helpeth much, and preventeth many inconveniences.

How to oppose, so as children may get both matter, words and phrase of each Lecture, with examples of it in the first Authors: and how to make use of each Author.

Parsing in the higher fourmes, and to do all in Latine.

The summe of all for parsing.

[147–158]

Chap. 10.

OF making Latine. How to enter children to make Latine, with delight and certainty; without danger of false Latine, barbarous phrase, or any other like inconvenience.

Particular points;

To enter children to make Latine, a matter ordinarily extremely difficult and full of toyle, both to Master and Scholler.

The usuall manner in Country Schooles, to enter children to make Latine.

The shortest, surest, and easie way, both to Master and Scholler, for entring to make Latine.

Making first the Latine of their Lectures, and giving a reason of each word. Example of it.

Continuall construing, parsing, and reading their Authors

THE CONTENTS.

thors out of Grammaticall translations, is continuall making pure Latine, to cause children to come on in it very fast.

Choosing fit sentences out of Authors, for the children to make of themselves.

The manner of the entrance of children to write Latine, so as to profit in English, Latine, Writing faire and true, all under one labor.

How to have their bookes ruled to this purpose.

Manner of dictating the English to Schollers, when they are to learne to write Latine.

Making and setting downe the Latine, by the Schollers.

Benefit of it for certaine direction both to Master and Scholler.

Further use to be made of the Latine so set downe, to make it fully their owne.

Composing the Latine into the order of the Author.

Tullies Sentences, the fittest booke to dictate sentences out of.

An example of the manner of dictating, and writing downe both English and Latine.

Translating into pure Latine, and in good composition of themselves, trying who can come neerest unto *Tully*.

How to prevent stealing, and writing after one another.

How to go on faster, and dispatch more in making Latine.

Translating into English of themselves after M. *Askam's* manner; and after, reading the same into Latine againe, or writing it.

The most speedy and profitable way of translating for young Schollers.

How to translate an Author into Latine, or any piece thereof.

Such translating onely for Schollers well grounded.

Summe of all for making Latine.

CHAP.

THE CONTENTS.

[158–165]   CHAP. 11.

OF the Artificiall order of composing, or placing of the words in prose, according to *Tully* and the purest Latinists.   Herein these particulars :

Pure composition a matter of difficulty.

The error of young Schollers, displacing sentences, in an imagination of fine composition.

Composition generally belonging to all Latine.

Rules of composition, as they are set downe by *Macropedius*, in the end of his Method of making Epistles.

More exquisite observation in placing and measuring sentences.

[165–171]   CHAP. 12.

HOw to make Epistles imitating *Tully*, short, pithy, sweete Latine and familiar, and to indite Letters to our friends in English accordingly. Herein these things;

Difficulty of making Epistles purely, and pithily.

The ordinary meanes of directing Schollers to make Epistles.

Difficulty for children, who have no reading, to invent variety of matter of themselves.

Helpes for making Epistles, by reading *Tullies* Epistles, and imitating them.

Making answers to Epistles.

Examples of imitating Epistles, and answering them.

[172–190]   CHAP. 13.

OF making Theames full of good matter, in a pure stile and with judgement.

Here-

THE CONTENTS.

Herein these branches;
The ordinary manner of directing Schollers how to enter to make Theames, according to *Apthonius*' precepts.
The inconveniences of that course for young Schollers; and that it is hard enough for many teachers.
Difficulty in making Theames, because Schollers are not acquainted with the matter of them.
The Scholler is oft beaten for his Theame, when the Master rather deserveth it.
To consider the end of making Theames.
The meanes to furnish the Schollers for Theames.
Presidents or examples for Theames.
Presidents for matter, to furnish Schollers with store of the best matter.
Reusneri Symbola, a booke meete to this purpose; and chiefly for training up young Gentlemen, and all of chiefe sort and condition.
How to use *Reusner* for Theames.
An easie direction for Theames, to be handled according to the severall parts thereof.
Imitation of Exordiums and conclusions.
Other Authors for matter.
Helpes for invention of matter.
The knowledge of the tenne grounds of Invention, the readiest way.
The Art of meditation most profitable and easie for helpe of invention.
Presidents for the forme and manner of making Theames.
Declamations and patternes for them.
Declamations fit for Universities, or for the principall Schollers in Grammar Schooles.
Manner of writing downe Theames by Schollers of judgement.
Making of Theames *ex tempore*, a matter of great commendations, if it be done Scholler-like.
The way to make Theames *ex tempore*.

A

THE CONTENTS.

A most easie & profitable practice, to help to make Theames *ex tempore.*
Where to be stored with matter and words for each part of the Theame.
Helpe for supplying words and phrases.
Common-place bookes, a singular helpe.
Orations.
Orations belong specially to the Universities.
Examples of Orations.
Orations *ex tempore.*
Summe for Theames.

[190-198]   CHAP. 14.

OF versifying. How to enter to make verses with delight and certainty, without bodging; and to traine up Schollers to imitate and expresse *Ovid* or *Virgil*, both their phrase and stile.
    Herein these particulars:
Poetry rather for ornament, then for any necessitie.
There may be commendable use of Poetry.
The ordinarie difficulty of Poetry.
The folly of some in this kinde.
The most plaine way how to enter to make verses, without bodging.
Turning the verses of their Lectures into other verses.
Of contracting or drawing seven or eight verses into foure or five; and the certaine benefit of this exercise.
To make verses of any ordinarie Theame.
To versifie *ex tempore.*
Helpes for versifying.

THE CONTENTS.

CHAP. 15. [198–201]

THe manner of examining and correcting exercises.
    Herein these particulars :
Examining exercises never to be omitted.
Generall faults wherein schollers doe commonly slip.
To reade over their exercises first in naturall order.
To parallel each thing by examples.
To looke to elegancie and finenesse of composition.
Never to thinke any thing laboured enough.
Adversaries to note faults in one another's exercises.
The manner of examining exercises by the Master.
Speciall faults in the highest fourmes.
Care that they doe correct their exercises presently.

CHAP. 16. [201–204]

HOw to answer any needfull question of Grammar or
    Rhetoricke.
    Herein these things :
To answer any Grammar question, a thing commendable.
How to answer any difficult Grammar question.
Most of the difficulties of the ancient Classicall Authours,
    collected briefly by M. *Stockwood*.
How to answer the questions of Rhetoricke.
How to answer the questions of *Tullies* Offices.

CHAP. 17. [205–210]

OF Grammaticall oppositions. How to dispute scholler-
    like of any Grammar question in good Latine.
    Herein these branches :

To

THE CONTENTS.

To use the helpe of Master *Stockwood's* disputations of Grammar.
Benefits of such Scholasticall oppositions.
Disputations of morall Philosophy belong rather to the Universities.
How these may be done, and how farre.
Objection answered, for disputing out of Master *Stockwood*.
Evils of inforcing Schollers to exercises, with the examples whereof they are not acquainted first.
Benefit of having the best patternes.

[211–214]   CHAP. 18.

OF pronouncing naturally and sweetly, without vaine affectation.
Herein these particulars:
The excellency of pronunciation.
Pronunciation ordinarily hard to bee attained in Schooles.
How Schollers may bee brought to pronounce sweetly.
Children to be trained up to pronounce right from the first entrance.
To utter every matter according to the nature of it.
What they cannot utter in Latine, to learne to do it first in English, then in Latine.
To cause sundry to pronounce the very same sentence in emulation.
To be carefull, chiefely for pronunciation, in all Authors wherein persons are fained to speak.
Poetry to be pronounced as prose, except in scanning.
Further helpes in pronouncing.
To marke in each sentence, in what word the Emphasie lieth.
Care in pronouncing exercises.

The

THE CONTENTS.

The more exquisite knowledge and practice of pronouncing, left unto the Universities.

Chap. 19. [214–222]

OF speaking Latine purely and readily.
Complaint of the difficultie to traine up schollers to speake Latine.
The Generall errour, for the time when schollers are to begin to speake Latine.
To learne to speake Latine should be begun from the first entrance into construction.
The surest course for entring young schollers to speake Latine.
How the Master himselfe may doe it easily before them.
The daily practice of Grammaticall translations, and chiefly of reading bookes of Dialogues out of English into Latine, is a continuall practice of speaking Latine.
Difficultie to cause schollers to practise speaking Latine amongst themselves.
Inconveniencies of *Custodes* for speaking Latine.
Inconvenience of one scholler smiting another with the Ferula.
The best meanes to hold schollers to speaking Latine.
How any one may by himselfe alone, attaine to speake Latine in ordinarie matters.
For them who desire to come to ripenesse and purity in the Latine tongue, *Goclenius* his observations of the Latine tongue, is of singular use.

Chap. 20. [222–243]

HOw to attaine most speedily unto the knowledge of the Greeke tongue.
Herein these branches ;

The

THE CONTENTS.

The Greeke may be gotten with farre lesse labour then the Latine.

One benefit of the perfect knowledge of the Greeke Testament alone, worthy all our labour to be taken in the Greeke.

M. *Askam's* testimonie concerning the Greeke tongue, and the excellent learning contained in it.

The way to the Greeke, the same with the Latine.

How schollers of understanding and judgement may take a shorter course.

To use M. *Camden's* Grammar.

Grammatica Græca pro Schola Argentinensi per Theophilum Golium, may serve in stead of a further exposition of *Camden*.

To begin construction with the Greeke Testament, and why.

To strive to have the Scriptures as familiarly in the Originals, as the Jewes had the Hebrew.

Those who purpose to have any smattering in the Greeke, to have it in the Testament, and why.

The Testament compared to other Greeke Authors.

The Testament a notable entrance to all other Greeke Authors.

How Schollers may be made most perfect in the Greeke Testament.

The speediest way to the Greeke; To get the *Radices* first.

The easiest way, how to learne the Greeke *Radices*.

How any may soone learne to reade the Greeke, before they learne the Greeke Grammar.

How the *Nomenclator* of the Greeke Primitives might be made of singular use.

Helpe for committing words to memory.

Caveat in remembring.

The Greeke *Radices* contrived into continued speeches, may be gotten soonest of all.

The readiest and surest way of getting the Testament, By a perfect verball translation, separate from the Greeke.

How

THE CONTENTS.

How by the helpe of such a translation, any who have but a smattering in the Greeke, may proceed of themselves in the Testament.

This cannot be so done by the interlineall, or having the Greeke and Latine together, and why.

How schollers of judgement may use the interlineall.

How to proceed in other Authors.

The benefit of such translations of some of the purest Greek Authors.

Parsing in Greeke.

Helpes for parsing in Greeke.

Helpes for knowledge of the Poets.

How to write in Greeke purely.

How to write faire in Greeke.

Versifying in Greeke.

Summe of all for the Greeke.

CHAP. 21. [244–252]

How to get most speedily, the knowledge and understanding of the Hebrew.

Herein these branches;

The knowledge of the Hebrew may be the soonest gotten, and why.

Manner of learning the Grammar, and what Grammar to be used.

The getting the Hebrew *Radices*, a chiefe helpe.

Manner of committing the *Radices* to memory.

Examples of helping the memory in learning the Hebrew *Radices*.

The benefit of comparing the tongues.

The best Epitome for learning the *Radices*.

The way might be more compendious by the rootes reduced to *Classes*.

Continuall practice of perfect verball translations, a singular helpe.

THE CONTENTS.

A Student having opportunitie, cannot be better imployed, then in getting perfectly, and imprinting the originals in memory.

The Latine, Greeke and Hebrew, may be the soonest gotten by such perfect translations in each tongue.

How much, and what to learne in all things.

[253–263]   Chap. 22.

OF knowledge of the grounds of Religion, and training up Schollers therein.
    Herein these heads;

Schollers are to be trained up in religion

Religion most neglected in Schooles.

The Popish Schoolemasters shall rise up in judgement against all who neglect it.

Teaching the Catechisme, and when.

Examining the Catechisme.

Taking notes of sermons.

Setting downe all the substance of the Sermons, in the higher fourmes.

Manner of noting, for helping understanding and memory.

To translate the Sermon into Latine, or to reade it into Latine *ex tempore*.

Examining sermons.

Repetition or rehearsall of the Sermons.

Benefit of strict examination of Sermons.

How the repetition may be done readily.

How to goe thorow the History of the Bible, and the manner of examining it.

Objections answered.

How to teach the schollers civilitie.

                                                          Chap.

THE CONTENTS.

CHAP. 23. [263-266]

How to understand and remember any Morall matter.
Herein these things;
A principall helpe of understanding, to cause children to understand and remember by questions.
An example hereof.
Helpe in private reading, by questions.

CHAP. 24. [267-269]

Some things necessarie to be knowne, for the better attaining of all the parts of learning mentioned before: as,
1 How the Schoolemaster should be qualified.
  Herein these branches;
The Schoolemaster ought to be sufficient to direct his schollers, or tractable and willing to be directed.
The Schoolemaster must be painfull and constant, of conscience to God.
He must cast off all other studies at schoole-times.
He must not poast over the trust to others.
The Schoolemaster must be of a loving disposition, to incourage all by praise and rewards.
He ought to be a godly man, and of good carriage.
To seeke to gaine, and maintaine authoritie, and how.

CHAP. 25. [69-272]

Of the Usher and his office.
   Herein these particulars;
An Usher necessarie in all greater Schooles.

Evils

THE CONTENTS.

Evils of lacke of an Usher.
The Master burdened with all, is, as the Husbandman overcharged with more then he can compasse.
Supply by Schollers, not sufficient.
Sufficiencie of the Usher.
The Usher to be at the Master's command.
To be used with respect.
The Usher not to meddle with correcting the highest schollers.
The Usher to use as little correction as may be, unlesse in the Master's absence.
The Usher's principall imployment with the younger, to traine them up for the Master.
To prevent all inconveniences by the Usher.

[272–275]

Chap. 26.

Helpes in the Schoole besides the Usher.
Seniours in each fourme.
Particular help, a Subdoctor in place of the Usher, or where one Usher is not sufficient.
Sorting the fourmes, so many into a fourme as may be.
Choise and matching each fourme equally, that all may sit as matches.
Benefits of this election.
This equall matching all, a chiefe meanes to make the Schoole *Ludus Literarius*.

[275–279]

Chap. 27

Of government, and of authoritie in Schooles.
 Herein these branches;
Government, the helpe of helpes.
Authoritie, the top of government.
Authoritie, how to be maintained.

The

THE CONTENTS.

The Masters and Ushers to be as living lawes, to maintaine their Authoritie.

Authoritie maintained by most strict execution of justice, by rewards and punishments.

Incouraging vertue, discouraging vice, to maintaine authoritie.

The evils of neglect hereof, and of partialitie.

Authoritie, to be maintained by a continuall demonstration of conscience, and love to the schollers.

By being Presidents of all vertue.

Extreme severitie, and whipping, to be avoided in schooles; and all meanes used to prevent it.

Reasons.

Difficultie for the Master to moderate his passions oftentimes, if he strive to doe good.

CHAP. 28. [280–286]

OF preferments and incouragements.
Herein these particulars:
Incouragements to be by these meanes ;
Often Elections.
Countenancing and gracing the Seniours, and all the best and most painfull.
Putting up into higher fourmes.
Giving places.
Commending every thing well done.
Caveat in commending.
Disputation for the victorship.
Præmia to be given to the two Victors.
Office of the Victors for their *præmia*.
Solemne examination to bee made once every yeere.
Exercises to be provided against that time.
To keepe their daily exercises faire written in bookes, to try their profiting, by comparing with the former.
A course of examination to be appointed: and the same first
to

.THE CONTENTS.

to be performed by the Masters and Ushers; after by others not satisfied.
All doing well to be praised, the best specially graced.
Benefits of this set solemne examination.
All Parents to have notice before such examination.
To labour by all meanes to worke a conscience in all the Schollers, to doe all of duty and love to God, and how.
Some excellent sentences to be oft inculcated, to worke in the Schollers a love of learning.

[286-296]

CHAP. 29.

OF execution of justice in Schooles, by punishments. Herein these particulars:
To punish unwillingly.
To proceed by degrees in punishing.
A note which may be termed the blacke Bill, of principall use, and most availeable in punishing and reforming.
Manner of the blacke Bill, to deprive all chiefe offenders of the benefit of play-dayes.
To cause all such to know aforehand, what to looke for.
To view the fourmes before play, and to separate all the disobedient and unworthy, to be left to their taskes.
Care that their taskes be strictly exacted.
Notorious offenders, or stubborne boyes, to sit so many dayes, untill that they shew good tokens of amendment.
Benefit of this punishment, strictly observed, and why.
Correction with rodde to be used more seldome, and chiefly for terrour.
Caveats in correcting.
Manner of correcting the stubborne, and unbroken.
Not to suffer any to goe away in their stubbornnesse.
To be wary to avoid all smiting or hurting the children.
Caveat

THE CONTENTS.

Caveat of threatening.
That the Master doe not abase himselfe, to struggle with any stubborne boy.
To avoid all furious anger and chafing.
How correction should ever be taken.
Sparing the rod where necessitie requireth, is to undoe the children.
Assurance of safety in correction, when it is done aright.
Anger necessarie in Schoolemasters, so it bee tempered aright.
Meanes to represse furious and raging anger.
Places of Scripture to be ever in our mindes, for the repressing and moderating our anger.
Danger of rash anger when it exceeds.
Occasions of anger, left to the calling of the Schoolmasters, to humble and exercise them.
Three lessons for preventing anger.
The danger of having the rod, or ferule ever in the hand of the Master or Usher.
The surest way to have nothing ordinarily, but gravity and authoritie.
The time of inflicting common punishments.
Such as in whom is no hope of reformation, to be sent from Schoole in time.

CHAP. 30. [296–302]

OF School-times, intermissions, and recreations.
Schoole-time to begin at sixe.
The Usher to be ever present at sixe of the clocke, though only to oversee all.
How to make children to strive who shall be first at schoole without correction.
Daily intermissions at nine, and three of the clocke, for a quarter of an houre or more.
To sing part of a Psalme before breaking up at night, and each

THE CONTENTS.

each to begin in order, and to give the tune.
Intermissions at nine of the clocke and three, not offensive, when they are once knowne.
Benefits of intermissions.
None to stirre forth of their places at Schoole-times, but upon urgent occasions.
The time of the intermissions may be gained dayly, and sundry inconveniences prevented.
Weekely recreations.
Before breaking up to play, to make Verses *ex tempore*, or to cap Verses.
The best manner of capping Verses.
The greatest commendation in these.
Manner of their recreations.
The recreations of the studious to be regarded.
Overmuch play, to be carefully avoided.

---

[303]   CHAP. 31.

INconveniences growing by diversitie of teaching and of Grammars.
How this helped.

[304–305]   CHAP. 32.

Evils by ordinarie absence of Schollers.

[305–306]   CHAP. 33.

DIscouragements of Schoolmasters, by unthankfulnesse of parents.
Remedies against such discouragements.

CHAP.

THE CONTENTS.

Chap. 34. [307-309]

What children to be set and kept to learning.
What Schollers to be sent to the Universities.
None to be sent to the Universities before fifteene yeeres of age at least.
The best courses to be practised.

Chap. 35. [310-312]

A Briefe rehearsall of the chiefe points and speciall helps, mentioned thorow the whole booke.
The principall heads of those things, which would be ever kept in memory by the Master, to be continually put in practice.
Master *Askam's* steps to good learning: with a briefe direction of *Melanctons*.

FINIS.

BIBLIOGRAPHICAL NOTES.

AGRICOLA (Rodolphus) [Roelof Huysmann], 1443-1485. Born near Groningen. Professor of Greek and Roman literature at Heidelberg, 1482.
De inventione dialectica libri iii. . 4°, Strasburg, 1521

ANTESIGNANUS (Petrus). Born in 16th century at Rabastiens, in Languedoc.
Praxis, seu usus praeceptorum grammatices graecae.
8°, Lugduni, 1572

APHTHONIUS (Sophista) of Antioch. Fl. 375 A.D.
Rhetores in hoc volumine habentur hi. Aphthonii Sophistae Progymnasmata; Hermogenis Ars rhetorica; &c. [In Greek. Ed. by Aldus Manutius]. . . . . f°, Venice, 1508
Progymnasmata, partim a R. Agricola, partim a J. M. Catanaeo Latinitate donata; cum luculentis et utilibus in eadem scholiis R. Lorichii Hadamarii . . . 8°, London, 1583

ARIAS MONTANUS (Benedictus), 1527-1598. Born in Estremadura. Son of a lawyer. Studied at University of Alcala, chiefly ancient languages. Entered Order of St. James, and accompanied the Bishop of Segovia to the Council of Trente, 1562. At request of Philip II. spent 4 years, 1568-72, directing the publication of the new Polyglott Bible, printed by Plantin at Antwerp. Accused of having altered the text, but finally absolved in 1580. Had charge of the Library of the Escurial, and taught oriental languages. Died at Seville.
Biblia sacra, Hebraice, Chaldaice, Graece et Latine. [Ed. by B. A. M.] . . . . 8 vols., f°, Antwerp, 1569-73
Sacra Biblia, Hebraice, Graece et Latine . . . Editio postrema . . . cui accessit . . . Novum Testamentum Graecoi latinum B. Ariae Montani . . 2 vols., f°, [Heidelberg], 1599.
Davidis regis ac prophetae aliorumque sacrorum vatum Psalmex Hebraica veritate in Latinum carmen a Benedicto Aria Montano . . . conversi . . . . 4°, Antwerp, 1574
Rhetoricorum libri iv. . . . . 8°, Antwerp, 1569
Humanae salutis monumenta . . . 4°, Antwerp, 1571
Antiquitatum Judaicarum libri ix. . . 4°, Leiden, 1593
Naturae Historia . . . . . 4°, Antwerp, 1601

ASCHAM (Roger), 1515-1568. Born at Kirby Wiske, Yorks. Taught in Cambridge c. 1537. Professor of Greek before 1540. Tutor to Princess Elizabeth. Secretary to Sir Richard Morrison, then Latin secretary to Queen Mary. Later canon in York Minster.
The Schoolmaster . . . . . 4°, London, 1570

ASKAM, see **ASCHAM.**

AVENAR (John Egrenus) [Johann Habermann].
Liber Radicum seu Lexicon Ebraicum . . . [With a preface by P. Eber] . . . . f°, Wittenberg, 1568
Grammatices Ebraicae sanctae linguae tres partes . . . [With a preface by P. Melanchthon] . . 8°, Wittenberg, 1575
Preces pro omnibus conditionibus . 1°°, Strassburg, 1578
Dictionarium Hebraicum. . . . 8, Wittenberg, 1589
The Enemie of Securitie, or a daily exercise of Godly Meditations, drawn out of the Holy Scriptures; trl. T. Rogers.
London, 1580
An Enemie to Atheisme, or Christian Godly praiers for all Degrees . . . . trl. T. Rogers. . . . 16°, London, 1591

BALDWIN (William).
A treatise of moral philosophy, containing the sayings of the wise . . . . 8°, London, [1547]
[Another edition]. Enlarged by T. Palfreyman.
8°, London, [1620?]

BARRET or BARET (John), d. 1580? Taught Latin in Cambridge c. 1555.
An Alveane, or triple dictionary, in Latin and French.
f°, [London 1573]
An Alvearie, or quadruple dictionary containing four sundry tongues, namely English, Latin, Greek and French.
f°, [London, 1580]

BERCHETUS (Tussanus), fl. in sixteenth century. Born at Langres. Taught grammar in the college at Sedan.
Elementaria traditio Christianorum fidei, ant catechismus . . . cum familiarissima . . . interpretatione . . . per T. B.
8°, Hanover, 1628
Versio et notae ad Stephani catechismum Graecum, cum alio catechismo compendiosiori . . . . London, 1646
First printed in 1615.

BERKET, see **BERCHETUS.**

BEZE (Théodore de), 1519–1605. Born at Vezelai, Burgundy. Professor of Greek at Lausanne, 1549, and at Geneva, 1558. Biographer and administrative successor of Calvin.
T. B. Vezelii Poemata . . . . . . 8°, Paris, 1548
Jesu Christi D. N. Novum Testamentum . . . cujus Graeco textui respondent interpretationes duae; una vetus, altera nova T. Bezae . . . ejusdem T. Bezae annotationes, etc. Gr. & Lat.
f°, [Geneva], 1565
There were many later editions.

BLEBEL (Thomas), 1539-1596. Born at Bautzen.
Progymnasma artis rhetoricae.
Grammatica Hebraea.
De Sphaera, et primis astronomiae rudimentis libellus . . .
denuo editus. . . . . . . 8°, Wittenberg, 1611

BODENHAM (John).
Politeuphuia: Wit's Commonwealth. Newly corrected and amended. [Commenced by J. B. Edited by N. L., *i.e.*, Nicholas Ling. Fourth edition.] . . . . 8°, London, [1600?]
[Tenth Edition] . . . . . 12°, London, [1605?]

BOND (John), 1550-1612. Born at Trull, Somersetshire. Master of the Free School of Taunton, *c.* 1580. Afterwards practised as a physician.
Quinti Horatii Flacci poemata, scholiis sive annotationibus, quae brevis commentarii vice esse possint illustrata.
8°, London, 1606
Auli Persii Flacci satyrae sex. . . 8°, London, 1614

BOWES (Thomas)
The French Academie, wherein is discoursed the institution of maners, and whatsoever els concerneth the good and happie life of all estates and callings, by preceptes of doctrine, and examples of the lives of ancient sages and famous men. By Peter de la Primandaye, Esquire, Lord of the said place, and of Barree, one of the ordinarie gentlemen of the king's chamber: dedicated to the most Christian King Henrie the third, and newly translated into English by T. B.
4°, London, 1586
[Second part] . . . . . . 4°, London, 1594

BRASBRIDGE (Thomas), born 1547 in Northants. Studied divinity and medicine at Oxford. Held a living at Banbury, where he also opened a school and practised medicine.
Abdias the Prophet. Interpreted by T. B., Fellow of Magdalen College in Oxford. . . . . . 8°, London, 1574
The Poore Man's Jewel. that is to say, a Treatise of the Pestilence . . . . 8°, London, 1578
8°, London, 1579
[Second edition] . . . . . 12°, London, 1592
Quaestiones in Officia M. T. Ciceronis, compendiariam totius opusculi Epitomen continentes. . . . 8°, Oxford, 1615

BRUNSWORD or **BROWNSWERD (John)**, 1540?-1589. Born in Cheshire. Educated at Oxford and Cambridge. Appointed headmaster of Macclesfield Grammar School, 1560. Tutor of Thomas Newton of Butley, who afterwards collected his works. A brass tablet was erected to his memory in Macclesfield Parish

Church by Newton, with the following inscription: "Joanni Brounswerdo Maclesfeldensi Ludimagistro viro pio pariter ac docto hic sepulto et repulverescenti Thomas Newton Butlensis pietatis gratitudinis et officij ergo. p. Alpha poetarum Coryphaesis Grammaticorum, Flos pedagogwn hoc sepelitur humo: obijit 15 April 1589."

Progymnasmata aliquot Poemata, . . . *c.* 1580.

Joannis Brunswerdi, Maclesfeldensis Gymnasiarchae, Progymnasmata quaedam Poetica: sparsim collecta et in lucem edita, studio et industria Thomae Newtoni Cestreshyrii.
4°, London, 1590

On back of dedication are four short poems to his memory by Hugh Winnington, William Hanford, Reginald Briscoe and Randle Barlow.

BUCHLER (Joannes). Born in Gladbach in the 17th century.

Thesaurus sacrarum profanarum phrasium poeticarum.
12°, Douai, 1633
[Another edition] . . . . . 8°, London, 1636
[Another edition] . . . . . 12°, London, 1652
[Another edition] . . . . . 12°, London, 1679
Originally printed at Cologne, in 1603

Gnomologia praecepuarum sententiarum linguae Germanicae ac Gallicae . . . . . . 8°, Cologne, 1602

Institutio Poetica, ex Jac. Pontani libris. 8°, Cologne, 1603

Laconicarum Epistolarum Thesaurus . 8°, Cologne, 1623

BUSCHIUS [Hermann von dem Busche], 1468-1534. Born at Minden, Westphalia. Studied at Heidelberg. Teacher in Cologne, 1494. Travelled in Italy, France and Germany. Lectured on classical literature at several German universities. Professor of History and Poetry at Marburg, 1526.

A Persii Flacci Satyrae luculentissima ecphrasi et scholiis J. Murmellii enarratae . . . H. Buschii epistola, qua Persiani prologi et primae satyrae argumentum explicatur.
4°. Cologne, 1522

A. Persii Flacci Satyrae Sex . . . Item H. Buschii . . . prologi ac primae satyrae explicatrix epistola . 4°, Paris, 1531

A. Persii Flacci Satyrae . . . Adjecta est epistola H. Buschii ad intelligentiam Persii multum conducens. 16°, Cologne, 1534

BUTLER (Charles), died 1647. Born at Wycombe. Schoolmaster in Basingstoke *c.* 1590. Vicar of Wotton *c.* 1597.

Rhetoricae libri duo. . . . . 16°, Oxford, 1600
[Fourth edition] . . . . 4°, Oxford, 1618

The feminine Monarchie; or, a Treatise concerning Bees.
8°, Oxford, 1609

BUXTORF (Johannes), the Elder, 1564–1629. Born at Kamen in Westphalia. Professor of Hebrew in Bâle.
   Epitome radicum Hebraicarum et Chaldaicarum. 8°, Bâle, 1607
   Thesaurus grammaticus linguae sanctae Hebraeae.
8°, Bâle, 1609
   Lexicon Hebraicarum et Chaldaicum. . . . Editio tertia . . . recognita . . . . 8°, Bâle, 1621
   This is another edition of the Epitome Hebraicarum et Chaldaicarum.
   Lexicon Chaldaicum, Talmudicum et Rabbinicum. f°, Bâle, 1639
   Completed and edited by his son
   Epitome grammaticae Hebraeae . . 12° London, 1653
   Revised and edited by his son, 1666. Translated by Nicholas Gray, 1627, and by John Davis, 1655.

CAMDEN (William), 1551–1623. Born in London. Antiquary and historian. Headmaster of Westminster School, 1593. Clarenceux king-of-arms 1597.
   Britannia . . . . 8°, London, 1586
   Institutio Graecae grammatices compendiaria.
8°, London, 1597
   Annales [1st part] . . . . . f°, London, 1615
   ,, [2nd part] . . . . . 8°, Leiden, 1625
   ,, ,, ... f°, London, 1627

CARMINUM PROVERBIALIUM totius humanae vitae statum breviter delineantium . . . loci communes, in gratiam juventutis selecti [by S. A. I.] . . . . . 8°, London, 1577
   [Another Edition] . . . . 8°, London, 1579
   [Another Edition] . . . . 8°, London, 1603
   There were several subsequent editions.

CASTALION, *see* **CHÂTEILLON**

CATANAEUS (Joannes Maria), d. 1529. Born at Novara. Secretary to Cardinal Bendinello Saulo at Rome.
   Isocrates Oratio Panegyrica . . . per. J. M. C. . . . translata
4°, Rome, 1509
   Aphthonii . . . prae-exercitamenta, J. M. Cataneo interprete.
8° [Paris, 1534?]

CEPORINUS (Jacobus), 1499–1525. Born at Dynhart, Zürich. Printer's reader in Bâle. Professor of theology, Greek and Hebrew, Zürich, 1525.
   Compendium grammaticae Graecae . . . jam tertium de integro ab ipso authore locupletatum. Hesiodi Georgicon ab eodem . . . brevi scholio adornatum [with the text]. . . . Epigrammata quaedam . . . adjecta . . . . . 8°, Zürich, 1526
   The Hesiod commentary was printed separately in 1533.
   [Another edition] . . . ex postrema authoris editione, nunc primum opera Joannis Frisii . . . castigatum et auctum.
8°, London, 1585

CEROPINE, *see* **CEPORINUS.**

CHARACTERY (? CHARACTERS), see HALL.

CHÂTEILLON (Sébastien), 1515-1553. Born in the Dauphiné: Professor of humanity, Geneva, c. 1540. Professor of Greek, Bâle, c. 1544.

Colloquia sacra . . . . . . 8°, Bâle, 1545
Dialogorum sacrorum ad linguam et mores puerorum formandos libri iv. . . . . 8°, Antwerp, 1552

CIVIL CONVERSATION, see GUAZZO.

CLEONARD, see KLEINARTS.

COGNATUS (Gilbert), 1506-1567. Born at Nozeroy, in Franche-Comté. Studied law and theology at University of Dôle. Secretary for five years to Erasmus. Returned to Nozeroy and opened a school which soon became famous. Canon to the chapter of Nozeroy in 1535.

A bok of the Office of Servantes, englyshed by Thomas Chaloner.
                8°, London, 1543
Martini Episcopis Dumiensis Formula honestae vitae
                12°, Basil, 1545
Brevis admodum totius Galliae Descriptio . 4°, Basil, 1552
Brevis ac dilucida Burgundiae Descriptio . 12°, Basil, 1552
Collectio Epistolarum veterum Authorum Gr. ac Lat.
                 Basil, 1554
ΤΙΜΗΤΗΣ, seu Censoria Virgula . . 8°, Basil, 1560
Sylva Narrationum . . . . . 12°, Basil, 1561
[Another edition] . . . . . 12°, Basil, 1567

Gilberti Cognati Nozereni Opera multifarii argumenti, lectu et incunda et omnis generis Professoribus, veluti Grammaticis, Oratoribus, Poetis, Philosophis, Medicis, Jureconsultis, ipsisque Theologis apprime utilia, in tres tomos digesta. Quorum serdem sequens pagella indicabit.

 Containing *inter alia*:
  Basilii Magni de Grammatica, Graece et Latine, e regione.
  [at heading of work itself]

ΜΣΓΑΛΘΥ	Basilii
ΒΑΣΙΛΙΘΥ ΠΕΡΙ	Magni de Grammatica
ΓΡΑΜΜΑΤΙΚΗΣ	Exercitatione
γυμνασιας	Gil. Cognato Noz. Interprete

Gilberti Cognati παροιμιᾶν συλλογὴ, quas Des Erasmus, in suas Chiliadis non rettulit.

Syntaxeos et Prosodiae Latinae Tabulae.

Collectanea ex Cicerone.

Oratoriae facultatis Distributiones.

Cum gratia et privilego Caes. Maiest	f°, Basil, 1562
In Horatium	Basil, 1580
Adagiorum Sylloge	Basil, 1599
[Another edition]	Col. Agr. 1612

COOTE (Edmund). Headmaster of the Free School at Bury St. Edmunds, 1597.

The English schoolmaster, teaching all his scholars . . . the most easy . . . order of distinct reading and true writing our English tongue . . . . . . 4°, London, 1596

CORDERIUS, see **CORDIER.**

CORDIER (Mathurin), c. 1480-1564. Born in Normandy. School-master in Paris and Geneva.

De corrupti sermonis emendatione libellus . 8°, Paris, 1530
Colloquiarum scholasticorum libri quatuor ad pueros in sermone Latino paulatim exercendos. . . . 8°, Geneva, 1563

COSARZUS, see **COGNATUS.**

CRUSIUS (Martin), 1526-1607. Born at Bamberg. Rector at Memmingen 1554. Professor of Morality and Greek at Tubingen 1559.

Commentarius Sturmianus in Olynthicam primam. Demosthenis, et Scholia in secundam . . 12°, Strasburg, 1554
Scholia in primam, secundam et tersiam Vergilii Eclogam Sturmiana . . . . . . 12°, Strasburg, 1556
Grammatica graeca cum latina congruens. 2nd ed.
                                                                                  8°, Bâle, 1563
Majoris Syntaxeos graecae Epitome . . . 8°, 1583
Commentationes grammaticae, rhetoricae, poeticae, historicae, et philosophicae in librum primum Iliadis, inserto textu graeco.
                                                                        8°, Heidelberg, 1612

CULMANN (Leonhard). Born 1497 at Crailsheim. Rector at Nuremberg.

Sententiae pueriles, pro primis Latinae linguae tyronibus, ex diversis scriptoribus collectae. His accesserunt pleraeque veterum theologorum sententiae de vera religione.
                                                                               8°, Leipzig, 1544

DRAKES, see **DRAX.**

DRAX (Thomas), d. 1618. Born near Coventry. Vicar of Dovercourt-cum-Harwich, Essex, 1601.

Calliepeia ; or a rich storehouse of proper, choice and elegant Latin words and phrases, collected for the most part out of all Tully's works . . . . . . 8°, London, 1612

ERASMUS (Desiderius), 1466-1536.
Adagiorum Chiliades tres . . . . f°, Venice, 1508
First printed in Paris in 1500
De copia verborum . . . . 4°, Strasburg, 1513
De ratione studii et instituendi pueros commentarii
4°, Paris, 1514
Novum Testamentum omne, ad Graecam veritatem, Latinorumque codicum emendatissimorum fidem, denuo diligentissime a Des. Erasmo Roterodamo recognitum. Cum nova praefatione Erasmi 8°, Bâle, 1520
De conscribendis epistolis . . . 4°, Cambridge, 1521
Familiarium Colloquiorum D. Erasmi . 8°, Florence, 1531
First published 1523-4.

ERYTHRAEUS (Nicholaus). Born in Venice, in 16th century.
Index Erythraei Virgiliano operi cujuslibet impressionis . . . accommodatus . . . . 8°, 1603
[Another edition] . . . . . . 8°, 1613

ESTIENNE (Henri), 1528-1598. Born in Paris, where he commenced printing in 1554.
Thesaurus Graecae linguae . . . . . f°, Paris, 1572
Publii Virgilii Maronis poemata, novis scholiis illustrata, quae H. Stephanus . . . dedit. Ejusdem H. Stephani schediasma de delectu in diversis apud Virgilium lectionibus adhibendo.
8°, 1576?
P. V. M. Poemata, H. Stephani scholiis illustrata . . . Tertia editio . . . . 8°, Geneva, 1599
Magno epigrammatu numero et duobus indicibus auctu. [Ed. with annotations by H. Estienne] . . 4°, Paris, 1566
Epigrammatum Graecorum . . . libri vii. Accesserunt H. Stephani in quosdam Anthologiae Epigrammatum locos annotationes . . . . . . f°., Frankfort, 1600

EUSTATHIUS, died c. 1193. Probably born in Constantinople, where he taught rhetoric. Bishop of Myra 1174, and of Thessalonica 1175.
Εὐσταθίου Ἀρχιεπισκόπου Θεσσαλονικῆς Παρεκβόγαι εἰς τὴν Ὁμήρου Ἰλιάδα καὶ Ὀδύσσειαν μετὰ εὐπορωτάτου καὶ πάνυ ὠφελίμου πίνακος [by M. Devarius.—With the text. Ed. by N. Majoranus]. 4 vol. . . . . f°, Rome, 1550
Eustathii . . . in Homeri Iliadis et Odysseae libros παρεκβόλαι, indice adjuncto perutili. . . . [By S. Guldenbeck.—With the text]. . . . . f°, Bâle, 1559-60

FLORES POETARUM de virtutibus et viciis ac donis sancti
spiritus . . . . 4°, [Cologne, 1480?]
  [Another edition] . . . . 4°, [Delphis, 1487]
  [Another edition] . . . . 4°, [Cologne, 1490]
Many later collections.

FRENCH ACADEMIE, see **BOWES**.

FRISIUS (Joannes), Tigurinus, 1505-1565. Born in the canton of Zürich. Head of College in Zurich; organised and encouraged there the study of Oriental languages. *See* **CEPORINUS**.

GOCLENIUS (Rodolphus), 1547-1628. Born at Corbach. Professor of Logic at Marburg.
  Observationes linguae Latinae . . 8°, Frankfort, 1609

GOLDEN GROVE, see **VAUGHAN**.

GOLIUS (Theophilus) [Gottlieb Goll], 1528-1600. Born in Strassburg. Teacher at the Gymnasium 1548. Professor of Logic at the University 1572.
  Onomasticon latino-germanicum in usum scholae argentoratensis, collectum a Theophilo Golio cum praefatione Joan. Sturmii.
                                        12°, Strassburg, 1579

GUAZZO (Stefano), 1530-1593. Born at Casale. Instrumental in founding there the Academy which went by the name of "les Argonautes." Secretary to Margaret, Duchess of Mantua, and later to Louis de Gonzaque, Duke Nevers.
  The Civile Conversation, translated by George Pettie, divided into four books . . . . . . 4°, Lond., 1581
  The Civile Conversation of S. G. written first in Italian, divided into four books, the first three translated out of French by G. Pettie . . . the fourth translated out of Italian by B. Young.
                                        4°, Lond., 1586

HALL (Joseph), 1574-1656. Born at Ashby-de-la-Zouch. Fellow of Emmanuel College, Cambridge. Took orders and held the living of Halsted, Suffolk, in 1601, and of Waltham, Essex, in 1608. Chaplain to Prince Henry, 1608. Sent by the King as chaplain to Lord Doncaster in his embassy to France, 1616. Nominated Dean of Worcester 1617. Selected as one of the King's representatives at the synod of Dort, 1618. Bishop of Exeter 1627, and of Norwich 1641. Author of *Christ Mysticall* and many other works of divinity.
  Characters of Virtues and Vices . . . 8°, London, 1608
  Divided into 2 parts: (1) *The Characterisms of Vertues;* (2) *The Characterisms of Vices.* One of the books inspired by Casaubon's Latin translation of Theophrastus, 1592. "An attempt to bring home to men's convictions the nobleness of virtue and the baseness of vice." (*Camb. Hist. of Eng. Lit.*, IV., 336.)

HEGENDORPHINUS [Christoph Hegendorff], 1500-1540. Born at Leipzig. Assisted at the colloquy between Luther and Eckius 1519. Professor of Greek at Leipzig 1525, and of Law at Frankfort-on-the-Oder c. 1531. Later professor of Literature at Lüneburg, where he died.

De instituenda vita et moribus corrigendis juventutis paraeneses . . . . 8°, Paris, 1529

Dialogi pueriles C. Hegendorphini xii lepidi aeque ac docti apud Wynkyndum de Worde . . . . London, 1532
First printed at Nurnberg, 1520.

Stichologia, seu ratio scribendorum versuum.
8°, Strasburg, 1535

De conscribendis epistolis Joannes Ludovicus Vives . . . libellus . . . C. Hegendorphini methodus . 8°, Cologne, 1537

HOLYOAKE (Francis), 1567-1653. Born at Nether Whitacre, Warwickshire. Taught at Oxford and in Warwickshire. Rector of Southam, 1604. Member of Convocation, 1625.

Dictionary etymological 2 pts. . . . 8°, London, 1617
Annexed to Rider's Dictionary.

[Another edition]. To which are joined many useful alterations, with additions, by N. Gray . . . . 4°, London, 1626

Dictionarium etymologicum Latinum. 3 pts.
4°, London, 1633

JUNIUS [DE JONGHE] (Adrianus), 1512-1575. Born at Horn. Studied medicine at Haarlem, Louvain, Paris and Bologna. Practised first at Haarlem. Called to Copenhagen in 1556, as chief physician to the King. Returned to Haarlem in 1564, and was appointed rector of the schools in that town.

Lexicon graeco-latinum auctum . . . f°, Bâle, 1548

Adagiorum ab Erasmo omissorum centuriae octo cum dimidia. Animadversorum libri 6 et de coma commentarius.
8°, Bâle, 1556

Emblemata et aenigmata . . . 8° Antwerp, 1565

Nomenclator omnium rerum propria nomina variis linguis explicata indicans . . . . . 8°, Augsbourg, 1555
[Another edition] . . . 8°, Antwerp, 1577
[Another edition] (in 8 languages) . . 8°, Geneva, 1619
[Another edition] (in 7 languages) . 8°, Frankfort, 1620

The Nomenclator, or Remembrances of A. J. . . . divided into two Tomes, containing proper names and apt terms for all things under their convenient Titles . . . Written . . . in Latine, Greeke, French and other forrein tongues; and now in English by J. Higins . . . with a Dictional Index, etc. Imprinted . . . for R. Newberie and H. Denham.
8°, Lond., 1585

KLEINARTS (Nicolaus), 1495-1542. Born at Diest, in Brabant. Professor of Greek and Hebrew in Louvain and Salamanca. Tutor to the brother of the King of Portugal. Later professor of Latin, Braga.

Meditationes Graecanicae in artem grammaticam, multo quam ante hac castigatiores . . . . . 8°, Venice, 1543
(Prescribed by Thomas Ashton, first master of Shrewsbury School (1562-8) for use of his scholars.)

Institutiones . . . in linguam Graecam . 8°, Antwerp, 1545

[Another edition] . . . meliore ordine digestae atque . . . locupletatae . . . opera G. J. Vossii . . 8°, Leiden, 1632

LEECH or LEACHE (John), 1565-1650? Came of an old Cheshire family. Probably "identical with the vicar of Walden mentioned by Strype (Life of Sir Thomas Smith, p. 6), who combined the occupations of his cure with the ushership of Walden school" (D. N. B).

A book of Grammar Questions [2nd ed.] . 8°, London, 1628

A book of Grammar Questions for the help of Young Scholars. . . . Now the fourth time imprinted. 8°, London, 1650

(To this is appended "Four Little Dialogues or Colloquies in Latine. Now verbally translated . . . but long since gathered. . . ."

LILY (William), c. 1468-1522. Born at Odiham, Hampshire. Private teacher of Grammar in London. First headmaster of St. Paul's School, 1510.

G. Lilii . . . De generibus nominum, ac verborum praeteritis et supinis, regulae . . . Opus recognitum et adauctum cum nominum ac verborum interpretamentis, per J. Rituissi, Scholae Paulinae praeceptoris [sic] . . . . . 4°, [1520?]

Brevissima Institutio, seu Ratio Grammatices cognoscendae.
4°, London, 1528
Prefixed to this edition are the epistle and directions for teaching the eight classes in Ipswich school, written by Cardinal Wolsey.

LORICHIUS (Reinhardus), born in Hadamar. Professor of Rhetoric in Marburg, 1535-48.

De Institutione princupum Loci Communes, ex . . . optimis auctoribus collecti . . . . . 8°, Frankfort, 1538

Tabulae de schematibus et tropis Petri Mosellani. . . . Jam recens compluribus figuris locupletatae, variisque novis autorum optimorum exemplis illustratae, per R. Lorichium.
8°, Frankfort, 1540

Aphthonii Progymnasmata . . . cum luculentis et utilibus in eadem scholiis R. Lorichii Hadamarii   8°, London, 1583

LUBIN (Ellhard), 1565-1621. Born at Werterstede, in Oldenburg. Professor of Literature, Rostock, 1595. Later professor of Theology.

A. Persii Flacci . . . Satyrae vi. . . . illustratae . . . commentariis E. Lubini. . . . . 8°, Amsterdam, 1595

D. Junii Juvenalis Satyrarum libri v. . . . Cum analysi et . . . commentariis . . . E. Lubini . . . 4°, Hanover, 1603

LYCOSTHENES (Conradus), 1518-1561. Born at Ruffach, in Alsace. Taught grammar and logic at Bâle, 1542.

Apophthegmatum ex optimis utriusque linguae scriptoribus per C. Lycosthenem . . . collectorum loci communes, denuo aucti et recogniti. . . . His accesserunt Parabolae . . . olim ex gravissimis auctoribus collectae [by D. Erasmus], nunc vero per C. Lycosthenem in locos communes digestae.
8°, Lyons, 1574.
[Another edition] . . . . . 8°, Geneva, 1602

MACROPEDIUS (Georgius) [Langeveldt], 1475-1558. Born at Bois-le-Duc. Entered the Order of St. Jerome, and taught in the monastic schools at Liège, Bois-le-Duc and Utrecht.

Epistolica G. M. studiosis Trajectinae scholae tyranculis nuncupata, quae nihilominus quicquid ad prima rhetorices elementa attinet, brevibus praeceptis plane complectitur.
8°, Antwerp, 1543

Graecarum institutionum rudimenta . . . nunc primum . . . edita . . . . 12°, Antwerp, 1571

Methodus de conscribendis Epistolis. . . . Accessit Chr. Hegendorphini epistolas conscribendi methodus.
16°, Lond., 1595

MANUTIUS (Aldus) the younger, 1547-1597. Born at Venice. Professor of Rhetoric, Bologna, 1585, and of Belles-lettres, Rome, 1589. Director of the Vatican press, 1590.

Phrases linguae Latinae, in Anglicum sermonem conversae.
16°, London, 1579

MARTINIUS (Petrus). Born in Navarre. Died 1594. Professor in the college at La Rochelle, 1572.

Grammaticae Hebraeae libri duo . . 8°. Paris, 1567
Grammatica Ebraea Martinio-Buxtorfiana. . . . S. Amama . . . mutavit, correxit et auxit. . . . 8°, Amsterdam, 1634

MELANCHTHON (Philipp), 1497-1560. Born in Baden. Taught in Tübingen, 1512. Professor of Greek at Wittenberg, 1518.

Elementa Latinae grammatices . . 8°, [Cologne] 1526
Grammatica Graeca . . . . . 8°, Hayn, 1527
Sintaxis P. M. recens nota et edita. . . 8°, Paris, 1529

In Hesiodi libros de opere et die enàrrationes P. M. Una cum authoris praefatione. . . . . . 8°, Paris, 1543
Vergilius. P. Melanchthonis scholiis . . . illustratus.
8°, Cologne, 1545
P. V. M. Poemata quae extant omnia. P. M. annotatiunculis illustrata . . . . 8°, Zürich, 1561

MINOS (Claudius) [Claude Mignault], c. 1536-1606. Born at Talant, near Dijon. Lectured in Greek and Latin at the College of Rheims. Later professor in Paris. Went to Orleans in 1578 and there studied law. Appointed advocate of the king at Etampes, and later professor of canonical law in Paris.

Omnia A. Alciati Emblemata: cum commentariis . . . per C. Minoem . . . . 8°, Antwerp, 1577
——— Editio tertia . . . . . 8°, Antwerp, 1581
Many other editions.

MORAL PHILOSOPHY, see BALDWIN.

MURET (Marc Antoine), 1526-1585. Born near Limoges. Taught Latin at Villeneuve and Bordeaux. Finally settled at Rome.

Orationes xxiii . . . ejusdem interpretatio quincti libri ethicorum Aristotelis ad Nicomachum. Ejusdem hymni sacri et alia quaedam poematia. 3 pts. . . 8°, Venice, 1575

MURMELLIUS (Joannes), c. 1479-1517. Born at Roermonde in the Netherlands. Teacher in Münster 1501, Rector of the Schule Ludgen 1509.

A. Persii Flacci Satyrae luculentissima ecphrasi et scholiis Murmellii enarratae . . . . . . 4°, Cologne, 1522
A. Flacci Persii . . . Satyrae cum quinq commentariis, et eorum indice amplissimo: ac satyrarum argumentis J. Badii Ascensii . . . J. Murmellii . . . additis . . . L. J. Scoppae . . . adnotationibus . . . . . . f° [Paris], 1523
[Another edition] . . . . . 4°, Paris, 1531
[Another edition] . . . . 16°, Cologne, 1534
[Another edition] . . . . . 8°, Paris, 1546

PAGET or PAGIT (Eusebius), 1551-1617. Born at Cranford, Northants. Rector of Lamport, 1572, and later of Kilkhampton. Suspended c. 1585 on account of his Nonconformist tendencies. Rector of St. Agnes, Aldersgate St., London, 1604, till his death.

The history of the Bible, briefly collected, by way of question and answer . . . . . . 12°, London, 1613

PAGNINUS (Sanctes), c. 1470-1541. Born at Lucca. Entered the Dominican order, 1486. Professor of Oriental languages at Rome. Finally settled at Lyons, of which he was made a citizen.
Thesaurus linguae sanctae . . . f°, Lyons, 1529
Thesaurus linguae Sanctae sive lexicon Hebraicum, auctum ac recognitum opera Jo Merceri, Ant. Cevallerii et B. Corn Bertrami . . . . Lugd., 1575
Thesauri Pagnini epitome . . . 8°, Antwerp, 1616
Epitome, Thesauri Linguae Sanctae, settia editio, per F. Raphelengium . . . . . 8°, Antwerp, 1578
[Another edition] cum appendice dictionum Chaldaic; acc. index dictionum Latinarum, sive lexicon Latino-Hebraicum.
4°, Lugd. Bat. 1599

PELEGROMIUS (Simon).
Synonymorum Sylva . . . recognita et multis in locis ancta
8°, Antwerp, 1555
Synonymorum Sylva olim a S. Pelegromio collecta, et Alphabeto Flandrico . . . illustrata: nunc autem e Belgarum sermone in Anglicanum transfusa et in alphabeticum ordinem redacta per H. F. et ab eodem . . . emendata et aucta. Accesserunt huic editione synonyma quaedam poetica . . 8°, London, 1609

POLANUS (Amandus).
Partitiones Theologicae . . . . 8°, London, 1591
[Another edition] . . . . . . Bâle, 1602
The Substance of the Xtian Religion, trl. by E. Wilcockes.
8°, London, 1595
Sylloge Thesium Theologicarum, ad methodi leges conscriptarum, et disputationibus R. Bellarmini praecipue oppositarum.
8°, Bâle, 1597
Analysis libelli Prophetae Malachiae aliquot praelectionibus Genevae proposita ab A. Polano . . . Adjunctae sunt orationes quatuor ab eodem auctore in Academia Basiliensi habitae . . . Heb. and Lat. . . . . 8°, Bâle, 1597
Treatise concerning God's Eternal Predestination; trl. by Roger Gostwicke . . . . . . 8°, Camb., 1599
Comm. in Danielem . . . . . 8° Bâle, 1599
Syntagina logicum Aristotelico-Ramoeum. . 8°, Bâle, 1605
Syntagina Theologiae Christianae. 2 vol.. . f°, Han., 1609
[Another edition] . . . . . . f°, Geneva, 1612

RAMUS [Pierre La Ramée], 1515?-1572. Born in Picardy. Owing to poverty became a servant at the college of Navarre, but studied to such effect that he took his degree there in 1536, afterwards opening a course of lectures in philosophy. In 1544 these were interdicted, on the grounds that they undermined the foundations of philosophy and religion. This decree was cancelled later. Professor of Philosophy and Eloquence at the

Collège de France, 1551. Adopted protestantism 1556 and had to flee from Paris. Lectured on Mathematics at Heidelberg 1568. Met his death in the Massacre of St. Bartholomew.

Institutiones dialecticae iii. libris distinctae.	8°, Paris, 1543
Animadversiones in dialecticam Aristotelis.	8°, Paris, 1543
Rhetoricae distinctiones in Quintilianum.	8°, Paris, 1549
Arithmeticae libri tres	4°, Paris, 1555
In quatuor libros Georgicorum et in Bucolica Virgilii praelectiones	8°, Paris, 1555-6
Ciceronianus	8°, Paris, 1556
Grammatica latina	8°, Paris, 1558
Scholae grammaticae libri duo	8°, Paris, 1559

RAVISIUS (Joannes), c. 1480-1524. Born at Saint-Saulge in the Nivernais. Professor of Rhetoric, Paris. Rector of the university, 1520.

Officina, partim historiis partim poeticis referta disciplinis.
f°, [Paris], 1520

Epithetorum J. Ravisii Textoris Epitome.	8°, Lyons, 1548
[Another edition]	4°, Bâle, 1592

RECORDE (Robert), 1510?-1558. Born at Tenby. Fellow of All Souls', Oxford, 1531. Taught at Cambridge, and later at Oxford, mathematics and medicine, rhetoric, anatomy, music, astrology and cosmography. Said to have been physician to Edward VI. and Mary. Comptroller of the Mint at Bristol, 1549. General surveyor of the mines and money for England and Ireland, 1551.

The ground of artes teachyng the worke and practise of Arithmetike, moch necessary for all States of men.
8°, Lond., 1543

Other editions in 1561, 1582, 1607, 1623.

The pathway to Knowledg, containing the first principles of Geometrie . . . . . 2 pts., 4°, Lond., 1551

The whetstone of witte, which is the seconde parte of Arithmetike . . . . 4°, Lond., 1557

REUSNER (Nicolas), 1545-1602. Born at Loewenberg. Professor of Belles-lettres, and later rector, of the college at Laningen. Subsequently rector of the academy at Jena.

Emblematum libri iv. . . . . 8°, Frankfort, 1581

N. Reusneri. . . . Symbolorum Imperatiorum classis prima (-tertia). Qua symbola continentur Impp. ac Caesarum Romanorum . . . a C. Julio Caesare usque ad Constantinum Magnum . . . . 8°, Frankfort, 1588

——— Secunda editio . . . . 8°, Frankfort, 1602
——— Tertia editio . . . . 8°, Frankfort, 1607

RHODES (Hugh), fl. 1550. Born in Devonshire. Gentleman of of the king's chapel.
The boke of Nurture, or Schoole of good maners.
London, 1577

RIVIUS (Joannes), 1500-1553. Born at Attendorn, in Westphalia. Teacher in Zwickau 1519. Rector in Annaberg 1527, in Marienberg 1530, and in Schneeberg 1536.
P. Terentii . . . comoediae ex. . . . J. Rivii castigationibus.
8°, Cologne, 1535
Many other editions

M. T. Ciceronis familiarium epistolarum libri xvi. cum . . . annotationibus (J. Rivii) . . . . . f°, Paris, 1549
De institutitione puerorum . . . 8°, Lugduni, 1550
De Rhetorica, libri II. De Periodis, libellus I. De Puerorum Institutione, liber I. . . . . 8° Louanii, 1550
C. C. Salustii . . . opera . . . omnia . . . cum . . . commentariis . . . J. Rivii . . . . . f°, Bâle, 1564
Many other editions.

[Murmellius (J.)] Tabulae . . . ad primam auctoris editionem diligenter recognitae, et ex eadem auctae. Adjecimus . . . de ratione distinguendi, ex Joanne Rivio . . . brevem praeceptionem.
16°, Cologne, 1596

SABINUS (Georgius), 1508-1560. Born in Brandenburg. Studied in Wittenberg. Professor in Frankfort-on-the-Oder, 1538.
Epithetorum J. Ravisii Textoris Epitome. Ex H. Junii . . . recognitione. Accesserunt ejusdem Ravisii Synonyma poetica multo quam prius locupletiora. (Synonyma propriorum nominum. —Accesserunt de carminibus ad veterum invitationem artificiose componendis praecepta . . . collecta a G. Sabino.)
12°, Lond., 1626

SCAPULA (Johann). Born in Germany in the sixteenth century.
Lexicon Graeco-Latinum . . . . f°, Bâle, 1579
Lexicon Graeco-Latinum novum. . . . Accesserunt opuscula . . . de dialectis, de investigatione thematum et alia.
f°, Geneva, 1609

SCHMIDT (Erasmus), 1560-1637. Born at Delitzch, in Misnia. Professor of Greek in Wittenberg.
Tractatus de Dialectis Graecorum principalibus quae sunt in parte λεξεως. Cum rerum et verborum indice, *etc.*
8°, Wittenberg, 1621
P. Melanchthonis Grammatica Latina. . . . Editio novissima . . . atque . . . aucta [with a preface by E. Schmidt.]
8°, Leipzig, 1689
Hypomnemata et alia quaedam, ad Grammaticam P. Melanchthonis . . . pertinentia . . . . 8°, Leipzig, 1696

SCHONAEUS (Cornelius), c. 1540-1611. Born at Gouda. Rector of Latin School at Haarlem, 1575.
Terentius Christianus. Utpote comoediis sacris transformatus.
. . . 4 pt. . . . . . . 8°, Colon. Agrippinae, 1592
Terentius Christianus, sive comoediae duae Terentiano stylo conscriptae ad usum scholarum seorsim excusae. . . . Tobias. Juditha . . . . 12°, London, 1595
[Another edition] . . . . . 8°, London, 1620

SCHOOLE OF GOOD MANNERS, see RHODES, SEAGER, WHYTYNGTON.
SCHOOLE OF VERTUE, see SEAGER.

SCHORUS (Antonius). Born at Hoogstraaten. Professor in Heidelberg. Died at Lausanne 1552.
De ratione discendae docendaeque Linguae Latinae et Graecae, libri duo. . . . 2 pts., 8°, Strasburg, 1549
[Another edition] . . . . 8°, Strasburg, 1571
Phrases Linguae Latinae: ratioque observandorum eorum in authoribus legendis, quae praecipuam ac singularem vim aut usum habent . . . . . 8°, Cologne, 1567
Thesaurus verborum linguae Latinae Ciceroianus in usum . . studiosae juventutis collectus, per A. Schorum, cum praefatione J. Sturmii . . . . . . 4°, Strasburg, 1570
[Another edition] . . . . 4°, Strasburg, 1618

SEAGER or SEGAR (Francis), fl. 1549-1563. Probably belonged to an old Devonshire family.
The schoole of vertue and booke of good nourture for chyldren and youth to learne theyr dutie by [In verse]. Newely perused, corrected and augmented by the fyrst auctour, F. S[eager].
8°, London, 1557.
The schoole of vertue [of F. Seager], the second part [by R. West] or the young schollers' paradice. Contayning verie good precepts . . . . . . 8°, London, 1619

SENTENTIAE PUERILES, see CULMANN.

SMETIUS (Henricus).
Prosodia H. Smetii . . . reformata . . . et, . . . adaucta. Editio postrema, emendatior, cum appendice aliquot vocum, ab ecclesiasticis poetis aliter usurpatarum (Methodus dignoscendarum syllabarum ex G. Fabricii . . . de re poetica lib. i. . . .
8°, [Paris?], 1621

STEPHENS, see ESTIENNE.

STOCKWOOD (John), d. 1610. Headmaster of Tunbridge Grammar School, 1578. Wrote and translated many religious works.

A plain and easy laying open of the meaning and understanding of the rules of construction in the English accidence.

4°, London, 1590

Quaestiones et responsiones grammaticales ad faciliorem earum regularum explanationem quae in grammatica Liliana habentur accomodatae . . . . 8°, London, 1592

Progymnasma scholasticum . . . 8°, London, 1597

Disputatiuncularum grammaticalium libellus.

12°, London, 1598

STURMIUS (Joannes), 1507-1589. Born at Schleinden. Taught in Paris, 1529. Rector of the college at Strasburg, 1538.

In partitiones Ciceronis oratorias dialogi quatuor.

8°, Strasburg, 1539

De universa ratione elocutionis rhetoricae libri quatuor.

8°, Strasburg, 1576

Epistolarum M.T. Ciceronis libri tres a J. S. ex universis illius epistolis collecti ad institutionem puerilem. . 8°, Prague, 1577

SUSENBROTUS (Joannes).

Epitome troporum ac schematum et grammaticorum et rhetorum.

8°, Zürich [1540?]

[Another edition] . . . . . 8°, London, 1621

SYLBURGIUS (Fridericus), 1536-1596. Born near Marburg, in Hesse. Studied Greek with Rhodoman at Jena. Head of the schools at Lich and at Neuhaus. Gave up teaching and became director and annotator of all editions of Greek and Latin authors printed by Wechel at Frankfort and by Commelin at Heidelberg.

Scriptores historiae Romanae . . f°, Frankfort, 1588

Epicae elegiacaeque minorum poetarum gnomae, Graece ac Latine: Pythagorae, Phocylidis, Theognidis, Solonis . . . opera et studio F. S. . . . . . . 8°, Frankfort, 1591

Alphabetum Graecum, in quo de Graecarum litterarum formis, nominibus, potestate, ac pronunciatione . . . disseritur,

8°, Frankfort, 1591

SYLVA SYNONYMORUM, see **PELEGROMIUS**.

SZEGEDIN, or **STEPHAN de KIS**, 1505-1572. Born in Szegedin, Hungary, whence he took his name. Teacher of Latin in that town. In Cracow 1540, and in Wittenberg 1541, where he studied dialectic under Melanchthon and divinity under Luther. Returned to Hungary in 1544. Started a school at Tasnad and attempted to establish a Lutheran church, but was punished and driven from the town.

Assertio vera de Trinitate adversus Servetum.

8°, Gen., 1573

Speculum Pontificum Romanorum . . . . 8°, 1586
Tabulae Analyticae, quibus exemplar illud Sanorum Sermonum de Fide, Charitate et Patientia, quod olim Prophetae, Evangelistae, Apostoli, literis memoriaeque mandaverunt, fidelitus declaratur. Authore Steph. Szegedino Pannonio . . 4°, London, 1593
· The Antithesis betweene the voyce of Christ and the Pope whereby is shewed that the Pope is Antichrist. In Latyn written by S. Szegedins and Englished by R. B. [*Stationers' Register*, 14 May, 1604].
Theologiae sincerae loci communes de Deo et homine. Editio quinta cum vita auctoris (auctore M. Scaricaeo) with preface by J. J. Grynaeus . . . . Bâle, 1608

TALAEUS (Andomarus).
Rhetorica . . . Quinta . . . editio, ex vera . . . authoris recognitione . . . . 8°, Paris, 1552
[Another edition] . . . . . . 8°, Frankfort, 1589

TERENTIUS CHRISTIANUS, see SCHONAEUS.

TEXTOR, see RAVISIUS.

TURNER (Robert), d. 1599. Born at Barnstaple. Ordained priest, 1574. Professor of Rhetoric in the English college, Douai. Taught classics in the German college, Rome, 1576. Later professor in Eichstadt and Ingolstadt, where he subsequently became rector of the university.
Roberti Turneri Devonii Panegyrici duo . . . ejusdem orationes xvi. . . . Additae sunt ejusdem epistolae. Editio secundo. . . . auctior . . . . 8°, Ingolstadt, 1599
Orationes, epistolae, tractatus de imitatione rhetorica, a R. Turnero . . . collecta, omnia nunc primum e MS. edita.
8°, Ingolstadt, 1602

VAUGHAN (Sir William), 1577-1641. Poet and colonial pioneer.
The Golden-Grove, moralized in three books. . . . Second edition . . . enlarged by the author . . 8° London, 1608

WIT'S COMMONWEALTH, see BODENHAM.

ZEGEDINE, see SZEGEDIN.

INDEX

AESOP, *see* Esop
Agricola (Rhodulphus), 183
Antesignanus, Praxis præceptorum grammatices, 240
Aphthonius, xvii., 121, 172, 173, 174, 178, 179, 180, 184, 185, 186, 187, 325; Progymnasmata, 181, 182, 183, 189, 190
Arias Montanus, 237, 248
Aristotle, 223
Ascham, xxv., xxvi., 49, 108, 148, 152, 223, 224, 277, 311, 323, 330, 339
Avenar, Hebrew Dictionary, 246, 247, 248

BARRET, Dictionary, 156
Berket, Commentary on Stephen's Catechism, 240
Beza, 236, 262
Blebelius, 245
Bond, Commentary upon Horace, 122
Brasbridge, Questions on Tullies Offices, 204, 207
Brinsley, Translations of schoole-authors, 121, 156
Brunsword, 88
Buchlerus, Thesaurus phrasium poeticarum, 196, 197
Buschius, Commentary upon Persius, 123
Butler, Rhetorick, 162 (margin), 196, 197, 204, 214
Buxtorphius, 247, 248, 249

CÆSAR, 161, 162
Camden, Grammar, 225, 226, 240, 241, 330
Carmina Proverbialia, 301
Castalion, Dialogues, 219
Cataneus, 183
Cato, xvii., 121, 131, 139, 144, 167, 175, 261, 301; Brinsley's translation, xxvii.
Ceporinus, Hesiod commentary, 240

Ceropine, *see* Ceporinus
Charactery, 182
Civil Conversation, 182
Cleonárd, 240
Coot, English Schoolemaster, 138
Corderius, xvii., 113, 213, 215, 217, 221, 237, 257; Dialogues, 121, 156
Cosarzus, 92
Crusius, 92, 93, 94, 100, 320

DEMOSTHENES, 223, 239
Drax, Phrases, 121, 187, 188, 218

ERASMUS, Adages, 182, 188; De Copia, 189, 218; Colloquium, 219, 221; Latin Testament, 262
Erythræus, Index, 196
Esop, xvii.; Fables, 116, 121, 131, 145, 156, 175, 213, 239
Eustathius, Homer commentary, 241

FABRICIUS, 196
Flores Poetarum, 121, 182, 187, 193, 195, 196, 198
French Academie, 182
Frisius (Johannes), Tigurinus, Hesiod commentary, 240

GOCLENIUS, 92, 209, 222, 329
Golden Grove, 182
Golius, Grammar, 226, 239, 330

HALL (Joseph), xii.
Hegendorphinus, De conscribendis epistolis, 166, 167
Hesiod, xv., 226, 311; Opera et Dies, 240
Holyoke, Dictionary, 156, 187, 218
Homer, xv., 226, 241
Horace, xv., xvi., 43, 44, 122, 317

ISOCRATES, xv., 223, 239, 242.

JUNIUS (Adrianus), Nomenclator, 218, 248
Juvenal, 122, 123

LEECH, 92, 320
Lillie's Rules, xvi., 23, 24, 71, 72, 202, 319
Lorichius, 183
Lubin, Commentaries upon Persius and Juvenal, 123
Lycosthenes, Apophthegmata, 182

MACROPEDIUS, 159, 166, 167, 173, 189, 218, 324
Manutius, 187, 218
Martinius, Grammar, 245, 249
Melancthon, 311, 339; Annotations on Virgil, 123; Hesiod commentary, 240
Minos (Claudius), Commentary on Talæus' Rhetorick, 162, 203
Morall Philosophy, 182
Muretus, 189
Murmelius, Commentary upon Persius, 123

OVID, xvi., 44, 107, 190, 193, 195, 301, 326; De Tristibus, 121, 131, 192; Metamorphosis, xvii., 121, 131, 146, 192, 213; De Ponto, 192

PAGET, History of the Bible, 259
Pagnine, Epitome, 247, 248
Persius, xv., xvi., 122, 123
Phocilides, 240
Plato, 223, 239
Polanus, 247
Propria quæ maribus, 69, 74, 79, 83, 142
Psalmes in metre, 17
Pueriles confabulatiunculæ, xvi., 121, 131, 145, 167, 212, 215, 217

RAMUS, Commentary, upon Virgil, 123
Record's Arithmetique, 26
Reusner, Symbola, 176, 179, 182, 183, 187, 188, 190, 325
Rivius, 218

SABINE, 196
Scapula, 231, 232, 241
Schmidt (Erasmus), 241
Schoole of Good Manners, The (or The New Schoole of Vertue), 18, 261
Schoole of Vertue, The, 18
Schorus (Antonius), De ratione discendæ linguæ Latinæ, 170
Sententiæ pueriles, xvi,, xxvii., 121, 131, 142, 167, 175, 257, 261, 264
Smetius, Prosodia, 196; Methodus dignoscendarum syllabarum ex Fabricio, 196
Socrates, 43
Solon, 276
Stephens (H.), Annotations on Virgil, 123; Greek epigrams, 240
Stockwood, Disputations of grammar, 181, 202, 203, 205, 206, 209, 217, 327, 328; Progymnasma scholasticum, 197
Sturmius, Tullies Epistles, 121, 145, 167, 169
Susenbrotus, 92
Sylburgius, Notes to Theognis, 234, 240
Sylva Synonimorum, 196

TALÆUS, Rhetorick, 162, 203, 204, 213, 214
Terence, xvi., xvii., 213, 221
Terentius Christianus, 114, 121, 156, 221
Textor, Epitheta, 196, 197
Theognis, xv., 118, 234, 240, 242

Tully, xiv., 44, 49, 103, 107, 114, 148, 153, 157-163, 165-7, 171, 172, 183, 193, 195, 199, 223, 241, 317, 324; Epistles, xiv., xvii., 121, 167, 168, 170, 324; De natura deorum, xvii., 114, 121; De officiis, xvii., 116, 121, 146, 204, 207, 261, 327; De oratore, xxv.; De senectute, 100, 121; Sentences, 114, 121, 153, 156, 173, 175, 178, 179, 182, 187, 188, 193, 237, 241, 323; Paradoxes, 121, 184; De amicitia, 121; Orations, 184, 189, 214

Turner, Orations, 189

VIRGIL, xv., xvi., 44, 107, 121, 123, 190, 192, 194, 195, 196, 198, 205, 213, 235, 301, 326

WHITNEY (John), xxvi.
Wit's Commonwealth, 182

XENOPHON, 223, 239, 242

ZEGEDINE, Philosophia Poetica, 182

Printed by J. MILES & Co. LTD.
68-70, Wardour Street, London, W.

UNIFORM WITH THIS VOLUME.
Crown 8vo, 8s. 6d. net.

A NEW DISCOVERY

Of the old Art of
TEACHING SCHOOLE,
In four small

TREATISES.

1. A Petty-Schoole.
2. The Ushers Duty   ⎫ In a
3. The Masters Method   ⎬ Grammar
4. Scholastick Discipline ⎭ Schoole.

concerning

By *Charles Hoole* Master of Arts, and Teacher of a Private Grammar School in *Lothbury* Garden, *London*.

Edited with
BIBLIOGRAPHICAL INDEX
By *E. T. Campagnac*

EXTRACTS FROM REVIEWS AND NOTICES

"Altogether his work, which brushes the dust off one of the foundations of the history and system of Education in England . . . . has been admirably done."—*The Scotsman.*

"A reprint of a treatise on education by a seventeenth-century Schoolmaster, who was recognised as one of the foremost teachers of his day. The Editor adds a valuable bibliography of school books and books on education available at the time the treatise was written."—*Educational Record.*

"Professor Campagnac is to be thanked for giving us the opportunity of reading this delightful work and for his admirable introduction to it."
Liverpool Daily Post.

"We have previously spoken of this ancient treatise or series of treatises on education as of surpassing interest."—*Journal of Education; Boston.*

"This admirable reprint should therefore meet with a warm welcome."—*Times: Educational Supplement.*

"Professor Campagnac has treated his text with fitting reverence, and has added a useful bibliography of the books mentioned by Hoole . . . . We shall not be content until we possess a reprint of the excellent Brinsley in the same series, to put on our shelves alongside of this carefully edited volume."
Manchester Guardian.

"All who care for school education, whether historically or practically, should welcome this very charming reproduction of one of the best books on the schoolmaster's art which the seventeenth century produced . . . . As Professor Campagnac says in his Introductory Note, 'Until the documents are collected and presented in a convenient form it will be impossible to write and idle to guess at the history of teaching.'"
Journal of Experimental Pedagogy.

"Hoole's famous book (too long inaccessible, but now at last reprinted) shows how uniform is the staff on which the educational theories of different ages are embroidered."—*Spectator.*

"We owe a debt of gratitude first to Professor Campagnac for his scholarly edition, and next to the Committee of the University Press of Liverpool for undertaking the publication."—*Journal of Education.*

LIVERPOOL
The University Press
57 Ashton Street

LONDON
Constable & Company Ltd.
10 Orange Street, Leicester Square, W.C.

1913

Lightning Source UK Ltd.
Milton Keynes UK
UKHW021858200622
404706UK00003B/230

9 781371 594992